## Why Visual Basic ? Why an Inst

Even with the aid of the early visual design libraries, Wind always a very new and steep challenge to DOS oriented de_____. ........ ......, even from version 1, gave a quick and moderately easy path to developing Windows applications. Without recourse to in-depth knowledge of the API, novice programmers were able to manipulate powerful Windows methods to achieve professional results. With Visual Basic 3, the product has matured into a robust development environment used by a nearly a million pro and amateur programmers. Whether you are an experienced Cobol maintainer or a C or Pascal user, you need a route to put Visual Basic to work, instantly. We have assumed in this book that you have a grip on normal programming behaviour and simply need a direct approach to putting the package through its paces.

## What is Wrox Press?

Wrox Press is a computer book publisher which promotes a brand new concept - clear, jargon-free programming and database titles that fulfill your real demands. We publish for everyone, from the novice through to the experienced programmer. To ensure our books meet your needs, we carry out continuous research on all our titles. Through our dialog with you we can craft the book you really need.

We welcome suggestions and take all of them to heart - your input is paramount in creating the next great Wrox title. Use the reply card inside this book or mail us at:

feedback@wrox.demon.co.uk
or
Compuserve 100063, 2152

Wrox Press Ltd.  Tel:  001 312 465 3559
2710 W. Touhy   Fax:  001 312 465 4063
Chicago
IL 60645
USA

# Instant Visual Basic 3

Steve Dolan

**Wrox Press Ltd.®**

# Instant Visual Basic 3

© 1995 Steve Dolan

All rights reserved. No part of this book may be reproduced, stored in a retrieval system or transmitted in any form or by any means - electronic, electro static, mechanical, photocopying, recording or otherwise, without the prior written permission of the publisher, except in the case of brief quotations embodied in critical articles or reviews.

The author and publisher have made every effort in the preparation of this book to ensure the accuracy of the information. However, the information contained in this book is sold without warranty, either express or implied. Neither the author, Wrox Press nor its dealers or distributors will be held liable for any damages caused or alleged to be caused either directly or indirectly by this book.

Published by Wrox Press Ltd. Unit 16, 20 James Road, Birmingham, B11 2BA UK
Printed in the U.S.A
ISBN 1-874416-48-6

# Trademark Acknowledgements

Wrox has endeavored to provide trademark information about all the companies and products mentioned in this book by the appropriate use of capitals. However, Wrox cannot guarantee the accuracy of this information.

# Credits

**Author**
Steve Dolan

**Technical Editor**
Darren Gill

**Series Editor**
Luke Dempsey

**Technical Reviewers**
Stephen Husak
Neil Bonnaud

**Beta Tester**
John Van Hoof

**Production Manager**
Deborah Somers

**Book Layout**
Eddie Fisher
Greg Powell
Lee Kelly

**Proof Reader**
Pam Brand
Jenny Nuttall

**Cover Design**
Third Wave

**Managing Editor**
John Franklin

**Operations Manager**
Gina Mance

For more information on Third Wave, contact Ross Alderson on 44-121 236 6616

Cover photograph supplied by The Image Bank

# About the Author

Steve Dolan has been programming in many different languages since 1974. His specialities include business analysis and database development, especially using Visual Basic. He is a director of Psynet Ltd. who develop multimedia and Internet products.

# Author's Acknowledgements

It's almost impossible to write a book in splendid isolation. Along the way there are many people that help you out, and some that support you throughout the process. This book was no exception, and there are a few people deserving of my thanks, and undying gratitude.

First and foremost in the roll of honor is Peter Wright, my friend and partner, without whom I'd never have written the book in the first place. Thanks for your splendid work on chapters 1, 9 and 10, as well as overall support as I worked my way through the book.

Next is Mike Gwilliam whose enthusiasm and interest in the book helped make it what it is. Thanks must also go to Dave McBain, and Martin Thomas, who dragged me from the screen when I most needed a break, even if I did have to buy the beer!

Finally, thanks to everyone at Wrox Press who had confidence in me, and believed in me, especially Darren Gill, and Luke Dempsey, whose positive support was greatly appreciated - what a Grude! Thank you all.

Steve Dolan

# INSTANT

## Summary of Contents

Introduction .................................................................................... 1

Chapter 1: Getting To Know Visual Basic ............................................... 7

Chapter 2: Projects and Forms ............................................................ 37

Chapter 3: Gaining Control ................................................................. 61

Chapter 4: Graphics, Text, and Time Controls ........................................ 89

Chapter 5: Variables in Visual Basic ................................................... 121

Chapter 6: Coding Visual Basic Style .................................................. 149

Chapter 7: Objects, Menus and Dialogs, and the MDI ........................ 175

Chapter 8: Introducing Graphics ....................................................... 205

Chapter 9: Input and Output ............................................................. 237

Chapter 10: Database Development ................................................. 265

Chapter 11: Debugging and Error Handling ........................................ 297

Chapter 12: Communicating With Other Windows Applications ......... 321

Appendix A: The Professional Version ............................................... 353

Appendix B: What Next? .................................................................. 361

Appendix C: Exercise Hints and Tips ................................................. 365

# INSTANT Visual Basic

# Table of Contents

**Introduction** .................................................................................................. 1
    What's in This Book ................................................................................. 1
    What You Need to Know ........................................................................... 2
    Conventions Used ..................................................................................... 2
        Program Code ................................................................................... 3
    Important Bits, Font Conventions ........................................................... 3
    Assumptions and Code ............................................................................. 4

**Chapter 1: Getting To Know Visual Basic** ................................................ 7
Visual Basic Concepts ................................................................................... 8
    Graphic Development, Driven by Events .................................................. 8
    Event-Driven Programming ...................................................................... 8
        Device Independence ........................................................................ 9
    Projects .................................................................................................... 10
    Forms ....................................................................................................... 11
    The Visual Basic Environment ............................................................... 11
        Opening Up ..................................................................................... 11
        The Title Bar ................................................................................... 13
    The Menu Bar .......................................................................................... 14
        The File Menu ................................................................................. 14
        The Edit Menu ................................................................................. 15
        The View Menu ............................................................................... 15
        The Run Menu ................................................................................ 15
        The Debug Menu ............................................................................ 16
        The Options Menu .......................................................................... 16
        The Window menu .......................................................................... 16
        The Help Menu ............................................................................... 16
    Using the Toolbar and the Toolbox ........................................................ 17

# Table of Contents

      Controls as Programs .................................................................................................. 18
      Reinventing the Wheel: the VBX ............................................................................... 18
   Starting a New Project ........................................................................................................ 19
      The Intelligent Code Window .................................................................................... 20
   Properties ............................................................................................................................ 21
      The Properties Window ............................................................................................. 22
      The Naming of Parts ................................................................................................. 22
      The Project Window .................................................................................................. 23
**Fundamentals: Implementation** ................................................................................**24**
   The Password Project ......................................................................................................... 24
   Changing Properties ........................................................................................................... 25
      What You See Is Not What You Get ......................................................................... 26
      Adding a Textbox ...................................................................................................... 26
      Changing the Text Property ...................................................................................... 27
      Hotkeys ..................................................................................................................... 28
      Adding Sparkle ......................................................................................................... 29
      Using the Image Control ........................................................................................... 29
      Loading up Graphics ................................................................................................. 30
   Saving to Disk ..................................................................................................................... 30
      Naming Conventions ................................................................................................. 30
      Early Functionality .................................................................................................... 31
      Tab Order .................................................................................................................. 31
   Coding ................................................................................................................................. 32
      User Input and Coding .............................................................................................. 33
      Resaving .................................................................................................................... 35
**Summary** .......................................................................................................................**35**

## Chapter 2: Projects and Forms ................................................................................ 37

**Visual Basic Projects: Concepts** ...............................................................................**38**
   Managing Your Projects ..................................................................................................... 38
      Adding Files to Your Project ..................................................................................... 38
      File Types ................................................................................................................. 41
   Saving Your Project ........................................................................................................... 41
   The Project .mak File ......................................................................................................... 42
   Setting the Options ............................................................................................................. 43
   Options - the Environment .... dialog ................................................................................. 43
      The Forms Design Grid ............................................................................................ 44
      Changing the Colors and Tabs .................................................................................. 44
      More Environment Options ....................................................................................... 45
   The Options/Project .... dialog ........................................................................................... 46
   Compiling Your Projects .................................................................................................... 47
   Form Styles ......................................................................................................................... 48
**MDI Application: Implementation** ...........................................................................**48**
   An Introduction to Dialogs ................................................................................................. 51
   Custom Dialogs .................................................................................................................. 51
   Common Dialogs ................................................................................................................ 51

|  |  |
|---|---|
| Using the Open Dialog | 52 |
| The Option Explicit Effect | 55 |
| The Stretch Property of an Image Control | 55 |
| New Forms | 57 |
| **Closing the View Forms** | **58** |
| **Summary** | **59** |
| Exercises | 59 |

## Chapter 3: Gaining Control ............................................................. 61

| | |
|---|---|
| **Controls: Concepts** | **62** |
| Control Values | 62 |
| Naming Conventions | 64 |
| Using Buttons | 65 |
| Command Buttons | 65 |
| Accelerator Keys | 66 |
| Changing the Tab Order | 68 |
| Setting Focus | 68 |
| How Disabling Affects Focus and Tab Order | 69 |
| The Default Command Button | 70 |
| Using the Value Property | 70 |
| Using the Cancel Property | 71 |
| Calling the Click Event Code | 72 |
| Check and Option Buttons | 73 |
| Option Buttons | 74 |
| Check Boxes | 75 |
| Control Arrays | 76 |
| Mouse Pointer Property | 82 |
| **File System Controls:** | |
| **Implementation** | **83** |
| **Summary** | **86** |
| Exercises | 86 |

## Chapter 4: Graphics, Text, and Time Controls ............................... 89

| | |
|---|---|
| Picture Boxes, Image Controls and Windows Resources | 90 |
| Lightweight and Heavyweight Controls | 90 |
| The Image Control Revisited | 91 |
| Using the Image Control as a Button | 91 |
| Image Controls as Hotspots | 94 |
| Introducing Variable Arrays | 97 |
| Improving the Project | 98 |
| Resizing a Hotspot Graphic | 101 |
| Container Controls | 104 |
| **Using Controls: Implementation** | **108** |
| The Timer Control | 108 |

xi

# Table of Contents

Text Controls .................................................................................................. 111
Textboxes ..................................................................................................... 111
List Boxes ..................................................................................................... 112
    Sorted Lists ............................................................................................ 114
    Multiple Selections ................................................................................. 114
    Multi-Column List Boxes ........................................................................ 115
Combo Boxes ............................................................................................... 115
    DropDown List Combo Boxes ................................................................. 116
    DropDown Combo Boxes ....................................................................... 117
    Simple Combo Boxes ............................................................................. 117
User Defined Properties ............................................................................... 117
    The ItemData Property .......................................................................... 117
    The Tag Property ................................................................................... 118
Summary ...................................................................................................... 118
    Exercises ................................................................................................. 118

## Chapter 5: Variables in Visual Basic ................................................. 121

Declaring Variables: Concepts ..................................................................... 122
    The Scope and Lifetime of a Variable ................................................... 122
        Using Static to Preserve Values ...................................................... 122
        Private and Public Variables ........................................................... 123
    Shadowed Variables ............................................................................. 124
    The Variant Data Type .......................................................................... 126
        Variant Types ................................................................................. 126
        Empty and Null Variants ................................................................. 126
        Default Storage Types and Conversions ....................................... 127
        Checking Text Box Input ................................................................ 130
        Date and Time Manipulation .......................................................... 130
    Other Data Types .................................................................................. 132
    String Manipulations and Functions ..................................................... 133
        Strings Within Strings ..................................................................... 134
    Changing the Case ................................................................................ 137
    Numerical Functions ............................................................................. 137
Using Variables: Implementation ................................................................. 137
        Random Numbers .......................................................................... 138
        Loan Repayments .......................................................................... 139
    Constants .............................................................................................. 141
    Arrays .................................................................................................... 142
        Array Declarations ......................................................................... 143
        Multi-Dimensional Arrays ............................................................... 144
    User-Defined Types .............................................................................. 144
    Summary ............................................................................................... 145
    Exercises ............................................................................................... 146

# Instant Visual Basic

## Chapter 6: Coding Visual Basic Style .................................................. 149

### Using Code Modules: Concepts .................................................. 150
- Project Structure .................................................. 150
- Procedures and Functions .................................................. 151
  - Using a .BAS Module .................................................. 151
- Writing a Procedure .................................................. 152
- Creating a Function .................................................. 153
- Module/Form Scope .................................................. 155
- Loops and Case .................................................. 156
- Select Case .................................................. 157
- On...GoSub and On...Goto .................................................. 160
  - GoSub .................................................. 161
- Looping and Program Control .................................................. 162
- For...Next Loops .................................................. 162
  - Controlling the Loop .................................................. 162
- Do Loops .................................................. 165
- Do...Until .................................................. 168
  - Placing the Test .................................................. 168
- DoEvents .................................................. 169
  - Idle Loops with DoEvents .................................................. 169

### Validation: Implementation .................................................. 170
- The Focus Events .................................................. 170

### The Change Event .................................................. 171
### Summary .................................................. 173
- Exercises .................................................. 173

## Chapter 7: Objects, Menus and Dialogs, and the MDI .................. 175

- Generic and Specific Declarations .................................................. 176
- Assigning an Object to a Variable .................................................. 178
  - Releasing Resources .................................................. 178
  - Creating New Instances .................................................. 178
- Testing the Object Variable .................................................. 179
- Object Variable Arrays .................................................. 184
- Multiple Form Instances .................................................. 185
- Collections .................................................. 185

### Menu System: Implementation .................................................. 186
- The Menu Design Window .................................................. 187
- Pre-Plannng Menus .................................................. 187
  - Top Level Menu .................................................. 188
  - The File Menu Structure .................................................. 189
- The Window Menu Structure .................................................. 191
  - Coding Menu Items .................................................. 193
  - Using the Arrange Method .................................................. 193
- PopUp Menus .................................................. 194

xiii

## Table of Contents

MDI Re-visited ............................................................................................................ 196
    Menus With the MDI ............................................................................................ 196
Multiple Viewer Form Instances ................................................................................ 196
Status Bar .................................................................................................................. 197
Common Dialogs ........................................................................................................ 198
Input Boxes ................................................................................................................ 198
Message Boxes .......................................................................................................... 199
The Color Common Dialog ........................................................................................ 200
The Font Common Dialog .......................................................................................... 201
Exercises .................................................................................................................... 203

## Chapter 8: Introducing Graphics .................................................................. 205

System Objects: Concepts ........................................................................................ 206
    The Coordinate System in Visual Basic ................................................................ 206
        Scale Width and Height .................................................................................... 207
Insert Fig. Coord ........................................................................................................ 207
        Cursor Positioning ............................................................................................ 208
        Scales and Measurements .............................................................................. 208
    Creating a Custom Coordinate System ................................................................ 209
    Simple Animation With Print and Move ................................................................ 210
    Animation With Print .............................................................................................. 210
        Unexpected Results With DoEvents ................................................................ 213
    Persistent Graphics .............................................................................................. 213
        Using the Paint Event ...................................................................................... 214
        Setting AutoRedraw ........................................................................................ 215
        Clipping ............................................................................................................ 216
    Animation With the Move Method ........................................................................ 217
    Lines and Shapes .................................................................................................. 220
        The Line and Shape Controls .......................................................................... 220
Graphics: Implementation .......................................................................................... 223
        Drawing at the Pixel Level .............................................................................. 223
        Using the Line Method .................................................................................... 226
        Drawing Circles and Arcs ................................................................................ 229
        Filling, Drawing and Coloring In ...................................................................... 231
        DrawMode Property ........................................................................................ 232
    How Colors Work in Visual Basic .......................................................................... 232
        Color Specification with QBColor .................................................................... 232
        The RGB Function .......................................................................................... 233
        Specifying Hex Values .................................................................................... 234
Summary .................................................................................................................... 234
    Exercises ................................................................................................................ 235

## Chapter 9: Input and Output ........................................................................ 237

File Handling: Concepts ............................................................................................ 238
    The Three Visual Basic File Types ...................................................................... 238
    Binary Access Files .............................................................................................. 238

| | |
|---|---|
| Sequential and Random File Access | 239 |
|     Sequential Files | 240 |
| Comma Separated Variables | 245 |
|     Random Access | 250 |
| I/O and Printing: Implementation | 255 |
| The Printer Object | 255 |
|     Using the Common Dialogs | 255 |
|     Printing to the Printer Object | 257 |
| Printing Forms | 261 |
| Summary | 262 |
|     Exercises | 262 |

## Chapter 10: Database Development ............................................. 265

| | |
|---|---|
| Relational Databases: Concepts | 266 |
| Access | 266 |
| What is a Relational Database? | 267 |
| Creating a Database | 269 |
| The Data Control | 276 |
| Binding | 277 |
|     Binding the Data Control | 277 |
|     Binding Other Controls | 279 |
| Data Control Events | 280 |
| Introducing the Recordset | 282 |
| Accessing the Recordset | 283 |
|     Accessing Fields in a Record | 284 |
| Moving Around | 286 |
|     BookMarks | 286 |
| Data Maintenance | 287 |
| SQL: Database Implementation | 289 |
| The Alternatives | 291 |
| The Professional Edition | 292 |
| Code Basic and Q+E | 293 |
| Summary | 294 |
|     Exercises | 294 |

## Chapter 11: Debugging and Error Handling ........................................ 297

| | |
|---|---|
| Good Program Design:Concepts | 298 |
| Modularity and re-Usability | 298 |
| Modules | 298 |
|     Design for Reuse | 299 |
| The Visual Basic Debugging Facilities | 300 |
| The Debug Window | 301 |
|     Setting BreakPoints | 303 |
|     Single Stepping | 303 |

## Table of Contents

   Altering the Running Order ............................................................ 304
   Using Stop .................................................................................... 305
  Watching ............................................................................................. 305
   Setting and Editing a Watch .......................................................... 306
   Tracing Procedure Calls ................................................................ 309
  Procedure Stepping ............................................................................ 309
   Instant Watching .......................................................................... 310
  Handling Errors at Runtime ................................................................ 311
  On Error Goto… .................................................................................. 311
   Setting Error Traps ....................................................................... 311
   Resuming Execution ..................................................................... 312
   Using Error ................................................................................... 312
Error Handling : Implementation ............................................................. 314
Summary ................................................................................................. 318
  Exercises ............................................................................................ 318

### Chapter 12: Communicating With Other Windows Applications ........ 321

  Clipboard Methods ............................................................................. 322
  Using the Clipboard for Text .............................................................. 323
  Other Clipboard Formats .................................................................... 328
  The Windows API ............................................................................... 329
  Declaring DLL Functions .................................................................... 330
   Passing Parameters to DLLs ......................................................... 330
   Declaring Functions and Procedures ............................................ 331
  Using .INI Files ................................................................................... 333
   INI File Structure ........................................................................... 334
   Getting Information From WIN.INI ................................................. 334
  Running and Controlling Other Applications ..................................... 339
  Running Other Applications ............................................................... 340
   Monitoring Shelled Tasks .............................................................. 341
  Activating Other Applications ............................................................ 343
  DDE and OLE ..................................................................................... 344
  DDE .................................................................................................... 344
  OLE ..................................................................................................... 346
Linkage: Implementation ........................................................................ 348
   Linking At Design Time ................................................................. 348
Summary ................................................................................................. 349
  Exercises ............................................................................................ 350

### Appendix A: The Professional Version ................................................ 353

  The Professional Version Extras ........................................................ 354
   The Animated
   Button Control .............................................................................. 355
   The Crystal
   Reports Control ............................................................................ 355

| | |
|---|---|
| The Gauge Control | 356 |
| The Graph Control | 356 |
| The Key Status Control | 356 |
| The MCI Multimedia Control | 356 |
| The Communications Control | 357 |
| The Masked Edit Control | 357 |
| The Outline Control | 357 |
| The Picture Clip Control | 357 |
| The Spin Button Control | 358 |
| The 3D Controls | 358 |
| The MAPI Control | 359 |
| The Pen Controls | 359 |

## Appendix B: What Next? ............................................................................. 361

| | |
|---|---|
| MultiMedia and Visual Basic | 362 |
| Client Server Visual Basic | 362 |
| Further Help | 362 |
| Talking to Other Visual Basic Users | 362 |
| Other Add Ons | 363 |

## Appendix C: Exercise Hints and Tips ........................................................ 365

| | |
|---|---|
| Chapter 2 | 366 |
| Chapter 3 | 366 |
| Chapter 4 | 368 |
| Chapter 5 | 369 |
| Chapter 6 | 370 |
| Chapter 7 | 371 |
| Chapter 8 | 371 |
| Chapter 9 | 373 |
| Chapter 10 | 374 |
| Chapter 11 | 376 |
| Chapter 12 | 377 |

# INSTANT

# Introduction

Welcome to the latest Instant Guide from Wrox Press to concentrate on the most up-to-date development packages for programming Windows. There has been an explosion of these products in the last few years and they look set fair to dominate the software market for the foreseeable future.

This book is a programmer's book. If you have ever programmed before in any language and you want to move into Visual Basic, then this book is aimed squarely at you. Many developers are migrating into Visual Basic as it is one of the easiest and quickest of the Graphical User Interface (GUI) designing tools on the market.

## What's in This Book

Developers are finding that they don't need to learn the essentials of programming every time they sit down to learn a new package. They know that there are plenty of similarities between different languages. Instant Guides have been developed to address this issue. These books are in no way an exhaustive 'bible' of information, instead they take you through the essentials of a language and its implementation so that you have enough information to begin to develop useful applications.

Hence, each chapter is split into a concepts section and an implementation section. The concepts section looks at some of the main theory behind Visual Basic, whilst the implementation section puts some of that theory into practice. To further aid comprehension, at the end of each chapter we

# Introduction

encourage you to experiment with some exercises. You will see that they don't have any answers. This is not an exercise in misanthropy - it is to make you think *into* Visual Basic as you will have to in order to begin to master using the language. Don't worry - we have given you heavy clues to the answers in Appendix C, but only a shirker would look there first!

## What You Need to Know

It will help you greatly if you have programmed before in another language. We don't assume too much and we do take you through the whole concept of event-driven programming and how this challenges more traditional approaches to programming. But you won't find explanations to fundamental aspects of programming in this book - we trust that you probably know why you want to say, use an array, and just want the Visual Basic method explained quickly.

The other two appendices in the book look ahead for you as you begin to move more deeply into Visual Basic. Appendix A looks at the Professional Edition of Visual Basic and its added functionality compared to the Standard Edition. This book has been written to the Standard specification. If you are serious about using Visual Basic professionally, especially in database connectivity and distributing applications, you will need to look hard at purchasing the Pro edition.

Appendix B gives further help beyond the Standard Edition with a brief run-through of some of the vendor add-ons which address Visual Basic. It seems that every week sees a new tool for the product and we can only point you in the direction of where to get hold of the most useful. The proliferation of these products is testament to the interest in visual programming. It can be safely assumed that those who believe Visual Basic a toy for beginners are now a small minority.

## Conventions Used

To enable you to find your way around this book easily, we have used various different styles to highlight different references.

# Conventions Used

## Program Code

All program code in the book is highlighted with a gray background so you can find it easily.

```
frmAuto.WindowState = 2
frmAuto.Show
iAutoNumber = FreeFile
```

When code features in the middle of sentences, we write it in `this_style`.

In some instances, we repeat parts of the code in an example in various places. This is deliberate, so that you can see the program develop. We have shaded lines which are new additions to the program, and left the lines that are repeated unshaded. This will enable you to see immediately where new stuff has been added:

```
This is repeated code.
This is new code.
This is repeated code.
This is new code.
This is new code.
```

# Important Bits, Font Conventions

> Bits that you really must read are in this style.

- Important words are in **this style**. These are significant words that we are meeting for the first time. Subsequently they will appear as normal text.

- File names are in **THIS_STYLE**. All file names appear like this in the text, even when they are conventionally written in lower case inside a program.

- Keys that you press are in *this style*, such as *Enter* or *Ctrl*.

- Properties are in this style.

# Assumptions and Code

Visual Basic is very friendly and enters skeletal code for you when you select a control or a form, etc. As the book progresses, we will assume that you will recognize these familiar entries and adjust your code entry accordingly. For example, this is a typical piece of code automatically generated for a click routine when selecting a control button, which you called "cmdQuit"

Sub cmdQuit_Click()

End Sub

The instruction to enter the code : `Unload frmTest` , for this button simply means to place it between Sub & End Sub. It will then be the instruction for this 'Click of the button'

As we progress, you will become very familiar with the initial stages of setting up a Visual Basic project. For example, re-naming and captioning various elements on your designed 'screen' will happen every time. You will become very familiar with this and the generated code, and so we will start to assume that you will alter your elements without prompting. A quick look at the code discussed will give you the necessary guide. In the paragraph above, for example, we would assume after a few chapters that you would understand that `frmTest`, means you would have named your Form ..... "frmTest".

Be careful to check those 'little things' when Visual Basic doesn't behave! Pasting in code from text editors can sometimes inject a rogue space or hidden code. Remember to give the end of newly entered code a *return* for safety.

You will find things easier if you have to hand the language reference manual from the Visual Basic box or, alternatively keep a close eye on the Help system for syntax details.

We also assume you will be using Visual Basic 3 as your compiler. Although there is enough congruency with Visual Basic 2 for you to get something out of the book, Version 1 users will find the differences too much to bear!

# Assumptions and Code

# Chapter 1

# Getting To Know Visual Basic

Welcome to the wonderful world of Visual Basic! This book is a guide to, and a route map through, the vast array of functions and facilities that Visual Basic offers for writing excellent systems under Windows. But enough of the hype - we're sure that you know how good Visual Basic is, or you wouldn't be reading the introduction to this book. So take it to the check out, get it home, and we can begin in earnest.

This initial chapter will take you quickly through the basics of the Visual Basic environment, and will introduce you to the overall concept of event-driven programming. To use this book you simply need some programming experience and a desire to move ahead in your programming career.

In this chapter we will cover:

- The graphic development environment of Visual Basic
- How Visual Basic fits into Windows
- Your first application
- Saving your work
- Entering code

## Chapter 1 - Getting To Know Visual Basic

## Visual Basic Concepts

Before we leap into the programming, and get too involved in the nitty-gritty, we will take a step back and find out exactly what Visual Basic is, and how it fits into the development of applications under Windows.

> A word of warning. We're going to assume that you have programmed before in some language, under some kind of operating system. If you haven't done so, then you may find the going a little tough. If you need to get yourself up to speed on the basics of programming, now is probably a good time to go back to the bookstore and pick up a beginner's guide (*The Beginner's Guide To Visual Basic 3* is a good bet).

# Graphic Development, Driven by Events

Visual Basic 3 is a graphical development environment for Windows. Using it, you can create powerful windows applications with all the flair and graphical panache you would expect to see in a normal 'out of the box' professional Windows application program (such as Word). Using Visual Basic, you create applications by first drawing the user interface (creating forms, placing graphics objects and controls on those forms) then writing code to make these objects respond to user events (such as being clicked with a mouse, or triggered by pressing a key).

# Event-Driven Programming

Windows is an event-driven operating system. What this means to you and me as developers is that applications in Windows are all written and designed to respond to events. Nowhere is this more obvious than in Visual Basic. In Visual Basic, you don't write code in the traditional sense. Using traditional methods (like those you might use in QBasic, or C) you write a long list of program code, compile it and then run it. The program starts to run at a predefined point (usually the first line of code in the list) and then steps through any subsequent lines of code until it hits one which causes the program to end.

# Event-Driven Programming

In Visual Basic, you write programs by first designing the forms (the user interface), and then attaching code to the elements of the user interface that need to respond to the user (by triggering events). For example, you may want a command button to display a message box onto the screen when it is clicked. In such a case, you would just write a small amount of code and attach it to the command button's `click` event. You can tell Visual Basic where to start running your code (that is, which module to run first, or which form to display first), but from then on the flow of program control is left entirely up to the user. He or she could close the window which contains your user interface at any time, and you often need to write code to cope with this event.

> Event-driven code also brings with it a number of expectations on the part of the user. He or she doesn't expect your program to force them down a preset route.

Event-driven programs (or more specifically Windows programs) should always provide a way for the user to cancel an operation, or suddenly jump from one operation to another, and return to the first at a later time. Thankfully, in Visual Basic, this is really a false complexity. It sounds really tricky to do, especially if you are coming from a programming background that is not graphical at all, but in reality it is surprisingly easy to accomplish. You will learn over time that most of the stuff a *traditional* coder would consider to be really hard to do is all done for you.

Some people have trouble with the event-driven concept, but the secret of good event-driven coding is to have a clear understanding of the requirements of your program, so that you can select the correct events to code to make your application respond to the user correctly.

> For those of you who have written modular code, event-driven programming is similar to writing code modules to undertake specific tasks, with Windows acting as the control module.

## Device Independence

Another very powerful feature of both Windows and Visual Basic is *device independence*. In traditional character-based environments such as DOS, your program may have to cope with being run on many different screen

# Chapter 1 - Getting To Know Visual Basic

resolutions and capabilities. One day it may be running on a dated EGA display with only 16 colors, the next it could find itself alive on a state-of-the-art True Color Super VGA display, with enough colors to produce an accurate reproduction of the Sistine Chapel!

In Windows, all the effort involved in handling these different devices is already done for you. Windows handles the color mapping from one video display to another. It also handles all the keyboard processing for you, and tracks the mouse in its spare time, leaving you and your program to get on with the job in hand. When you need to know about the mouse you just ask Windows. If you want to display something you just write code to tell Windows where to put it and how high to make it - it then worries about whether or not it will fit, and what colors are best used in the display.

## Projects

All the work that you do for an application is held as a **project** within Visual Basic. The project will hold all the code that you write, all the forms that you design, and all the controls that you use on the forms. These details are held in a project file called a `.MAK` file. A project is really the Visual Basic term for an application in development.

Visual Basic is a compiler, of sorts, so you can turn a project into an `.EXE` application by compiling it. This is in fact an item on the File menu, a menu which contains items allowing you to deal with the files in your project and the project itself. This is a fairly simple concept: a project consists of files. Although a project is a single application, and ultimately a single executable program, the project is actually made up of files. Each Form or Window in a Visual Basic project is a file, which is usually stored on your hard disk with an `.FRM` suffix. You may also have pure code modules (defined with a `.BAS` suffix - as per regular Basic). You may also use VBX files these are pre-written or defined mini-modules or controls.

> Controls are the objects, such as command buttons and textboxes, that you use when writing a Visual Basic program. They build up the user interface of the program, and give the user something he or she can interact with on the screen. We'll see these in use later in this chapter.

# Projects and Forms

## Forms

Visual Basic forms are the windows in your program that provide your users with information they need to see, as well as places to enter and maintain their data. Think in terms of a game for a moment: you need at least one form to show the player the playing area containing their ship and the bad guys. You'll probably also want a separate form to display the game's title screen and another for the high scores table. Each one of these forms will appear as different file in your project (with .FRM extensions), but all will be compiled into the final executable program.

## The Visual Basic Environment

Before we dive in to the real stuff of Visual Basic programming, there is a more pressing matter at hand - how on earth do you get started? After you have endured the withering delay that is the Visual Basic setup, you will be presented with a fairly confusing array of menus, icons, toolbars, and forms, all of which represent the tools at your disposal to allow you to quickly create powerful Windows applications. We'll introduce you to all of these things and also show you some of the code behind the fancy graphics. At the end of the chapter you will find yourself jumping around the Visual Basic environment, diving into properties window and writing in the code window along with the best of them. Enough delay, we're sure that you're itching to get clicking with that mouse, so sit back, relax and enjoy!

## Opening Up

The first time you run up Visual Basic you are confronted with what you might find to be a terrifying sight - icons everywhere. Let's take a look at each part of the display in turn.

## Chapter 1 - Getting To Know Visual Basic

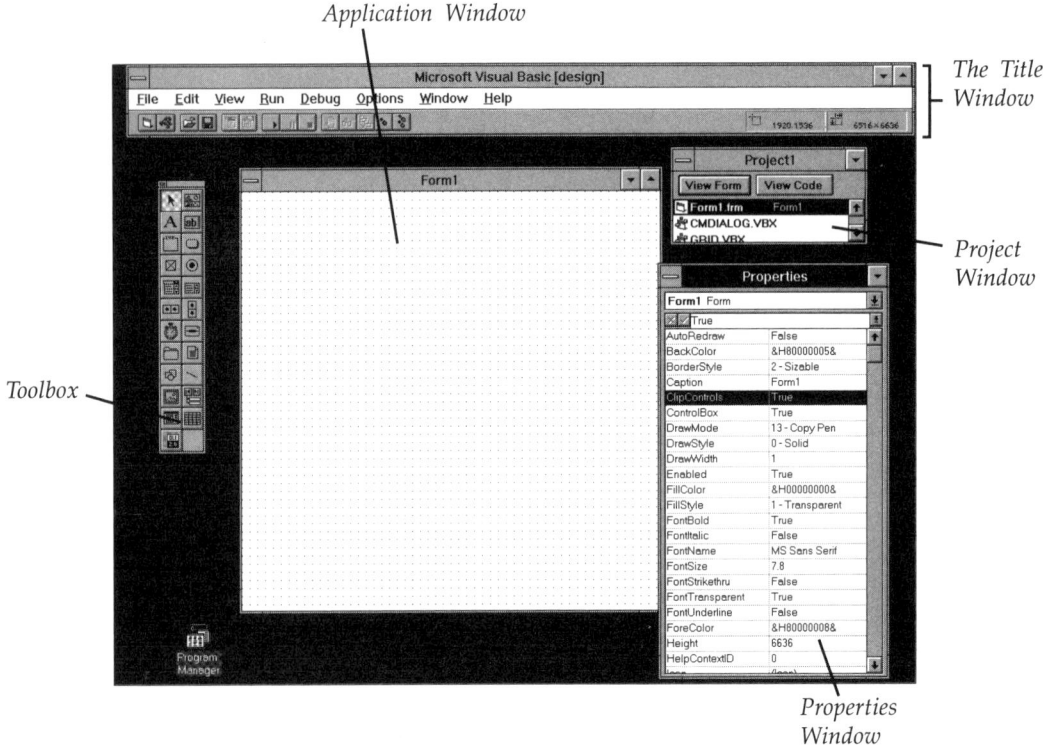

At the top of the display you have the main Visual Basic title, menu and toolbar:

*This is the title bar. It shows you are in Visual Basic, that you have a project loaded, and which operating mode you are in (in this case, design mode).*

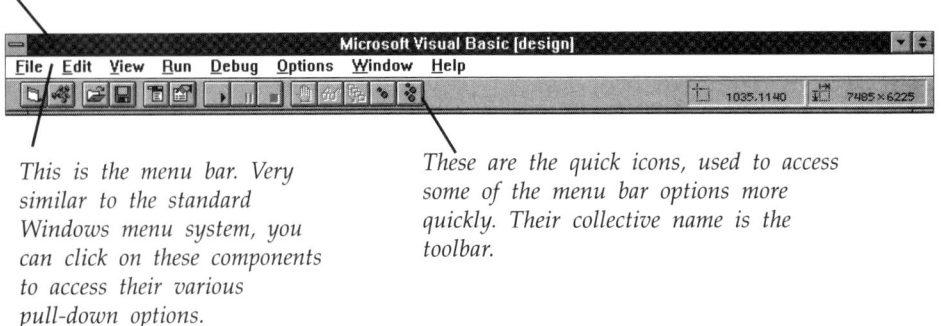

*This is the menu bar. Very similar to the standard Windows menu system, you can click on these components to access their various pull-down options.*

*These are the quick icons, used to access some of the menu bar options more quickly. Their collective name is the toolbar.*

# Visual Basic Enviroment

We'll now introduce you to each of these fundamental components of Visual Basic a little more fully.

## The Title Bar

The title bar itself is much the same as it is in any other Windows program. Its most obvious function is to show you that you have Visual Basic loaded and, if you have a project loaded, it tells you  its name and which operating mode you are working in.

## *Operating Mode*

The operating mode is important. Visual Basic works in three modes:

- design
- run
- break

Initially you will spend most of your time in design mode. This is the mode where you can place controls onto forms, write code to take control of the application and generally alter the way the program will run and look.

Try pressing *F5* to run the default program and the mode will change to run indicating that the program you are working on (the default one in this case) is now running. This program doesn't do much, but you have a window that you can maximize, minimize, re-size, and which also has a control button in the top left corner to close it. Not too bad for no code! You'll find that much of what may seem to be difficult or complex is handled by Visual Basic for you.

The final mode is break. While the program is running press *Ctrl* and *Break* together or click on the Pause icon on the toolbar and the mode display will say break. In this state the program is essentially paused. From here you can examine exactly where in the code (if it has any) Visual Basic has got to, the value of any variables in the project, and much more besides.

13

# Chapter 1 - Getting To Know Visual Basic

We look at break mode in a lot more detail in Chapter 11. For the time being we will concentrate on design and run modes. If the program is still running select End from the Run menu to stop it.

## The Menu Bar

Immediately beneath the title bar is the menu bar. Just as with the menus you come across in any other Windows program, you can *drop* the menus down by pointing at a heading and clicking once with the left mouse button. Take a look at the menu bar for a moment. There are 8 menu items:

- File
- Edit
- View
- Run
- Debug
- Options
- Window
- Help

As you might expect, each of these has a plethora of menu items underneath (in the drop down menus), which allow you to take control of the Visual Basic environment, as well as more general aspects of your project.

## The File Menu

The File menu lets you deal with projects, allowing you to load and save entire projects or individual files, print out the code and forms in your project and compile a stand-alone executable program which you can distribute to your users without the need for them to have Visual Basic.

# The Menu Bar

> In fact, Microsoft positively object to programmers giving away free copies of Visual Basic with their applications, but we will look at a more legal alternative later in the book.

## The Edit Menu

The Edit menu provides you with all the normal menu options you would expect to find in a Microsoft Windows application. With the items on this menu you can cut and paste both code and graphical elements of your user interface, search and replace specific chunks of text within your application's code, undo any mistakes you might make and redo things that you don't want to have to do by hand (great if you need to quickly put 50 command buttons onto a form).

## The View Menu

The View menu lets you toggle the toolbar on and off, bring up the code window to allow you to edit the code for the application, and move about the various pieces of code in your application.

> Remember, Visual Basic applications consist of both forms (containing the graphical stuff that your users will interact with) as well as the code that controls these elements.

Both the forms and the code have their own windows, and you can bring these windows into view using the Project window from the Window menu. You can also get to the code window from the View menu using the hotkey, F7. As with all the other menus, we will cover how to use the menu items in much greater depth through the course of the rest of this chapter.

## The Run Menu

The Run menu, unsurprisingly, contains menu items which let you control the running of the project on which you are working. It only has three entries: running a project, stopping a project, or restarting a project (used when you are debugging your code). To run a program you can either press F5, click

*F5*, click the Run icon (you'll see that in a moment) or select Start from the Run menu. To stop the program you simply select End from the Run menu, as you did when you followed the earlier example.

## The Debug Menu

The Debug menu also lets you take control of Visual Basic's built-in debugger, letting you step through your application one line of code at a time, set breakpoints which trip up the program and pause it, examine variables, and much more besides. Debugging and controlling the running of a program is a whole topic in itself and is covered in greater detail in Chapter 10, *Debugging*.

## The Options Menu

The Options menu has only two entries. These allow you to change the default settings for your Visual Basic environment, and to alter some of the project options. These will both be discussed in greater detail in the section on options in the next chapter.

## The Window menu

The Window menu acts a little differently to the window option in most other Microsoft products, in that it brings into view the different windows you'll be using to write your application, such as the code window, or the project window. You will find that there are times when you will close some of the main Visual Basic windows to make the desktop less cluttered. It is the Window menu that you will use (or the short cut keys) to bring these closed windows back into view.

## The Help Menu

The final menu is the Help menu. Just like Help in any other Microsoft application, Visual Basic comes with a complete help system giving you quick and easy access to information that would otherwise take hours of searching through the manuals to find. Visual Basic is a very complex and powerful tool, and you will find over time that the help system becomes one of the features of it that you use most often.

# The Toolbar

## Using the Toolbar and the Toolbox

While menu items are very useful and provide a fairly easy way to control Visual Basic, they are quite cumbersome to use once you get used to Visual Basic. For that reason, many of the more common menu items are also displayed on a toolbar beneath the menu bar.

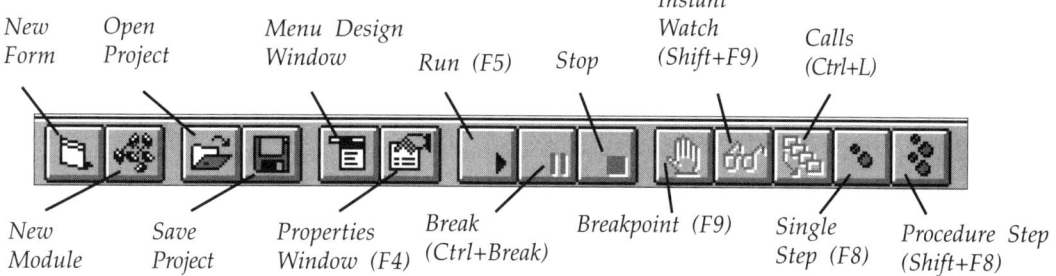

*Top labels:* New Form, Open Project, Menu Design Window, Run (F5), Stop, Instant Watch (Shift+F9), Calls (Ctrl+L)

*Bottom labels:* New Module, Save Project, Properties Window (F4), Break (Ctrl+Break), Breakpoint (F9), Single Step (F8), Procedure Step (Shift+F8)

Despite Windows' brief that programs should be intuitive and easy to use, newcomers to Visual Basic often complain that the icons are a little tricky to understand. For example, would you have guessed just by looking at these icons that the far left hand icon creates a new form in your project, or that the far right icon is used in debugging to ignore a section of code in the program? By the time that you've completed this book, you'll know what every icon does, and you'll have used them extensively throughout the exercises.

### The Toolbox

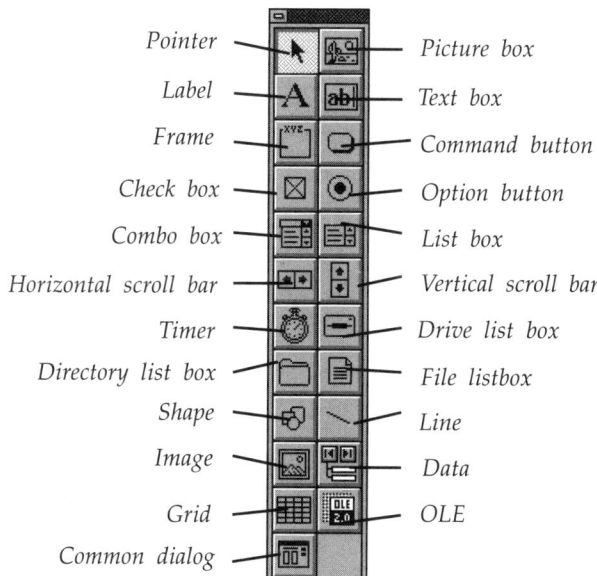

*Left labels:* Pointer, Label, Frame, Check box, Combo box, Horizontal scroll bar, Timer, Directory list box, Shape, Image, Grid, Common dialog

*Right labels:* Picture box, Text box, Command button, Option button, List box, Vertical scroll bar, Drive list box, File listbox, Line, Data, OLE

**17**

Chapter 1 - Getting To Know Visual Basic

You can bring the toolbox into view at any time by selecting Toolbox from the Window menu. Each icon in the toolbox, as you may have already guessed, is called a control. Controls are the objects that you use when writing a Visual Basic program. They build up the user interface of the program, and give the user something he or she can interact with. However, just saying that controls are the stuff users see and interact with is a little like saying computers add numbers - it doesn't quite show how useful they really are.

## Controls as Programs

Each control is in effect a separate program, (for the object-oriented literate amongst you, a control is actually an object). Once you draw a control onto a form you are adding the functionality of that control to your project. For example, you could draw a textbox on a form and tell Visual Basic to link it to an item in a table in an Access database. From that point on, your users can see and change information in that database, adding new details, deleting existing ones and so on, but without you having to do any coding at all. Of course, most Visual Basic programmers do end up writing a little bit of code, but this is really just to refine the way the controls work out of the box and make them fit into the application a little better. The placing of a control onto a form allows you to use its functionality.

## Reinventing the Wheel: the VBX

You could think of controls as being like parts on a car. If you were a car manufacturer and a customer asked you for a hi-tech CD stereo system in the car, you wouldn't go away and design a new one from scratch. You would probably use an existing model and simply plug it into the car. Controls work exactly the same way. Visual Basic lets you add controls to a project (using the Add File... item on the File menu) as well as remove unnecessary controls from a project. Most of these controls live on your hard disk as .VBX files (files ending in .VBX).

> There are literally thousands of plug in controls available to you from third-party developers. These controls can do absolutely anything from providing complete word processing capabilities, to giving you the ability to play sounds and music, to being able to display the latest computer movie and animation files. Later, you'll see how to use these controls yourself, how to add them to a project and actually write code to let your programs (and users) interact with them.

# Starting a Project

# Starting a New Project

```
File  Edit  View  Run  Debug  Options  Window  He
New Project
Open Project...
Save Project
Save Project As...
New Form
New MDI Form
New Module
Add File...                                Ctrl+D
Remove File
Save File                                  Ctrl+S
Save File As...                            Ctrl+A
Load Text...
Save Text...
Print...                                   Ctrl+P
Make EXE File...
1 \BLAST\SMALLCAP.MAK
2 \BEESETUP\BEESET.MAK
3 AUTOLOAD.MAK
4 H:\DEVELOPS\OWN\PEDESTAL\PEDRUN.MAK
Exit
```

When you first start up Visual Basic, and when you create a new project (using the New Project item on the File menu) Visual Basic always gives you one new form, called Form1 by default. The form as you now see it is the size that it *should* appear when the program is running, and also any controls that you have selected from the toolbox and dragged into position on the form itself. If you point and double click on a form, or a control on the form, then another window called the code window (shown below) comes into view. This will contain the Visual Basic code that you have written or Visual Basic has written for you, which is working behind the form (or control), and responds to the events that your users trigger. You can also bring the code window into view by pressing F7, or by selecting Code from the View menu.

19

# Chapter 1 - Getting To Know Visual Basic

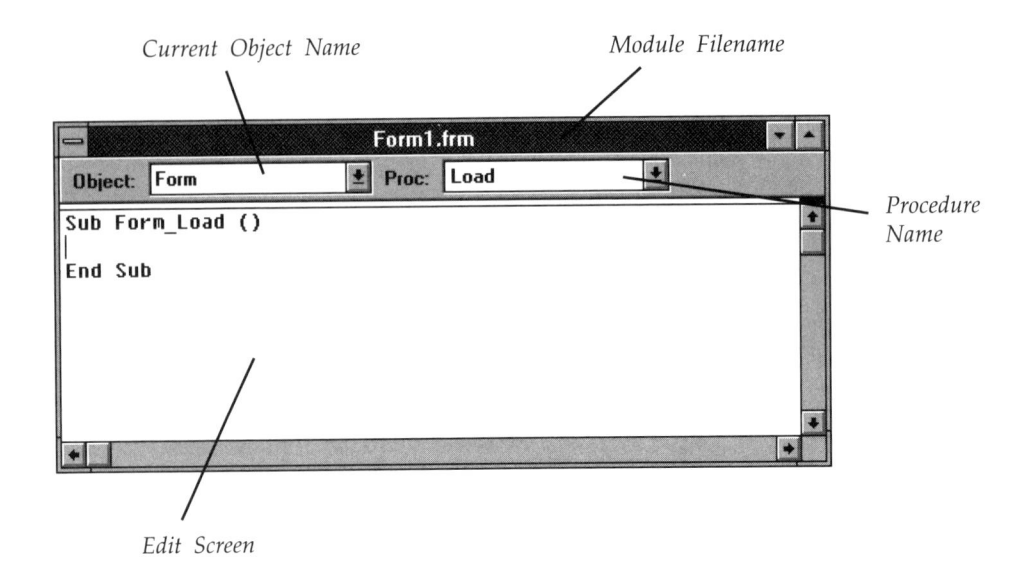

*Current Object Name*

*Module Filename*

*Procedure Name*

*Edit Screen*

## The Intelligent Code Window

The code window acts just like any other text editor you may be used to using, but with one major difference: the code window is intelligent. By this we don't mean that every now and then it will start a conversation with you, or go off in a sulk when you insult it (which will happen a lot, believe me). By intelligent we mean that if you type in something that doesn't comply with the Visual Basic syntax, the editor will stop and tell you so. Similarly, if you decide to indent a line of code using the *Tab* key, then any subsequent lines you type into the editor also get indented.

### Code and Event Combo Boxes

At the top of the code window there are two combo boxes. The left combo box tells you the object that you are currently dealing with, (remember that controls are objects). If you double click on the form itself, rather than on a control (to bring up the code window), then this combo box will tell you that you are dealing with the form object - that is, you are writing code or looking at the code that controls the form. The right hand combo box tells you the event you are dealing with. You can write code into the code window to do anything you want, but you will spend most of your time writing code to respond to Windows events. Again, if you have just double clicked on the form then this will say Load, meaning that you are looking at the code that takes place when the form 'loads'.

# Properties

## Properties

Let's take a look at the form itself again for a moment. You may have asked yourself 'How can I change the color of the form?' 'How can I change the border style?' 'What about the awful caption in the title bar, I want to change that straight-away'. All these things, the colors, captions, borders and so on, are called **properties** and can be controlled using the Properties window.

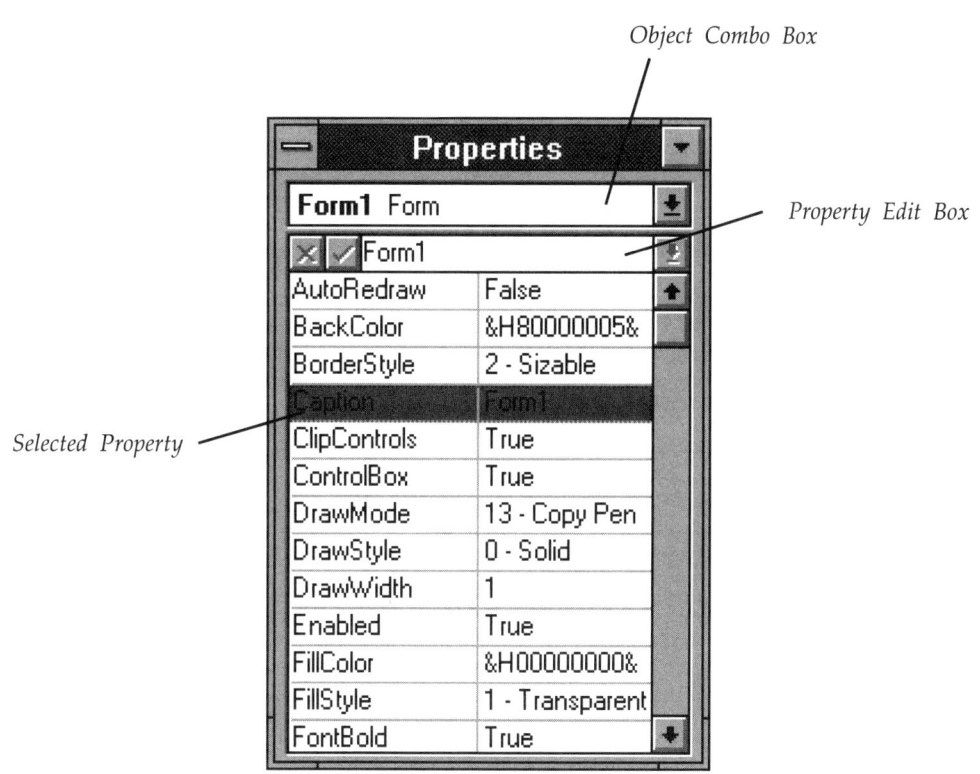

*Object Combo Box*

*Property Edit Box*

*Selected Property*

| Properties | |
|---|---|
| **Form1** Form | |
| X ✓ Form1 | |
| AutoRedraw | False |
| BackColor | &H80000005& |
| BorderStyle | 2 - Sizable |
| Caption | Form1 |
| ClipControls | True |
| ControlBox | True |
| DrawMode | 13 - Copy Pen |
| DrawStyle | 0 - Solid |
| DrawWidth | 1 |
| Enabled | True |
| FillColor | &H00000000& |
| FillStyle | 1 - Transparent |
| FontBold | True |

> There are a several ways to get to the **Properties** window. You can select the element whose properties you want to see and press *F4*, or select **Properties** from the **Window** menu. Use the method you feel most comfortable with.

**21**

# Chapter 1 - Getting To Know Visual Basic

Almost every object in your Visual Basic project (forms and controls on a form) has properties which you can look at and change using the Properties window. Over time you will find yourself spending a great deal of time with the Properties window since it is one of the key tools available to you to help refine and define the user interface of your project.

## The Properties Window

The Properties window is split into two main parts. Beneath the title bar, a combo box tells you which object you are dealing with and its name. In the case of the previous screenshot, the object is a form, and its name is Form1. You can drop down the combo box by clicking on the arrow to the right of the objects name, at which point you will see a list of all the objects used in the current form.

> In the case of this form, the list will only have an entry for Form1, because it's a new project, and there are no other controls on the form.

By default, whenever you create a new form, a module, or draw a control onto a form, Visual Basic gives it a name which is made up of the type of control plus a number. For example, the first textbox on a form is usually called Text1, the first command button, Command1, and so on. Clearly, with a great many forms and controls this can get a little confusing, and this is where the second part of the Properties window comes in.

## The Naming of Parts

Directly beneath the combo box is the value or setting of the currently highlighted property. In the case of the screenshot, the `caption` property is highlighted and it is set to its default value of Form1. Below this is the list of property names, and their values. These are the actual properties, and you can examine and set many of them both in design mode (the mode in which Visual Basic starts up) and at runtime through your code. You can navigate around the list of properties very easily:

- Using the scroll bar on the right of the Properties window.
- By clicking in the Properties window and using the cursor keys.

# The Properties Window

> By clicking in the window and pressing *Ctrl*, *Shift* and the first letter of the property you require.

Try it - click in the Properties window and press *Ctrl*, *Shift* and *N* and you will see a property appear called **Name**, which contains the name of the form (in this case Form1).

> Using names that mean something to you is an obvious advantage when using forms. In the above case, a better name for say, a login screen would probably be **frmLogin**, or **frmSecurity**. You can change the name by clicking on the current name in the window and typing over it with the new one. We'll come back to naming conventions in Chapter 3.

## The Project Window

The final, and very important window you will come across regularly is the Project window.

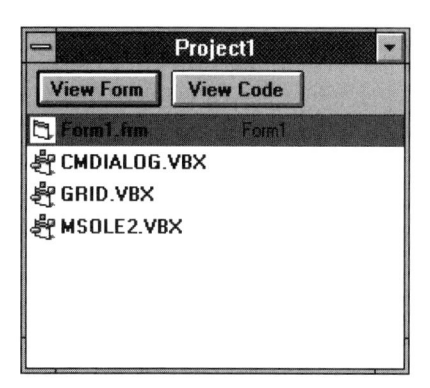

A Visual Basic project, as we've already said, can hold a great many forms, and code modules. Rather than have them all open on the screen at once, Visual Basic lets you navigate around them using the Project window. At the top of the window you will see two buttons: View Form and View Code. If you select a form from the list (you should only have one at the moment) and click the View Code button, then the code window for the selected form will appear, along with any code that the form may contain. Equally, if you select a form and click the View Form button then the form itself, and any controls you have drawn onto the form, will appear.

# Chapter 1 - Getting To Know Visual Basic

> If at any time you can't find the **project** window (for example, if it is hidden behind some of the other windows that you have open), then you can bring it into view by selecting **Project** from the **Window** menu.

You will also see from the screenshot that there are three extra controls in the project. These are the common dialog control, the grid control, and the OLE control. These are loaded as part of our default settings. We'll show you how to alter these using the `AUTOLOAD.MAK` file in the next chapter.

## Fundamentals: Implementation

Enough of the theory - let's try it out. We will now move to producing a real application in Visual Basic.

## The Password Project

What you are going to do now is create a form that looks like this:

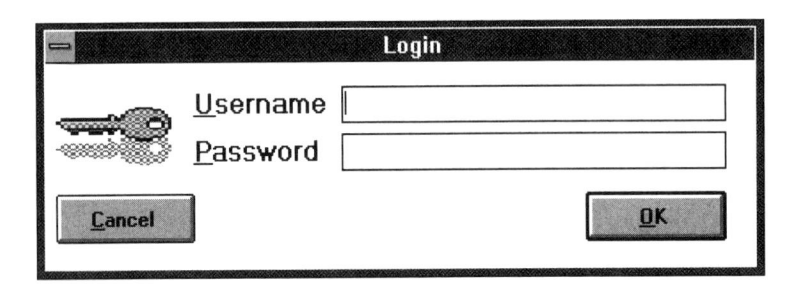

[Login dialog with Username and Password fields, Cancel and OK buttons]

We'll then write the code to control it. As we said before, the first stage to creating a Visual Basic project is to create the user interface. Load up Visual Basic, or if it is already loaded select the New Project item from the File menu. Whichever route you chose, Visual Basic will create a new project consisting of a single blank form. Just as with any other window, you can resize the form by clicking and dragging its borders. Click on the bottom right corner of the form, and with the left mouse button held down, drag the form so that it looks roughly the same size as the one in the screenshot.

24

# The Password Project

You have just done your first bit of programming: you have resized the form and Visual Basic will record the new dimensions in the Properties window, in the **Height** and **Width** properties. However, at the moment the form itself looks nothing like the one in the screenshot. To make it look a little more slick we need to change some of its properties.

## Changing Properties

Press *F4* to bring up the Properties windows and use the scroll bar to move to the **BorderStyle** property.

> If you have had much experience with Windows as a user, then you will know that it is possible for a window to not actually be resizeable, or to have no border, or to have a single line border, or the more common double width resizeable border.

Click on the word **BorderStyle** once and you will see that its value is now shown at the top of the properties list, with a downward arrow displayed on the right hand side.

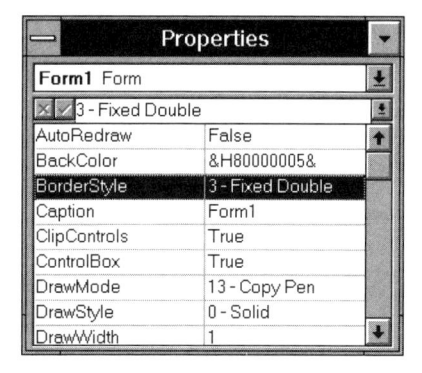

| Properties |  |
|---|---|
| Form1 Form | |
| 3 - Fixed Double | |
| AutoRedraw | False |
| BackColor | &H80000005& |
| BorderStyle | 3 - Fixed Double |
| Caption | Form1 |
| ClipControls | True |
| ControlBox | True |
| DrawMode | 13 - Copy Pen |
| DrawStyle | 0 - Solid |
| DrawWidth | 1 |

Click on the down arrow to drop down the combo list and a list of border styles will appear. What we want to do here is select a **Fixed Double** border, so click on that entry.

The form still doesn't look right - it still has maximize and minimize icons on its top right corner but the form in the screenshot doesn't have these.

**25**

# Chapter 1 - Getting To Know Visual Basic

Find the `MaxButton` and `MinButton` properties in the Properties window. These are both `True` or `False` properties. In each case just double click the property name to change the setting from the default `True` value to `False`. (The max. and min. buttons will still be shown at design time).

One final change is the caption. If you take a look at the screenshot again you will see that the title bar of that form says Login, but yours probably says Form1. Find the `Caption` property, and change it to `Login` (you can do this by clicking on the word `Form1` to the right of the word `Caption`).

## What You See Is Not What You Get

If you have followed everything up to now very closely you are probably beginning to get very confused: the form still doesn't look that different to when you first resized it. Visual Basic is not a true 'what-you-see-is-what-you-get' environment. However, if you run the program at this stage you will see the form takes on quite a different appearance. To stop the program running simply double click on the control box on the top left corner of the form.

> To many people, this particular 'feature' of Visual Basic is most annoying. However, having forms with a slightly different look at design time and run-time does help you to see instantly whether or not the program is running.

## Adding a Textbox

The next step in our small program is to put two textboxes onto the form, into which the user can enter his or her username and password. Click on the Textbox icon on the Visual Basic toolbox (remember, if the toolbox is not visible then you can bring it into view by selecting Toolbox from the Window menu). You have selected a text box by moving your mouse to the Form body, and it will then change to a crosshair. Hold down the left mouse button and 'drag out' a textbox.

Once you have a textbox looking just the way you want, you can easily create a copy of it. When you create a control you will see resize handles all around it (a thin border with small black squares on each edge and corner). This tells you that the control is currently selected, and that if you bring up the Code window or the Properties window you will see

26

# The Text Property

information relating to the textbox as opposed to the form. With a control selected you can also use the Copy and Paste items on the Edit menu to quickly create new copies of the control. Do it now: select Copy, then select Paste. A dialog box will appear:

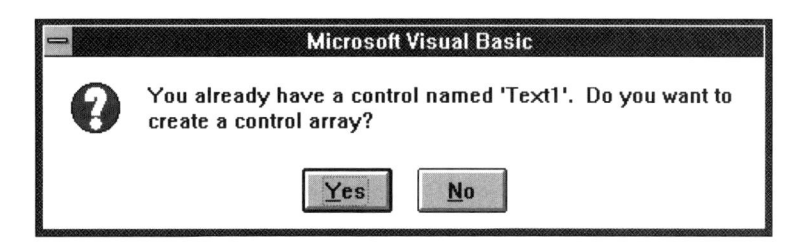

**Microsoft Visual Basic**

You already have a control named 'Text1'. Do you want to create a control array?

[ Yes ]   [ No ]

For the time being, don't worry too much about what this means, just click on the No button. A second textbox will appear on your form which you can now drag to beneath the first to create the two text entry areas we need.

## Changing the Text Property

However, there is still a problem with both textboxes. Firstly, both have the words Text1 in them. If you run the program this will appear in the textboxes to the users. The reason for this is the **Text** property. Whenever a user keys data into a textbox, whatever they key in appears in the **Text** property. When you create a textbox (and then a copy from it), Visual Basic puts some dummy text into the **Text** property so that you can get an idea for how the text will look. To get rid of this click on the first textbox and then, holding down *Ctrl*, click on the second. Both textboxes are now selected. Press *F4* to display the Properties window and find the **Text** property. Click on the word **Text,** press *Space* and then *Backspace*, followed by *Enter*. This clears out the text from the **Text** properties of both selected controls, and thus has the effect of clearing the textboxes. Click anywhere else on the form to now deselect the textboxes.

As you know, Visual Basic gives each control a default name, using the **Name** property of the control. If we wanted to set the **Text** property, or find out what is in it, from within program code (which you will do later) then you are going to end up with code looking like this:

```
Text1.Text = "My Name"
Text2.Text = "My Password"
```

27

Not very intuitive is it! The solution is to give each textbox a more meaningful name. Select the first textbox (the one that will ultimately hold the username) by clicking on it once with the left mouse button. When it is selected (shown by the resize border appearing around the control) bring up the Properties window again and find the **Name** property. To change the property just click on the name itself (which should be something like **Text1**) and type over it with the word **txtUsername**. Now do the same for the second textbox, changing the name to **txtPassword**. Now when we use the textbox controls in our code, it will be much easier to understand. For the above, our code would read:

```
txtUsername.Text = "My Name"
txtPassword.Text = "My Password"
```

Now you know how to draw controls on a form, and set their properties, see if you can do the rest yourself. Using the label control and the command button control, draw two labels (which will be your user clues) and two command buttons (which will eventually be 'OK' and 'Cancel') on the form so that their size and position looks roughly like the ones in the screenshot. To display the text shown in the command buttons and the labels in the screenshot, you simply need to change the **Caption** property of each. There is a slight difference though between these captions and the caption you set up for the form's title bar. Look closely at the screenshot again - notice how the first letter of each of the captions is underlined.

*Command button* — *Label control*

We'll solve this now.

## Hotkeys

If you are a regular Windows user then you will know that these underlined letters represent hotkeys. Pressing *Alt-O* for example would click the OK button for you. Pressing *Alt-U* would move the cursor to the label control, but since labels only display information and can't accept any input from the user, the cursor would move to the next control in the sequence (which we will look at in a moment). To set the hotkeys, simply prefix the caption with **&**. For example, the **Caption** property of the **Username** label should actually be **&User Name**, the **Password** caption should be **&Password**, and so on. You can use this technique to set the hotkey of any control that has a **Caption** property (not all do), with the obvious exception that you can't do it to the form's caption.

At this point, your form should look something like the following:

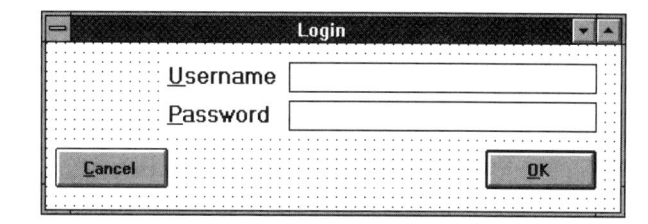

## Adding Sparkle

It still doesn't look quite like the screenshot earlier since the colors are wrong (something Visual Basic corrects when you run the program, as you've seen) and our form has a graphic on it, whereas yours does not. Since the whole Visual Basic ethos is graphics and lots of them, it shouldn't come as much of a surprise that putting a graphic illustration of some kind onto a form is not that hard to do. Visual Basic gives you two controls to let you add a little sparkle to your application's look and feel: the picture box control  and the image control:

Each has its own strengths and weaknesses (as you will see in Chapter 4), but each performs basically the same task. For now, let's just use the image control.

## Using the Image Control

Select the image control from the toolbox. Once you have selected the control simply move to the form and drag it out there as you did with the command buttons, labels and textboxes. You should see a blank outline appear on the form, showing you where the graphic will go.

> Don't worry too much about getting the dimensions right since the image control will resize itself when you load in the graphic image.

## Loading up Graphics

Loading up a graphic is really easy. Simply bring up the Properties window of the graphics box you just created, find the `Picture` property and either double click it or press *F4*. A common dialog (in this case the Load Picture dialog) will appear asking you for the name of the graphic that you want to display. Visual Basic comes with a vast number of sample graphics for you to play with: these are all stored on your hard disk in the icons directory within your Visual Basic directory. The one we are after is stored in `ICONS\MISC` and is called `SECUR08.ICO`. Move to that directory and find the file, click on it and then click O<u>K</u>. Miraculously, the icon will appear on your form! If you don't like it try choosing one of the others - again it's all a matter of personal taste.

# Saving to Disk

Now it's time to see how your application works so far. Before we run it, it is a good idea to save it to the hard disk. Windows, as you know, can sometimes be a little temperamental. There is nothing worse than spending hours working on a top-dollar user interface, only to have the dreaded GPF dialog appear (for non-Windows programmers, this is a General Protection Fault, and crashes your application at the very minimum), informing you that Windows has crashed, taking your work with it. To save, either click on the Save icon on the main toolbar or select Sa<u>v</u>e Project from the <u>F</u>ile menu. You will then be asked to select directory and file names for both the form in your project, and for the project itself.

## Naming Conventions

Normally, forms have a name ending in `.FRM` and projects have a name ending in `.MAK`. There is nothing forcing you to stick to this standard - it's just the accepted practice, and makes for a less confusing life later on.

> For example, if you decide to buy an add-on code manager for Visual Basic then you will find that many of the available ones expect forms to have a `.FRM` extension, and the projects to have a `.MAK` extension, and so on.

# Saving

## Early Functionality

Having saved your work, press *F5* or click the Run icon to start the program running. Although we haven't done any real code yet, the application is surprisingly functional. You can press *Tab* to move from one control to the next, type information into the textboxes, highlight that information and use Cut (*Ctrl-C*) and Paste (*Ctrl-V*) to copy and paste information from the textboxes to each other, and so on. Visual Basic, or more precisely Windows, also deals with the more mundane stuff that most people take for granted, but which can be really difficult to code. For example, click on the command buttons at the bottom of the screen and you will see them depress and then come back up again. Each of them will also get a solid black border to show you which one currently has the focus (that is, which one is currently receiving user input).

## Tab Order

If you are lucky, pressing *Tab* will move you first from the username textbox to the password textbox, then to the OK button and finally to the Cancel button. This is something called the tab order - but rarely is the default tab order the one you want. The way that a user is able to move around your forms will affect their usage of that form. Most people would expect your application to either tab from left to right, or from top to bottom. In the case of our Login application, we'd expect the tab order to be Username, Password, then the OK button. We'll show you how to do this now, and we go into much more detail in Chapter 3 which deals with controls.

Stop the program running by either selecting End from the Run menu, or by pressing the Stop icon on the main toolbar You set the tab order using the `TabIndex` property of the controls. Simply select each control in turn and using the Properties window set up the `TabIndex` property. The first control to receive the highlight in a form is always numbered 0, with each control in turn after that being incremented by one. Be sure to number the label controls also. Even though they can never be selected by the user, or receive input from the user, they are useful in defining the tab order. For example, the Username label has a hotkey as *Alt-U*. Pressing *Alt-U* will attempt to move the focus to the label control, at which point Visual Basic will say 'hang on, this can't happen, move to the next control'. Then, providing the tab order is set correctly, the focus moves to the username textbox.

**31**

The order you'll need to set them is: **label1**, **Tab Index** (0), **txtUsername**, **label2**, **txtPassword**, **cmdOK**, **cmdCancel**. The image control doesn't have a tab index.

# Coding

Time now to add some code. Before we do, let's think about what we want to do. In a real world program this form would represent the entry point to a major application. Therefore, if the user presses the Cancel button (indicating that they don't want to enter a username and password) then the program should stop. You can stop a Visual Basic program from code in a number of ways, the easiest being to get rid of all forms. Forms have two states: they can either be loaded (in which case they are normally on display and accepting input) or they can be unloaded (removed from memory totally, until the next time your code loads them of course). A Visual Basic program will normally end as soon as all the forms have unloaded. So, when the Cancel button is clicked we want to unload Form1 (since Form1 should still be the name of this form, unless you decided to change it earlier on). In code this looks like this:

```
Unload Form1
```

Pretty simple, really! To key this in, double click the Cancel button - the code window will appear with an empty subroutine in it waiting for you to key in your code:

```
Sub Command2_Click()

End Sub
```

Just type in **Unload Form1** between the **Sub** and **End Sub** statements

```
Sub Command2_Click()
    Unload Form1
End Sub
```

Visual Basic automatically checks the code for obvious errors as you type it, warning you of problems as it goes. In addition, when you press *Enter*, or otherwise move the cursor to a new line of code, Visual Basic will color code it, using colors to highlight which parts of the code are Visual Basic keywords, expressions and so on.

# Coding

## User Input and Coding

Now, what about when the user clicks the OK button? Well, first we need to check the username textbox (which can be done by looking at the **Text** property). Unless they enter, for example, Me (case sensitive) we will want to display an error message and give them the opportunity do it again. You can display messages using the **MsgBox** command as code attached to an action. Like **Print** in normal Basic, **Cout** in C++ and **printf** in C, this simply displays text on screen. However, in Visual Basic, think of it as displaying text with attitude. The **Msgbox** command puts up a complete new window with your text in, and command buttons to get out of the window. Later in the book you will see how it can be used to also display graphics, and get options from a user. Let's look at the code to direct a user.

```
If txtUsername.Text <> "Me" Then
    MsgBox "Sorry, you entered an invalid username"
    txtUsername.SetFocus
```

Having programmed before, you shouldn't be too daunted by this code. If the **Text** property of the **txtUsername** control is not equal to **"Me"**, then display the message box and set focus back to the username textbox. If this is confusing don't worry, we're just trying to introduce you to what coding in Visual Basic entails - you don't have to understand the syntax totally at this stage to appreciate the theory behind it.

We also need code to do the same sort of thing to the password textbox. Unless the user enters noidea then we need to display the message box again, and set the focus back to the password.

```
ElseIf txtPassword.Text <> "noidea" Then
    MsgBox "Sorry, you entered an invalid password"
    txtPassword.SetFocus
```

Finally, if both those checks got through alright, then we need to tell the user (with a message box) that they got everything correct. After that we can simply unload the form to end the program, although in the real world we would probably load up another form instead. We can give the user a friendly pat on the back, thus;

```
Else
    MsgBox "Access granted...."
    Unload Form1
End If
```

## Chapter 1 - Getting To Know Visual Basic

The `EndIf` at the bottom marks the end of the condition (`If`...`ElseIf`...`Else`...`End If`). We will cover this in a lot more detail later in the book (Chapter 6 to be precise). Let's now put the full code behind our OK control. Double click the OK command button and change the code in the editor so that it looks like this:

```
Sub Command1_Click()
    If txtUsername.Text <> "Me" Then
        MsgBox "Sorry, you entered an invalid username"
        txtUsername.SetFocus
    ElseIf txtPassword.Text <> "noidea" Then
        MsgBox "Sorry, you entered an invalid password"
        txtPassword.SetFocus
    Else
        MsgBox "Access granted...."
        Unload Form1
    End If
End Sub
```

Both sections of code that you just entered tell the command buttons what to do when the click event occurs (`Sub Command1_Click()`, and `Sub Command2_Click()`).

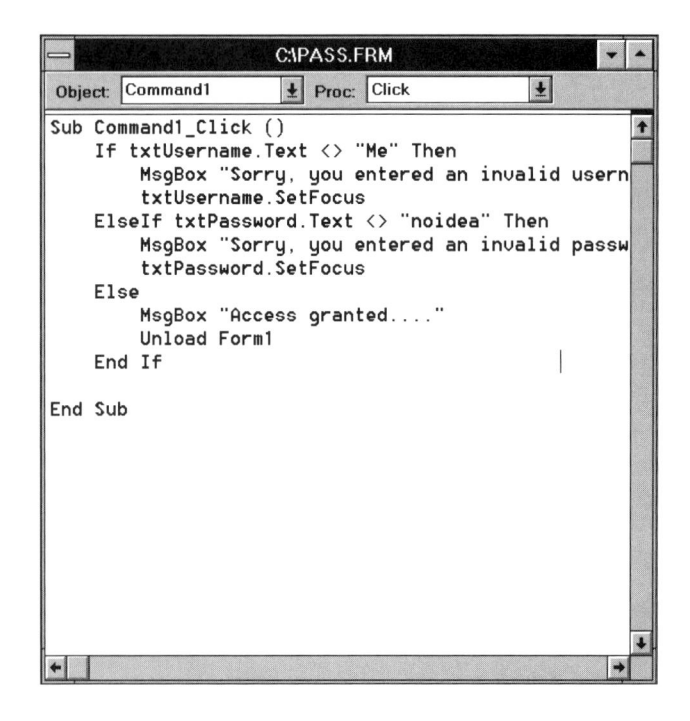

```
                    C:\PASS.FRM
Object: Command1         Proc: Click

Sub Command1_Click ()
    If txtUsername.Text <> "Me" Then
        MsgBox "Sorry, you entered an invalid usern
        txtUsername.SetFocus
    ElseIf txtPassword.Text <> "noidea" Then
        MsgBox "Sorry, you entered an invalid passw
        txtPassword.SetFocus
    Else
        MsgBox "Access granted...."
        Unload Form1
    End If

End Sub
```

# Summary

You could also have coded double click code, code to respond to keypresses and much more. All these things we will cover in depth during the rest of the book. For now though, congratulations are in order - you just wrote your first Visual Basic program. Run it (press *F5*, select §tart form the Run menu, or press the Run button from the toolbar) and try it out.

## Resaving

An important point to finish with - because you saved the work earlier you can now just click on the Save icon on the main toolbar and Visual Basic will quite happily go away and write the updated program to the disk without any prompts or dialogs appearing. Later you will see how to make Visual Basic automatically save the code for you before running your project. Gone are the days when you can talk your way past a deadline with the 'I forgot to save my code' excuse.

## Summary

In this chapter you learnt:

- What all the menus, toolbars and icons are there for
- What event driven programming is and why it is important
- How to create a user interface in Visual Basic
- How to set up the tab order of your user interface
- How to set up the properties of the controls
- How to display a graphic
- How to write code for your project
- How to save your work to disk

Take a rest now, the rest of the book gets a little more detailed!

# Chapter 2

# Projects and Forms

In Chapter 1 we looked briefly at the main components of a project, some properties, forms, and did a little coding. In this chapter we'll look at projects in greater detail, and alter the default settings that came with Visual Basic to customize our environment.

We'll be trying out all the different form styles available in Visual Basic, and considering when and where we should use each, and trying out an example using the Multiple Document Interface (MDI). So let's not dally here, time to get our feet wet!

In this chapter you'll learn about:

- Project files
- Compiling your projects
- Form styles
- Dialogs

# Visual Basic Projects: Concepts

We've already seen how to start a new project in the first chapter. Now, we want to be able to add and delete files in our project, then save our project at the end.

## Managing Your Projects

The project window holds all the files that go to make up our project. To remove a file, just highlight it in the project window, then from the drop down File menu, select Remove File. You will see the file name deleted from the project window; however, the actual file has not been deleted. So don't worry if you accidentally remove a file, just follow the steps below in adding a file, and you'll get it back. The down side of this is that you could end up with lots of forms and files in your directories that are no longer used.

> When we start a new project, we always create a new directory to hold all the files associated with the project. When the project is complete, we check the .MAK file against all the files in the directory, and delete any that are no longer used. This is a good habit to get into, as you'll always know where to find the files required for your project.

### Adding Files to Your Project

As the project is made up of many different files, there are different ways to add them to the project. To add a new form or code module, select the appropriate icon from the toolbar. You'll find that the first icon on the toolbar adds a new form to your project, and the second adds a code module.

OK, run up Visual Basic, and let's add a form and a module to your project. Apart from the fact that you've now got another blank form and empty code module on the desktop, you'll see that your project window now has three entries that do not end in .VBX.

# Projects

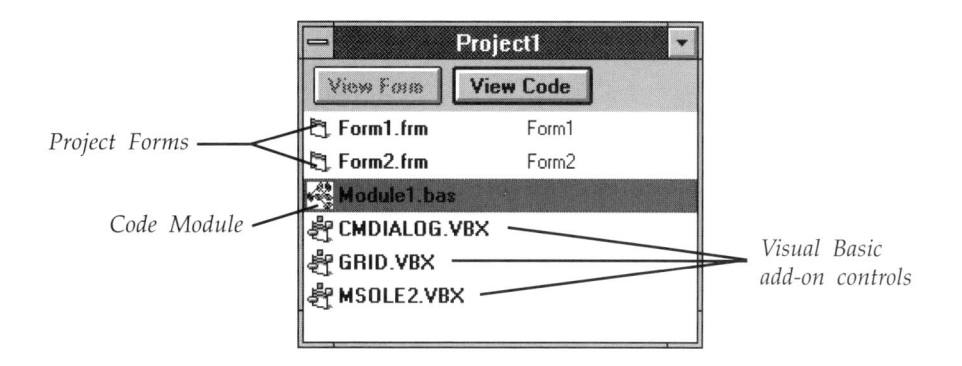

*Project Forms* — Form1.frm / Form2.frm
*Code Module* — Module1.bas
*Visual Basic add-on controls* — CMDIALOG.VBX / GRID.VBX / MSOLE2.VBX

However, we just realized that for this project, we didn't want a code module, so go ahead and remove it. In this case because it wasn't saved, the removal of the module has deleted it.

To add custom controls to your project, select Add File... from the File menu:

From here, you are able to add all sorts of goodies to your project, the easiest being custom controls. These are not available in the standard version, so a little investment is required. A custom control is a **.VBX** (**V**isual **B**asic e**X**tension) file that adds to the functionality of Visual Basic.

> For those of you who have the Professional version of Visual Basic, you'll see custom controls such as the Sheridan 3D Controls, and the graph control. You'll find that .VBX files are available as freeware and shareware, as well as in commercial form. Bulletin Boards such as CompuServe are good areas to find these custom controls. You'll also see that your toolbox will expand to accommodate the new tools.

39

## Chapter 2 - Projects and Forms

We've added the **THREED.VBX** custom control to my project (it's one of the extras with the professional version of Visual Basic), and you'll see from the screenshot that six new controls have been added.

This is the **THREED.VBX**. These are 3D versions of other controls in the toolbox, such as the check box. They can then be selected and drawn as per vanilla controls.

If you have the Professional version, try drawing some of these controls on one of the forms (don't worry if you haven't got the Professional edition, the book concentrates on the Standard edition). Now draw on their 2D equivalents. You can see the difference, but the 3D controls don't really look all that 3D. To get the full effect, we need to change the background color of the form to light gray. Click on the form so that the Properties window has the form in the title. Now select **BackColor** in the properties window, and click on the arrow to the right. The color palette is displayed, from which you select light gray by clicking on it. The form color has changed, and now the 3D controls look really good. You'll find that most applications written in windows have light gray backgrounds, so that these 3D effects can be used. Try using the Backcolor property within the standard edition.

You can also add existing forms (**.FRM** files), and code modules (**.BAS** files) to your project by using the Add File... option from the File menu. The project window will be updated with the file that you have added.

> You may find that you create some forms that can be used in other projects, so by adding them to your current project you will not have to re-create them. All the code associated with the form is also added with the form. However, if you have to change the form or the code at all, it will alter the original, which you will probably not want to do. All you need to do is select the Save Project As... option from the File menu, and save the added form to your new project. This will create a copy which you can safely edit.

# Saving Projects

## File Types

There are several different types of file that make up a Visual Basic project. The **.BAS** files are code modules that contain Visual Basic code not directly associated to a form, the **.FRM** file holds the form that you have drawn, and its associated event code, and the **.VBX** file is a Visual Basic extension file, better known as control, such as the common dialog control. All the files that are used to make up your project are held in the project **.MAK** file.

# Saving Your Project

The final (and most important) thing that you will want to do is to save your project. There are several ways to save your project. The quickest way is to choose the save icon on the toolbar (the fourth one along). If you've not saved the project before, a dialog will be displayed asking you where you want to save the project details.

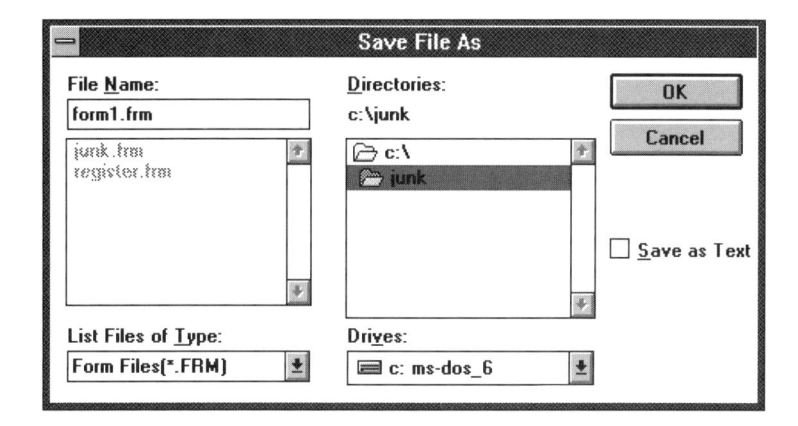

Note that each element of your project will be saved individually, so you'll have to go through this dialog for every file in the project, then the project file itself (**.MAK**). The other methods of saving your work are to select Sa*v*e Project, or Sav*e* Project As... from the *F*ile menu, or press *Ctrl* and *S*.

## *Save as Text*

You'll notice the *S*ave as Text check box in the Save File *A*s... dialog. If you check this box, then all your files will be saved in text format, and you'll then be able to edit in any text editor. You'll need to do this if you wish to make use of the code managers currently available, or the set up wizard, as these tools scan text files of Forms. Also, you may have a favorite text

## Chapter 2 - Projects and Forms

editor that you prefer to use, although we wouldn't really recommend one other than the one in Visual Basic, because this provides syntax checking, and validation of the entries in the properties of controls.

# The Project .mak File

All the files in your project are held in the `.MAK` file. This is a text file, and you can edit it with a text editor. It holds all kinds of interesting stuff, like the version information, `.EXE` file name, and the files that make up the project. Don't worry too much, you should never really need to edit the `.MAK` file, although we're sure that it will appeal to the hackers amongst you!

When Visual Basic starts, it reads a special `.MAK` file that tells it what to load at startup. This file is called the `AUTOLOAD.MAK` file, and it can be altered in the same manner as any of the `.MAK` files. To load it, select Open Project... from the File menu. This will display the Open Project dialog, from which you should select the `AUTOLOAD.MAK` file.

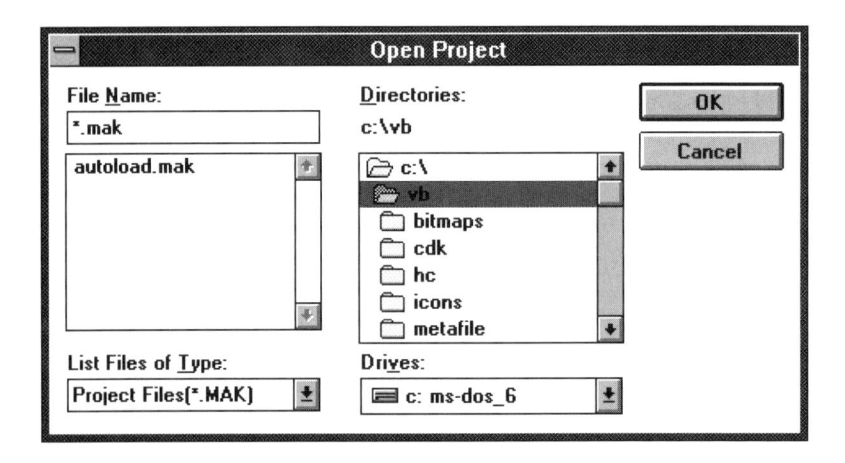

You can now add files and custom controls to the file, and then save it. The next time you start a project, all the new files that you've added will be included at the start of the project. Similarly, if you remove files, they will not be added by default. The `AUTOLOAD.MAK` file acts as a startup template.

# Environment Options

For Visual Basic to use the **AUTOLOAD.MAK** file as the project template, it must be saved in the same directory as Visual Basic **.EXE**, otherwise Visual Basic will load with only a single new form.

## Setting the Options

Let's look at the way that Visual Basic looks on our desktop, and the way that it initially sets up our projects. Most of the defaults that are set up when you installed Visual Basic will be OK, but there are a few that you'll be changing from time to time. Of course, if you love clashing colors, then you'll be able to change the look to satisfy those surrealist instincts! There are two options dialogs off the Options menu. We'll go through each in turn.

## Options - the Environment .... dialog

The first of the options dialogs is the Environment Options dialog. This gives you some control over the Visual Basic development environment options.

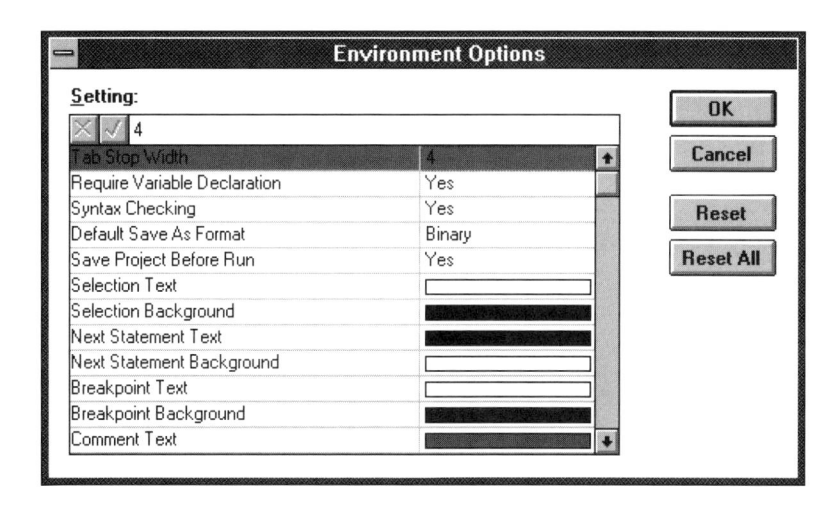

| Setting: | |
|---|---|
| Tab Stop Width | 4 |
| Require Variable Declaration | Yes |
| Syntax Checking | Yes |
| Default Save As Format | Binary |
| Save Project Before Run | Yes |
| Selection Text | |
| Selection Background | |
| Next Statement Text | |
| Next Statement Background | |
| Breakpoint Text | |
| Breakpoint Background | |
| Comment Text | |

> If you make a complete mess of the options, you can reset a selection of options with the **Reset** button, or reset all the defaults with the **Reset All** button.

43

# Chapter 2 - Projects and Forms

## The Forms Design Grid

The form design grid controls the way the controls are drawn, moved and re-sized on your form. You probably noticed that the form was loaded with a grid of dots that looks like a cool template for a game of squares. These can be switched on and off with the Show Grid set to Yes. This won't affect the alignment of your controls, it's just a matter of personal preference. The width and height of the grid is altered by entering a number between 30 and 1185 in the boxes. Setting the width and height to 30 allows for such small adjustments that it's probably not worth using a grid at all, and the other extreme will give a very chunky appearance to your project. Values between 100 and 200 will prove to be the most useful. Try setting both the grid width and grid height to 30, then click OK. The form appears to have gone a mottled gray color if you had the Show Grid set to Yes, and it looks terrible. Set them both back to 120, or a number that you feel comfortable with.

> It's not necessary to set width and height to the same number, but we can't think of a good reason not to!

Sometimes, it's useful to have full control over the size and position of a control, especially for very fine adjustments. Just change Align To Grid to No. Now you can move and re-size controls to within a pixel. Remember however, that these options will stay set until the next time you change them. Visual Basic will save your settings in the `VB.INI` file, and use them every time you reload Visual Basic. So unless you've got a keen eye and a steady hand, you'll probably find it useful to have the Align To Grid option switched on.

## Changing the Colors and Tabs

The Color options will allow us to alter all the colors on the desktop. Great fun to mess about with, but not too cool after a hard night on the town!

Now the fun starts with the colors. For each text type used in the code (comment text, keywords and so on), you can set a foreground and a background color to make the style easily identifiable. However, you'll find that not too many people alter the colors beyond recognition, so that reading code on another system isn't too difficult.

# Forms Design Grid

> The **Tab Stop Width** is the number of characters that will be skipped by pressing the tab key. This range is 1 to 32 characters.

## More Environment Options

The Default Save As Format option tells Visual Basic which format to save your files in. You can change this to text, so that all your files are saved as text.

The Require Variable Declaration option will add the two keywords **Option Explicit** to your code modules if you have set this to Yes. This will force you to declare all the variables you use in your modules, before those variables can be used. This may sound like a bad idea, but it's really useful. Imagine that you've written a fairly large system with quite a few forms, and code modules. You decide to add some code to a function to change a variable in another part of the system, perhaps setting a flag for some reason, but you misspell the variable. Without **Option Explicit** Visual Basic will run with no problems, but your system will not run as expected. This type of bug can be really hard to find and can lead to baldness because you'll end up pulling out your hair trying to find it, especially as everything looks OK! With **Option Explicit** set, Visual Basic won't run, the offending variable will be highlighted, and a message box will pop up:

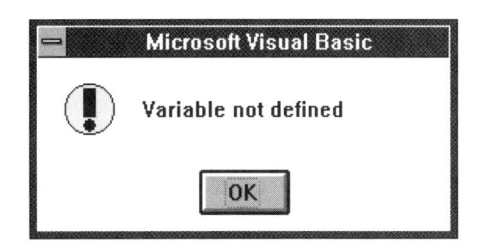

*Microsoft Visual Basic*
*Variable not defined*
*OK*

> This is also useful where you do not have your variables scoped correctly, but that's a subject for Chapter 5 where we discuss variables and their usage.

The Save Project Before Run option is quite useful. It gives you the chance to save your project before you run it. Generally, you'll want to save in case your code causes windows to crash. If you've not saved your project, all your hard work will be lost! However there are times, especially during testing, where you may not want to continually save your project before running it.

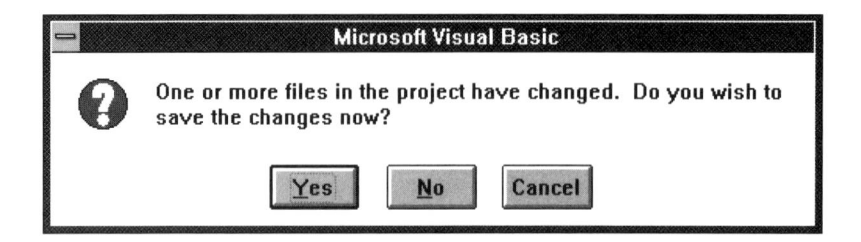

The final option that we've not covered is the Syntax Checking, and we would recommend that it's always set to Yes. This will tell Visual Basic to check all the code you enter for syntax errors, and it's a real boon for all two finger typists!

# The Options/Project .... dialog

The project options will differ from project to project, depending on the requirements. The main option you'll be setting here is the Start Up Form. If you have a Windows help compiler (shipped with the Professional edition, and with Visual C++), then you may also use the Help File option.

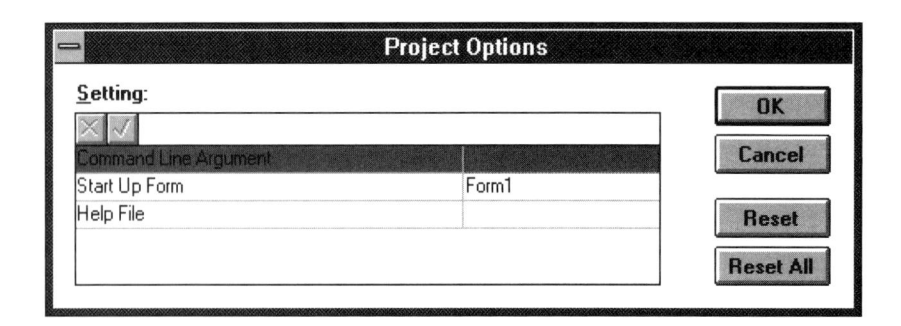

The Start Up Form will be the form that is loaded when the project starts. In some cases, you may not want a form to load when the project is first loaded - perhaps you have some project set up code that you want to run

# Project Options

before the first form is loaded. This can be achieved by choosing Sub Main (). The Sub Main () function must be part of a `.BAS` module, not part of a form, so you must remember to load forms in this procedure, or nothing will happen!

If you have created a help file for your project, enter its path and name in the Help File text box. Visual Basic will then call the Windows help system with the specified file loaded when *F1* is pressed in the project. If you leave this blank, then no help will be called when *F1* is pressed. This will usually be filled in at the end of the project, after it has been developed and tested, so that the Help system can include screenshots, and the most up to date details of the project.

In the Command Line Arguments text box, enter any arguments that you want Visual Basic to pass to a project. These will be sent only if you choose Start from the Run menu.

## Compiling Your Projects

When you've finished your project, you'll want to compile it, to produce an executable. This is simply a case of selecting the Make EXE File... from the File menu within Visual Basic. A dialog box will be displayed asking for the name of the `.EXE`, and where it should be stored.

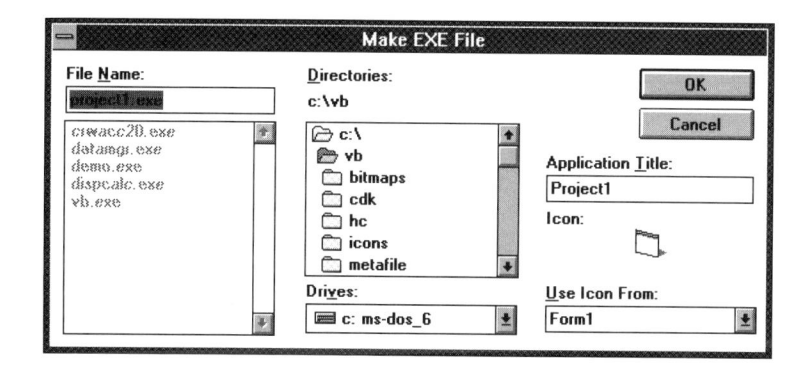

You will also be able to enter some further options, such as linking an icon to the `.EXE`. This is the icon that will be loaded into program manager when you add the executable to your desk top. You are also able to give your application a title. An executable file will now be produced that you can run from within Program Manager without Visual Basic running.

47

## Form Styles

Within Visual Basic you can have several different form types or styles. Actually there isn't really any difference between a form and a window. Most projects produced today are Multiple Document Interface (MDI) applications. This means that there is a container form, called the parent form, and within this there are sub forms, called child forms. Microsoft Word is an example of an MDI application, with a parent form which has the menu and toolbar on it, and the child forms which are the document windows where you write your documents. There are also common dialogs, such as open a file, and custom dialogs such as format columns.

These dialogs can be **modal** or **non-modal**. What this means in English is that for modal forms, no other window function can be run until some action has been undertaken, and the form unloaded.

All these different form types can be used in Visual Basic, and we'll have a brief look at each of these.

## MDI Application: Implementation

If you don't have Visual Basic running, run it up. If it is currently running, select New Project from the File menu, so that we can start from scratch. Every MDI application has one parent form, and at least one child form. It's not essential that you have any child forms, but there's no point in having an MDI application without any forms!

To create the parent form, select New MDI Form from the File menu. A new form will be added to your project called MDIForm1. You'll notice that the form will inherit the color attributes that you have set up in the Control Panel. You can override these in the Properties window for the form if you wish. If you do this, changes to the Control Panel colors will not affect your MDI parent form. The New MDI Form option in the File menu is now grayed out, so that you can't create another parent for this project.

Now our project has an MDI parent form and a normal form. To change Form1 to an MDI child form, we need to change the **MDIChild** property of Form1 to **True**.

# MDI Application

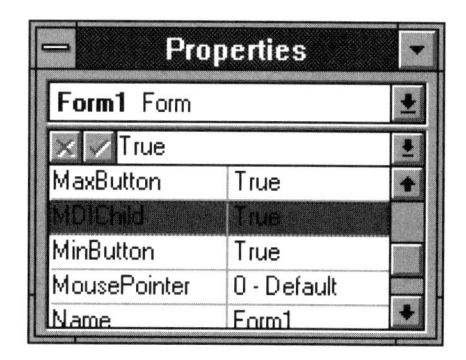

[Properties window showing Form1 properties with MDIChild set to True]

That's all there is to it! Let's see how a child form acts in an MDI application. To do this, we need to change the Start Up Form in the project options and write some code.

Firstly, we need to select the MDIForm1 as the Start Up Form. (If you've forgotten, it's in the Project... option under the Options menu). Simply double click on the Start Up option to change it.

Now we need to write some code to display the child form. In the project window, select the MDIForm1 and press the View Code button. This will bring up the Code window for the MDI form. The event we need is the **Form_Load** event. To display this event in the Code window, select the MDIForm in the Object list box at the top of Code window as follows:

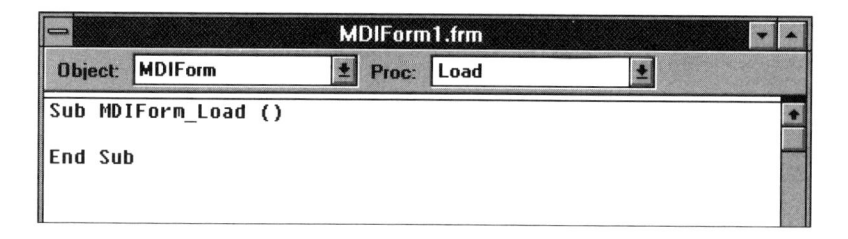

[Code window showing MDIForm1.frm with Object: MDIForm, Proc: Load, containing Sub MDIForm_Load () / End Sub]

The **Form_Load** event is displayed as the default.

Now we need to add the following code:

```
'This is the MDI parent form load event.
    Load Form1
    Form1.Show
End Sub
```

**49**

## Chapter 2 - Projects and Forms

> Note that you do not need to type End Sub - **Visual Basic supplies this for you.**

The two lines that you've typed tell Visual Basic to load the form into memory, and then display it on the screen. The load statement does not display the form, although the show method will load the form if it is not already loaded, so you could just type `Form1.Show`. Before we run the application, create a directory where we can save the project, and then change the Save Project Before Run option in the Environment... options to Yes.

Now try running your project (click the Run button on the toolbar, or press *F5*). You'll find that Visual Basic has noticed that you've changed the project in some manner, and will ask if you wish to save it. Click the Yes button, and the Save File As dialog is displayed for each form and then the project. By default, Visual Basic calls the forms the same name that you have set in the Properties window. Save the **FORM1.FRM** as **VIEW.FRM**, **MDIFORM1.FRM** as **MDI.FRM**, and the project as **MDIVIEW.MAK**. Now the application is running and the Visual Basic title has changed to Microsoft Visual Basic - MDIVIEW[run]. You should see a screen similar to this:

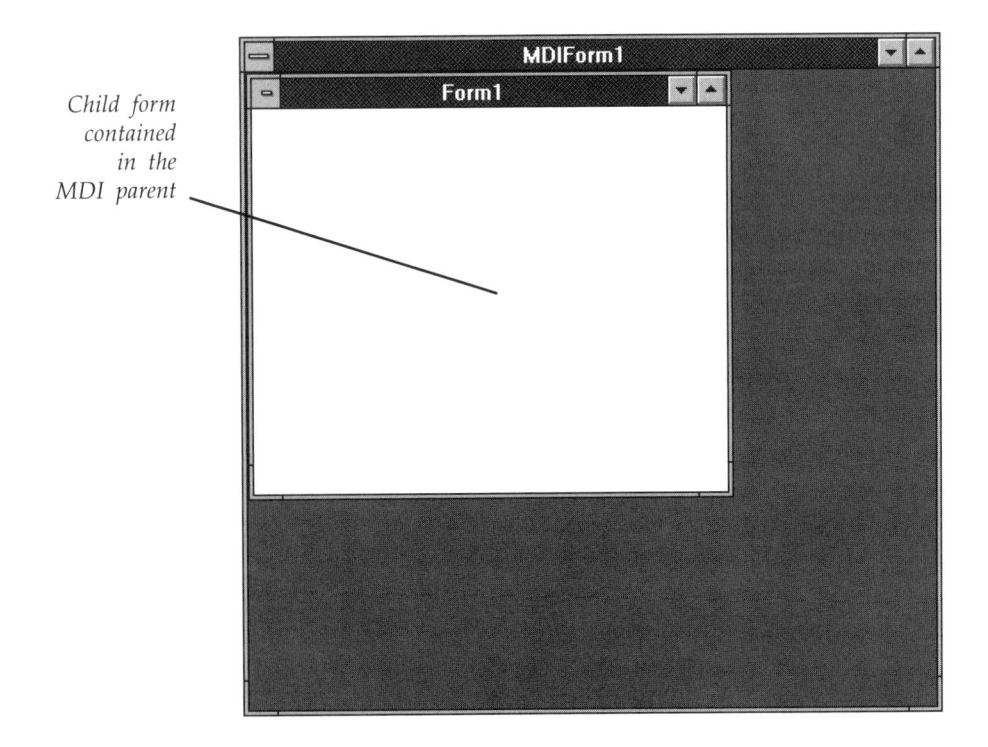

*Child form contained in the MDI parent*

You can move the child form around the screen, re-size it, maximize it and minimize it. The form stays within the parent form. When you close the application, Windows will first unload all the child forms that are running, then close the parent form. Stop the application by pressing the End button on the toolbar. The Visual Basic title has now changed back to [design]. This is all OK as far as it goes, but it's hardly a world beating application is it? Don't worry, we'll look at the other form types, and then come back to it.

## An Introduction to Dialogs

So far, we seem to have mentioned dialogs quite a lot, so it comes as no surprise that not only are they very useful, but that Visual Basic has predefined dialogs that you can use via the common dialog control, and also allows you to write your own custom dialogs. In fact, the password form you developed in Chapter 1 is an example of a custom dialog.

## Custom Dialogs

A custom dialog is a dialog that you design and write which allows the user to supply some information to your application. In the above case, a password is supplied. This would be an excellent dialog to make a modal form, so that the user can't continue until the password is entered. To achieve this you will need to add a **1** to the **Show** statement for the form, when you have defined it in the parent/child context:

```
frmPassword.Show 1
```

## Common Dialogs

Visual Basic supports five operations as common dialogs: Open, Save As, Color, Font, and Print. You've already seen the Open and Save As dialogs from the user point of view, so let's try out the custom dialog control, to add our own Open dialog box. We don't intend to cover all the dialog types here (we've saved that pleasure for Chapter 7), so if you can't contain your excitement we'll forgive you for leaping ahead - but don't forget to come back!

# Chapter 2 - Projects and Forms

## Using the Open Dialog

Load up Visual Basic if it's not already running, and then open the MDIVIEW application. If you've not already discovered it, the File menu has the last four projects that were loaded at the bottom:

| Make EXE File... |
|---|
| 1 ALIGN.MAK |
| 2 ..\CALLDLLS\CALLDLLS.MAK |
| 3 ..\CONTROLS\CONTROLS.MAK |
| 4 ..\CALC\CALC.MAK |
| Exit |

All you need to do is to click on the MDIVIEW entry to load the project. This time, when the project is loaded there are no forms displayed, so we'll need to use the Project window to display our forms and code. Visual Basic ships with an extensive icon library, so we'll put together an icon viewer using an image control, and the Open common dialog.

Firstly, let's re-name **FORM1** with a more meaningful name. Highlight the **Form1 Form** and click View Form to display it. The Properties window will now have the form properties loaded. Select the **Name** property, and change it to **frmView**. Also change the **Caption** property to **VB Icon Viewer**. Now we need to add four controls to the form: two command buttons, a common dialog control, and an image control.

For **command1**, change the **Name** property to **cmdView**, and the **Caption** property to **&View**. For **command2** change the **Name** property to **cmdClose**, and the **Caption** to **&Close**.

For the common dialog control, we need to change the properties individually. The **Filename** property should be set to **\*.ico** (to display all the icon files), the **InitDir** property should be set to **C:\VB\ICONS** (or wherever you've loaded Visual Basic). We've also given the dialog a title in the **Dialog Title** property (Open Icon File), and called the dialog **dlgOpen** in the **Name** property.

52

# Icon Viewer

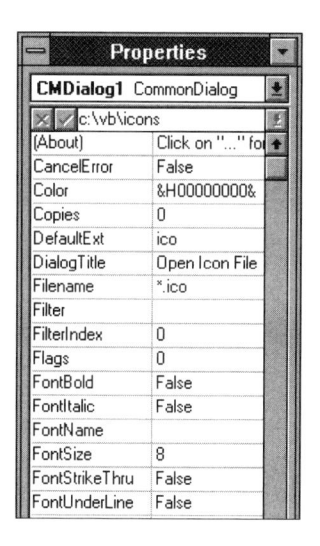

We've also renamed the image control **imgIcon** in its **Name** property. Here is a summary of the controls used and the properties that we are changing:

| Control Type | Properties |
|---|---|
| Form | **Name** = frmView <br> **Caption** = VB Icon Viewer |
| Command button | **Name** = cmdView <br> **Caption** = &View |
| Command button | **Name** = cmdClose <br> **Caption** =&Close |
| Image control | **Name** = imgIcon |
| Common dialog | **Name** = dlgOpen <br> InitDir1=c:\vb\icons <br> FileName = *.ico |

53

## Chapter 2 - Projects and Forms

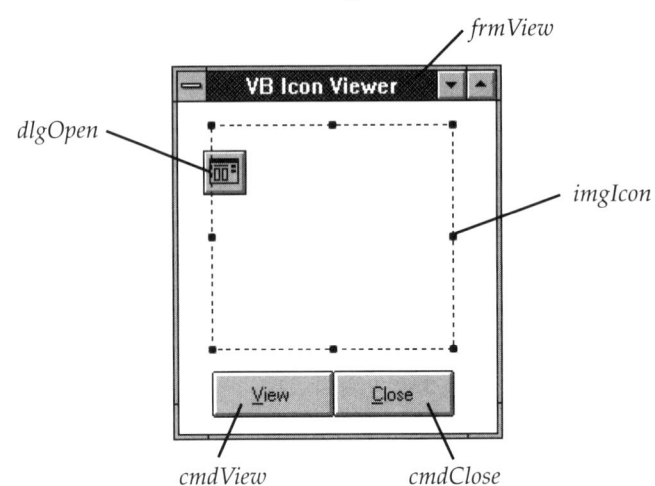

Your form should now look something like this:

*frmView*
*dlgOpen*
*imgIcon*
*cmdView*
*cmdClose*

Don't worry about the common dialog button being partially covered by the image control - this button is not displayed at runtime anyway. To display our Open File dialog we need to write some code, so without further ado, add the following code in the Code window for each separate **frmView** event:

```
Sub cmdClose_Click()
    Unload frmView
End Sub
```

```
Sub cmdView_Click()
  'When the cancel button is pressed, an error is
  'generated. This code handles the error
    On Error GoTo ErrCode

    'Set the Action property to 1 for an Open Dialog This is
  'A property only available at run time
    dlgOpen.Action = 1

  'set the image picture property to the value in
  'the open dialog's file property
    imgIcon.Picture = LoadPicture(dlgOpen.FileName)

  'This code will run if an error occurs, or the
  'user presses cancel in the open dialog
ErrCode:
    Exit Sub
End Sub
```

# Stretching Images

## The Option Explicit Effect

Now run the project. However, if you've set Option Explicit, then you should have an error message saying Variable Not Defined, and the **Form1** part of the **Load** statement will be highlighted. This is because we changed the name of the form in the Properties window, and Visual Basic can no longer find a form named **Form1** in our project. Take care that if you change the names of forms or controls after you have typed code that refers to them, or if you have entered code into their events, Visual Basic will not rename the references in your code, or copy all the code from the events. You'll have to cut and paste the code into the new set of events that Visual Basic has set up for the form or control under the new name. OK, change the **MDIForm** code to look like this:

```
Private Sub MDIForm_Load()
   'Load and show the child form
      Load frmView
      frmView.Show
End Sub
```

## The Stretch Property of an Image Control

Now run the project again; this time it should run after going through the save procedure. Try clicking on the View button. You'll get the Open dialog, with the defaults loaded that we entered into the properties. Select a sub directory (this is where all the **.ICO** files are) and an icon file, then click OK. It has loaded the icon but it's pretty small, especially as we have quite a big image control on the form. This is because it has loaded the actual size of the icon file. We'll want to change this so that the icon fills the image control as we have set it up on the form. It's really easy to do this - just stop the project from running, and change the **Stretch** property in the image control to **True**, then run the project again. Now when you select an icon to display, the icon will stretch to fill the whole size of the image control. This is an improvement and no code was required. Click on the Close button, and the form is unloaded, but the MDI application is still running. Stop the project, and we'll go through the code, and see what it's doing.

```
Sub cmdClose_Click()
    Unload frmView
End Sub
```

## Chapter 2 - Projects and Forms

This is the code that is run when you click the Close button. It stops the form **frmView** from running, and unloads it from memory.

```
Sub cmdView_Click ()
        On Error GoTo ErrCode
```

The **On Error** statement is run whenever a runtime error is encountered in this event. (We'll be covering runtime error handling in Chapter 11.) The **GoTo ErrCode** tells Visual Basic to jump to the label **ErrCode** when an error occurs.

> `Gotos` are generally disliked by programmers (especially structured programmers), as they can quickly cause code to be impossible to follow and debug (it is known as *spaghetti code*). This is a fairly valid use of `GoTo`, and one of the rare times (hopefully) you'll actually need to use it.

```
dlgOpen.Action = 1
```

This line alters a property of the common dialog that is only available at runtime. The valid action settings range from 0 to 6, with 1 being the action that tells the common dialog control to display a file open dialog. By changing the action number, we can display the other common dialog types.

```
imgIcon.Picture = LoadPicture(dlgOpen.FileName)
```

Here we are setting the **Picture** property of the image control **imgIcon**. **LoadPicture** (amazingly enough) tells Visual Basic to load the picture named in the brackets into the image control. The **dlgOpen.FileName** is the property that is set to the path and file name that you selected in the Open File dialog. If you pressed Cancel, then this would have been set to the file name that was specified as the default (in this case **\*.ICO**) and would have generated an error:

```
ErrCode:
    Exit Sub
End Sub
```

This final section of code is run whenever a runtime error occurs. It tells Visual Basic to exit this event code subroutine, whenever an error occurs, such as an invalid file name being entered, or the Cancel button of the dialog being clicked.

# New Forms

With a grand total of six lines of code, we've managed to design an MDI application that allows us to view `.ICO` files. This is an good illustration of the power of Visual Basic.

## New Forms

At the moment, we can only view one icon at a time. With just another couple of lines of code we can have more than one child form open at once. Don't worry about fully understanding exactly what's happening as we'll cover MDI applications fully in Chapter 7. For now, add a new command button to the child form called cmdNew, with a caption of &New. It should look something like this:

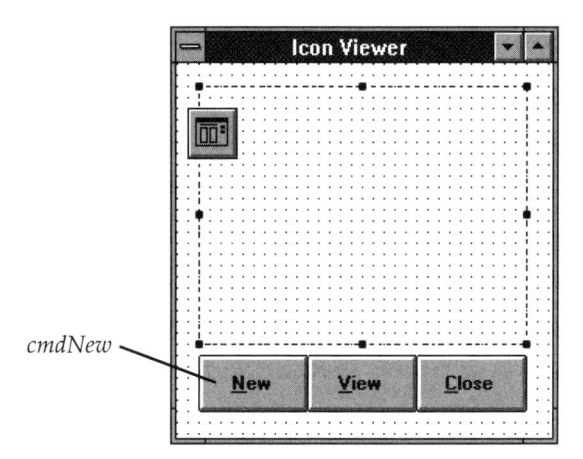

*cmdNew*

Now add the following code to the `cmdNew_Click` event:

```
Sub cmdNew_Click()
    Dim frmNewView As New frmView
    frmNewView.Show
End Sub
```

The **Dim** statement is telling Visual Basic to create a new **instance** of our form **frmView**. This is a copy of **frmView** in every way. The next statement tells Visual Basic to load and display the new instance of the form. You can now click the New button, and another icon view form is created, so that we can see more than one icon at a time.

**57**

Chapter 2 - Projects and Forms

## Closing the View Forms

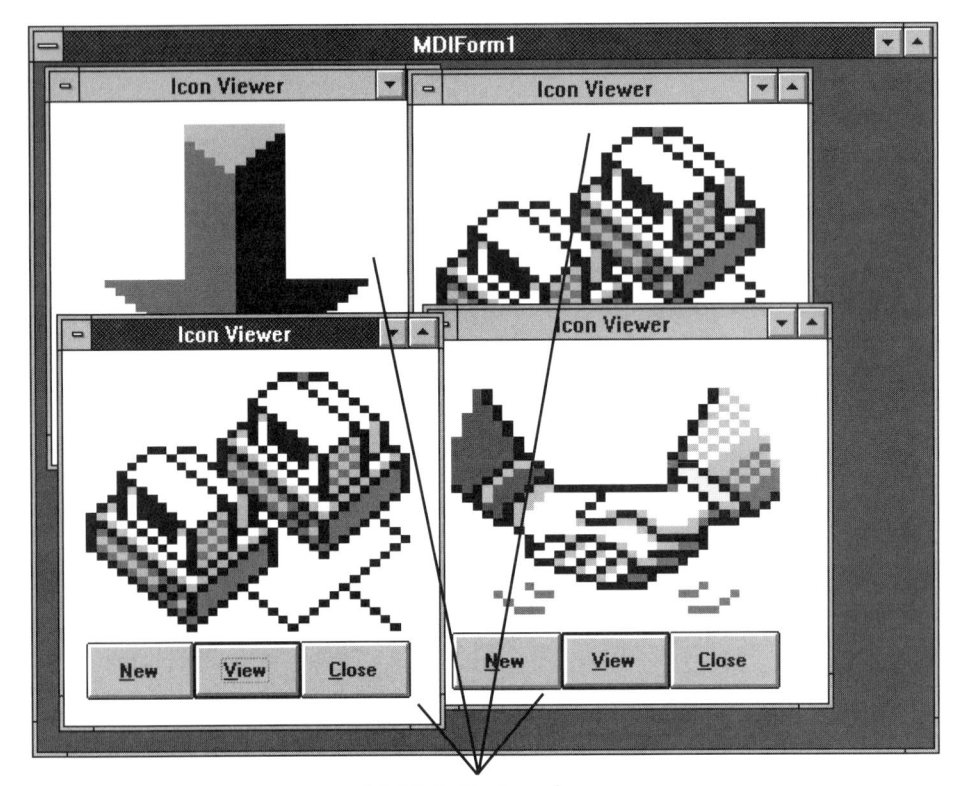

*Multiple frmIcon forms*

If you try to close the forms with the Close button, you'll find that it only works on the first form that you loaded. (We'll go through this in the discussion on MDI applications.) For now, we need to change the code in the `cmdClose_Click` event as follows:

```
Sub cmdClose_Click ()
    Unload Me
End Sub
```

This tells Visual Basic to close the particular instance of the view form in which the code is running. This is usually (but not always) the form that is currently active. Loading multiple instances of a form is not restricted to MDI children. You can use this method wherever required, except on an MDI parent form.

# Summary and Exercises

## Summary

We've managed to cover quite a lot of ground in this chapter, and been introduced to some of the fundamentals of Visual Basic. You learnt how to add files to a project, how to delete files from a project, and how to alter the basic project template via the **AUTOLOAD.MAK** file. We looked at the other options that affect the Visual Basic environment, and how to customize Visual Basic to our own requirements by using the Environment... and Project... options from the Options menu. You've learnt how to save your project and turn it into an executable. You've been introduced to the different form styles available in Visual Basic, and managed to produce a working MDI application with just six lines of Visual Basic, then extended it with a further two lines.

## Exercises

Using the MDIView application, do the following:

**1** Set the **Filename** property to the default **\*.ICO** when the View button is pressed.

**2** Extend the viewer to also view **.BMP** files and **.WMF** files.

**3** Add the password dialog you designed in Chapter 1, make it the Start Up Form, and only load the **MDI** form if a valid password is entered.

**4** Save the project and compile it, so that it can be run from Program Manager.

INSTANT
INSTANT
INSTANT
INSTANT
INSTANT
INSTANT

# Chapter 3

# Gaining Control

So far, we've taken a rapid roller coaster ride through the different areas of Visual Basic, and been introduced to most of its building blocks. At this point, we'll briefly catch our breath and spend a little time looking at how to use **controls** in Visual Basic. You have had a short introduction to controls in Chapter 1, and actually used some of the more useful controls (such as command buttons), in the examples and exercises of the previous two chapters.

Controls are the objects used in Visual Basic to communicate with the outside world. They are used to get and to display data and pictures, as well as to control how the application works. There are two basic categories of controls: **standard controls** which are part of Visual Basic and will always be available in the toolbox, and **custom controls** which are the add-on *Visual BasicX* controls.

In this chapter, we'll be looking at some of the standard controls which are available, as well as how they behave, and the most commonly used properties of these controls. We'll cover:

- Controls
- Buttons, tabs and focus
- Control arrays
- File system controls

# Chapter 3 - Gaining Control

## Controls: Concepts

So what is a control? Basically, every control is really an **object** that you use to add functionality to your Visual Basic application. By dragging the control from the toolbox, you are inserting a pre-written program into your application. You can then customize this program by altering the properties, and control how it reacts through coding its events. This component (object-oriented) method of programming has long been discussed, and C++ programmers are familiar with objects and how to use them. For the more humble amongst us, an example might help to put it into context.

> **Visual Basic is not an object-oriented language. Rather, it uses some of the ideas behind object orientation, such as creating instances of an object (like controls) which can then be altered as required.**

If our application were, perhaps a garage, then a fairly useful control to add would be a car. The properties that would customize the car are the engine size, number of doors, color and so on. The events that could 'happen' to the car include when it is sold and when it gets its six monthly service. It could even be assumed that there is a possibility that the car could crash (events can be coded for even if they might never be utilised). From within the events, it is possible to change some of the properties, such as color, but not others, such as number of doors.

Controls in Visual Basic act in much the same way in that you have the properties, such as size, foreground and background color, and events such as click and double click; and you specify what is to happen at the event by entering Visual Basic code.

## Control Values

For every control, there is a property that is most commonly used, and could be considered the default property. In Visual Basic every control has one of these default properties set up, called its **Value**, and when you use the **Value** of a control, you do not need to specify the property name. So for the text box control, its value is the **Text** property. The following two snippets of code have the same effect in that they assign the string **"Steve Dolan"** to the text control **txtName**:

# Control Values

```
txtName.Text = "Steve Dolan"

txtName = "Steve Dolan"
```

In fact, the second example runs slightly faster because Visual Basic knows that the value of the textbox control is `Text`, therefore it does not have to resolve the properties identifier. However, this can make your code less readable, and therefore more difficult to understand and maintain.

The following table lists the values for all of the standard controls:

| Control | Value Property | Naming Convention |
|---|---|---|
| Check Box | `Value` | `chk` |
| Combo Box | `Text` | `com` |
| Command Button | `Value` | `cmd` |
| Common Dialog | `Action` | `dlg` |
| Data | `Caption` | `dat` |
| Directory List Box | `Path` | `dir` |
| Drive List Box | `Drive` | `drv` |
| File List Box | `FileName` | `fil` |
| Frame | `Caption` | `fra` |
| Grid | `Text` | `grd` |
| Horizontal Scroll Bar | `Value` | `hsb` |
| Image | `Picture` | `img` |
| Label | `Caption` | `lbl` |
| Line | `Visible` | `lin` |
| List Box | `Text` | `lst` |
| Menu | `Enabled` | `mnu` |
| OLE Container | `Value` | `ole` |
| Option Button | `Value` | `opt` |
| Picture Box | `Picture` | `pic` |

*Continued*

## Chapter 3 - Gaining Control

| Control | Value Property | Naming Convention |
|---|---|---|
| Shape | `Shape` | `gph` |
| Text Box | `Text` | `txt` |
| Timer | `Enabled` | `tim` |
| Vertical Scroll Bar | `Value` | `vsb` |

For the values of custom controls, you'll need to refer to the documentation or help file that you received with the control. Don't be surprised however, if you don't actually find any information!

## Naming Conventions

You might have spotted that we've sneaked in an extra column to the table! Using standard prefixes for your controls and variables will help make your code much more readable, and also give you important information at a glance. For instance, you might well have a couple of text boxes, a list box and a combo box on the same form. In the code you might enter:

```
details.Text = "Invoice Number 1"
```

This line is equally valid for all of the above controls, whereas this:

```
txtInvoiceNo.Text = "Invoice Number 1"
```

will give you a far better idea of what is going on. We've also given the control a meaningful name, to further explain the code. After all, using `details` as a name does not really help explain the code.

> The naming conventions that you'll see throughout the book are the ones that we use - you may find that they differ from the quoted Microsoft conventions. You can use your own, of course; it's the principle that's important, not the usage. OK, time to get off the soapbox, and back to the real fun stuff.

# Buttons

# Using Buttons

Where would we be without buttons? Star Trek just wouldn't be the same without all those colored buttons to press. You may well be tempted to create the bridge of the Starship Enterprise in your form, but this is not a good idea (although we've seen some applications that would put sci-fi film producers to shame). You may think that it looks really cool, but imagine for a moment that you'd never used a computer before, and suddenly you are presented with a daunting array of buttons. It can be very off-putting and ultimately counter productive. Try to keep your user interface simple and easy to use. People will be much more impressed with an intuitive and easy to use application, rather than one that looks complex. Having said that, you'll find that the button controls are amongst the most used controls. So let's take a closer look at the buttons available in Visual Basic.

## Command Buttons

You've already used command buttons in the first two chapters. They are probably the most used control in Visual Basic. They are also one of the simplest to use. Generally speaking, all a command button does is click (although there are a lot more events associated with them).

### Clicking a Command Button

There are several ways to cause a command button to click, the most obvious being to move the mouse pointer over the button and press the left mouse button. The button depresses, and the `Click` event code is run.

The other methods we'll be looking at introduce some important concepts that apply to many of the Visual Basic controls. We'll write and then alter a small project to illustrate these methods and concepts as we go through the different ways to generate a click for a command button.

Start a new project, and draw three command buttons on the screen.

> A quick way to draw controls on the form is to double click on the control. This will copy a control to the center of the form of default dimensions. All you need to do is drag them to their locations on the form. It will look like there is only one control on the form as they are loaded one on top of the other, until you move them to their final locations.

## Chapter 3 - Gaining Control

Change the Form1 **Name** property to **frmCommandTest**, and the **Caption** to **Command Buttons**.

Put the **Command3** button at the top, **Command2** button in the middle, and **Command1** at the bottom. This may sound strange but don't worry, there's method in our madness! Now, in the Properties window change the **Name** of **Command1** to **cmdQuit**, and type **&Quit** in the **Caption**. For **Command2** change the **Name** to **cmdPress** and alter the **Caption** to **&Press**, and finally for **Command3** change the **Name** to **cmdMe**, and the **Caption** to **&Me**. Your form should now look something like this:

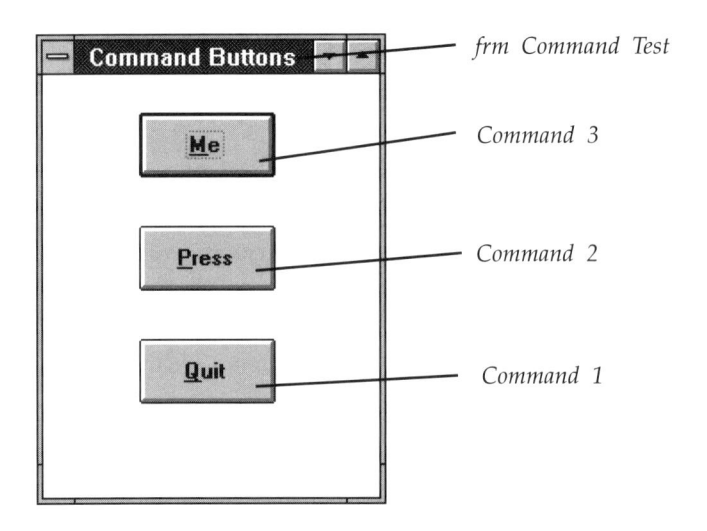

*frm Command Test*

*Command 3*

*Command 2*

*Command 1*

## Accelerator Keys

You'll notice that the first character of each command button is underlined. This is caused by the **&** character in the caption. The underlined character is called the **accelerator key**. It gives the user a short cut to causing a **Click** event by pressing *Alt+* the underlined character.

> Although it may seem obvious, you'll need to check your form when you use accelerator keys to make sure that the same key has not been used twice. This is easily done, even by experienced Visual Basic programmers. It doesn't cause an error, but passes focus to the next key with the accelerator letter. The Click event code is not run.

# Focus

Give the control **cmdQuit** the focus, and View the code for its Click event (Proc:). Enter the following middle line of code in the Click event:

```
Sub cmdQuit_Click()
    Unload frmCommandTest
End Sub
```

Now save and run the project. Try pressing *Alt+Q*. You'll find that the project stops running, just as if you'd clicked the Quit button.

## Focus

Run the project again without making any changes, and press the *Enter* key. The project quits again. This is because you should have left the Quit command button *with the focus*. If you look at the button closely, you'll see a dotted box around the caption, and the sides of the button are darker than the other command buttons:

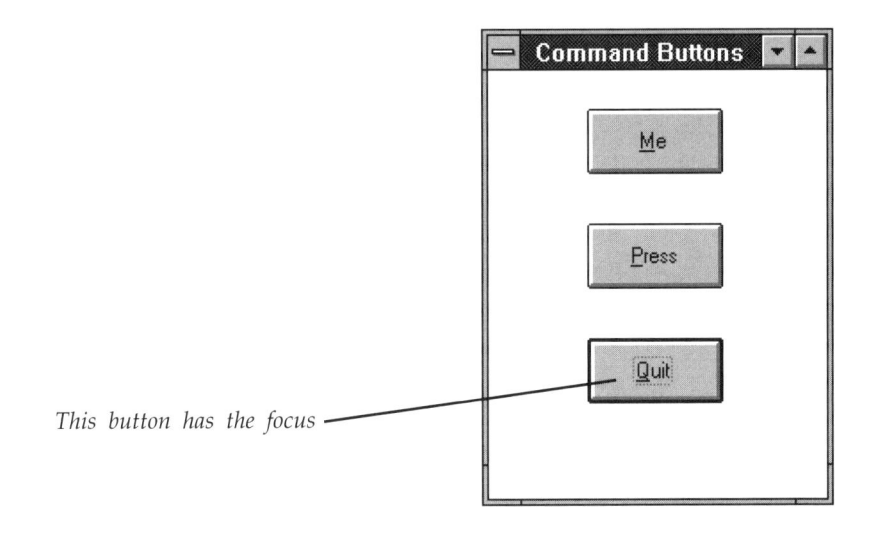

*This button has the focus*

Run the project again, and press the *Tab* key. You'll see the focus move up the command buttons, from Press to Me. The order (called the **tab order**) is determined by a property called the **tab index**, and most controls have a tab index, (whether or not the control can actually get the focus). The actual order is sequential, and starts from 0. As you add a control, it is assigned the next number, so as the Quit button was the first one we placed on the form, it has **TabIndex 0**.

## Changing the Tab Order

The tab order can be changed either in the Properties window, or at run time. Give the Form body focus and add the following code to the **Form_Load** event in the project:

```
Sub Form_Load()
    cmdQuit.TabIndex = 2
    cmdMe.TabIndex = 0
    cmdPress.TabIndex = 1
End Sub
```

Now when you run the project, the tab order is reversed. However, when you stop the project, the tab indexes in the Properties window have not changed. Setting properties at runtime does not alter the default properties for the control.

If you change the **TabIndex** property in the Properties window, Visual Basic will re-index all the other controls to reflect your change. Delete the new code from the **Form_Load** event, and alter the **cmdMe TabIndex** in the Properties window to **0**. If you look at the **TabIndex**es for the other two, you'll see that they have been altered to reflect your changes. Change the other two so that the tab order is from top to bottom (as would generally be expected).

## Setting Focus

There are other issues that will affect the tab order of controls, and what the user sees when the project is running. What happens when the *Tab* key is pressed is that focus is passed to the next control in the **TabIndex** order.

You may have noticed in the Properties window that there is a **TabStop** property below the **TabIndex** property. This is a **True/False** property. Try setting the **TabStop** property of the **cmdQuit** button to **False**, then run the project.

If you press the *Tab* key now, focus jumps between **cmdMe** and **cmdPress**. The **cmdQuit** can no longer be tabbed to by the user, but you can still *Alt+Q*, or use the mouse to press the Quit button. With the **TabStop** property set to **False**, it doesn't stop the control from getting focus from the normal tools of mouse and ALT key.

To prove this, add the following code to the `cmdMe_Click` event:

```
Sub cmdMe_Click()
    cmdQuit.SetFocus
End Sub
```

Now run the project, and press the *Tab* key. Focus is still only between **cmdMe** and **cmdPress**, until you click on **cmdMe**. Focus now jumps to **cmdQuit**. The `SetFocus` method is very useful and you'll often come across it when passing the focus to a particular control.

## How Disabling Affects Focus and Tab Order

Change the code in the two controls to the following:

```
Sub cmdMe_Click()
    cmdPress.SetFocus
End Sub
```

```
Sub cmdPress_Click()
    cmdPress.Enabled = False
End Sub
```

Now run the project. Pressing the *Tab* key still moves the focus between Me and Press, but clicking the Me button now passes focus to the Press button. Nothing special there until you click the Press button. You'll notice that the caption on the button has gone pale:

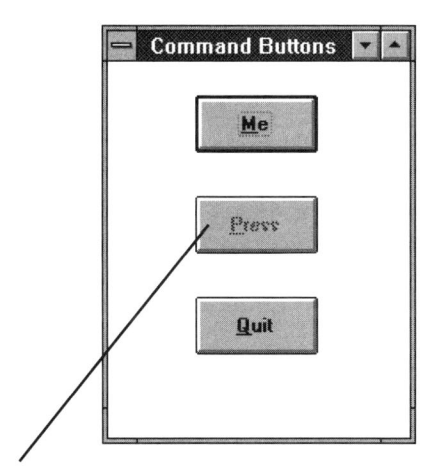

*The 'graying' of this button shows that it is disabled*

Now when you click the Me button what happens? If you set the **Enabled** to `False` either in the Properties window of the control, or at runtime in the code, the caption of the control will be **grayed out**, and you won't be able to click it. The control will also not be able to receive focus (as you've noticed) and a runtime error (illegal function call), will occur. You can stop the project from running by pressing the stop button on the toolbar, or by selecting End from the Run menu.

> You'll find that this method of setting focus is used on controls and menu items throughout many Windows applications. You'll need to take care not to pass focus to a button or menu item in code that has been disabled to avoid runtime errors.

# The Default Command Button

When you have more than one command button on a form, you can specify one (and only one) as the default command button. This property is not affected by the `TabStop` or `TabIndex` properties. Providing that the focus is not on another command button, pressing the *Enter* key will run the `Click` event of the default command button.

Let's give it a try. Change the default property to `True` for the `cmdQuit` button, and remove the code from the `Click` events in `cmdMe` and `cmdPress`. Now run the project. You'll find that pressing the *Enter* key doesn't actually do anything at the moment. This is because another command button has focus. Try adding a text box, and altering the `TabIndex` of the text box to `0`. Now try pressing the *Enter* key. The project will end because none of the command buttons has the focus when you pressed the *Enter* key, so the `Click` event of the default command button (`cmdQuit`) is executed.

## Using the Value Property

The `Value` property of the command button is only available at runtime. Just to confuse you the `Value` property is also the value (or default property) of the command.

# Command Buttons

You can't set runtime properties at design time, and if you look in the Properties window, you'll see that there isn't an entry for **Value**. For many of the controls in Visual Basic, there are properties that can be set at design time only, properties that can be set at runtime only, and properties that can be set both at design and runtime. This also applies to custom controls. To find out about the runtime properties (and all the other properties) you'll have to refer to the documentation for the control.

> No, we're not trying to duck the issue - it's just that there are a large number of controls, and properties for the controls, and it would take another book to describe them and their usage in detail. But don't worry, we'll go through some of the more interesting and useful properties later in the chapter.

Let's get back to the plot. Change the **cmdPress** event code to the following:

```
Sub cmdPress_Click()
    cmdQuit.Value = True
End Sub
```

Now when we run the project, every time we click the Press button, the project ends. This is because the **cmdQuit_Click** event is executed as soon as the **cmdQuit** button value is set to **True**. You could have also entered this line:

```
cmdQuit = True
```

Remember that the default property for the command button is **Value**.

## Using the Cancel Property

Only two more ways to click the command button left to look at! If you look at the Properties window for the command buttons, you'll see a property called **Cancel**. Only one command button on a form can have its **Cancel** property set to **True**. Set the cancel property to **True** for the **cmdQuit** button, then run the project. If you press the *Esc* key on your keyboard, the project ends. This is because the **Click** event code for the command button that has its **Cancel** property set to **True** will be executed when the *Esc* key is pressed.

# Calling the Click Event Code

At last, we've got to the final method of clicking a command button. Every one of the events where we have entered code is a sub procedure, and can be called from code within other procedures and functions. This applies to all of the events, not only the `Click` event.

Change the code in the three controls to the following:

```
Sub cmdMe_Click()
    MsgBox "You Clicked Me"
End Sub
```

```
Sub cmdPress_Click()
    cmdMe_Click
End Sub
```

```
Private Sub cmdQuit_Click()
    Unload frmCommandTest
End Sub
```

When you click the Me button, a message box with an OK button on it is displayed.

> Message boxes are a form of common dialog, and are very useful. We'll come back to them in Chapter 7.

When you click on the Press button, the message box is displayed again. This is because you are calling the `Click` event code for the Me button in the code. If you add the line:

```
cmdQuit_Click
```

after the `MsgBox` line in the `cmdMe_Click ()` event, when you click on the Press button, the message box is displayed and then the project ends.

> A few words of warning: it's possible to set up infinite loops by calling other events (try changing: `cmdQuit_Click()` to `cmdPress_Click()` in the `Me_Click` event). Now when you run the project, it will loop indefinitely, displaying the message box. To stop the project, press *Ctrl* and *Break* and Visual Basic will drop into **break** mode - we will discuss this more thoroughly in Chapter 11, *Debugging*.

# Grouping Buttons

Click the Stop button from the tool bar to stop the project and return to design mode.

## Check and Option Buttons

There are two other button controls available within Visual Basic. The **option** button, which is sometimes also called the radio button, because only one can be selected at a time, rather like the frequency buttons on a radio. The other is the check box - you are able to select any number of check boxes on a form. These are used to allow the user to select from the available options and functions. We feel an example coming on, so start a new project in Visual Basic, and let's get going.

Change the form name to **frmButtons**, change the caption and then draw a label at the top of the form. Enter a test caption in the **Caption** property of the label and change the name to **lblTest**.

### Grouping Buttons

Now, to logically group sets of buttons on the screen, draw two frames next to each other on the form. This isn't necessary in this example as the two button groups are different, but if you needed more than one option group, you'd use a frame or picture box. It's best to draw the frame first, then draw the buttons, so that moving the frame will also move the buttons. Note, creating controls with double click or cut and paste will make them behave independently of the frame.

Change the caption of the first frame to **Option Buttons**, and the caption of the second to **Check Boxes**. Add three option buttons to the first frame, and three check boxes to the second. Now change names and captions as follows:

| Control | Name | Caption |
| --- | --- | --- |
| Option1 | optRed | Red |
| Option2 | optYellow | Yellow |
| Option3 | optBlue | Blue |
| Check1 chkBig | Big Text | |
| Check2 chkBold | Bold | |
| Check3 chkItalic | Italic | |

73

# Chapter 3 - Gaining Control

Your form should now look something like this:

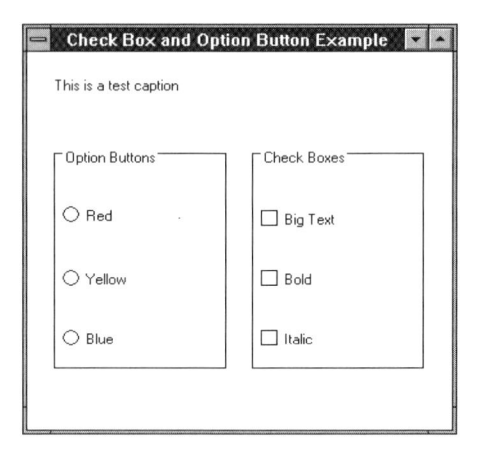

## Option Buttons

The code for the option buttons is as follows:

```
Sub optRed_Click()
 'Const is a constant declaration, in this case I've
 'assigned the number 4 to the constant called red
    Const red = 4
    lblTest.ForeColor = QBColor(red)
End Sub

Sub optYellow_Click()
    Const Yellow = 6
    lblTest.ForeColor = QBColor(Yellow)
End Sub

Sub optBlue_Click()

    Const blue = 1
    lblTest.ForeColor = QBColor(blue)

End Sub
```

If you run the project now, you'll see that the text in the label starts out as red (if the **optRed** radio button has **TabIndex** =0, and if you choose one of the other options then the color will change). It isn't possible to select more than one option at a time - the black spot that shows which one has been selected moves as each option button is clicked.

# Check Boxes

We've used the `QBColor` function to change the color of the text. `QBColor` can be set to 15 values, each of which specifies a different color.

> For the full range of colors you'll need to use the RGB function. This will be more fully covered in Chapter 8.

## Check Boxes

To try out the check boxes, add the following code to the project:

```
Sub chkBig_Click()
    lblTest.FontSize = 20
End Sub

Sub chkBold_Click()
    lblTest.FontBold = True
End Sub

Sub chkItalic_Click()
    lblTest.FontItalic = True
End Sub
```

When we run the project, we can now select any or all of the check boxes, and the text alters accordingly, until we have something like this:

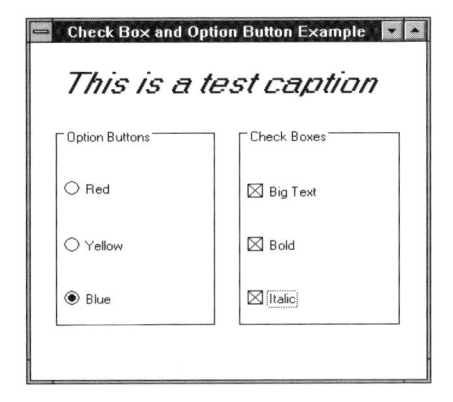

What happens if we deselect one of the check boxes, such as the italic check box? Nothing happens. This is because we are not actually checking the value of the check box in the `Click` event, we are just setting the properties of the label. We need to add some **If**...**Then**...**Else** statements to the code that check the state of the check boxes in their `Click` event code as follows:

**75**

# Chapter 3 - Gaining Control

```
Sub chkBig_Click()
    If chkBig.Value = 1 Then
        lblTest.FontSize = 20
    Else
        lblTest.FontSize = 14
    End If
End Sub

Sub chkBold_Click()
    If chkBold.Value = 1 Then
        lblTest.FontBold = True
    Else
        lblTest.FontBold = False
    End If
End Sub

Sub chkItalic_Click()
    If chkItalic.Value = 1 Then
        lblTest.FontItalic = True
    Else
        lblTest.FontItalic = False
    End If
End Sub
```

The project will now behave as expected, with the text changing depending on whether or not a check box is checked.

> We can't use the `True` keyword to see whether or not the box is checked because the value of the `True` keyword is -1. The values in the `Value` property for check boxes are: 0 for unchecked (this is the default), 1 for checked, and 2 for grayed out.

## Control Arrays

This may sound like your worst nightmare (hands up those who love array handling), but **control arrays** are very useful. A control array is an array of controls that all have the same name, and which share events (Visual Basic also supports the standard data arrays which we'll go through in Chapter 5). Visual Basic will index each control as it is added to the array, so that the individual controls can be accessed. When you name the second control, Visual Basic will ask if you wish to create a control array:

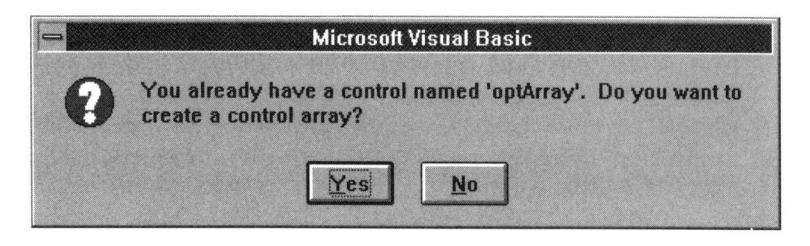

> **Microsoft Visual Basic**
>
> ? You already have a control named 'optArray'. Do you want to create a control array?
>
> [Yes] [No]

There is only one set of events for the control array, rather than individual events for each control, as the following figure illustrates:

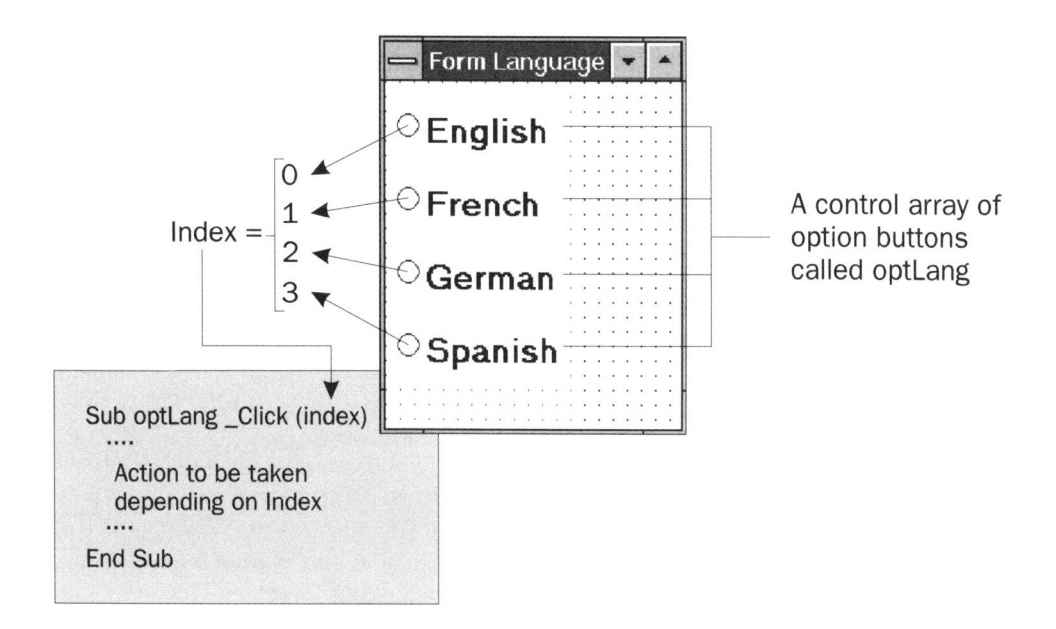

```
Form Language
  ⊙ English         ── Index = 0
  ⊙ French          ── Index = 1
  ⊙ German          ── Index = 2
  ⊙ Spanish         ── Index = 3
```

A control array of option buttons called optLang

```
Sub optLang _Click (index)
   ....
   Action to be taken
   depending on Index
   ....
End Sub
```

Using the current project, we'll change the options buttons to a control array, and look at the impact of the changes required in the code.

Change the name property of the **optRed**, **optYellow**, and **optBlue** to **optArray**. Visual Basic quite happily changed the **optRed** name, but when you altered the **optYellow**, it detected that there was a control called **optArray** and asked if you wanted to create a control array. When you renamed the **optBlue** option button, Visual Basic added it to the array, and gave it an index number of 2.

77

## Chapter 3 - Gaining Control

If you look in the code window for the (general) code of the form you'll notice that Visual Basic has not deleted the **Click** event code for **optRed**, **optYellow** and **optBlue**, or attempted to rename it. The code is no longer associated with a control, so can only be run if it's called from within other code. You can delete this code, as we'll need to write code for the **optArray_Click** event as follows:

```
Sub optArray_Click(Index As Integer)
  'define all the constants
  Const blue = 1
  Const yellow = 6
  Const red = 4
  'check the value of each element in the array
  If optArray(0).Value = True Then lblTest.ForeColor = QBColor(red)
  If optArray(1).Value = True Then lblTest.ForeColor = QBColor(yellow)
  If optArray(2).Value = True Then lblTest.ForeColor = QBColor(blue)
End Sub
```

Here, we are checking the value of each element of the control array to determine which has been clicked, and then setting the **Color** property of the label. We no longer have separate events for each button. That's great, but why use them? Well, with a control array, we can create generalized code, and code that will allow for the creation of controls at runtime.

To do this we need to make some further changes to the form. Firstly, we'll add three command buttons to the form, with captions **&Add**, **&Delete**, and **&Quit**, and called **cmdAdd**, **cmdDelete** and **cmdQuit**.

Next, we need to delete the third option button, and extend the frame to allow for the extra buttons to be added at run time. Alter the caption of the first two option buttons to **Mouse Pointer 0** and **Mouse Pointer 1** respectively. Your form should look something like this:

# Control Arrays

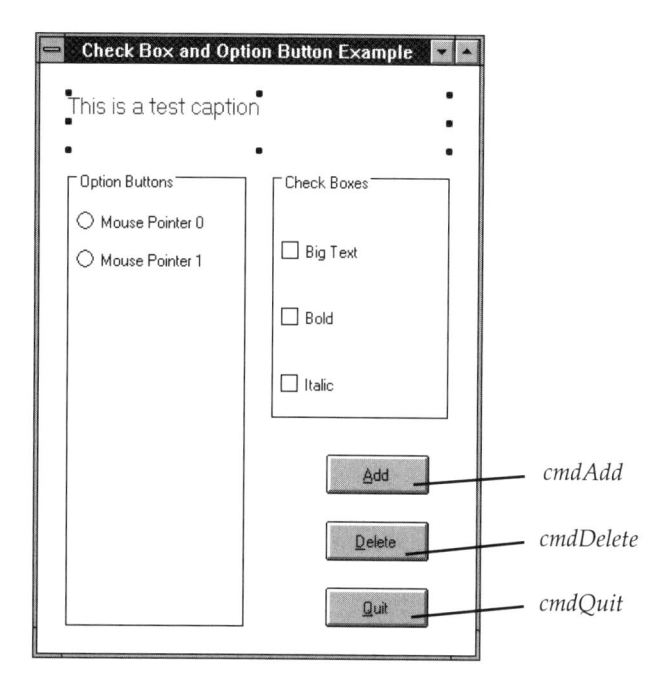

To limit the addition and deletion of controls at runtime, add the following line after the **Option Explicit** line in the (general) code window:

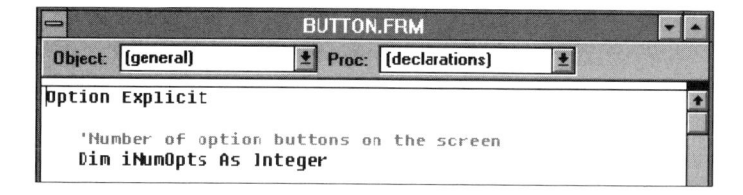

This integer will be used to keep track of how many option buttons are currently on the form. Delete the code from the **optArray_Click** event, and add the following code to the project:

```
Sub Form_Load()
    'When the form loads, set iNumOpts
    iNumOpts = 1
End Sub
```

## Chapter 3 - Gaining Control

```
Sub cmdAdd_Click()
   'check that there are not yet 13 option buttons
    If iNumOpts > 11 Then
        MsgBox "The limit is 13 controls"
        Exit Sub
    End If

    'Add another Option Button
    iNumOpts = iNumOpts + 1
    Load optArray(iNumOpts)

    'Set the properties for the new button Position first
    optArray(iNumOpts).Top = optArray(iNumOpts - 1).Top + 350
    optArray(iNumOpts).Caption = "Mouse Pointer " & iNumOpts
    optArray(iNumOpts).Visible = True
    optArray(0).SetFocus
End Sub

Sub cmdDelete_Click()
    'check how many option buttons are on the screen
    If iNumOpts <= 1 Then
        MsgBox "Sorry you must have at least two options on the form"
        Exit Sub
    End If

    'Delete the last button, and reset the focus
    Unload optArray(iNumOpts)
    iNumOpts = iNumOpts - 1
    optArray(0).SetFocus
End Sub

Sub cmdQuit_Click()
    'end the project
    Unload frmButtons
End Sub

Sub optArray_Click(Index As Integer)
    Frame1.MousePointer = Index
End Sub
```

When we run the project, we can now add and delete option buttons at runtime, but they don't do anything until you click on them, when you'll notice that the mouse pointer changes (but only while it's in the Option Buttons frame).

There's quite a lot of code here, so let's take it a step at a time. We've taken out the comments, and the **Sub**...**End Sub** lines, so we can concentrate on the code that does the business. In the **Form_Load()** event we have the following line:

# Control Arrays

```
iNumOpts = 1
```

This sets the `iNumOpts` integer to `1`, which means that there are two option buttons on the form (remember that indexes start at `0` in Visual Basic).

Next we have the `cmdAdd_Click` event as follows:

```
If iNumOpts > 11 Then
        MsgBox "The limit is 13 controls"
        Exit Sub
    End If
```

The `If` statement checks if you've reached the maximum number of controls to be added. A message box is displayed telling the user that the maximum has been exceeded if there are more than 13 controls, and then the sub procedure is exited.

```
        iNumOpts = iNumOpts + 1
    Load optArray(iNumOpts)
```

We would have only reached here if the maximum has not yet been reached, so we can add another option button. First we add `1` to `iNumOpts`, as we are going to add another control. Then a new control is added using the `Load` statement. This is the same as loading a form, and doesn't display the newly loaded option button, so we need to set some properties at runtime. This is what the following code does:

```
    optArray(iNumOpts).Top = optArray(iNumOpts - 1).Top + 350
    optArray(iNumOpts).Caption = "Mouse Pointer " & iNumOpts
    optArray(iNumOpts).Visible = True
    optArray(0).SetFocus
```

The first line tells Visual Basic to place the top of the new option button 350 Twips from the top of the previous option control. (The Visual Basic coordinates system, including Twips, will be covered in Chapter 8). The second line sets the `Caption` property for the new option button, the third line makes the option button visible, and the forth gives the focus to the initial option button.

The `cmdDelete_Click` event code comes next, and handles the removing of option buttons from the frame:

```
If iNumOpts <= 1 Then
        MsgBox "Sorry you must have at least two options on the form"
        Exit Sub
End If
```

**81**

This code checks if you are trying to remove the first two option buttons, and displays a message box informing you that you can't delete the first two option buttons.

```
Unload optArray(iNumOpts)
    iNumOpts = iNumOpts - 1
    optArray(0).SetFocus
```

It should come as no surprise that the opposite of `Load` is `Unload` (as per forms). Having deleted the option button, `1` is subtracted from `iNumOpts` so that it still reflects the number of option buttons on the frame. Finally, focus is passed to the first option button.

The code for the `cmdQuit_Click` event unloads the form, thereby ending the project as follows:

```
Unload frmButtons
```

Finally we have the code that changes the mouse pointer in the `optArray_Click` event:

```
Frame1.MousePointer = Index
```

When you click on one of the option buttons, Visual Basic passes the index of the button clicked to the `Click` event. We are using this number to change the mouse pointer for the frame that holds the option buttons (`Frame1`). As the mouse pointer property is a number between 0 and 12, we do not have to determine which option has been chosen, we just change the pointer. This code will still work if Microsoft decided to add or change the mouse pointer codes.

## Mouse Pointer Property

The reason that the mouse pointer reverts back if you move it off the frame is because we've only altered the mouse pointer for the frame `Frame1`.
You'll see that every control has a `MousePointer` property, so it's feasible that you can have a different mouse pointer set for every control, as well as the form (although this may confuse the user!).

# File System Controls

## File System Controls: Implementation

So far, we've only briefly touched upon common dialogs, and used the File/Open dialog in the MDI View project in Chapter 2. There are times when you'll want to access drive, directories and files, but none of the common dialogs quite fit the bill. Visual Basic has a useful set of controls for just this type of occasion called the **File System Controls**. There are three associated controls that are used to imitate File Manager:

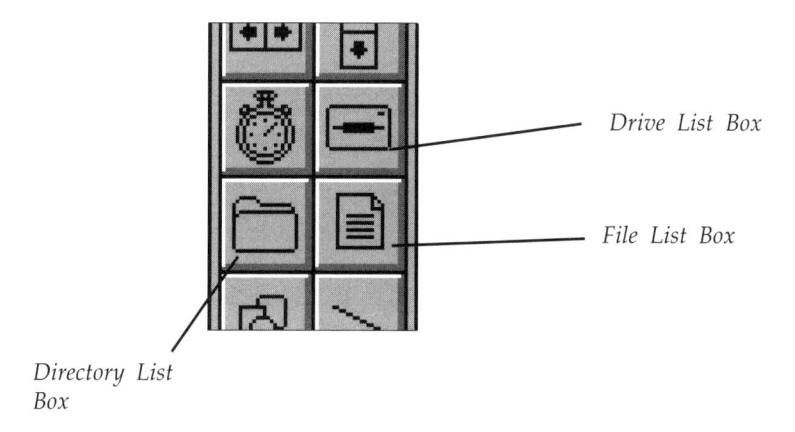

*Drive List Box*

*File List Box*

*Directory List Box*

As we saw in the MDI View application, Visual Basic comes with an impressive library of icons, so we'll write a better graphic viewer than the MDI View project, using the file system controls, and the image control. Time to fire up Visual Basic, and start a new project, then draw a drive, directory, file and image control on the form. At the top of the form add a label and a text box, then add two command buttons, so that it should now look something like this:

## Chapter 3 - Gaining Control

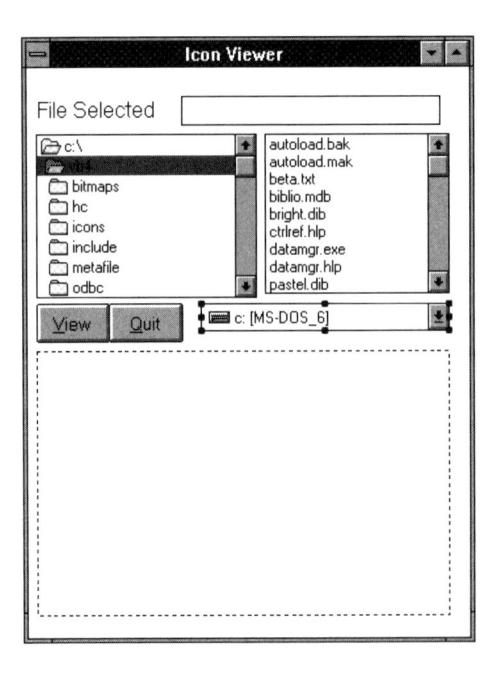

Name the form **frmView**, and give it a caption. We've called the file control **filSel**, the directory control **dirSel**, and the drive control **drvSel**. The textbox is called **txtSelection**, and we've set the **Text** property to nothing. The two command buttons are **cmdView** and **cmdQuit**, with captions of **&View** and **&Quit**. Finally, we've called the image control **imgSelected**.

You'll notice that Visual Basic loads the details of the current drive and directory into the boxes at design time. Now we need to write some code to tie the file system controls together, and display the selected icon:

```
Sub Form_Load()
    filSel.Pattern = "*.bmp;*.ico;*.wmf"
    txtSelection = filSel.Pattern
End Sub
```

In the **Form_load()** event we'll set the **Pattern** property of the file list box so that only graphic files are displayed. To show the user what's happening, the pattern is also displayed in the selection text box when the form is loaded.

```
Sub drvSel_Change()
    dirSel.Path = drvSel.Drive
End Sub
```

# File System Controls

If a different drive is selected from the drive list box, then the **change** event will be triggered. We want to change the contents of the directory list box to reflect the change in drive, so we assign the **Drive** property of the drive list box to the **Path** property of the directory list box. Visual Basic will use the currently selected directory of the drive that you've changed as the place from where to start the list, rather than the root directory of the drive:

```
Sub dirSel_Change()
    filSel.Path = dirSel.Path
End Sub
```

Similarly, if the directory is changed, we'll want the file list to be updated, so the file list path is changed to the new directory list path.

```
Sub filSel_Click()
    txtSelection.Text = filSel.Path & "\" & filSel.FileName
End Sub
```

Having got our file list up to date, if the user clicks on a particular entry, we'll want to update the **txtSelection.Text** with the selected file. You'll notice that the **Filename** property of the file list box doesn't include the path, so we need to add the path to the front of the file name (not forgetting to add a \) to produce the fully qualified file name. Now, having selected the file name, we'll want to look at the image:

```
Sub cmdView_Click()
    imgSelected.Picture = LoadPicture(txtSelection.Text)
End Sub
```

When we wish to assign a picture to a picture control, image control or a form, (yes, we *can* have a background picture on a form), we need to tell Visual Basic to load the picture. The fully qualified file name that is displayed in the **txtSelection.Text** control is used, rather than the **filSel.path** and **filSel.FileName**, so that the user can type a file name directly into the text box, and also use the file selection process.

```
Sub filSel_DblClick()
    cmdView_Click
End Sub
```

The code in the **DblClick** event will allow the user to view the selected file without having to select the file and then click the View button. Finally, we need to be able to end the project, so the last section of code unloads the form in the following way:

85

# Chapter 3 - Gaining Control

```
Sub cmdQuit_Click()
    Unload frmView
End Sub
```

When you run the project, you'll see that the bitmaps and icons are only button size, and appear in the top left hand corner, but when you load a metafile, it expands beyond the limits of the image box. This is easily fixed by altering the **Stretch** property of the image control to **True**. Now, when you run the project, all of the images re-size to fit the image control.

# Summary

In this chapter we have looked at the different button types available in Visual Basic, and seen various ways of clicking command buttons to illustrate many of the methods used to manipulate controls. We saw how to change the properties of controls within our code and in the Properties window, and looked in detail at how focus is controlled within code as well as using the **Tab** properties of the controls.

You've learnt about grouping buttons, and extended this concept to control arrays. Finally, we looked at the file selection controls, and were introduced to some of the properties and uses of the image control. In the next chapter we'll be looking at the other graphic and text controls, and the timer. Before we go rushing off into Chapter 4, try a few of the following exercises on the projects we worked on in this chapter.

In Chapter 4, *Graphics, Text and Timer Controls*, we'll cover the other controls and their usage.

# Exercises

Using the Buttons project:

**1** Change the check boxes into a control array, and re-code the **Click** event

**2** When a new option is added, set the focus to the new button, and automatically change the mouse pointer.

# Summary

**3** Add a new control array of options that change the color of the label text, using `Qbcolor`. Allow the user to add and remove controls at runtime.

Using the View Icon project:

**4** In the drive change event add an **error handler** to stop the project from crashing if a floppy drive is selected without a disk in the drive.

**Hint: we saw how to trap runtime errors in the MDI View project in Chapter 2.**

**5** Add the View Icon form to the MDI View project replacing the old viewer, and recompile.

**87**

# Chapter 4

# Graphics, Text, and Time Controls

There are still quite a few controls in the toolbox that we've yet to get our hands on. In this chapter we'll be taking a look at some more of the graphic controls available in Visual Basic. We'll also be trying out the timer control, and finally we'll be manipulating data by using the text, list, and combo boxes.

By now you should be getting familiar with manipulating the properties of controls (especially the **Name** and **Caption** properties), so from now on, we'll only be discussing the properties that you have not yet used.

In this chapter we'll cover:

- Image controls
- Variable arrays
- Picture box control
- The timer control
- Text, list and combo boxes

# Chapter 4 - Graphics, Text, and Time Controls

## More Graphic Controls

One of the questions often asked with using Visual Basic is when to use a picture box, and when to use the image control. Generally, you'll find that using an image control is often recommended, but nobody says exactly why.

# Picture Boxes, Image Controls and Windows Resources

Before we look at the differences between the two controls, we need to determine why image controls are generally preferred.

Under Windows, we are all sharing the resources available to the PC, such as memory. You may well have noticed that the more applications you have running, the slower the screens load and repaint, and occasionally the PC will crash. Windows has a finite amount of resources available to it, and when we write Visual Basic applications, we are taking a share of these resources. So if we can minimize the amount of memory and resource that we use, our applications, and other Windows applications that may be running, will run faster.

## Lightweight and Heavyweight Controls

You'll remember from the previous chapter that controls are really small programs, but some are larger than others. The controls that use less resource are called **lightweight** controls, whilst those that use more resource are **heavyweight** controls. The image control is a lightweight control, so when all you want to do is display a picture, use the image control, and save resources. As you may have guessed, the picture box is a heavyweight control.

Other heavyweight controls include list boxes, combo boxes, grids, timers, data controls and textboxes. The lightweight controls are labels, images, lines and shapes. Generally speaking, the more properties a control has, the more resources it will use.

Wherever possible use a lightweight control. For instance, if you want to display some text, then use a label rather than a textbox. Whilst this may not make a great difference in a small project, it can make a huge difference

# Windows Resources

in the larger projects (and don't forget that other applications will also be vying for those precious resources).

You can look at the resource usage on your PC at any time by going into Program Manager, and selecting the About Program Manager... option from the Help menu. You'll get a dialog similar to this:

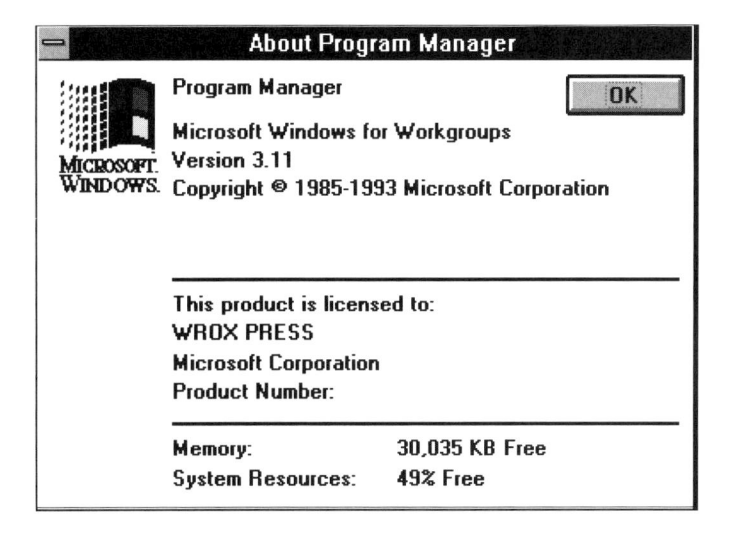

```
About Program Manager

Program Manager                              [ OK ]
Microsoft Windows for Workgroups
Version 3.11
Copyright © 1985-1993 Microsoft Corporation


This product is licensed to:
WROX PRESS
Microsoft Corporation
Product Number:

Memory:            30,035 KB Free
System Resources:  49% Free
```

As you can see, on our system we have about 30M of free memory (most of that is the virtual memory file), and 49% of resource free. This is getting quite low, but at the moment we have quite a few applications running.

## The Image Control Revisited

You have had a couple of brief visits to the image control, so it's time that we took a detailed look at this control. It's actually quite a versatile control, and by using its properties and events, it can be used for more than just displaying pictures.

### Using the Image Control as a Button

One of the events of the image control is the `Click` event. This makes it possible to use image controls as graphical buttons, and it also allows you to animate the button when it is pressed. Let's try it out. Start a new project, and place an image control and a command button on the form.

## Chapter 4 - Graphics, Text, and Time Controls

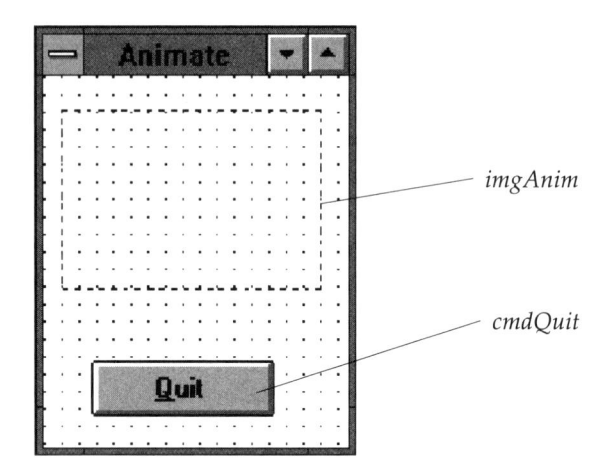

*imgAnim*

*cmdQuit*

Set the **Stretch** property of the image control to **True**, then add the following code to the project (after altering the **Name** properties of the controls to **cmdQuit** for the command button, **imgAnim** for the image control, and **frmAnim** for the form):

```
Dim iHot As Integer
```

This line should be entered in the (general) declarations Code window for the form. The rest of the code should be entered in the respective event procedures.

```
Sub cmdQuit_Click()
    Unload frmAnim
End Sub

Sub Form_Load()
   imgAnim.Picture = LoadPicture("c:\vb\icons\computer\trash02a.ico")
   iHot = False
End Sub

Sub imgAnim_Click()
    If iHot Then
        imgAnim.Picture = LoadPicture("c:\vb\icons\computer\trash02a.ico")
        iHot = False
    Else
        iHot = True
        imgAnim.Picture = LoadPicture("c:\vb\icons\computer\trash02b.ico")
    End If
End Sub
```

# The Image Control

> In the `Form_Load` event, we're loading the `TRASH02A.ICO` from the Visual Basic icon library. The location of this icon may differ on your PC. You can use the Icon Viewer that you wrote in the last chapter to locate it.

In the `imgAnim_Click` event the integer `iHot` is being used as a boolean (or flag), to determine which of the two icons is currently loaded, so that the other can be loaded over it. This gives the illusion of animation, but it's not incredibly effective. The `Click` event doesn't respond quickly enough, but it works well if we want to indicate a state to the user, such as whether we have mail or not. Try changing the icons to the `MAIL16A.ICO`, and `MAIL16B.ICO` in the mail subdirectory under `ICONS`, so that the code looks like this:

```
Sub Form_Load()
   imgAnim.Picture = LoadPicture("c:\vb\icons\mail\mail16b.ico")
   iHot = False
End Sub

Sub imganim_Click()

        If iHot Then
        imgAnim.Picture = LoadPicture("c:\vb\icons\mail\mail16b.ico")
        iHot = False
    Else
        iHot = True
        imgAnim.Picture = LoadPicture("c:\vb\icons\mail\mail16a.ico")

        'Call the "new mail received" function here

    End If
End Sub
```

When the form is loaded, it indicates that you have mail, and you would be told to click the icon in order to read the mail. The icon changes to show that the mail has been read, and you would be presented with all the new mail. The `iHot` indicator is now used to tell you if there is new mail or not. Within the receive mail function, `iHot` and the mail icon are reset to indicate that new mail has been received.

> We've also seen image controls used as graphical switches, with the switch icon being in an up state to indicate off, and down to indicate on. This works very well on the screen, and can be thought of as a graphical check box in this case.

# Image Controls as Hotspots

Image controls can also be used as hotspots on a form. A hotspot is an invisible area on a graphic which the user can click on to make something happen. You may have seen them used in Windows help files where clicking on a hotspot will give you further information about the area that the cursor is over. We'll be covering some useful concepts, such as displaying status details, and looking at some of the other events during the following example.

Firstly, we need to set the background 'picture' upon which we are going to put the hotspots. We shall be using a control array of 7 image controls, called **imgNation()** which we will use to display icons of various nations. Set the **Stretch** property of the image controls to **True**, and ensure that the controls are square. The reason for this is to keep the icons in their correct proportions. We also require an array of 7 labels, **lblNation()**, to complement our hotspot in displaying information. Initially, we don't want to display these labels, so set their **Visible** property to **False**. We have also included an extra label which we will use as a status indicator for the application. The icons to use for the various images can be found in your **\VB\ICONS\FLAGS\** directory. Set out the images and labels in a similar way to the screenshot.

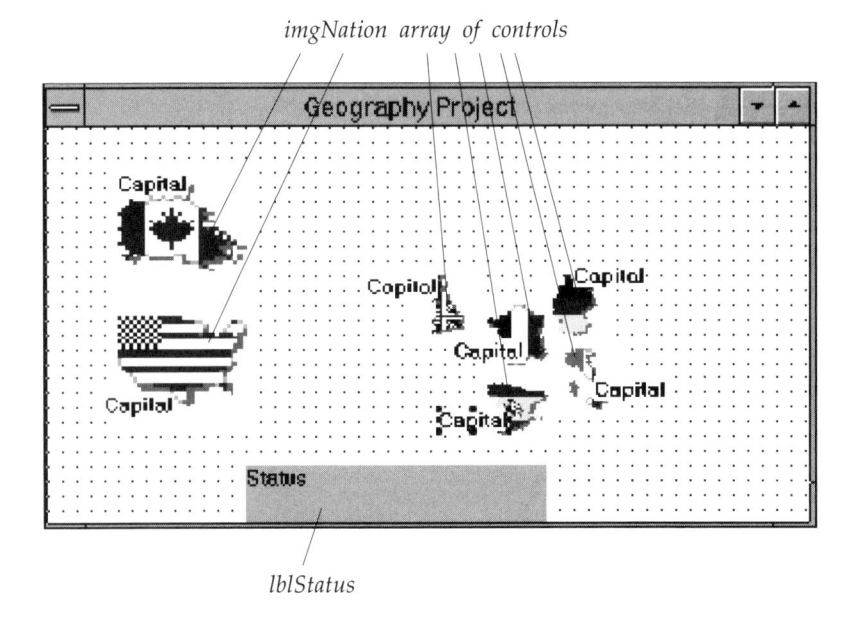

*imgNation array of controls*

*lblStatus*

# Hotspots

The properties that we have used are as follows:

| Type | Name | Property Setting |
|---|---|---|
| Form | **frmMap** | **BorderStyle = 3 Fixed Double**<br>**Caption = "Map Project"** |
| Images | **imgNation(0)**<br>**Stretch = True**<br>(this applies to all the images of the array) | **Picture = CTRCAN.ICO** |
|  | **imgNation(1)** | **Picture = CTRFRAN.ICO** |
|  | **imgNation(2)** | **Picture = CTRGERM.ICO** |
|  | **imgNation(3)** | **Picture = CTRITALY.ICO** |
|  | **imgNation(4)** | **Picture = CTRSPAIN.ICO** |
|  | **imgNation(5)** | **Picture = CTRUK.ICO** |
|  | **imgNation(6)** | **Picture = CTRUSA.ICO** |
| Labels | **lblStatus** | **Caption = " Status"** |
|  | **lblNation(0)** | **Caption = " Ottawa"**<br>**Visible = False**<br>(this applies to all of the array labels)<br>**Autosize = True**<br>(this applies to all of the array labels) |
|  | **lblNation(1)** | **Caption = " Paris"** |
|  | **lblNation(2)** | **Caption = " Berlin"** |
|  | **lblNation(3)** | **Caption = " Rome"** |
|  | **lblNation(4)** | **Caption = " Madrid"** |
|  | **lblNation(5)** | **Caption = " London"** |
|  | **lblNation(6)** | **Caption = " Washington, D.C."** |

# Chapter 4 - Graphics, Text, and Time Controls

Now we need to add some code as follows:

```
Dim iVisible As Integer
```

We'll set up a boolean in the (general) declarations code window to indicate whether or not the label is visible (this is similar to the previous example).

```
Sub imgNation_Click (index As Integer)
  'Display or hide the label depending on the iVisible Boolean
  If iVisible Then
    lblNation(index).Visible = False
    iVisible = False
  Else
    lblNation(index).Visible = True
    iVisible = True
  End If
End Sub
```

For the **Click** event of the **imgNation** image controls, we have the following code. This must be placed into the 'MouseMove' procedure of the **imgNation** object, in code view:

```
Sub imgNation_MouseMove(Index As Integer, Button As Integer, Shift As Integer, X As Single, Y As Single)
    'Change the mouse if you're over a hot spot
    imgNation(Index).MousePointer = 4
    'update the status label with where the cursor is
    If Index = 0 Then lblStatus = "You are over Canada"
    If Index = 1 Then lblStatus = "You are over France"
    If Index = 2 Then lblStatus = "You are over Germany"
    If Index = 3 Then lblStatus = "You are over Italy"
    If Index = 4 Then lblStatus = "You are over Spain"
    If Index = 5 Then lblStatus = "You are over the U.K."
    If Index = 6 Then lblStatus = "You are over the U.S.A."
End Sub
```

Firstly, use the **MouseMove** event for the image control to check whether or not the label is visible by referring to the **iVisible** variable which we are using as a boolean to indicate a **True** or **False** value for the property. This is a control array, so we use the index of each control to determine which of the images we are dealing with. Let's break the code down for clarity:

```
Sub imgNation_MouseMove(Index As Integer, Button As Integer, Shift As Integer, X As Single, Y As Single)
    'Change the mouse if you're over a hot spot
    imgNation(Index).MousePointer = 4
```

# Variable Arrays

This section changes the mouse pointer if you are over one of the hot spots, using the **MouseMove** event. Visual Basic will call this event code whenever the mouse pointer passes into an image control. We could have changed the mouse pointer property to **4** for every control, which would have achieved the same effect, but we could not achieve the results of the next section of code without using this event.

```
'update the status label with where the cursor is
    If Index = 0 Then lblStatus = "You are over Canada"
    If Index = 1 Then lblStatus = "You are over France"
    If Index = 2 Then lblStatus = "You are over Germany"
    If Index = 3 Then lblStatus = "You are over Italy"
    If Index = 4 Then lblStatus = "You are over Spain"
    If Index = 5 Then lblStatus = "You are over the U.K."
    If Index = 6 Then lblStatus = "You are over the U.S.A."
End Sub
```

This section of code will alter the caption of the status label in the notes section of the picture, depending on where the cursor is.

```
Sub Form_MouseMove (Button As Integer, Shift As Integer, X As Single, Y As Single)
    lblStatus = ""
End Sub
```

Similarly, we use the **MouseMove** event of the form to blank out the caption when the cursor is moved off the image hotspot.

As you can see, by using control arrays, we can achieve a lot of functionality with very little code, but you may have noticed the bug in our code, when you ran the project. Try making a label visible, then click on another hotspot. Nothing happens, because **iVisible** was set to **True** when you made the first label visible.

## Introducing Variable Arrays

What we need is a variable array to match the control array - we can then check to see if each individual label is visible or not. We'll be looking in depth at variables and arrays in Chapter 5, but for now we need to alter the following code:

```
Dim iVisible(6) As Integer
```

The `Dim` statement (general) declarations section has changed to tell Visual Basic that there will be seven elements to the `iVisible` integer array (0 to 6 because Visual Basic indexes start at 0 by default). This will match the `lblNation` control array.

```
Sub imgNation_Click (index As Integer)
  'Display or hide the label depending on the iVisible Boolean
  If iVisible(index) Then
    lblNation(index).Visible = False
    iVisible(index) = False
  Else
    lblNation(index).Visible = True
    iVisible(index) = True
  End If
End Sub
```

All we need to do is reference the individual `iVisible` array elements with the index integer that Visual Basic passes when a particular control array element is clicked. Now when you run the project, it will display and hide each individual nation label.

Is this the best method of displaying the hidden text, though? After all, we now have two arrays (a control and a variable array), just to display the hidden text. We'd only code it this way if all the hidden text had to be on screen together and was never going to change. Don't forget that we are also using up valuable Windows resources with these arrays. It would be better for each control to write its hidden text at runtime to a single label control. This is also more flexible, as the text could be picked up perhaps from a file or a database at runtime.

# Improving the Project

We'll need to alter the screen, and change the code to add these improvements. You'll find yourself doing this quite a lot at the beginning, as you discover better and more efficient ways to do the things you want to do, and deliver the best solution to the users.

We need to delete all the labels in the `lblNation` control array, and all the code associated with this array, then change some of the code in the image array `Click` event, and add a new larger label at the bottom of the form. The form should look something like the following after these changes:

# Trial and Error

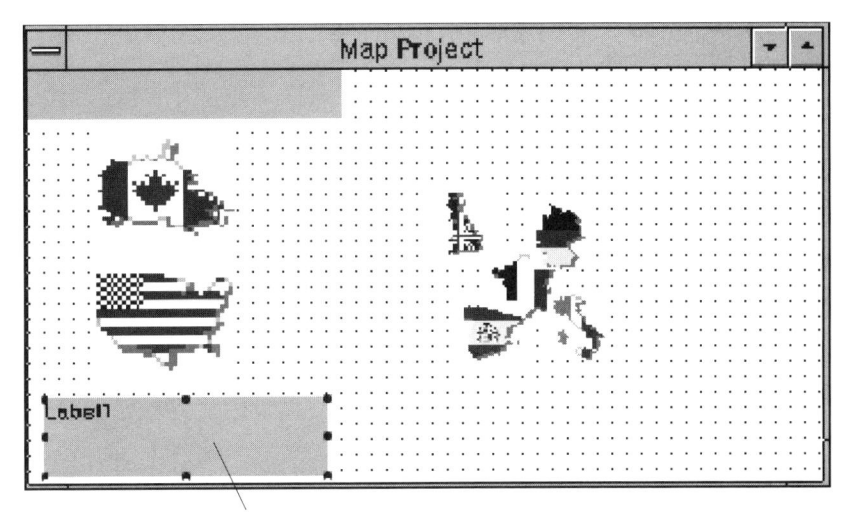

*This replaces the array of labels used to display the nation's capital*

Now change the code as follows:

```
Dim iVisible as Integer
```

We again change the declaration of the **iVisible** variable to a simple integer in the (general) declarations since we now only have one label to display information in. Now we also have a new large label instead of 7 seperate ones. Leave its name as the default **label1**.

For the image control array we need to change the code to the following:

```
Sub imgNation_Click (Index As Integer)
    'Display or hide the label depending on the iVisible Boolean
    If iVisible = Index Then
        label1.Visible = False
        iVisible = 7
    Else
        If Index = 0 Then label1 = "Ottawa"
        If Index = 1 Then label1 = "Paris"
        If Index = 2 Then label1 = "Berlin"
        If Index = 3 Then label1 = "Rome"
        If Index = 4 Then label1 = "Madrid"
        If Index = 5 Then label1 = "London"
        If Index = 6 Then label1 = "Washington, D.C."
        label1.Visible = True
        iVisible = Index
    End If
End Sub
```

99

We're not using the `iVisible` integer as a boolean anymore. We're now checking to see if the user is re-clicking the same hotspot. If they are re-clicking, then we hide the label and set the value of `iVisible` to 7 so that the next time the image is clicked the `Else` section of the code is run:

```
Sub imgNation_Click (Index As Integer)
   'Display or hide the label depending on the iVisible Boolean
    If iVisible = Index Then
        label1.Visible = False
        iVisible = 7
```

The second section of code changes the caption of our label depending on which image control was clicked, and then sets the `iVisible` integer to the index of the image clicked, ready for the next time an image is clicked

```
    Else
         If Index = 0 Then label1 = "Ottawa"
         If Index = 1 Then label1 = "Paris"
         If Index = 2 Then label1 = "Berlin"
         If Index = 3 Then label1 = "Rome"
         If Index = 4 Then label1 = "Madrid"
         If Index = 5 Then label1 = "London"
         If Index = 6 Then label1 = "Washington, D.C."
         label1.Visible = True
         iVisible = Index
    End If
End Sub
```

## Resizing Controls at Runtime

The project seems to run fine now, but you may well be a little puzzled, looking at the properties table for the project. Why did we set the `Border` style of the form to `Fixed Double`?

Well, you may have noticed that when you run the project, there are no maximize or minimize buttons on the form, nor can you change its size. This is as a result of the border style change for the form. Try changing it back to `2-Sizable` and then run the project. It all works fine until you start to resize the form. The images simply stay where they are, when what you would actually want is for them to be scaled appropriately for the new size of the window. Imagine what would happen if you had a metafile graphic loaded onto the form itself (the form also has a `Picture` property). A metafile picture will automatically resize itself to match the form.

# Resizing

Think of what would happen if you had a map of the world in such a graphic. When the form is resized the graphic will re-scale, but any image controls that you are using will remain in the same absolute position on the form with their original **Left** and **Top** properties. This would mean that clicking your hotspots would now be very confusing and bear no relation to what the user would expect. With this in mind there are two solutions. You can keep the form at a fixed size and not allow the user to change it, or change the size and location of your hotspots at runtime from the code. This would have to be done using the form **Resize** event.

This is quite tricky (especially if you have a background picture as you have no control over this image). We'll go through the necessary calculations to resize and relocate the controls, but it is slow, so unless you have a particular reason to allow the user to resize a hotspotted graphic, then we recommend that you keep the size of the form fixed.

## Resizing a Hotspot Graphic

Some of the important things you will have to consider are the change in size of the control, and the change in its position reflected in its **Left** and **Top** properties. The best way to calculate these is to consider the center of the control:

```
Dim iVisible   As Integer
Dim iOldfrmWidth As Integer
Dim IOldfrmHeight As Integer
```

These are the variables that you should place in the (general) declarations section. The code we are using for the **Load** event of the form is as follows:

```
Sub Form_Load()
  iOldfrmWidth = frmMap.Width
  iOldfrmHeight = frmMap.Height
' move the label for our click information to the bottom of the screen
  label1.Left = 0
  label1.Top = frmMap.Height - label1.Height

  lblStatus.Top = 0
  lblStatus.Left = 0
End Sub
```

## Chapter 4 - Graphics, Text, and Time Controls

The two variables will be used to hold the size of the form before any resize events occur. We will be using this to calculate by how much the form has changed size.

```
iOldfrmWidth = frmMap.Width
iOldfrmHeight = frmMap.Height
```

We are setting the status and information labels to the top left of the form and the bottom left of the form respectively. This way when a **Resize** event occurs we will be able to keep the labels out of the way of the newly placed image hotspots. Now let's think about what must be done when we want to resize the form. Initially, we need some code entered into the 'resize' procedure of the Form object:

```
Sub Form_Resize()
' variables to hold the proportional change of the window
    Dim dWidthRatio As Double
    Dim dHeightRatio As Double
    Dim iCount As Integer
' Calculate the ratio of size change
    dWidthRatio = frmMap.Width / iOldfrmWidth
    dHeightRatio = frmMap.Height / iOldfrmHeight
    For iCount = 0 To 6
        'Move the top and left of each hotspot
        imgNation(iCount).Left = (imgNation(iCount).Left * dWidthRatio)
        imgNation(iCount).Top = (imgNation(iCount).Top * dHeightRatio)

        'Resize each image proportionally
        imgNation(iCount).Width = (imgNation(iCount).Width * dWidthRatio)
        imgNation(iCount).Height = (imgNation(iCount).Height * dHeightRatio)
    Next iCount
    label1.Top = frmMap.Height - label1.Height
    'Finally reset the form level variable ready for the next resize
    iOldfrmWidth = frmMap.Width
    iOldfrmHeight = frmMap.Height
End Sub
```

Let's take a look at what is behind some of the code fragments.

Firstly, we have declared two variables as type **Double** - these will be used to hold the ratio of the change in size of the window. **Double**s are the most precise variable available to us in Visual Basic (we will discuss variables in more depth in the next chapter). We need to use floating point calculation for this because the dimensions of the screen are measured in **Twips** by default (one **Twip** is approximately 1/567 of a centimeter). Consequently, the numbers we are dealing with are large, but the changes are comparatively small. Without floating point arithmetic our scaling factor would be rounded to 0, 1 or 2 if we were using integer arithmetic, which would not be particularly useful in trying to make fine movements of the hotspots!

```
' Calculate the ratio of size change
dWidthRatio = frmMap.Width / iOldfrmWidth
dHeightRatio = frmMap.Height / iOldfrmHeight
```

To calculate the required ratio of size change we have to use the forward slash for floating point division. Using a back slash would carry out integer division and give us a rounded result to our high precision variables.

```
For iCount = 0 To 6
  'Move the top and left of each hotspot
  imgNation(iCount).Left = (imgNation(iCount).Left * dWidthRatio)
  imgNation(iCount).Top = (imgNation(iCount).Top * dHeightRatio)

  'Resize each image proportionally
  imgNation(iCount).Width = (imgNation(iCount).Width * dWidthRatio)
  imgNation(iCount).Height = (imgNation(iCount).Height * dHeightRatio)
Next iCount
```

We are using a **For**...**Loop** to scale each of the image hotspots using the ratios calculated above. Although the value produced by the calculation will be of floating point, the result assigned to the integer properties for the controls are automatically converted to an integer.

```
label1.Top = frmMap.Height - label1.Height
'Finally reset the form level variable ready for the next resize
iOldfrmWidth = frmMap.Width
iOldfrmHeight = frmMap.Height
End Sub
```

Finally, we are moving the information label to the bottom of the form and resetting the values of the `iOldfrmWidth` and `iOldfrmHeight` to the current values of the form width and height, ready for the next time that the form is resized.

Now, when you run the project, you will be able to resize the form, and the hotspots will relocate and resize automatically, but even after all that code the result is not perfect. The relocation is slow and a little ugly. However, this method of resizing controls is quite common, and very useful when used in the right application.

## Container Controls

With all the functionality available to the image control, why bother with the picture boxes at all? Well, the image control does have a few limitations. Image controls can't receive focus, and they can't be placed on top of another control, unless it's a **container** control. A container control is a control that can hold other controls within it, such as the frame control (as seen in the previous chapter), and surprise surprise, the picture box. The controls inside the container are affected by the actions on the container. For example, making the container control invisible will also make all the controls inside the container invisible. Try it out with the Buttons application that we wrote in the last chapter.

### Picture Boxes

Picture boxes can be considered as a form within a form. You can place controls on them, display graphic images, they can receive focus, and they can also display text, and can be used to be printed to. Picture boxes can be used as toolbars or status bars. We'll be looking at the picture box as a status bar when we re-visit the MDI in Chapter 7, so let's build a toolbar. This will in fact use an image control array drawn inside the picture box to hold the toolbar icons.

### Creating a Toolbar

We'll add a toolbar to the View Icons project that we developed in Chapter 3, so load the project now. We've used the Save File As... and the Save Project As... options from the File menu in Visual Basic to create a new form and project, so that we don't overwrite the View Icons project.

Firstly, we need to expand the form, then move all the controls down. An easy way to select all the controls is to hold down the left mouse button, and drag the dotted rectangle that appears over all the controls. Any control that is within the selection rectangle, or touched by the dashed line defining the rectangle, will be selected.

# The Picture Box Control

*Delete these two buttons*

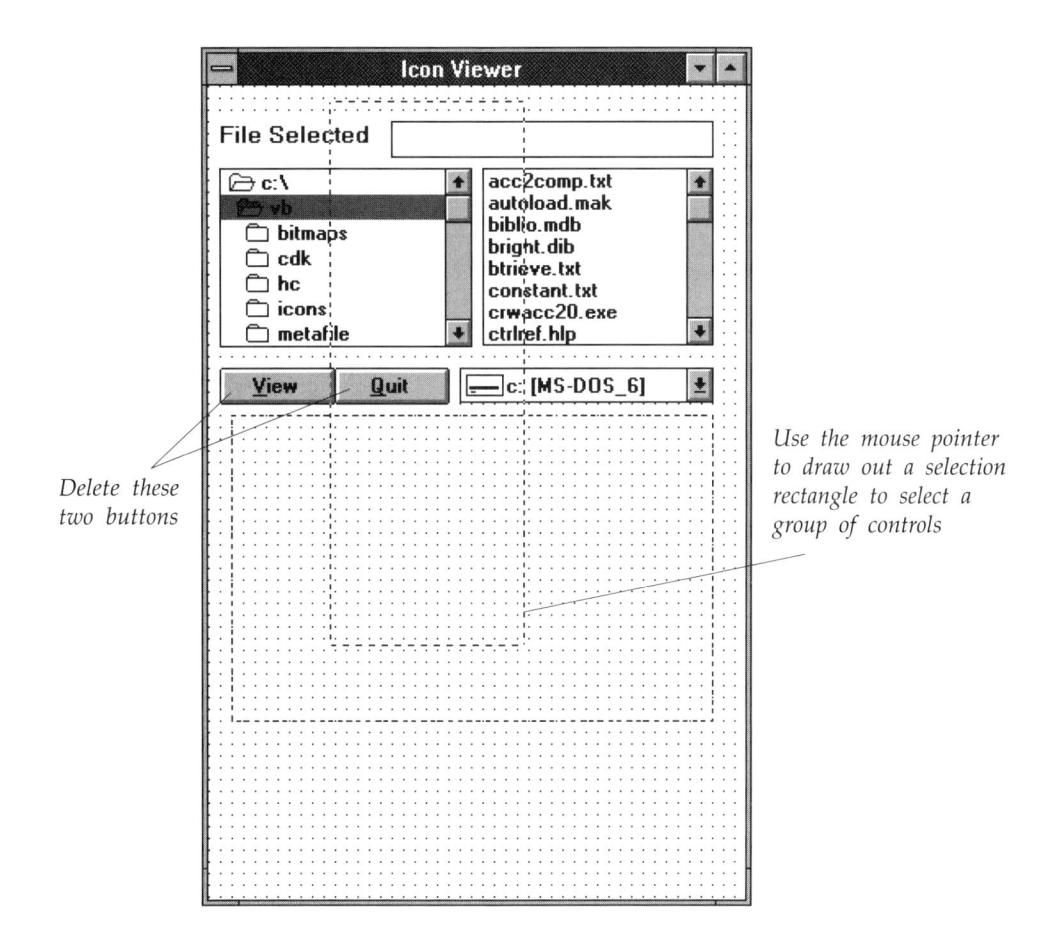

*Use the mouse pointer to draw out a selection rectangle to select a group of controls*

Now drag the controls down, and they will all move together, leaving a space at the top of the form to draw our toolbar. Draw a picture control at the top of the form. Don't worry about getting it exactly the right width, or exactly at the top - simply set the **Align** property to **Top**. The picture box now aligns to the top of the form, expands to the width of the form, and will automatically resize itself to the width of the form.

## Chapter 4 - Graphics, Text, and Time Controls

Now delete the two command buttons (they're going on the toolbar), and add three image controls to the picture box. Your form should look something like this:

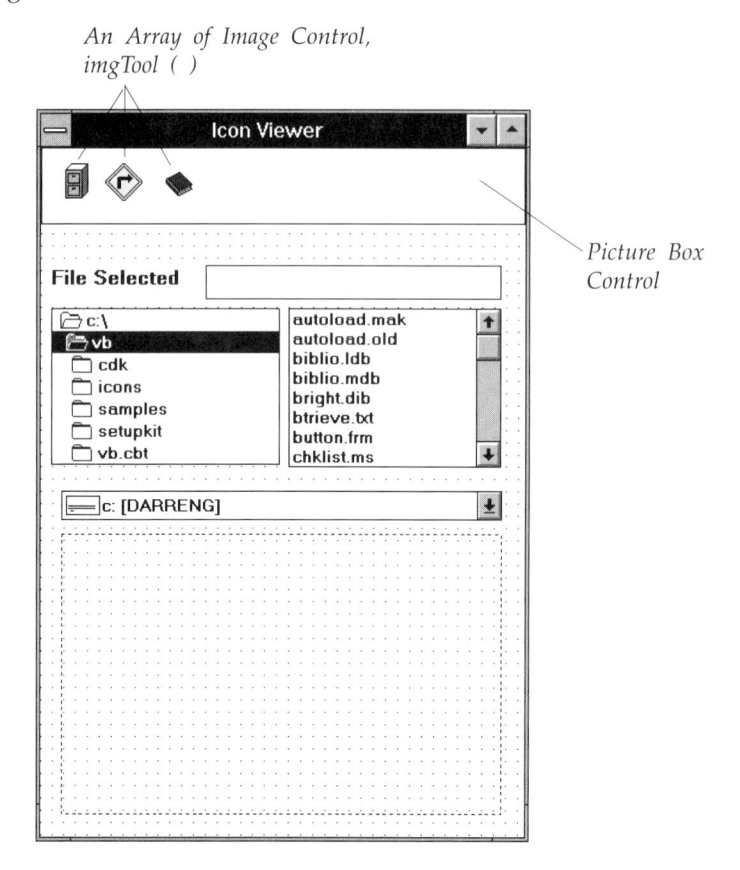

*An Array of Image Control, imgTool ( )*

*Picture Box Control*

Change the **Name** properties of the image controls to **imgTool**. This will create a control array, and set the **Stretch** property to **True** for each image. Set the **Picture** property of **imgTool(0)** to the **\OFFICE\FILES03A** (under the **\VB\ICONS** directory) - this will be our view button. Set **imgTool(1)** to **\TRAFFIC\TRFFC05.ICO**, as out exit button, and **imgTool(2)** to **\WRITING\BOOKS01A.ICO** as a help button. It's time to write some code which will align the images on the toolbar, and make them work.

Firstly, delete the **Click** event code for the command buttons - this will now be in the procedure area of the (general) object because we've deleted the buttons! Now let's see how the code needs to be changed:

# Coding Clicks

```
Sub imgTool_Click(Index As Integer)
    If Index = 0 Then imgSelected.Picture = LoadPicture(txtSelection.Text)
    If Index = 1 Then Unload frmView
    If Index = 2 Then MsgBox "Help Not yet Available for this application"
End Sub
```

If the user clicks the first icon, then we need to load the picture. If the second button is clicked, then we quit the project. These lines are exactly the same as the code that was in the command button **Click** events. At the moment we have no help system, so we are displaying a message box.

```
Sub imgTool_MouseDown(Index As Integer, Button As Integer, Shift As Integer, X As Single, Y As Single)
    If Index = 0 Then imgTool(0).Picture = LoadPicture("c:\vb\icons\office\files03b.ico")
    If Index = 1 Then imgTool(1).Picture = LoadPicture("c:\vb\icons\traffic\trffc02.ico")
    If Index = 2 Then imgTool(2).Picture = LoadPicture("c:\vb\icons\writing\book01b.ico")
End Sub
```

We want to give the illusion of the button being clicked, so we need to change the icon in the image. For the icons that we are using, there is a set of bitmaps that correspond to the button in a down state. We are using the **MouseDown** event so that the user has the illusion of the button going down when a mouse button is pressed.

```
Sub imgTool_MouseUp(Index As Integer, Button As Integer, Shift As Integer, X As Single, Y As Single)
    If Index = 0 Then imgTool(0).Picture = LoadPicture("c:\vb\icons\office\files03a.ico")
    If Index = 1 Then imgTool(1).Picture = LoadPicture("c:\vb\icons\traffic\trffc05.ico")
    If Index = 2 Then imgTool(2).Picture = LoadPicture("c:\vb\icons\writing\book01a.ico")
End Sub
```

When the left mouse button is released, we want to reload the original bitmaps. This is done in the **MouseUp** event. This event will not be triggered until the user releases the mouse button, so will remain in the down state if the user keeps the button down. This currently works for both mouse buttons.

```
Sub filSel_DblClick()
    imgSelected.Picture = LoadPicture(txtSelection.Text)
End Sub
```

Finally, since we have removed the command button to view the icon, we give the user a second method to view the icon by loading the picture from the double click event of the file list box.

Try running the program now. You have the beginnings of some simple and slick user controls. Note how the 'View' icon has to have text to act upon, otherwise the program hangs.

## Using Controls: Implementation

Let's put some of our knowledge of controls into practice by looking in some detail at the timer control.

## The Timer Control

The timer control is the only control in Visual Basic that doesn't respond to events, but in fact causes them! If you have a section of code or a function that needs to be run at regular intervals, then the timer control fits the bill. It does have a few limitations and drawbacks though:

**1** It's a resource hungry control. In fact, Windows limits the number of timers to sixteen for ALL applications that are running. The more often a timer event is triggered, the more processor time is used, and this can slow down overall performance.

**2** The interval is in milliseconds from 1 to 64,767 (about 1 minute 5 seconds).

**3** The actual interval between one timer event and the next may not be exact because Windows may be occupied with other tasks and not trigger the timer event at the exact time interval. Also, the system clock only ticks 18 times per second, so eighteenths of a second are the most accurate that you can be.

It's a really easy control to use - let's start a new project and try it out. Draw an image control, three command buttons, and a timer on the form. Don't worry about the size and location of the timer control, it'll be invisible at runtime so it doesn't matter. Your form should look something like the following:

# Timer Application

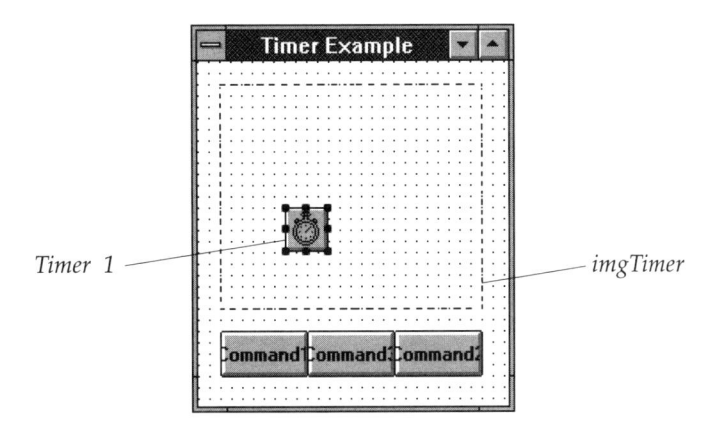

*Timer 1* — *imgTimer*

[Figure: Timer Example form showing Timer1 control, imgTimer image, and three command buttons]

Now change the **Stretch** property of the image to **True**, the **Enabled** property of timer to **False**, and **Interval** to **500**. By setting the **Enabled** property of the timer to **False**, we are switching off the timer. We'll be switching it on in the **Click** event code for **cmdGo**.

Change the properties of the other controls as follows.

| Control | Name | Caption |
| --- | --- | --- |
| command1 | cmdGo | &Go |
| command2 | cmdStop | &Stop |
| command3 | cmdQuit | &Quit |
| image1 | imgTimer | |
| form1 | frmTimer | Timer Example |

Add the following code to the project, and see what happens:

```
Dim iFaceLoad As Integer
```

This variable should be declared in the (general) declarations Code window.

```
Sub Form_Load()
    iFaceLoad = 1
End Sub
```

**109**

Set up an integer called **iFaceLoad**, and set it to **1** in the **Form_Load** event. This integer will be used to keep track of which image is loaded.

```
Sub cmdGo_Click()
    Timer1.Enabled = True
End Sub
```

This switches on the timer control. The timer events will now be executed about every half second (remember we set the interval to **500** in the Properties window).

```
Sub cmdStop_Click()
    Timer1.Enabled = False
    imgTimer.Picture = LoadPicture("")
End Sub
```

This code switches the timer off, and also clears the **imgTimer** image.

```
Private Sub cmdQuit_Click()
    Unload frmTimer
End Sub
```

As usual, we're stopping the project by unloading the form in the **cmdQuit_Click()** event.

```
Sub Timer1_Timer()
    If iFaceLoad = 3 Then
        iFaceLoad = 1
        imgTimer.Picture = LoadPicture("C:\vb\icons\misc\face03.ico")
        Exit Sub
    End If
    If iFaceLoad = 2 Then
        iFaceLoad = 3
        imgTimer.Picture = LoadPicture("C:\vb\icons\misc\face02.ico")
        Exit Sub
    End If
    If iFaceLoad = 1 Then
        iFaceLoad = 2
        imgTimer.Picture = LoadPicture("C:\vb\icons\misc\face01.ico")
    End If
End Sub
```

Finally, we have the code for the timer event. You'll find that this is the only event available for the timer control. All this block of code does is check which of the icons is currently loaded by using the **iFaceLoad** integer, then loads the next icon in the series and updates **iFaceLoad** with the number of the new icon. The **Exit Sub** is a new command, and tells Visual Basic to leave the sub procedure without executing any more code. You'll run into this command on many occasions, and use it regularly yourself.

# Text Controls

We'll wind up this chapter by looking at the three most common text controls:

- The textbox
- The list box
- The combo box

One of the controls that's covered in most other books, and in the manuals is the grid control. We won't be covering this control because there are better custom grid controls available, such as *Sheridans Data Widgets*, which are quicker and easier to use.

> If you feel that you've spent enough on Visual Basic, and don't want to spend more on a custom control, have a look at **Chapter 13** of the *Programmers Guide* manual.

If you only want to display text use a label control (it saves resources), use a textbox if you need to let the user update the text, or enter some text. List boxes allow the user to select from a list of items, but they can't type into the list box. If this is what's required use the combo box, which is a combination of the list and textboxes.

# Textboxes

Let's try them out in yet another new project. On the form, draw two textboxes, two labels, and a command button that'll be used to quit the application. We've changed the caption of the labels to tell the user what the textboxes are used for, and we've changed the **BackColor** properties of the form and the labels to light gray (**&H00C0C0C0&**) so that the textboxes stand out. The form now looks like the following:

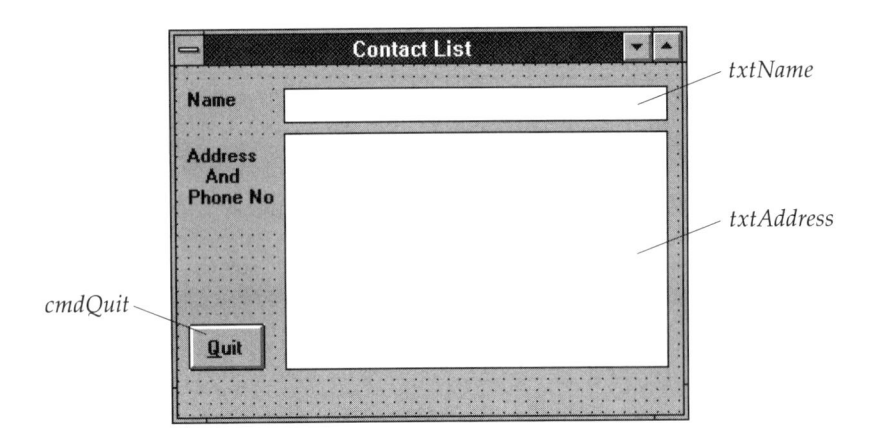

# Chapter 4 - Graphics, Text, and Time Controls

*txtName*

*txtAddress*

*cmdQuit*

Try running the project without any code. You can type text into the name textbox, then tab (if you have the tab order from top to bottom), and type text into the address box. But when you get to the end of the line, it doesn't wrap. This can be fixed in the properties - simply set the **MultiLine** property to **True** in the address textbox. Now when you try it, the text wraps, and you can also press *Enter* for a new line. That's about it. Visual Basic handles the tricky stuff, so now you've got a fully functional text input screen. To make it a little better, change the **ScrollBars** property of the address textbox to **2-Vertical**, so that the user can scroll through the textbox.

## List Boxes

Clearly the project has limited functionality. Let's extend it by adding two more command buttons and a list box, so that we can see what a list box can do for us. Before you start to embelish the project with some functionality, don't forget to change the name property in the **Form** to **frmContact** and in **Text1** to **txtName**. The form now looks like the following:

# List Boxes

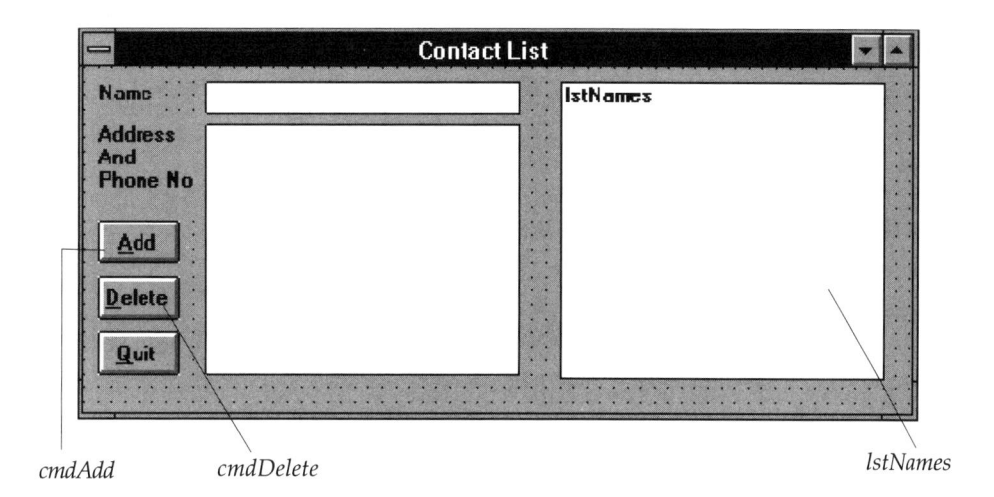

*cmdAdd*  *cmdDelete*  *lstNames*

We've added the following code to the project, so that we have some data loaded into the list box, and can add and remove entries in the list:

```
Sub Form_Load()
    lstNames.AddItem "Luke Dempsey"
    lstNames.AddItem "Darren Gill"
    lstNames.AddItem "Peter Wright"
    lstNames.AddItem "My Mum"
    lstNames.AddItem "WROX"
    lstNames.AddItem "Benny Many"
End Sub
```

The **AddItem** method adds an entry to the specified list. We're loading six entries into the list box as the form loads.

```
Sub cmdDelete_Click()
    lstNames.RemoveItem (lstNames.ListIndex)
End Sub
```

This code will remove the highlighted entry from the list box. The **ListIndex** property returns the index of the currently selected entry in the list, and the **RemoveItem** method deletes it.

```
Sub cmdAdd_Click()
    If Not txtName = "" Then lstNames.AddItem txtName.Text
End Sub
```

To add an entry to the list at runtime, we're checking if anything has been entered in the textbox, and if it's not an **empty string**, (""), then it's added to the list box.

# Chapter 4 - Graphics, Text, and Time Controls

> You may also see the `""` string called a `Null` string, because it has nothing in it. In Visual Basic, `Null` is a special case, and can only be allocated to database fields and a variable type called `Variants`. This will be covered in the next chapter.

```
Sub cmdQuit_Click()
    Unload frmContact
End Sub
```

Finally we have the unload code to end the project.

## Sorted Lists

The project isn't too bad, but we all like to see things in order. Now sorting the list may sound like a difficult task, but Visual Basic does it all for us. All we need to do is set the **Sorted** property of the list to **True** and hey presto, it's in alphabetical order. Any new items will also be added in the correct place.

> A word of warning - it doesn't sort in numerical order, so if you had a list with numbers from 1 to 12, the first three entries would be 1,11,12.

## Multiple Selections

The list box control also supports multiple selections of entries in the list using the **MulitSelect** property. This property can be set to **0** for no multi selection, **1** for **simple** multi selection, and **2** for **extended** multi selection. Simple multi selection will select and deselect entries in the list by pressing the space bar. The extended multi selection is more complex, in that holding *Shift* and clicking the mouse button will select all entries between the current and previous selections, and *Ctrl* and click will select or deselect a single item in the list.

The problem with this is that our deletion code no longer works, because the **ListIndex** property only returns the index of the last item selected. We need to add some code to the **cmdDelete_Click()** event.

# Sorting and Selecting

```
Dim iIndex As Integer
    For iIndex = lstNames.ListCount - 1 To 0 Step -1
        If lstNames.Selected(iIndex) = True Then lstNames.RemoveItem
(iIndex)
    Next iIndex
```

The line that does the business here is the first line. The **ListCount** property returns the size of the list. We reduce it by one and set the integer **iIndex** to the value. The deletion starts at the bottom of the list, and works backwards up the list to the top. The **Step -1** section subtracts one for each iteration of the loop. We can't go forward, as the **ListCount** property is updated every time an item is deleted, so the loop wouldn't work properly.

The deletion line has also changed. We need to see if the particular list item is selected (using the **Selected** property), before we delete it, otherwise we'd end up deleting all the entries in the list!

A quicker and better way to remove all the items in the list is with the **Clear** method:

```
lstNames.Clear
```

This is also a lot quicker than deleting each entry individually with a loop.

## Multi-Column List Boxes

As you've probably guessed, all we need to do to make the list box multi-column is to set the **Columns** property of the list box. A value of **0** (the default) is a single column list box with vertical scrolling, a value of **1** is a single column list box with horizontal scrolling, and a value above **1** is a multi column list box with horizontal scrolling. No coding required, just give it a go.

## Combo Boxes

On the face of it, list boxes and combo boxes are very similar. You can add items, delete items, sort, select, and clear. But combo boxes allow for selections that are not in the list by entering a selection in the text field. They also save space on a form, because the list is not displayed until the

115

user clicks on the down arrow of the combo box. There are three styles of combo box, assigned through the **Style** property of the combo box.

## DropDown List Combo Boxes

To use this style, set the **Style** property to **2**. This style is the one most similar to the list box, and it can be used in place of the list box where space is tight on the form. Beware though - combo boxes do not allow for multiple selections. Let's alter our project by removing the list box, and replace it with a combo box with the **Style** set to 2. The form now looks like this:

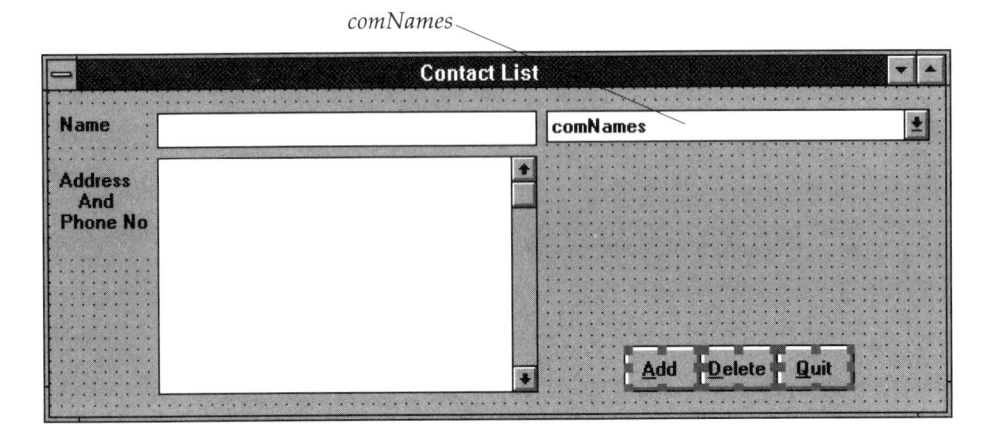

### Global Replace

Because we've deleted the list box, and replaced it with a combo box, we'll need to alter the code. A quick way to alter all the references of **lstNames** to **comNames** is to click on the Code window, then from the Edit menu select the Replace... option. Enter **lstN** in the find textbox, **comN** in the replace list box. Visual Basic will alter all the references for you (select All Modules & deselect Whole Word.). The only code that needs to be altered is in the **cmdDelete_Click()** event. Delete all the code, and add the following line to delete the selected item:

```
comNames.RemoveItem (comNames.ListIndex)
```

You'll notice when you run the project that you can't enter details in the combo box, but the Add and Delete buttons work fine.

# Combo Boxes

## DropDown Combo Boxes

The DropDown combo box (**Style 0**), is the default for combo boxes. The full list will still not be displayed until the down arrow is clicked, but we can now enter text in the combo box as selection criteria. You'll need to clear the **Text** property of the combo box in the Properties window, otherwise it will be displayed at runtime. Try entering a single letter, then the down arrow. If it matches any of the first letters in the list, it will auto select the first entry that matches the letter. This can be extended beyond the first letter to any length string. If it doesn't find a match, it will leave the text you typed in the combo box, so you don't need to actually make a selection from the list.

## Simple Combo Boxes

This style combo box (**Style 1**) is a combination of a list box and a combo box. You'll find that the down arrow has disappeared, and you'll need to expand the combo box to show the list (this is similar to the list box). You can still enter text into the combo box, and the list will adjust as you enter text, so that matching entries are displayed. Also like the DropDown combo, you can enter text that is not on the list, and you'll find that the Add and Delete buttons still work as expected.

# User Defined Properties

## The ItemData Property

The combo box, and list box have a property that you can use as a reference, called **ItemData**. This property is an array of long integers, with each element of the array matching an element in the list or combo box. In our example, it could be used to hold the telephone number of each contact that you add, so that you can subsequently display the phone number without having to search for it.

Once you've started using the **ItemData** property, when you use the **AddItem** method, a new **ItemData** element will be added by Visual Basic for the new item. It will contain the same value as the previously accessed **ItemData** entry. This may well not be what is required, so you need to make sure that you enter the correct value after you've added a new item.

**117**

## The Tag Property

Most, if not all, controls have a property called **Tag**. This property is never used or accessed by Visual Basic itself, and is therefore available for you to use in any manner that you wish. The property holds string data, so it could be used for almost any purpose, such as creating identifiers for controls on a form.

# Summary

We've managed to cover a lot of ground in this chapter. We had a brief look at Windows resources, and then looked in depth at the image control. You learnt how to set up hot spots, and use the resize event to resize and relocate controls on a form. You were also introduced to variable arrays, and we'll be looking at these in more detail in the next chapter. You also learnt about the picture box, and how to create a toolbar using this control.

We then examined the text controls, and you learnt about textboxes, list boxes, and finally the different styles of combo boxes that are available in Visual Basic. We'll be using most of these controls as we continue to learn about Visual Basic in the following chapters.

# Exercises

Using the Hot Spots project:

**1** The resizing/relocating looks messy on the screen. Hide this activity from the user.

**2** If the user changes the size of the window disproportionately, the icons won't be square. Write code to prevent this from happening.

**Hint: you will only need to use one ratio variable**

# Summary and Exercises

Using the Contact project:

**3** Change the combo style back to a drop down style, and sort it. When you add an item from the textbox, empty the textbox.

**4** Disallow duplicate entries from being added to the combo box.

**5** Allow the user to add a name by double clicking the textbox and pressing the *Enter* key.

# Chapter 5

# Variables in Visual Basic

So far we've seen the integer data type, and used it as an index and as a boolean in some of the examples. Visual Basic has a rich range of data types, and in this chapter we'll be looking at all the different types, and their uses.

We'll also be looking at the default variable type, the **Variant**, which is a very flexible data type that can contain different data types. We'll see how to manipulate variables using some of the functions built into Visual Basic, and how to convert data between the different types.

We'll also be looking at the **scope** and the **lifetime** of a variable, and take a deeper look at arrays. Finally, you'll find out how to create your own data types (similar to structs in C), and how to use them.

In this chapter we'll cover:

- Declaring variables
- Scope and lifetime
- Variants, and other data types
- String manipulation and functions
- Numerical fuctions
- Constants, more about arrays, and user-defined types

Chapter 5 - Variables in Visual Basic

# Declaring Variables: Concepts

The variables we use in our code can be declared either implicitly, or explicitly. If you've set the Require Variable Declaration option in the Options/Environment... dialog, then you'll have to explicitly declare all your variables (we covered this in Chapter 2). If you haven't set this option, then Visual Basic will create the variable for you if you have not declared it (of the data type `Variant`), providing it is a valid name. Every valid variable name must start with a letter, must be less than 40 characters long, must not contain a period, and must be unique within its **scope**.

## The Scope and Lifetime of a Variable

When you declare a variable in a procedure with the `Dim` statement, it can only be accessed within that procedure. This is known as the **scope** of the variable. When the procedure has finished, the variable is removed from memory. This is the **lifetime** of the variable, and usually the scope and the lifetime are the same. You can alter the lifetime of the variable by declaring the variable with the `Static` keyword. This preserves the value of the variable when the function or procedure finishes, although it will still be scoped to the procedure or function from where it was declared.

## Using Static to Preserve Values

You may remember that the `Timer` interval can be set to a maximum interval of just over a minute - so how would you trigger an event every hour? We can use a `Static` variable to preserve a value each time the `Timer` event is called. Assume that we've set the interval to `60000` (one minute), then we could use the following code snippet:

```
Sub Timer1_Timer()
        static iEntryTime as Integer
        iEntryTime = iEntryTime + 1
        if iEntryTime = 60 Then
              iEntryTime = 0
              'Do the hourly code
        End If
End Sub
```

Each time the `Timer` event is triggered, we add `1` to `iEntryTime`. If it's `60`, then an hour has elapsed, so reset it to `0` and run the hourly code. If we'd used a normal integer, it would've lost its value when the `Timer` event

# Variables

exited, so it would only ever be **1**, and the hourly code wouldn't be run. `iEntryTime` is still scoped to the `Timer` event and can't be accessed by any other procedure or module.

## Private and Public Variables

All the variables declared in a procedure (event code) are local variables, and the scope of these can't be altered. They are declared using the `Dim` statement, as we've already seen in the example projects that we've written so far.

We may find that in other projects we need variables whose scope goes beyond the module or form in which they are declared (these are the variables that we enter in the (general) declarations Code window). If we don't extend the scope, then when the form or module exits, the variable is no longer available. In these cases we need a `Global` variable. To declare a `Global` variable, use the `Global` keyword instead of the `Dim` statement.

> You can't declare a `Global` variable in a form - it must be in a code module. If you still wish to keep the variable scoped to the module in which it's declared, then you can use the `Dim` statement, (as we have done in the Timer project).

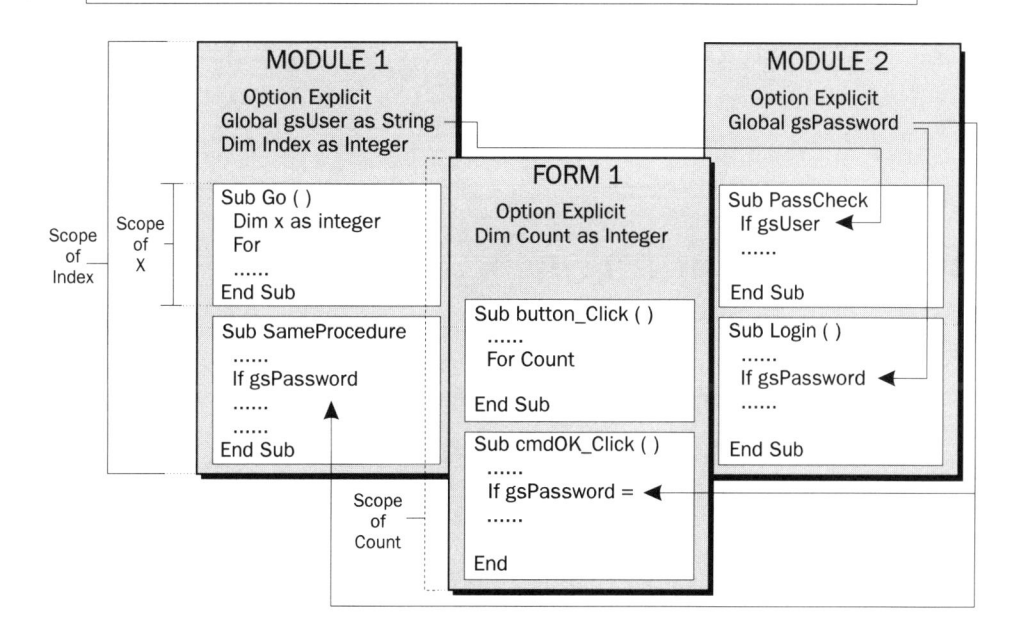

```
MODULE 1
Option Explicit
Global gsUser as String
Dim Index as Integer

Sub Go ( )
    Dim x as integer
    For
    ......
End Sub

Sub SameProcedure
    ......
    If gsPassword
    ......
    ......
End Sub
```

```
FORM 1
Option Explicit
Dim Count as Integer

Sub button_Click ( )
    ......
    For Count
    ......
End Sub

Sub cmdOK_Click ( )
    ......
    If gsPassword =
    ......
End
```

```
MODULE 2
Option Explicit
Global gsPassword

Sub PassCheck
    If gsUser
    ......
End Sub

Sub Login ( )
    ......
    If gsPassword
    ......
End Sub
```

Scope of Index, Scope of X, Scope of Count

123

# Chapter 5 - Variables in Visual Basic

Let's look at an example. Load the Timer project from the last chapter:

```
Dim iFaceLoad As Integer
```

```
Sub Form_Load()
    iFaceLoad = 1
End Sub
```

```
Sub Timer1_Timer()
      If iFaceLoad = 3 Then
        iFaceLoad = 1
         ....
```

`iFaceLoad` is currently scoped to the form (because it's declared in the (general) declarations, so it's a form level variable). The variable can be used in all the procedures within the form such as `Form_Load()` and the `Timer` event. Its lifetime is also linked to the form, and it will no longer be available when the form is unloaded. However, it will be available if the form is loaded, but not shown.

If we had declared the variable in the `Form_Load()` event, then it would have been scoped to that procedure, and couldn't have been used in the `Timer` event. Try it out by cutting it from the (general) declarations, and pasting it into the `Form_Load` event and see what happens:

```
Sub Form_Load()
    Dim iFaceLoad As Integer
    iFaceLoad = 1
End Sub
```

You'll find that Visual Basic cannot scope the variable to be used in the if...else loops in Timer.

## Shadowed Variables

Try the project again after adding back the declaration for `iFaceLoad` at the form level, but this time make it a `Global` variable. To do this, add a code module, and the following statement in its (general) declarations section:

```
Global iFaceLoad As Integer
```

The project runs, but when you press the Go button nothing happens! At first you may think that it's the change of the declaration to `Global`, but try the project again after commenting the `Dim` statement in the

# Shadowed Variables

`Form_Load()` event (turn the line into a comment line by adding an inverted comma (`'`) to the start of the line).

It works! So what was wrong? The **Global** variable **iFaceLoad** was **shadowed** by the local variable **iFaceLoad**. In Visual Basic, you can have variables of the same name providing that they have different scopes. This also applies to properties and controls, user-defined types, constants, and procedures, so you can write really difficult-to-read and impossible-to-debug code by giving everything the same name!

If you feel that you want to have the same names for variables or controls, then the locally declared variable will have precedence. This means that Visual Basic will use the local variable instead of the one with the wider scope.

In our example, the **iFaceLoad** declared in the **Form_Load** event shadowed the global **iFaceLoad**, and was set to **1**. The global **iFaceLoad** has been shadowed by the local level variable. At the end of the **Form_Load** event, the local **iFaceLoad** scope ended. The global **iFaceLoad** that we use to determine which icon to load was never set to **1**, so the code in the **If** statements for the **Timer** event is never executed.

Shadowing also applies to variables and controls, and control properties. If you have a control on a form called **TextIn**, and declare a variable in an event on the form called **TextIn**, the variable will shadow the control. You will need to add a **qualifier** to access the control. The qualifier is the name of the form, followed by an exclamation mark (**!**). If you use a reasonable set of naming conventions, this problem should never occur.

> This convention of adding a qualifier is also used where you have two forms loaded, and you wish to access controls on one form from the code in the other.

The following code snippet shows how to access both the control and the variable:

```
Sub cmdSave_Click()
    Dim TextIn As String    'Shadows the control on the form
    If frmEntry!TextIn.Text <> "" Then   'This accesses the control
        TextIn = frmEntry!TextIn.Text
    End If
End Sub
```

# The Variant Data Type

As its name suggests, the **Variant** data type is the 'Jack-of-all-trades' in its ability to hold all types of data, and automatically convert between them. It allows you to perform arithmetic operations (providing the **Variant** holds a number), string manipulations and date operations all on the same variable.

## Variant Types

You can determine which type of data that a **Variant** variable holds by using the **VarType** function. The following table lists the types and their **VarType** return values:

| VarType Return Value | Data Type |
|---|---|
| 0 | Empty |
| 1 | Null |
| 2 | Integer |
| 3 | Long |
| 4 | Single |
| 5 | Double |
| 6 | Currency |
| 7 | Date/Time |
| 8 | String |

## Empty and Null Variants

From the **Variant** table, you'll see that the first two types are: **0**, **Empty**, and **1**, **Null**. These are both special cases.

If the **Variant** has never had a value assigned to it, then using the **VarType()** function will return a value of 0. You can also use the **IsEmpty()** function to determine if the **Variant** has been used. This will return **True** or **False** depending on whether or not the **Variant** has been used. You can also set a **Variant** to **Empty** to mimic this effect.

# Variant Data Type

`Null` is similar to `Empty`, in that you can check a `Variant` for `Null` with the `IsNull()` function, and assign `Null` to a `Variant`. The `Null` value is generally encountered in database applications. Where values have not been entered in the database fields, Visual Basic will assign `Null` to them. Outside of databases, only the `Variant` data type can hold the `Null` value, which has to be assigned explicitly. If you don't assign `Null` to variants, then you won't need to write code to handle it outside of database applications.

> Null also propagates through a calculation or functions. Generally, if any variable or field in an expression has a `Null` value, then the result will be `Null`. If a variable passed to a function has the value of `Null`, then the result will be `Null`.

## Default Storage Types and Conversions

If you assign a decimal number to a `Variant`, then Visual Basic will use the `Double` data type. If you don't need this level of precision (it's slower, and takes up more memory than a single data type), then you can change it with the `CSng()` function. For all other numbers, Visual Basic will use the most compact numeric data type. If you do require a different data type use the following conversion functions:

| Function  | Converts To |
|-----------|-------------|
| `CCur()`  | Currency    |
| `CDbl()`  | Double      |
| `CInt()`  | Integer     |
| `CLng()`  | Long        |
| `CSsng()` | Single      |
| `CStr()`  | String      |
| `CVar()`  | Variant     |
| `CVDate()`| Date/Time   |

With such a flexible data type, why use any other? Well, the `Variant` does

## Chapter 5 - Variables in Visual Basic

have some disadvantages. It's slow to use (we don't get all that automatic re-formatting for free), and it also takes up much more memory than any other variable type.

Let's put together a quick project that tries out the **Variant** data type. Start a new project, and on the form, place a text box, two labels and five command buttons in a similar way to the following:

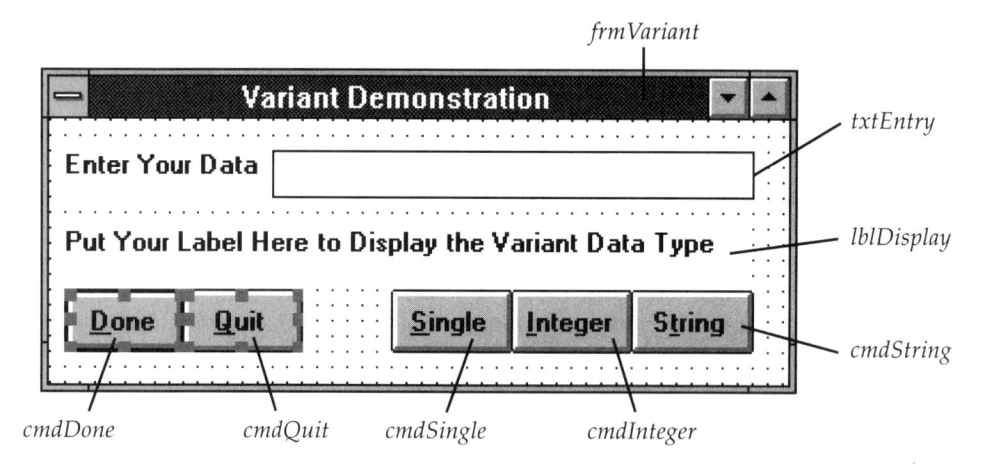

*frmVariant*

*txtEntry*

*lblDisplay*

*cmdString*

*cmdDone*   *cmdQuit*   *cmdSingle*   *cmdInteger*

Don't forget to name your form, **frmVariant** and label, **lblDisplay**. Add the following code as a form level variable:

```
Dim vEntered As Variant
```

We'll be using it in several of the events throughout the form.

```
Sub cmdDone_Click()
    Dim iType As Integer
    vEntered = txtEntry.Text
    iType = VarType(vEntered)
    lblDisplay.Caption = "The variant type is " & iType
End Sub
```

Here, we are declaring a local level variable **iType** as an integer. This is used to hold the result of the **VarType()** function. We then use the label to display the **Variant** type.

```
Sub cmdQuit_Click()
    Unload frmVariant
End Sub
```

# Data Type Conversion

Unload the form to end the project. No surprises here.

```
Sub cmdSingle_Click()
    Dim iType As Integer
    vEntered = CSng(vEntered)
    iType = VarType(vEntered)
    lblDisplay = "The variant is now type " & iType & " Single"
End Sub
```

This code converts the data held in the **Variant** to the data type single, once again using an integer called **iType**. This is not the same as the **iType** we used in the **cmdDone_Click** event, because each is a local level variable, and scoped to its own **Click** event.

We could have declared a form level variable called **iType**, and the project would still work fine. The reason for keeping variables local is that they take up memory, so we only want to keep them for the minimum amount of time, then free up the memory. If we had declared **iType** at the form level, it would stay in memory for the duration of the project. By declaring it locally in each **Click** event, it's removed after we've finished with it, freeing up valuable resources.

Use the **VarType()** function to check the data type and to prove that the conversion actually worked!

The following **Click** events do the same, except that they convert the **Variant**, to integer and to string respectively. If you try to convert a non-numeric string to a number, you'll get a run time error 13 'type mismatch' error:

```
Sub cmdInteger_Click()
    Dim iType As Integer
    vEntered = CInt(vEntered)
    iType = VarType(vEntered)
    lblDisplay = "The Variant is now type " & iType & " Integer"
End Sub
```

```
Sub cmdString_Click()
    Dim iType As Integer
    vEntered = CStr(vEntered)
    iType = VarType(vEntered)
    lblDisplay = "The Variant is now type " & iType & " String"
End Sub
```

When you run the project, you'll notice that the **Variant** type is always **8** (a string), when you click the Done button. Don't panic, this is a common mistake. The reason is that we are taking the data from a text box control, which always passes a string in its **Text** property, so the **Variant** is always a string rather than what you'd expect it to be. So if we need our **Variant** to be a certain type, we need to check the input from the text box, and then convert the **Variant** to the required format.

## Checking Text Box Input

We can check if the text box input is a number with the **IsNumeric()** function, or if it's a date with the **IsDate()** function, then convert it to the required data type, using the conversion buttons:

```
Sub cmdDone_Click()
    Dim iType As Integer
    vEntered = txtEntry.Text
    If IsNumeric(vEntered) Then vEntered = CDbl(vEntered)
    If IsDate(vEntered) Then vEntered = CVDate(vEntered)
    iType = VarType(vEntered)
    lblDisplay.Caption = "The Variant type is " & iType
End Sub
```

If the input is numeric, it's converted to a **Double**, and if it's a date to a **Date**.

## Date and Time Manipulation

You may have noticed that you can convert dates to numbers without error. Visual Basic holds dates as numerics, so you can add and subtract numbers from dates. Integer values subtract from the date part of a date/time variable, while fractions subtract time. To add a week from a date add **7**, and to add an hour add **1/24**. Visual Basic is very flexible on date/time entry - the following are all valid: **12-12-94**, **12 Dec 1994**, **12/12/94**, **12:00am**, **18:10**.

The order of the day and date will depend on the settings in the Control Panel. If you don't enter a time, Visual Basic sets it to midnight, and if you don't enter a date, then the date is set to Dec. 30th 1899. Date/time strings are delimited by the '#', so to assign a date to a **Variant** use **vdate = #12-12-94#**. This also applies to comparisons, so to check a date you'd use **If vDate = #12-12-94# Then**...

# Date and Time

## Date and Time Functions

Visual Basic has a wide variety of functions that can be used to set, check, and manipulate dates and times. There are just too many to go through each one, so we'll look at some of the more useful ones.

Two that are closely associated are the **DateAdd()** and **DateDiff()** functions, in that you have to specify the unit type when using the function. To add 6 weeks to a date you would enter the following:

```
dDateCalc = DateAdd("ww", 6, vStartDate)
```

The **"ww"** string tells the function that the units we are using are weeks. To determine the difference in days between two dates, you would need to add the following:

```
iDifference = DateDiff("d", dDateCalc, vStartDate)
```

The **DateDiff()** function returns the difference between the two dates, and the **DateAdd()** returns a date value. The unit types available with these functions are as follows:

| Symbol | Unit Type |
| --- | --- |
| yyyy | Years |
| q | Quarters |
| m | Months |
| y | Day of the Year. For example, 2 = 2nd January |
| d | Days |
| w | Weekday |
| ww | Weeks |
| h | Hours |
| n | Minutes |
| s | Seconds |

You may wish to determine the value of any part of a date/time field. Visual Basic has a set of built in functions to do this. Here they are:

| Function | Returns |
|---|---|
| **Year** | Number of years |
| **Month** | Number between 1 and 12 representing the month |
| **Day** | Number between 1 and 31 representing the day in the month |
| **Weekday** | Number between 1 and 7 representing the day of the week |
| **Hour** | Number between 0 and 23 representing the hour |
| **Minute** | Number between 0 and 59 representing the minutes |
| **Second** | Number between 0 and 59 representing the seconds |

For example, if we wanted to find out the day of a date, then we'd use the following:

```
iDay = Day(dDateCalc)
```

Finally, if we want to assign the current date and time from the system date and time fields, use the **Now** function, for example:

```
dCurrDate = Now
```

# Other Data Types

As we've seen, the **Variant** data type can handle all the various data types in Visual Basic, but at a cost. The vast majority of the time, you'll know what type of data you're going to work with, so to save space, and to speed up your application, it is advisable to declare your variables as specific data types. Following is a table of all the other data types, their ranges, and the amount of memory used:

# Strings

| Data Type | Memory Used | Range |
|---|---|---|
| Integer | 2 Bytes | -32,768 to 32,767 |
| Long | 4 Bytes | -2,147,483,648 to 2,147,483,647 |
| Single | 4 Bytes | -3.402823E38 to -1.401298E-45 (negative values) |
|  |  | 1.401298E-45 to 3.402823E38 (positive values) |
| Double | 8 Bytes | -1.7976931346232E308 to -4.94065645841247E-324 (negative values) |
|  |  | 4.94065645841247E-324 to1.7976931346232E308 (positive values) |
| Currency | 8 Bytes | -922337203685477.5808 to 922337203685477.5807 |
| String | 1 byte per char | 0 to approximately 65,500 |
| Variant | 16 Bytes + 1 | **Null**, **Error**, any numeric up to the range of Byte per **Char Double**, or strings |

## String Manipulations and Functions

The other main data type that you'll be manipulating is strings. As you'd expect, Visual Basic has a myriad of functions to convert and analyze strings. When you declare a string, Visual Basic will give you a variable length string, which expands and shrinks as you assign data to it. You can also declare a fixed length string by assigning a size to it. For example, to declare a fixed length string of twenty characters, you'd use:

```
Dim sSurname as string * 20.
```

If you then assign a shorter length string, such as **sSurname = "Dolan"**, the rest of the string will be space filled. To extract the data into another string without the spaces you'll need to use the **RTrim()** function to remove trailing spaces (**Trim()** and **LTrim()** are similar in functionality and usage).

```
sNoSpaces = RTrim(sSurname)
```

The string **sNoSpaces** will be five characters long in this case, and will contain the string **"Dolan"**. Similarly, **Trim()** removes leading and trailing spaces, and **LTrim()** removes leading spaces.

## Strings Within Strings

In most cases, you'll need more complex string manipulation to analyze the data held in a string. We'll try out some of the functions available using the contacts project we wrote in the last chapter, so now would be a good time to load it! To start with, we'll separate out the first name and surname for loading into the combo box. We'll be changing round the names in the **Form_Load()** event to **Surname** and **First Name** for consistency:

```
Sub Form_Load()
    comNames.AddItem "Dempsey Luke"
    comNames.AddItem "Gill Darren"
    comNames.AddItem "Wright Peter"
    comNames.AddItem "Mum My"
    comNames.AddItem "WROX"
    comNames.AddItem "Many Benny"
End Sub
```

The **Add_Click** event code should be altered as follows:

```
Sub cmdAdd_Click()
    Dim sNames As String, iSpace As Integer
    If Not txtName = "" Then
        iSpace = InStr(txtName.Text, " ")
        sNames = Right(txtName.Text, Len(txtName.Text) - iSpace)
        sNames = sNames & " " & Left(txtName.Text, iSpace)
        comNames.AddItem sNames
    End If
End Sub
```

We'll need a string, **sNames**, to hold the name in the new format and an integer, **iSpace**, to hold the position of the space character in the string. We'll be using this to split the two parts of the name.

```
If Not txtName = "" Then
```

> Only reformat and add to the combo box if there's been something entered in the text box.

# Trimming Strings

```
iSpace = InStr(txtName.Text, " ")
```

The **InStr()** function will search for a string within another string, and returns the position of the first occurrence. In this case, we are checking for a space in the text box, and holding the position of the space in the integer **iSpace**.

```
sNames = Right(txtName.Text, Len(txtName.Text) - iSpace)
```

The **Right()** function returns a string of specified size from the right side of the string. The **Len()** function returns the length of the string. By subtracting the position of the space from the total length of the string, we have the length of the surname, which we extract using the **Right()** function, and assign it to **sNames**.

```
sNames = sNames & " " & Left(txtName.Text, iSpace)
```

Similarly, the **Left()** function returns a string of specified size from the left of the string. The position of the **Space** character tells us the end of the first name, so all we need to do is to add a space and then the first name to the surname in **sNames**, and then add the newly formatted name to the combo box as below:

```
        comNames.AddItem sNames
    End If
End Sub
```

If you now run the project, whatever name you enter in the text box will be reformatted. If you enter a name without a space, no reformatting will occur, because **InStr()** will not be able to find a space character and will return **0**.

## Using the Mid Function

A close cousin to the **Left()** and **Right()** functions is the **Mid()** function. This is used to extract a string from within another string by using a start position, and specifying a length. Generally, **Mid()** is used to extract details from the middle of a string.

We could replace the **Left()** and the **Right()** functions with the **Mid()** function in the above example:

**135**

```
If Not txtName = "" Then
    iSpace = InStr(txtName.Text, " ")
    sNames = Mid(txtName.Text, iSpace + 1)
```

To extract the surname, we tell the `Mid()` function to start at the next position after the space. By not specifying the length of the string to extract, `sNames` is passed the rest of the string.

```
sNames = sNames & " " & Mid(txtName.Text, 1, iSpace)
```

To extract the first name, the starting position is the start of the string, and the length we require is up to the space (which delimits the first name).

```
        comNames.AddItem sNames
    End If
```

Then add it to the list, and exit the `If` statement.

## Using the Mid Statement

We can also use `Mid()` as a statement to replace a section of a string with another string, in a similar manner. Let's see how it behaves:

```
sExample = "Test the Mid Function"
```

Initialise the string to some text.

```
Mid(sExample, 10, 3) = "Ins"
```

Replace the 10th character for three characters with the string `"Ins"`. `sExample` is now `"Test the Ins Function"`.

```
Mid(sExample, 10) = "Del"
```

If we don't specify the number of characters to replace then the whole of the replacement string is used, so `sExample` is now `"Test the Del Function"`.

```
Mid(sExample, 10) = "Right and Left Function"
```

In this case, the length of our replacement string is greater than `sExample`, so the extra characters are truncated. `sExample` is now `"Test the Right and Le"`.

# Numerical Functions

## Changing the Case

Although Visual Basic as a language is case insensitive, when you compare strings the comparison is case sensitive. Visual Basic has two function that will change the case of a string: **UCase()** and **LCase()**.

In our contact project we may want to compare a surname, to locate a particular person, such as **"Wright"**, but we can't be sure that the surname starts with an upper case character, or if the name was entered entirely in upper case. To produce a test that is case insensitive, we need to convert the name either to all upper or all lower case (either will do):

```
If UCase(sSurname) = "WRIGHT" Then
```

It now doesn't matter how the surname has been entered. For the purpose of the test, all the lower case characters are converted to upper case, and compared to an upper case string.

## Numerical Functions

Most languages have a varied array of numerical functions, and Visual Basic is no exception. There are the usual mathmatical functions such as **sin**, **cos**, **tan**, **log**, **sqr**, and some more unusual financial functions such as **FV** (Future Value), which will return the future value of an investment based on fixed value periodic payments, and an interest rate. There are functions to work out loan costs, pensions and mortgage repayments.

> It's really outside the scope of this book to explain all these functions, so to find out about the mathmatical functions search the on-line help for *Math Functions*, and for the financial functions search the on-line help for *Financial Functions*.

## Using Variables: Implementation

Let's have a look at an example of each, so that you get an idea of how to use these functions, and we'll implement a dice game and a loan repayment program to illustrate how to use variables.

**137**

## Random Numbers

Many games depend on the generation and use of random numbers. Within Visual Basic, one of the math functions is a random number generator. We'll be using the random number facilities to generate dice throws, so start a new project, and add two labels and two command buttons to the form until it looks like this:

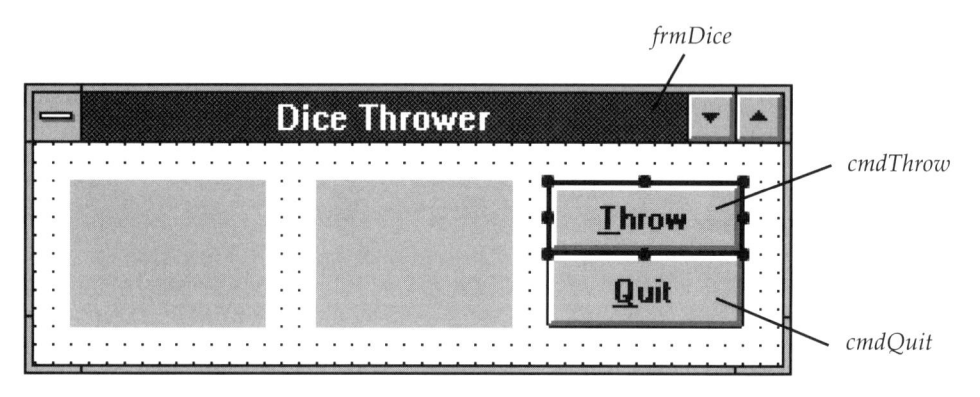

*frmDice*

*cmdThrow*

*cmdQuit*

We've altered the **FontSize** property of the labels to **24**, so that the numbers are much larger, and the **ForeColor** property to **Blue** so that they stand out.

Now to generate the dice throws, we'll need to add the folowing code to the project:

```
Sub Form_Load()
    Randomize (246)
End Sub
```

In the **Form_Load** event, we are seeding the random number generator, so that it generates a list of random numbers. The actual integer in the parentheses (called the **seeder**) can be any valid integer. If we leave the brackets blank, Visual Basic will use the system clock as the seeder.

```
Sub cmdThrow_Click()
    Dim iThrow As Integer

    iThrow = Int((6 * Rnd) + 1)
```

# Random Numbers

In the `Throw_Click` event, we declare an integer to hold the value of the die throw. The `Rnd` function returns a value between 0 and 1, so we need to use the following formula to get a number between 1 and 6:

```
Int((High No - Low No. + 1) * Rnd + Low No.)
```

The `Int()` function returns an integer number, so the formula will return a whole number. In our case, the `High No.` was 6, and the `Low No.` was 1, so the formula will return a number between 1 and 6.

```
    lblDice1.Caption = iThrow
```

The value of the throw is displayed in the first label.

```
    iThrow = Int((6 * Rnd) + 1)
    lblDice2.Caption = iThrow
    Randomize
End Sub
```

The next two lines generate a die throw for the second die, and the `Randomize` statement reinitialises the random number generator (this time using the system clock).

```
Sub cmdQuit_Click()
    Unload frmDice
End Sub
```

The quit button holds the form unload code which ends the project.

## Loan Repayments

Let's look at one of the financial functions. The `Pmt()` function calculates the loan repayment required for a loan, based on a fixed interest rate, and a fixed repayment. Let's take out a 3 year car loan for $6000 at a rate of 8.5% per annum, with monthly repayments. We'll write a project that calculates the monthly repayment amount. Start a new project, and design a form similar to the screenshot:

139

## Chapter 5 - Variables in Visual Basic

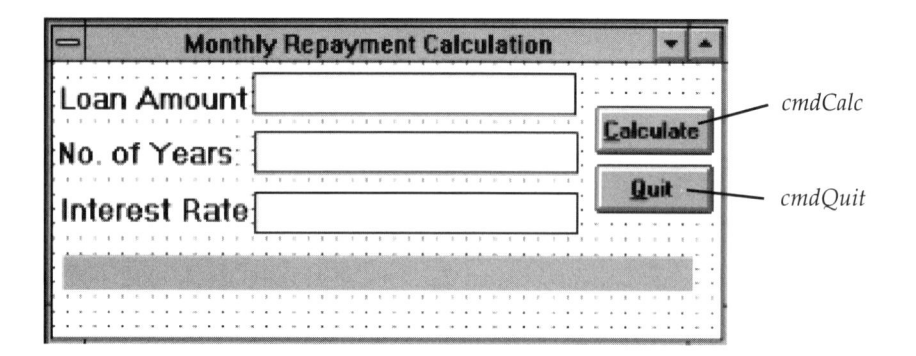

[Monthly Repayment Calculation form with Loan Amount, No. of Years, Interest Rate fields, Calculate button (cmdCalc) and Quit button (cmdQuit)]

You'll notice that we're actually writing a generic monthly repayment calculator, rather than a specific example - this is more useful. Add the following code to the project:

```
Sub cmdCalc_Click()
    Dim cRepay As Currency, sDispFmt As String, cBorrow As Currency, iPayments As Integer, cAPR As Currency
```

These are the variables used in the calculations. You'll notice that we are using the currency data type for the decimal calculations. This is because the currency type is not subject to rounding like the single and double data types.

```
    sDispFmt = "###,###,##0.00"
```

We are setting up a **format mask** for displaying the results using the `Format` function. The '`#`' tells `Format` to display nothing if there is no digit in the position, and the '`0`' will display a digit (if present), or a zero in the position.

```
    cBorrow = Val(txtLoan.Text)
```

This line assigns the value entered in `txtLoan.Text` to `cBorrow`. The `Val()` function returns a number from a string.

```
    iPayments = Val(txtPeriod) * 12
```

140

Because we have decided that the payment period is monthly, we need to multiply the number of years by `12` to give the total number of payments to be made for using in the `Pmt` function.

```
cAPR = Val(txtRate.Text)
If cAPR > 1 Then cAPR = cAPR / 100
```

The rate of interest is converted to a decimal if a whole number is entered rather than a percentage.

```
cRepay = Pmt(cAPR / 12, iPayments, cBorrow, 0, 1)
```

`Pmt()` expects the interest rate per period, so we are dividing the `APR` by `12` to give a rate per month as the first parameter. The next parameter is the number of repayment periods, followed by the amount borrowed. The `0` in the next parameter indicates the amount that should be left at the end of the payments. In our case it will be `0` because we're repaying a loan. (This function can also be used to calculate investment amounts.) The final parameter can be `0` or `1`, where `0` is payment as the end of each loan period, and `1` is payment at the start of each loan period.

```
lblRepayment.Caption = "Your Monthly payment is " & Format(cRepay, sDispFmt)

End Sub
```

Finally, we are displaying the results in the label on the form. The `Format` function uses the mask we declared in `sDispFmt` to display the amount. You'll notice that the value displayed is negative. This indicates that the amount is to be paid out, (debited), as opposed to positive numbers which indicate those rare amounts paid in (credited).

# Constants

There are cases when we are coding when a constant figure is required. To make the code easier to understand, we can declare these values as constants, as we did for the colors in Chapter 3. There is a complete set of constants declared that comes with Visual Basic called `CONSTANTS.TXT`. We'd advise against loading the whole file, as it's quite large, and will substantially increase the size of your project. Simply cut and paste the constant declarations that you need from the file.

There are also cases where we may wish to declare our own constants. For instance, our repayment project is currently working on monthly repayments, so we could declare a constant **kPaymentsPerYear** in our project, and use this instead of the number **12** in our calculations.

This has two advantages. The first is code readability, and the other is that if we wish to move to six monthly payments, we only need to change the constant to 2, instead of going through all our code changing the 12 to 2. The code for our repayment project now looks like this :

```
Const kPaymentsPerYear = 12
```

Constants are declared with the **Const** keyword. They have to follow the same naming standards as variables, and the same scoping rules apply. This constant has been declared in the (general) declarations Code window for the form, so it's a form level constant, and can be accessed by all the events associated with the form.

```
Sub cmdCalc_Click()
    Dim cRepay As Currency, sDispFmt As String, cBorrow As Currency, iPayments As Integer, cAPR As Currency

    sDispFmt = "###,###,##0.00"
    cBorrow = Val(txtLoan.Text)
    iPayments = Val(txtPeriod.Text) * kPaymentsPerYear
    cAPR = Val(txtRate.Text)
    If cAPR > 1 Then cAPR = cAPR / 100
    cRepay = Pmt(cAPR / kPaymentsPerYear, iPayments, cBorrow, 0, 1)
    lblRepayment.Caption = "Your Monthly payment is " & Format(cRepay, sDispFmt)
End Sub
```

All areas where the number of payments per year was used (in the calculation for the total number of payments, and in the interest calculations), have been changed to use the constant.

# Arrays

We first met variable arrays in the last chapter where we used a fixed length integer array. An array must be of the same data type, so if you need to hold different data types in an array use a **Variant** array (as variants can hold different data types).

## Array Declarations

Arrays, like variables also have a scope, and can be declared with the `Dim` or `Static` keywords. An array can be of fixed or variable length, and you can declare the upper and lower bounds (the index range) for the array.

Remember that in Visual Basic all indexes start at `0`. This can be altered for the lower bound of variable arrays with the `Option Base` statement, which must be placed in the (general) declarations section of the module. This will then apply to all the arrays declared in the form or module. For example, to have the lower bound of all your arrays to start at `1`, enter `Option Base 1` in the declarations section. The upper bound of the array must be an integer between -32,768 and 32,767.

Let's look at some examples of array declarations. The following declares an array of strings which have an index starting at 1, rather than zero, and has 52 elements, (useful for poker):

```
Dim sCards (1 to 52) as string
```

If we wanted the index to run from 100 to 200 in an array of variants, we would use the following:

```
Dim vArray (100 to 200) as Variant
```

To declare a variable length array, we leave the parentheses blank:

```
Static iSome () as integer
```

This would declare a local array of variable length. To allocate the actual number of elements to the array, we'll need to use the `ReDim` statement. Within the procedure that uses the `iSome` array, to allocate 15 elements the following statement would need to be included:

```
ReDim iSome(15)
```

The problem with `ReDim` is that when it's executed, the contents of the array are re-initialized to zero. To keep the details, we need to include the `Preserve` keyword. So if we have another `ReDim` statement in our procedure, and want to keep the contents of `iSome`, use the following:

```
ReDim Preserve iSome(30)
```

You can determine the upper and lower bounds of a variable array at runtime by using the `LBound()` and `UBound()` functions. This is very useful for determining the size of dynamic arrays, and controlling loops.

## Multi-Dimensional Arrays

Visual Basic will support multi-dimensional arrays of up to 60 dimensions, but beware - they use a lot of memory resource. The following code snippet will declare a three dimensional array 10 by 10 by 10. The number of elements in this array is 1000 (the product of 10 * 10 * 10).

```
Dim iMulti (9,9,9) as integer
```

This array will take up 2000 bytes. If it were a **Variant** array, the minimum size of the array would be 16000 bytes, so use multi-dimensional arrays with care.

# User-Defined Types

As if there were not enough data types in Visual Basic, you can also declare your own. If you are familiar with C, these types are similar to structs, or records in Pascal or COBOL. A user-defined type is made up of the other data types in Visual Basic, and must be declared in the (general) declarations section of a standard module. It's also possible to nest user-defined types within other user-defined types. The variables that you declare with your user-defined types can be local, module level or global.

The following code snippet will declare a **Payroll** data type:

```
Type Payroll
        EmpNo as long
        EmpName as String * 30
        HrsWorked as Integer
        RatePerHour as currency
        GrossPay as currency
        Tax as currency
        Insurance as currency
        NetPay as Currency
End Type
```

We would then use this as we would any other data type:

```
Dim CurEmpPay as Payroll
```

The **CurEmpPay** variable is subject to all the same rules of lifetime and scoping as the other variables in Visual Basic. To access the individual elements of the type we add the element to the end of the variable name as follows:

```
CurEmpPay.EmpNo = txtEmpNo.text
CurEmpPay.HrsWorked = txtHrs.text
CurEmpPay.RatePerHour = txtRate.text
CurEmpPay.GrossPay = CurEmpPay.HrsWorked *
   CurEmpPay.RatePerHour
```

# Summary

In this chapter we looked at the different data types available in Visual Basic, and their scope and lifetime. You learnt about the flexibility of the **Variant** data type, before going on to look at the other data types. We reviewed how to use some of the built in functions in Visual Basic to manipulate dates and times, strings and numbers.

You also learnt how to declare and use arrays, and finally how to define and use your own data types. Before we leap into the next chapter, there are a few exercises to have a go at.

# Chapter 5 - Variables in Visual Basic

## Exercises

**1**  In the Variant project we occasionally get a type mismatch error when converting between the different types. Write some code in the `Click` events to prevent this.

**2**  In the Contacts project, assume that the end of each address line is delimited by a comma. Using this delimiter write some code to extract each individual address line, and the phone and fax numbers.

**3**  When entering a name in the Contacts project, ensure that the first character of the first name and surname is upper case, and the rest of the name is lower case.

**4**  In the Dice project, generate dice throws between 6 and 12.

**5**  In the Financial project, validate the input from the text boxes to make sure that it's in the correct format.

ated at the same time-scale as the geologic map, so we can clearly see areas where geomorphic activity is ongoing.

## Exercises

INSTANT
INSTANT
INSTANT
INSTANT
INSTANT
INSTANT

# Chapter 6

# Coding Visual Basic Style

So far we've taken a fairly detailed look at how to put together a form, use the controls that are available in Visual Basic, and the variable types that are supported, so now it must be time to look at some of the coding constructs that are available in Visual Basic, and how they behave.

In this chapter we'll review the statements that support decision making, and we'll go through the methods of looping and flow control. We'll use these constructs to try out some validation, and look at some of the other events that are available in Visual Basic.

In this chapter we'll cover:

- Code modules
- Procedures and functions
- Decision making
- Validation

## Using Code Modules: Concepts

Before we leap into the intricacies of decision making and loops, let's tie down a definition of what a code module is, as they've been mentioned in several places. There are times in Visual Basic when you'll want to run some code which is used in many different procedures, or perhaps write some code which is loosely associated with an event and would be better off in its own window. Visual Basic will allow you to do this by creating a code module for your project (as we did in Chapter 2).

> The code module is not associated with a form. Any functions that are written in the code module will not be executed until they are called from event code for your forms.

## Project Structure

There have been, and indeed still are many discussions going on amongst users of Visual Basic as to where code should be written. For instance, you could put all of your code that initializes all your form level variables and controls in a code module and call it from the **Form_Load** event, as in the following code snippet:

```
Sub Form_Load ()
    InitializeForm
End Sub
```

This could be extended to all of your forms, by passing the name of the form as a parameter to an initialize function as follows:

```
Sub Form_Load ()
    InitializeForm frmPassword
End Sub
```

The advantage of this is that anyone who needs to maintain the code in the project will know that the initialization code for the project is all held in a **.BAS** file in a function called **InitializeForm**. For those of you who are used to structured programming such as *Jackson Structured Programming* this method gives you a way to create some form of structure.

# Code Modules

So why aren't we leaping about with joy? It all comes back to the way that Windows works, and the way it handles its resources. Because a **.BAS** file can be used throughout the project, it's loaded when the project starts, and isn't unloaded until the project ends. This could be quite an overhead in a large project - even in a smaller project - whereas if the code was kept with the form, it would be unloaded with the form.

In reality, you'll probably mix and match, using the event code to handle the user interface, whilst write special or re-usable procedures or functions in **.BAS** modules. It depends on whether memory resources are more important than easily maintainable code in your project.

> Bear in mind that a .BAS file can be added to any project, so as well as writing a function that's used in more than one form in a project, you may well be able to use the same code in other projects.

## Procedures and Functions

By now, you're probably wondering what the difference is between a procedure and a function. It's actually quite simple. A function will return some value (such as a function to calculate monthly repayments), whereas a procedure is simply a collection of code that is executed, such as the **InitializeForm** procedure described above.

### Using a .BAS Module

To illustrate some of the uses of the code modules, we'll try them out in an example. Start a new project, and add a code module to the project. When you do this, a file called **MODULE1.BAS** is added to the project, with only the (general) declarations available in the Code window.

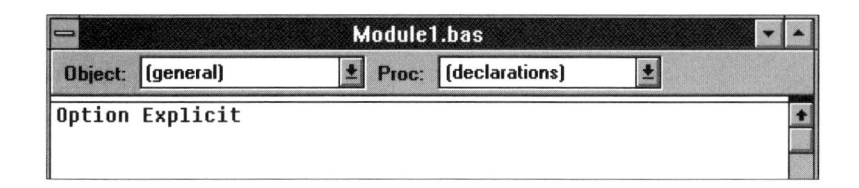

151

# Writing a Procedure

To declare a new procedure or function, all we need to do is to type in a header line. Enter the following into the Code window:

```
Sub TopForm
```

On pressing return, Visual Basic will create a template for your procedure automatically entering the **End Sub** line, and add it to the Proc combo box in the Code window. From the name of the procedure, you may have figured out that we're going to write a procedure which places a form on the top of the screen. In the procedure, enter the following code:

```
Sub TopForm ()
    Form1.top = 0
End Sub
```

In the **Form_Load** event enter the following:

```
Sub Form_Load ()
    TopForm
End Sub
```

Now when you run the project, you'll see that the form is at the top of the screen. This is not a very useful procedure as it stands - perhaps it would be more useful if we could use it for all forms. To achieve this we'll need to pass a parameter to the **TopForm** procedure. Add another form to your project, with File, New Form and reduce its size. Now go to Module1 add the following code to your project:

```
Sub TopForm (frmForm As Form)
    frmForm.Top = 0
End Sub
```

This is the variable that we'll use to receive details from the procedure. As it's an object variable, it holds all the details of the form, such as its properties. In the procedure, all we are doing is setting the **Top** property to 0 which is the top of the form.

> You'll notice that the variable type that we've used is fairly new to you (we saw it in the Chapter 2 MDI application). This is known in Visual Basic as an object variable, and we'll cover these in the next chapter.

# Procedures

Now for the **Form1_Load** event code:

```
Sub Form_Load ()
    TopForm Form1
    Form2.Show
End Sub
```

The first line calls our procedure to set the form at the top of the screen. We are passing the **Form1** form as an argument. The next line loads and displays our second form. Now we need the code to load Form2:

```
Sub Form_Load ()
    TopForm Form2
End Sub
```

Well, there are no surprises here. We're passing **Form2** to the procedure, so that it's also placed at the top of the screen.

# Creating a Function

Now you've got the idea, we'll create a function which returns the age in years from a date passed to the function. Start a new project, and on the form add a text box and a couple of command buttons. Our form looks like this:

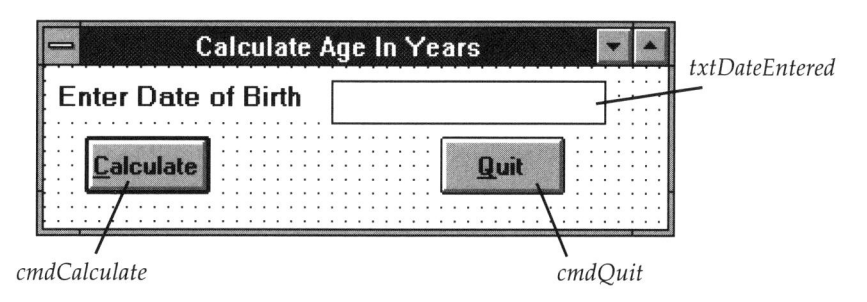

*Calculate Age In Years*

**Enter Date of Birth** — txtDateEntered

[Calculate] — cmdCalculate   [Quit] — cmdQuit

The code for the form (**frmYears**) looks like this:

```
Sub cmdQuit_Click ()
    Unload frmYears
End Sub
```

We've seen this before, so let's get to some of the interesting stuff:

**153**

# Chapter 6 - Coding Visual Basic Style

```
Sub cmdCalc_Click ()
    Dim iAge As Integer, dDOB As Variant
    If Not IsDate(txtDateEntered) Then
        MsgBox "The date you have entered is not valid, please re-try"
        txtDateEntered.Text = ""
        txtDateEntered.SetFocus
        Exit Sub
    End If
    dDOB = CVDate(txtDateEntered.Text)
    iAge = AgeInYears(dDOB)
    MsgBox "You Are " & iAge & " Years old"
End Sub
```

The integer **iAge** will be used as the return variable from the function, and the **dDOB** variant will be used to convert the date entered in the text box from a string to a date.

```
If Not IsDate(txtDateEntered) Then
```

This line checks to see if the entry in the text box is a date. If it's not a valid date, then the following lines are executed:

```
MsgBox "The date you have entered is not valid, please re-try"
```

This line displays a message box telling the user that the entry isn't a valid date.

```
txtDateEntered.Text = ""
```

Then the entry in the text box is cleared to save the user from having to delete the last entry.

```
txtDateEntered.SetFocus
Exit Sub
End If
```

Finally, the focus is set back to the text box, so that the user can enter a new date, and the sub procedure is exited.

```
dDOB = CVDate(txtDateEntered.Text)
```

This line assigns the date entered in the text box to the **dDOB** variant after converting it to a string.

```
iAge = AgeInYears(dDOB)
```

# Functions

Well, here it is! Our function returns an integer that is the age in years determined from the date of birth entered. As you can see, it's really no different from all of the other built in Visual Basic functions.

```
    MsgBox "You Are " & iAge & " Years old"
End Sub
```

Finally in this event, we display a message box with the result of our function. Now add a code module to the project, and enter the following code into the declarations section:

```
Function AgeInYears (dDatePassed As Variant) As Integer
```

When this line is entered you'll see that Visual Basic will automatically enter the **End Function** line, and change the Proc combo boxes at the top of the Code window to the name of the function. **AgeInYears** is the name of the procedure, **dDatePassed** is the variable that will receive the date from the calling procedure, and the **As Integer** tells Visual Basic that the return value of this function is an integer. Now add the following into the Module1 function:

```
    AgeInYears = Year(Now) - Year(dDatePassed)
```

To pass the result of our calculation back to the calling procedure, we assign the function name the result of our calculation. The **Year()** function is a built in Visual Basic function which returns the year section of a date as an integer. Here, we are giving the current date to **Year()** with the **Now** function. There are similar functions for day, month, hour, minute and second.

```
End Function
```

Visual Basic puts this line in for us. Obviously, this is a fairly simple example to demonstrate the principle, but you can have much more complex functions for complex calculations, string manipulation, and so on.

## Module/Form Scope

Before we leave functions and procedures, a brief word on their scope. So far, all the procedures and functions that we've written have been entered into a code module. These will all have global scope (also called **Public**), and be available to the whole project.

**155**

It's also possible to write procedures and functions within a form. These are local to the form, and can't be accessed from within other forms (these are called **Private**). They also shadow any procedures or functions that are declared in code modules, in a similar manner to variables.

## Loops and Case

So far all our decision making has been written using the **If...Then** construct, which we'll look into next. Visual Basic also supports **Case** statements, which can save effort coding large **If...Then...Else...If...** statements. We'll go back over some of the code in previous projects to see how this works. But first let's go through all the different **If...Then** styles that Visual Basic supports.

So far, we've looked at some fairly simple **If...Then** statements. An **If** statement must always evaluate out to either **True**, in which case the statements between the **If** and **End If** are executed, or **False**. As per previous versions of BASIC, Visual Basic allows the simplest form of **If** statement, all on one line:

```
If iMale = true Then iRetireAge = 65
```

In this case, an **End If** statement is not required as only one statement is being executed. Obviously, we also need to set the retirement age for females, so what we really need is the **If...Then...Else** construct. Because the **If** statement is now going to be larger than one line, we need to use the block **If**, which requires the **End If** statement.

```
If iMale = true Then
    iRetireAge = 65
Else
    iRetireAge = 60
End If
```

Generally, to make the code easier to read, all the statements within the **If** block are indented. The above snippet of code is much easier to read than the following:

```
If iMale = true Then
iRetireAge = 65
Else
iRetireAge = 60
End If
```

# Making Decisions

In all the previous examples, we could have entered the following:

```
If iMale Then......
```

This is because we are using the **iMale** integer as a boolean, and the **If** statement will evaluate out to **True** or **False**. The numeric equivalent of **True** in Visual Basic is **-1**, and **False** is **0**.

Suppose that the check were based on a string input, then we may well require a further test to check for correct input, as follows:

```
If sSex = "M" Then
    iRetireAge = 65
ElseIf sSex = "F" Then
    iRetireAge = 60
Else
    Msgbox "You have not entered a Valid Sex. Please Re-try"
    Exit Sub
End If
```

The **ElseIf** statement is deemed to be part of the overall structure of our block **If**, so only one **End If** is required to close the block. This is about the most complex that the **If** structure gets, aside from the complexity of the statement being tested. Obviously you can extend the **If**...**Else**...**If**...**Else** structure to support the testing of many expressions in one structure. In these cases, you'll find that you're usually testing the same expression for different values (as above). This is where the **Case** statement comes in useful.

## Select Case

Jumping straight into the fray, the last example could be written with the **Select Case** statement as follows:

```
Select Case sSex
    Case "M"
        iRetireAge = 65
    Case "F"
        iRetireAge = 60
    Case Else
        Msgbox "You have not entered a Valid Sex. Please Re-try"
        Exit Sub
End Select
```

**157**

# Chapter 6 - Coding Visual Basic Style

The **Select Case** tells Visual Basic the expression that we wish to test, then the **Case** statements tell Visual Basic what to do for each value of our test expression (in this example **sSex**). The **Case Else** statement at the end is a catch-all, so that if an invalid entry is made, it will run the message box statement, and exit the procedure. The **End Select** is similar to the **End If** and must be placed at the end of the case block after all the **Case** statements.

Some of our earlier projects could be better served by using the **Select Case**. Load the Hotspot project from Chapter 4. In the **imgNation()** events, there are two banks of **If** statements that should really be **Case** statements. Have a go at altering the code yourself.

> Another advantage of the **Case** statement is that it's more easily maintained than the equivalent **If** statements because you only need to add another **Case** block for new choices.

OK, how did you do? If you got stuck, below are the two sets of **Select Case** statements to replace the **If** statements:

```
Sub imgNation_Click (Index As Integer)

    Select Case Index
        Case iVisible
            lblText.Visible = False
            iVisible = 7
            Exit Sub
        Case 0
            lblNation = "Ottawa"
        Case 1
            lblNation = "Paris "
        Case 2
            lblNation = "Berlin"
        Case 3
            lblNation = "Rome"
        Case 4
            lblNation = "Madrid"
        Case 5
            lblNation = "London"
        Case 6
            lblNation = "Washington, D.C."
    End Select
    lblStatus.Visible = True
    iVisible = Index
End Sub
```

# Case Statements

The expression that we are going to test is the index of the array control.

```
Select Case Index
    Case iVisible
            lblText.Visible = False
            iVisible = 7
            Exit Sub
```

This one's a bit more tricky. You don't have to have a constant as the test expression, you can have almost anything, so long as you're comparing like with like, such as strings and strings, integers and integers and so on. You'll also notice that you can have more than one statement after the **Case** statement. All the lines up to the next **Case** statement (or **End Select**), will be executed.

```
        Case 0
            lblNation = "Ottawa"
        Case 1
            lblNation = "Paris "
        Case 2
            lblNation = "Berlin"
        Case 3
            lblNation = "Rome"
        Case 4
            lblNation = "Madrid"
        Case 5
            lblNation = "London"
        Case 6
            lblNation = "Washington, D.C."
```

Here are the replacement lines for the **If** statements, checking the value of the index for each day.

```
        End Select
```

This line denotes the end of the **Case** statement, much like the **End If** for the **If** statement.

```
        lblStatus.Visible = True
        iVisible = Index
Exit Sub
```

The final block of code shows the label, and sets **iVisible** to the index.

For each **Case** statement, the default comparison statement is **Is**, and the comparison operator is '='. Ranges can also be checked with the **To**

159

keyword. For instance, if we wished to check for European countries in the example above, the `Case` statement would be:

```
Case 1 To 5
```

You can also specify a selection and a range in a `Case` statement, such as checking for Monday, Wednesday, and Friday through Sunday where the days of the week were represented as an enumerated set where `0` represents Monday, through to `6` for Sunday. The `Case` statement would look like this:

```
Case 0,2,4 To 6
```

In all our examples we've use the default comparison (`=`); the full range of valid comparison operators for the `Case` statement are as follows:

| Comparison Operator | What it Means |
| --- | --- |
| < | Less than |
| <= | Less than or equal to |
| > | Greater than |
| >= | Greater than or equal to |
| <> | Not equal to |
| = | Equal to |

> As you'd expect, logic rules apply, so take care with the <> operator.

## On...GoSub and On...Goto

The `On...GoSub`, and `On...Goto` statements are included mainly for backward compatibility. They are less flexible than the `Select Case`, in that they can only evaluate a numeric expression, and also require more coding (especially if using `Goto`s). The structure of both statements is the same, and in our Hotspot example would have been as follows:

```
On Index + 1 Gosub Can, Fran, Germ, Italy, Spain, UK, USA
```

160

# OnGoto
# OnGoSub

`Can`, `Fran` and so on are labels that indicate the start of subroutines to display the correct text. For example:

```
Exit Sub
Can:
 label1= "Ottawa"
    Return
Fran:
    label1 = "Paris "
    Return
                :
                :
```

The `Exit Sub` statement designates the end of our normal code, and the start of our subroutines. If this statement was missed off, Visual Basic would continue processing, setting the label to each string in turn until the end of the sub procedure.

The `Can`: is a label recognized by the colon at the end (and designates the start of a subroutine in this case). With a subroutine, processing will continue until the `Return` statement is encountered. Processing will then continue from the line that called the subroutine.

If `Goto` is used instead of `GoSub`, then code will need to be written to control the program flow (and as ever with the `Goto`, this is not recommended!). We've had to add 1 to the `Index`, because indexes start from 0, but the `On` statement runs numerically down our label list starting at `1`. If it encounters a `0`, then control passes to the next statement in your code.

> You can't code for unexpected results with a general catch-all statement. If your numeric expression evaluates out to a number greater than your list, then control drops to the next statement - if it's negative or greater than 255, an illegal function call is generated.

## GoSub

As you've probably guessed from the above, `GoSub` is also supported in Visual Basic, again mainly for backward compatibility. Generally, if you have a section of code that needs to be executed, then its control returned, use a procedure or a function. This will make your code more maintainable, by being able to find the relevant code more easily, and will, perhaps, allow for some re-use. This takes us nicely into the branching and looping statements in Visual Basic.

# Looping and Program Control

Visual Basic really has only two commands which loop. We've seen the **For**...**Next** loop in the Hotspot project, and if you've done any form of BASIC before, these will be familiar to you. The other command to control loops is the **Do**...**Loop**. This will execute a block of code until some condition, specified by you, is met. Visual Basic also supports the **While**...**Wend** looping structure, but this is less flexible than the **Do**...**Loop**, and is not used as extensively. If you feel a burning urge to learn **While**...**Wend** loops, then they are described in the *Language Reference*, or you can search the Help file for **While**.

# For...Next Loops

Although you can use **Do**...**Loop** to do everything that **For**...**Next** loops can do, **For**...**Next** loops are more efficient. Obviously, you'll need to know the number, or be able to calculate the number of times that the loop will be executed to use the **For**...**Next** loop. You can, however, terminate the loop before it's finished with the **Exit**...**For** statement.

## Controlling the Loop

The actual control of the loop is fairly flexible. We saw in the multiple selection of lists in Chapter 4 that you don't have to specify an upward count, neither do you have to specify steps of 1 (although this is most common, and therefore the default). For example, if we wanted to display all the even numbers between 1 and 20 in descending order, we'd use the following loop:

```
Sub Form_Load ()

    Dim iNumber
    For iNumber = 20 To 1 Step -2
        MsgBox Str(iNumber)
    Next iNumber
    Unload form1

End Sub
```

# Looping and Control

Try it out. Start a new project, and enter the above. Because we are using a step of -2, we don't need an `If` statement to check if the number is even or not, and we're moving backward to zero, so the numbers will be displayed in descending order.

We could extend this to allow the user to enter the start/end number, and whether the display should be ascending or descending. All these will be controlled by a single `For...Next` statement.

On the form in your project, draw a check box, a text box, and two command buttons. The form now looks like this:

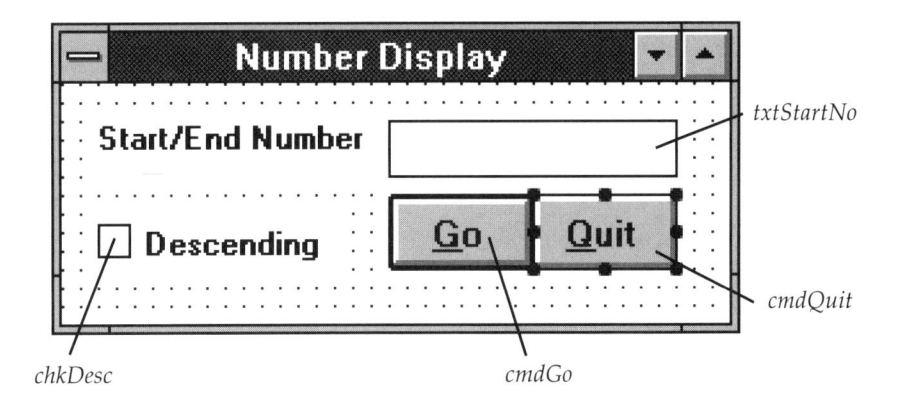

*txtStartNo*

*chkDesc*     *cmdGo*     *cmdQuit*

Now delete the code in the `Form_Load()` event, and add the following code to your project. Don't forget to rename TextBox and Form.

```
Sub cmdGo_Click ()
    Dim iNumber As Integer, iStart As Integer
    Dim iEnd As Integer, iStep As Integer, iCount As Integer
        If IsNumeric(txtStartNo) Then
            iNumber = txtStartNo.Text
        Else
            MsgBox "Ah, You've not entered a number. Try again", , "Error...error!"
            txtStartNo.SetFocus
            txtStartNo = ""
            Exit Sub
        End If
        If chkDesc = 1 Then
            iStep = -2
            iStart = iNumber
            iEnd = 1
        Else
```

163

# Chapter 6 - Coding Visual Basic Style

```
        iStep = 2
        iEnd = iNumber
        iStart = 0
    End If
    For iCount = iStart To iEnd Step iStep
        MsgBox Str(iCount)
    Next iCount
End Sub
```

Initially, we need to set up variables for each element of the `For` statements to hold our values.

```
        If IsNumeric(txtStartNo) Then
            iNumber = txtStartNo.Text
        Else
            MsgBox "Ah, You've not entered a number. Try again", , "Error...error!"
            txtStartNo.SetFocus
            txtStartNo = ""
            Exit Sub
        End If
```

Here, we're checking that a number has been input in the text box. From our validation, we'll be able to enter a decimal number. This doesn't matter, because we're assigning the input to an integer, which will remove the decimal part of the number. In real life, you'd probably need to check that this would be appropriate - for our demonstration purposes it doesn't matter.

```
        If chkDesc = 1 Then
            iStep = -2
            iStart = iNumber
            iEnd = 1
```

Next we need to see if the descending check box has been checked. If it has, then we set the start to the number entered by the user, the end number to `1`, and the step to `-2` to count backward to the number entered.

```
        Else
            iStep = 2
            iEnd = iNumber
            iStart = 0
        End If
```

Otherwise, we set the step to `2` for an ascending count, the start to `0`, and the end to the number entered by the user.

```
    For iCount = iStart To iEnd Step iStep
        MsgBox Str(iCount)
    Next iCount
End Sub
```

Then all that's left to do is to put our variables into the **For** statement, display the counter, and loop.

```
Sub cmdQuit_Click ()
    Unload frmLoop
End Sub
```

Oh, and allow the user to quit the application of course!

## Do Loops

**Do** loops are more flexible than the **For**...**Next** loop. The block of statements executed is bounded by the **Do** statement, and its corresponding loop statement. You can execute a block of statements an undetermined number of times, by testing a condition either at the **Do** statement, or on the loop statement. There are two statements that are used to test our condition: **While** and **Until**. The condition that we are checking must evaluate out to either **True** or **False**, in the same manner as an **If** statement.

Let's try an example, by using the password application that we wrote in Chapter 1. What we're going to do is use a **Do** loop to control the input. If after three tries the entry is still incorrect, the application will exit. In reality, it would probably lock out the user after three failed tries. To make the input easier, we'll also make the user name and password case insensitive. OK, load up the project, and alter the code to the following:

```
Dim iTries As Integer
```

This variable will count the number of tries that the user has had. It needs to go in the (general) declarations section of the form because we'll be exiting the OK **Click** event if an invalid entry is made. We need to keep the value between tries, so it has to be a form level variable.

```
Sub Form_Load ()
    iTries = 3
End Sub
```

In the **Form_Load** event, set **iTries** to three.

# Chapter 6 - Coding Visual Basic Style

```
Sub cmdCancel_Click ()
    Unload frmLogin
End Sub
```

End the application if the Cancel button is clicked.

```
Sub cmdOk_Click ()
    Do While UCase(txtUsername.Text) <> "ME"
        iTries = iTries - 1
        MsgBox "Sorry, you entered an invalid username, you now have " & _
Str(itries) & " Tries left"
        txtUsername.SetFocus
        If itries = 0 Then
            MsgBox "You have run out of tries, Exiting..."
            Unload frmLogin
            Exit Sub
        End If
        Exit Sub
    Loop
    Do While UCase(txtPassword.Text) <> "NOIDEA"
        itries = itries - 1
        MsgBox "Sorry, you entered an invalid password you now have " & _
Str(itries) & " Tries left"
        txtPassword.SetFocus
        If itries = 0 Then
            MsgBox "You have run out of tries, Exiting..."
            Unload frmLogin
            Exit Sub
        End If
        Exit Sub
    Loop
        MsgBox "Access granted...."
        Unload frmLogin
End Sub
```

The `Do` statement at the start of the procedure checks the users entry. If it isn't "ME", then the loop is executed.

```
iTries = iTries - 1
```

We have entered the loop, so subtract one from the number of tries allowed.

```
MsgBox "Sorry, you entered an invalid username, you now have " & _
Str(itries) & " Tries left"
```

Display a message telling the user that an invalid entry has been made, and also the number of tries left.

# Do Loops

```
txtUsername.SetFocus
```

Set the focus to the user name text entry box.

```
If itries = 0 Then
    MsgBox "You have run out of tries, Exiting..."
    Unload frmLogin
    Exit Sub
End If
```

This block **If** will be executed if the user has run out of tries. It tells the user that there are no more tries, and exits.

```
Exit Sub
```

The final line of code within the loop exits the procedure because we wouldn't be here unless there'd been an invalid user name entry.

```
Loop
```

This line signifies the end of the **Do** loop structure.

```
Do While UCase(txtPassword.Text) <> "NOIDEA"
    itries = itries - 1
    MsgBox "Sorry, you entered an invalid password you now have " &
Str(itries) & " Tries left"
    txtPassword.SetFocus
    If itries = 0 Then
        MsgBox "You have run out of tries, Exiting..."
        Unload frmLogin
        Exit Sub
    End If
    Exit Sub
Loop
```

These lines are identical to the ones above, except for the password text box.

```
        MsgBox "Access granted...."
        Unload frmLogin
End Sub
```

Finally, if the entries in the two boxes are valid, then the loops are not executed, and the user is granted access. Before you run this project, save the form and the project to new files, so that you do not overwrite the current project. (Use the Save File As..., and Save Project As... options from the File menu as we'll be using it again.)

167

## Do...Until

We can tidy up the code in the project above by using `Do...Until`. The actual style of `Do` loop that you use will depend on exactly what you need. We find that the one to use is the one which sounds most like its plain English correlative. So for the password, we'd like to continue until the correct password is offered. Let's see how that looks in code:

```
Sub cmdOk_Click ()

    Do Until UCase(txtUsername.Text) = "ME" And UCase(txtPassword.Text) = "NOIDEA"
        itries = itries - 1
        MsgBox "Sorry, you have made an invalid entry. You now have " & Str(itries) & " Tries left"
        txtUsername.SetFocus
        If itries = 0 Then
            MsgBox "You have run out of tries, Exiting..."
            Unload frmLogin
            Exit Sub
        End If
        Exit Sub
    Loop

        MsgBox "Access granted...."
        Unload frmLogin

End Sub
```

In the `Do` statement, we're now checking for both the username, and the password, so we need a lot less code. The down side of this is that we now no longer know which of the entries is incorrect if the user makes a mistake.

## Placing the Test

In all our examples so far, we've checked all our conditions at the `Do` stage. If the condition is `True`, then the loop is not executed. If the code needs to be executed at least once, then you can place the test on the loop statement. In this case, Visual Basic will encounter the `Do` statement, and continue executing statements until the loop statement. The condition is checked, and depending on the result, the loop is re-executed, or execution will continue at the next statement.

# DoEvents

As we've seen before, Windows is a task sharing environment, and we want to write Windows-friendly code. If you've written a loop that does nothing except calculations, and doesn't cause any Windows events, then you'll probably grind to a halt every other Windows application running. This is because Windows will allocate some time to the other programs when your code triggers an event. If you don't trigger any events, then all other applications have a chance to process their events.

This problem is solved with the **DoEvents** statement. This statement will relinquish control (but not focus) back to Windows, so that the events that have been waiting can be processed, and control is then passed back for the calculations to continue.

## Idle Loops with DoEvents

There may be times when you are waiting for a non-Windows event to occur (such as polling a serial port for information). In such cases, you'll only want to check the port when nothing else is happening in Windows. This can be achieved by using an **idle** loop with the **DoEvents** function, as demonstrated in the following code snippet:

```
Do While DoEvents ()
    'Idle loop Code, such as Serial port polling
    'which is executed when the system has free time
    If SomeCondition then Exit Do
Loop
```

> You'll need to check a condition within the loop to allow you to exit the loop, otherwise you'll be stuck within the loop indefinitely.

## Validation: Implementation

So far, all of our validation of user input has been undertaken when the OK button has been clicked. One of the problems with this is that the code will only highlight the first error that is on the form, and only then when input is complete.

As you've entered code, you may well have noticed that there are several events that could be used for validation, the `GotFocus`, `LostFocus` (these events are triggered when the focus is moved from a form or control), and the `Change` event. The `Change` event is triggered whenever details are changed.

We are going to use the password application from Chapter 1 again, so load it now. Check that it has the `If` statements in the `OK Click` event. If it hasn't been included, start a new project, and add the password form to the project. Now use the Save File As... option to save it to a new file. You'll have to retype the code from Chapter 1 (which is what we had to do!).

## The Focus Events

It would seem that the obvious place to enter validation code would be in the `LostFocus` events. So without further ado, let's do it.

Move the validation checks from the `cmdOk Click` event to their respective `LostFocus` events as follows:

```
Sub txtUsername_LostFocus ()
    If txtUsername.Text <> "Me" Then
        MsgBox "Sorry, you entered an invalid username"
        txtUsername.SetFocus
        Exit Sub
    End If
End Sub
```

```
Sub txtPassword_LostFocus ()
    If txtPassword.Text <> "noidea" Then
        MsgBox "Sorry, you entered an invalid password"
        txtPassword.SetFocus
        Exit Sub
    End If
End Sub
```

# Validation

All looks to be in order, so run the project, and enter an incorrect user name. Shoot - you've got stuck in an infinite loop! To stop, press *Ctrl* and *Break*, then select **E**nd from the **R**un menu.

So what went wrong? Well, the `LostFocus` event can cause problems as you've now seen. Let's review what's happening here.

Having entered the invalid user name, you moved to the password text box. It now gets the focus. The `txtUserName` text box has lost the focus, so the `LostFocus` event is triggered by Windows. Because there's been an invalid entry, the message box is displayed. (At this stage, the `txtPassword` text box has the focus.)

When you click on the OK button in the message box, the next line `UserName.SetFocus` is executed. Now, focus is passed back to the `UserName` text box, so the `LostFocus` event for `txtPassword` is executed.

But we've yet to enter anything in this box, so it's also invalid. This means that the error check code is executed, which displays a message box, and sets the focus back. So as you saw, the focus is swapped between the two.

> This is a trap that has been encountered by many people, and overall we'd not recommend using the `LostFocus` events for validation.

## The Change Event

We could move all our validation code to the `Change` events. These are triggered whenever a change is made to the details. Give it a try. You'll find that it works, but not really in the way you'd want. For every letter you enter, the event is triggered, and until you've entered the correct password, the error message box is displayed.

The `Change` event is useful for some forms of validation, for instance allowing only numbers to be input, or just ignoring incorrect entry. To finish, we'll amend the Password project one more time to demonstrate the last method. If you've not already done it, move the code for the text boxes to the `Change` events, and amend it to the following:

## Chapter 6 - Coding Visual Basic Style

```
Sub txtUsername_Change ()
    If LCase(txtUsername.Text) <> "me" Then
        txtUsername.SetFocus
        Exit Sub
    Else
        txtPassword.SetFocus
    End If
End Sub
```

Invalid entries are ignored but not notified. However, the user is still able to click another button, or tab off the field. The only way that you'll know that you've made a valid entry is when the system moves focus to the password text box.

```
Sub txtPassword_Change ()
    If LCase(txtPassword.Text) <> "noidea" Then
        txtPassword.SetFocus
        Exit Sub
    Else
        MsgBox "Access granted...."
        Unload frmLogin
    End If
End Sub
```

This code is almost identical, except we've moved our **"Access granted...."** message here, so that as soon as the correct password is entered, the user is granted access.

```
Sub cmdOk_Click ()
    txtPassword.SetFocus
End Sub
```

This does mean that we've had to remove the code from the **cmdOk** button. The way that we've now got the events coded means that we don't need this button anymore.

```
Sub cmdCancel_Click ()
    Unload frmLogin
End Sub
```

In this case we're still giving the user a way out. In real life, you'd probably still want to do this, in case the username and password have been forgotten.

# Summary

In this chapter we learnt how to create and use code modules to enter procedures and modules. Using these we looked at ways of creating re-useable code, and introducing some form and structure to our projects.

We looked at the decision making constructs within Visual Basic with the `If` and `Case` statements, as well as the `On Goto` and `On Gosub` statements. You also learnt how to use the looping constructs of `For...Next`, and `Do...Loop`, and how to write Windows-friendly code.

Finally, we reviewed some of the other events, and when they may cause problems or be useful. Before going onto the next chapter, there are a few exercises to try out.

# Exercises

**1** Extend our top of form procedure to also center a form when it's loaded.

**2** You'll notice that the age calculation isn't accurate, because it doesn't take into account when in the birth date the year occurs. Extend the function to check the system day and month against the date entered day and month, and adjust the date of birth accordingly.

**3** In our looping number project, you'll notice that if you use an odd number and set the descending check, the numbers displayed are odd. Write a check to make sure that even numbers are displayed.

**4** Extend the check by turning it into a function that will be passed an integer, and return an indicator saying whether the number is odd or even. You can now extend the loop numbers project to allow the user to select whether odd or even numbers are displayed.

**5** Create a project that uses `Sub Main` as its start. Now add a `.BAS` file, and in the `Sub Main` procedure load the password form. Using a loop in the `Sub Main` procedure, allow for five tries. (This code could be used to restrict access to your applications.)

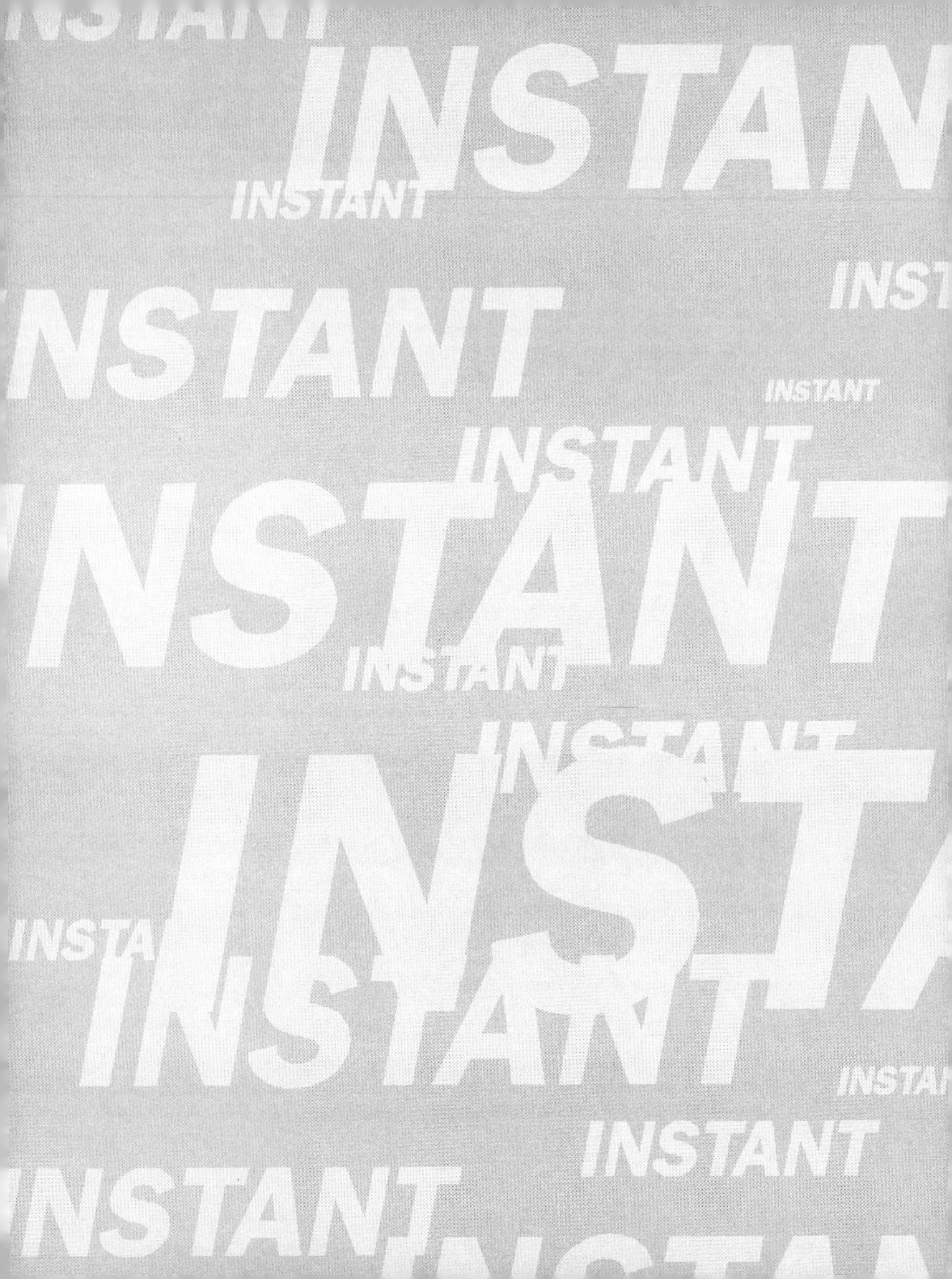
INSTANT
INSTANT
INSTANT
INSTANT
INSTANT
INSTANT
INSTANT

# Chapter 7

# Objects, Menus and Dialogs, and the MDI

In this chapter, we'll find out how to create the drop down menu structures that are widely used throughout Windows applications. We'll also build on our knowledge of common dialogs, and go through all of the other available types.

We'll also take an in-depth look at the MDI, and extend our Icon Viewer program, with some command buttons, and build a status bar. But first we'll cover the other variable type that's available within Visual Basic, the object variable.

In this chapter, we'll cover:

- Object variables
- Object variable arrays
- The Visual Basic menu system
- Status bars and common dialogs
- Input and message boxes

## Using Object Variables: Concepts

Up to this point in the book we've made constant reference to objects, so we might again ask whether or not Visual Basic is an object-oriented language? The answer remains that it is *not* object-oriented, but it *is* object based. The forms and the controls *on* the forms are actually objects, and Visual Basic does allow for some control of these objects. This is achieved through declaring object variables in a similar manner to string and integer variables, and then manipulating these variables. The main use of object variables is to create a new **instance** of a form in your application.

> An instance of a form is a specific copy of the form that is independent of the original.

These variables have a scope and a lifetime in the same way as the other variable types, and can be declared at any level, with the **Dim** or **Static** keywords.

## Generic and Specific Declarations

In Chapter 2 we created the MDI icon viewer, which allowed us to create new instances of our child icon viewer form. The declaration in the **cmdNew_Click** event is actually declaring a form type object variable.

```
Dim frmNewView As New frmView
    frmNewView.Show
```

This is an example of a specific declaration, based on our form **frmView**, because the object variable can only be applied to **frmView**. The form has to exist within the project, otherwise you'll get an error when you try to run the project.

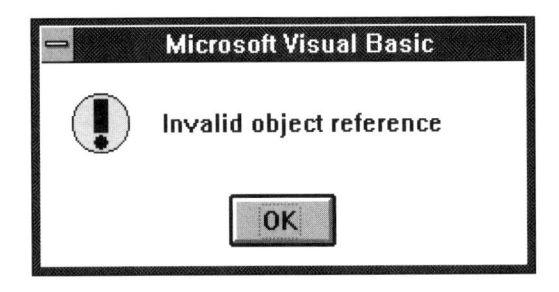

# Object Variables

> The **New** keyword in this statement tells Visual Basic to create a new instance of the object if the object variable doesn't already reference one. Because the next statement after the **Dim** is a **show** statement, **frmNewView** will not refer to any **frmView** form instances, so a new one will be created, loaded, and then shown.

We can also declare generic objects for forms, controls and MDI forms (although only one MDI form is allowed). For example, to declare a generic form variable and a generic control variable, we'd use the following code:

```
Dim frmGeneric as Form
Dim ctlGeneric as Control
```

By using a generic form or control variable, you are able to reference any form or control in your project, but these variables are slightly slower to use than ordinary variables, because Visual Basic has to resolve the references for the generic types.

The specific declaration for controls is slightly different from forms, in that you can't declare a control variable for a specific control, but only for a control type, such as a text box:

```
Dim txtObjVariable as Text Box
```

Visual Basic allows you to specifically declare object variables for the following controls:

| Controls For Which You Can Declare Object Variables ||||| 
|---|---|---|---|---|
| Vertical Scroll Bar | Horizontal Scroll Bar | Command Button | Common Dialog | Data |
| Option Button | Drive List List Box | File List Box | Grid | Frame |
| Directory | Image | Label | Line | List Box |
| Menu | Combo Box | OLE | Picture Box | Shape |
| Text Box | Timer | Check Box | | |

**177**

## Assigning an Object to a Variable

To assign an object to an object variable, Visual Basic uses the `Set` statement. You can then refer to the object variable instead of the object that it's based on. For instance, you may have a text box called `frmInput!txtSurnameEntry`. To reference it with an object variable, you'd use the following `Set` statement:

```
Set objSurname = frmInput!txtSurnameEntry
```

You can now use the object variable to change properties, and use the methods associated with the text box:

```
objSurname.SetFocus
If objSurname.text = "some text"
```

When you use the `Set` statement, you're not actually copying the object to the variable, rather you are assigning a reference to it. If you have several object variables that reference the same object, then each will reflect any changes to that object.

> For those of you that have used C, the `Set` statement is similar to pointers in C, where the object variable points to the object to which it refers.

## Releasing Resources

Object variables, like normal variables, take up resources. It's good practice to free the resources taken by the variable when you've finished with it (if it's a module, globally scoped, or `static` variable). This uses a special keyword, `Nothing`, with the `Set` statement. When you first declare an object variable, and when a procedure ends for a local object variable, it is set to `Nothing`. To set our `objSurname` above to `Nothing` we'd use this:

```
Set objSurname = Nothing
```

## Creating New Instances

Using the `Set` statement, we can also create new instances of an object. In our MDI viewer program, instead of using the `New` keyword in `Dim` statement, we could have used the following code:

# Assigning Objects

```
Dim frmNewView As frmView
Set frmNewView = New frmView
frmNewView.Show
```

By using **New** with the **Set** statement, we are able to set the object variable to **Nothing**. This is not the case with the **Dim** statement because Visual Basic will always ensure that the variable refers to a loaded object instance. Therefore, next time you reference the object, Visual Basic will load a new instance, so it will never be **Nothing**.

Try it out by loading the MDI viewer application from Chapter 2, then altering the **cmdNew_Click** code as above. Save the project to a new project as we'll be using it throughout this chapter.

## Testing the Object Variable

There are two tests that you may wish to use on object variables. For the generic control object variable, you may need to determine which type of control to which it is currently set. In this case you'd use the **TypeOf** keyword. To compare two object variable references, or to test for **Nothing** use the **Is** keyword.

Using our textbox example, we could test to see if the object variable is actually set to **Nothing**:

```
If objSurname Is Nothing Then..
```

We can also check the generic variable type to see what control it is set to:

```
If  TypeOf objPassed Is TextBox then..
```

Let's extend the functionality of our icon viewer, and use it as an example. Load the new version for this chapter, and if you've not done all the exercises, you'll need to replace the view form with the version that we developed in Chapter 4, with the toolbar (done by using Remove File and Add file from the File menu). Don't forget to make the form an MDI Child form (change its **MDIChild** property to **True**), and save it to a new name, so that you don't overwrite the old one.

## Chapter 7 - Objects, Menus & Dialogs, and MDI

What we're going to do is allow the user to select the up and the down icons for the toolbar, so we'll need to add a new form, then make it an MDI child. We've added two command buttons, two image controls, three labels, and a text box, so that the form looks like this:

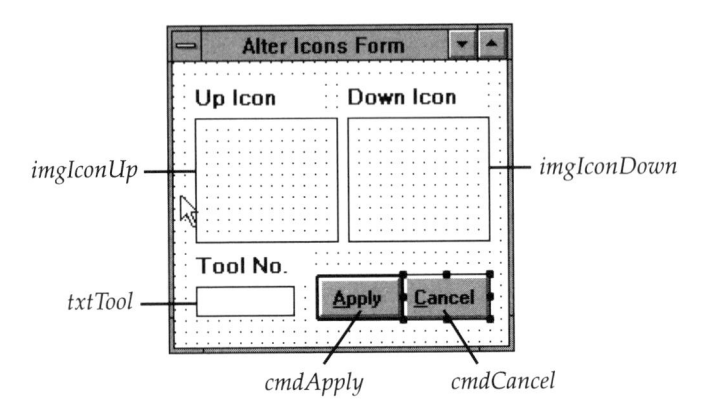

*Alter Icons Form*

- *imgIconUp* — Up Icon
- *imgIconDown* — Down Icon
- *txtTool* — Tool No.
- *cmdApply* — Apply
- *cmdCancel* — Cancel

Now we need to add two image control arrays to the toolbar of the viewer form to correspond to the up and down states of the buttons. We've called these **imgUp()** and **imgDown()**. Set the **Visible** properties of the new controls to **False**, and the picture properties to correspond to the up and down states of our toolbar as used previously, so the **Picture** property of **imgUp(0)** is set to **C:\VB\ICONS\OFFICE\FILES03A.ICO**, and **imgDown(0)** is set to **C:\VB\ICONS\OFFICE\FILES03B.ICO**. We've set the **Picture** properties of the **imgTools** array to **None**. Finally on this form, we've altered the **DragMode** property of **imgSelected** to **1 - Automatic**. This will allow us to drag the control around the screen - we will be using this to demonstrate the **TypeOf** object.

# Testing Object Variables

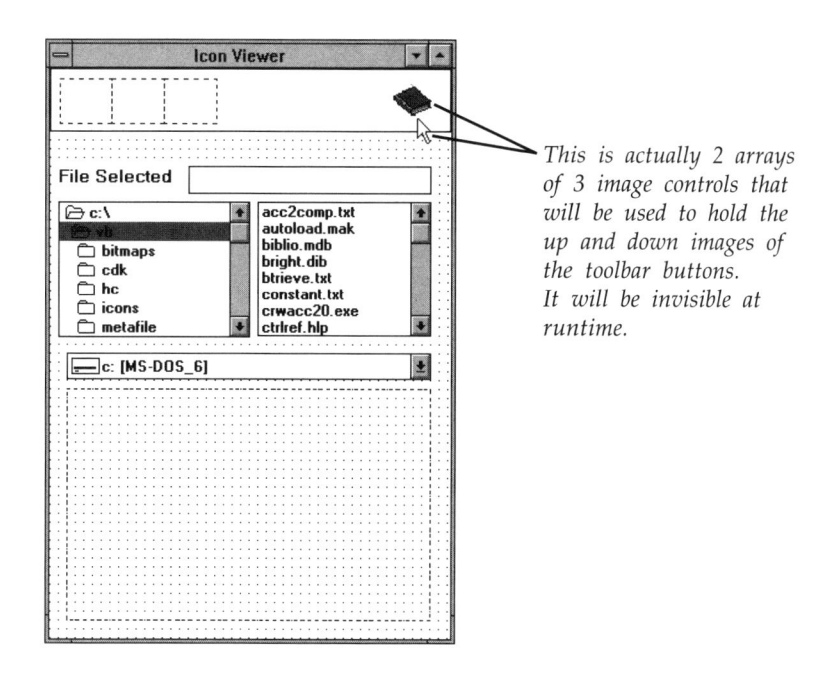

*This is actually 2 arrays of 3 image controls that will be used to hold the up and down images of the toolbar buttons. It will be invisible at runtime.*

Having made the amendments to the Viewer form we need to alter the code somewhat. In the **Form_Load** event we now require the following:

```
Sub Form_Load ()
    filSel.Pattern = "*.bmp;*.ico;*.wmf"
    txtSelection = filSel.Pattern
```

These lines remain the same.

```
    imgTool(0).Picture = imgUp(0).Picture
    imgTool(1).Picture = imgUp(1).Picture
    imgTool(2).Picture = imgUp(2).Picture
```

Because we've removed the pictures loaded in the Properties window, we now have to set them when the form loads. This is because the icons could change in a later version, and we now only need to worry about the up and down image control arrays. The tool image control array is entirely set from within the code to maintain flexibility, and keep the hard coded details to a minimum.

```
    frmAlter.Show
End Sub
```

181

# Chapter 7 - Objects, Menus & Dialogs, and MDI

Finally we want to display our new form to allow the user to select the new icons for the toolbar. The code for the **MouseDown** and **MouseUp** events now looks like this:

```
Sub imgTool_MouseDown (index As Integer, Button As Integer, Shift As Integer, X As Single, Y As Single)
    imgTool(index).Picture = imgDown(index).Picture
End Sub
```

```
Sub imgTool_MouseUp (index As Integer, Button As Integer, Shift As Integer, X As Single, Y As Single)
    imgTool(index).Picture = imgUp(index).Picture
End Sub
```

We no longer need to test the value of the index to see which icons to load, because we've set the up and down pictures in the hidden control arrays. When the user presses the mouse button down while over a button, the down icon is loaded, and when it is released, the up icon is loaded. It is this runtime allocation which will allow us to alter the icons at runtime.

Now we need to write some code for the alter icon form:

```
Sub imgIconUp_DragDrop (source As Control, X As Single, Y As Single)
   If TypeOf source Is Image Then imgIconUp.Picture = source.Picture
End Sub
```

To allow the user to drop the image control on the view form on our **imgIconUp**, we write some code in the **DragDrop** event. If you look at the first parameter received by this event, you'll notice that it is a generic control object variable. This will contain the reference of the object that's being dragged and then dropped, so our code will need to check that it is the right type of control for the operation that we're undertaking. In this case we check that the control is an image control, and then alter the picture setting of the **imgIconUp** on our icon alter form to the one that's in the source control. In a similar manner, we'll also set the **imgIconDown** control:

```
Sub imgIconDown_DragDrop (source As Control, X As Single, Y As Single)
    If TypeOf source Is Image Then imgIconDown.Picture = source.Picture
End Sub
```

There's some minimal validation on the **Change** event for the text box, to ensure that it is a number:

# Runtime Allocation

```
Sub txtTool_Change ()
        If Not IsNumeric(txtTool) Then
            txtTool.SetFocus
            txtTool = ""
        End If
End Sub
```

If non-numeric values are entered, this code clears the entry and resets the focus to the text box to allow for a valid entry. Finally, we have the code for the two command buttons:

```
Sub cmdApply_Click ()
    If imgIconUp.Picture = 0 Then
        MsgBox "You have not loaded an 'Up' picture. Please re-try"
        frmView.SetFocus
        Exit Sub
    End If
    If imgIconDown.Picture = 0 Then
        MsgBox "You have not loaded a 'Down' picture. Please re-try"
        frmView.SetFocus
        Exit Sub
    End If
```

These two `If` statements check to see if an icon has been dragged and dropped into our up and down image controls. If not, then it displays a message box, and gives focus back to the viewer form. The following code will check if the number entered is within the range of icons for the toolbar.

```
If Val(txtTool) >= 0 And Val(txtTool) <= 2 Then
```

If it is then set the images in the two control arrays on the view form to the up and the down pictures that are loaded in the up and the down images.

```
frmView!imgUp(Val(txtTool.Text)).Picture = imgIconUp.Picture
frmView!imgDown(Val(txtTool.Text)).Picture = imgIconDown.Picture
```

Also set the tool bar icon to the up image, so that it's changed on the toolbar.

```
frmView.imgTool(Val(txtTool.Text)).Picture = imgIconUp.Picture
```

Finally set the focus back to the viewer form, to allow the user to select another.

183

# Chapter 7 - Objects, Menus & Dialogs, and MDI

```
            frmView.SetFocus
        End If
End Sub

Sub cmdCancel_Click()
  Unload frmAlter
End Sub
```

We will use the Cancel button to unload the Icon Changer form.

# Object Variable Arrays

As with other variable types, you can also set up an array of object variables. This is very similar to our control arrays, but does have a few differences. With it you can create an array of forms, which you can't do with control arrays, and the array is always contiguous - it can't have any gaps, though gaps *are* allowed with control arrays.

The following table shows the differences between control arrays, and arrays of object variables:

| Action/Method | Control Array | Array of Object Variables |
| --- | --- | --- |
| Create the array | Set the **Index** property at design time | **Dim**, **ReDim**, **Global** or **Static** |
| Add/remove elements | Load or unload at runtime | **ReDimPreserve** |
| Find bounds of array | Must track each element | **Ubound** and **Lbound** |
| Contiguous elements | No | Yes |
| Range of index | 0 to 32,767 | -32,768 to 32,767 |

From the above table, you'll notice that you can create a dynamic object array, and alter its dimensions at runtime with the **RedimPreserve** statement. Also, if you use the **New** keyword in the declaration of the array, Visual Basic will produce a new instance for you.

# Object Variable Arrays

## Multiple Form Instances

When you create a new form instance with the **New** keyword, you are creating an independent copy of the form. Although it will share the same code as the original form and copy the property values of the original, you are able to change its properties at runtime. This is because it contains its own copy of the data (properties and variables). Therefore, if you wish to share data between form instances, you'll need to use **Global** level variables. When an event is triggered for the form, it will use the data that is contained in the instance. Generally the code doesn't need to worry which instance triggered it, but there are exceptions, such as when closing the form instance.

If you look at the MDI project we wrote in Chapter 2 you'll see a reference to the keyword **Me**. This tells Visual Basic to reference the particular form instance that is active. We used it to close the view form with the following code in the **Close_Click** event:

```
Sub cmdClose_Click ()
    Unload Me
End Sub
```

You can also use **Me** as a form variable. Consider it as always containing the reference to the active form.

> In certain circumstances, such as when a timer event is triggered, **Me** may not refer to the active form. In these cases it will refer to the instance of the form in which the code is being executed.

## Collections

Both the forms and the controls have **collections** created and maintained for them by Visual Basic. A collection is an array of loaded forms or controls, starting with an index of **0**. We can reference a form, or a control by its collection index, although this will change as forms and controls are loaded and unloaded. For example, if we wish to change the background color of all the loaded forms, we would use the following code snippet:

**185**

```
For iCount = 0 to Forms.Count - 1
    Forms(iCount).BackColor = &H00C0C0C0&
Next iCount
```

The forms collection is referenced with the name `Forms`. Beware - this is not a reserved word, so it can be shadowed by a variable named `Forms`. In the first line, we're starting a loop at `0`, and stopping at `Forms.Count - 1`. The `Count` is a runtime property in which Visual Basic maintains the number of members in the collection. In the next line, we're setting the `BackColor` of each form in turn. The strange number is the RGB (Red, Green, Blue) value expressed as a hexadecimal number. You'll see these numbers in the `Color` properties for forms and controls.

> We'll look at color in more detail in the next chapter.

In a similar way, we can use the control collection for a form. To change the background color of all the text boxes on a form, we'd use the following code:

```
For iCount = 0 to frmEntry.Controls.Count - 1
    If TypeOf frmEntry.Controls Is TextBox Then
        frmEntry.Controls(iCount).BackColor = &H00C0C0C0&
    End If
Next iCount
```

If the code was part of `frmEntry`, then you could leave the reference off, and just use `Controls(iCount).BackColor`. Because we're only changing the text boxes `BackColor`, we need to check which type of control the current one is.

## Menu System: Implementation

Most of the applications that you see and use under Windows have drop down menus at the top of the screen. From a users point of view, they're very useful, and Visual Basic has a very simple interface to allow us to create very complex menu structures for our applications. To run up the menu dialog select the menu icon of the toolbar:

# Menu Systems

Select Menu Design from the Window menu, or press *Ctrl* and *M*. The menu tool will only be active when a form is displayed. If more than one is displayed, the menu will be added to the currently selected form. The menu is a control, and you can create object variables for it in the same way as other controls, and create control arrays of menu items.

## The Menu Design Window

The best way to learn about the menu designer is to use it. We are going to put a menu bar on our MDI Viewer application, so without further ado, load the project, and we can begin. When the project has loaded, make the MDI parent form visible, then select the menu tool. You will be greeted with a window like this:

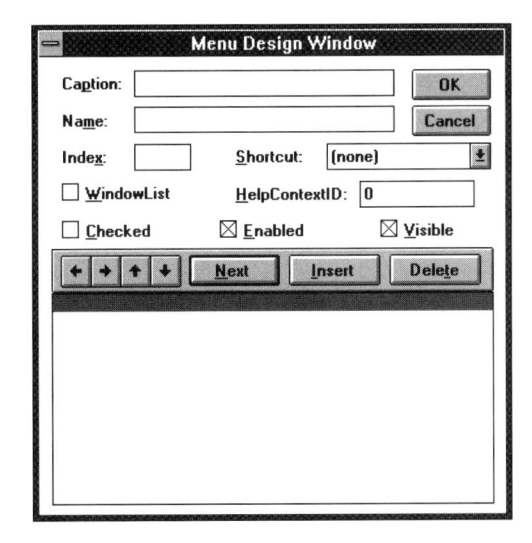

## Pre-Plannng Menus

Before we go launching into designing a menu, we need to decide what functions are required, and where they will go in our menu hierarchy. With our viewer, we need to be able to open and close the Icon Viewer, and also the Alter Icon form. We also need to be able to exit the application, and

**187**

call the help file (if it's available). It would be nice also to allow the user to open more than one icon viewer file at a time. There's also some functionality that we can add for very little effort, such as tiling or cascading open MDI child windows, and selecting one from a list of open windows, so we'll add this too.

> You'll notice that the Microsoft menus all follow the same structure, so that no matter what product you are using, the interface is familiar. We would recommend that you follow this convention so that users will know where to look for menu items.

## Top Level Menu

The top level menu is the one that will be visible at the top of the screen, and the other items will drop down from this. Our top level menu for our viewer application looks like this:

*File   Window   Help*

To start with, enter **&File** in the **Caption** property. This will create a menu control for you, and you'll see it in the menu design list box. Next we need to give it a name - we have called ours **mnuFile**, so our menu design window now looks like this:

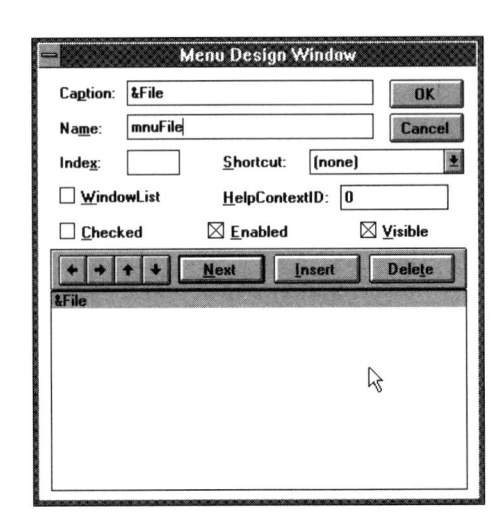

# Menu Design Window

That's the first menu entry done. To complete the top level, click the Next button, then enter **&Window** in the `Caption`, and **mnuWindow** for the name, and for the last entry click the Next button, then set the `Caption` to **&Help**, with a name of **mnuHelp**. Click the OK button, and the menu design window closes. You should now see the top level menu on your MDI parent form.

## Menu Properties

For the majority of your menu items, the only properties you'll need to set are the `Caption` and the `Name`. Don't be fooled by the different interface - the menu properties are exactly the same as on other controls: Index is the index number if you've created a control array, Enabled will control the graying out of an item, and Visible will show or hide the item. You'll also notice that the **&** gives you the quick access key in the caption in the same way as other controls.

Checked, WindowList and Shortcut apply only to menus, and we'll see some of these in action as we go. Checked will place a tick next to the menu item, WindowList displays a list of open windows in an MDI application, and Shortcut is a hot key. Remember that Checked, Enabled, and Visible can be altered in code at runtime, to control your menu system.

# The File Menu Structure

The next step is to build our menu structure that we require below the File menu. Our final structure looks like this:

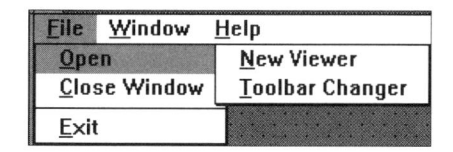

| File | Window | Help |
|---|---|---|
| Open | | New Viewer |
| Close Window | | Toolbar Changer |
| Exit | | |

To achieve this we need to insert five entries below the **&File** entry in the menu list box. Click the menu tool to load the menu, and then highlight the **&Window** entry in the list box by clicking it. Now click the Insert button five times, and you'll see five blank lines inserted above the **&Window** entry. Now enter **&Open** in the `Caption`, and **mnuOpen** in the `Name` properties. Press the Next key to go to the next blank entry and repeat the operation using the names and captions from the table below. Finally, press OK.

189

## Chapter 7 - Objects, Menus & Dialogs, and MDI

| Menu Caption | Menu Name |
|---|---|
| &Open | mnuOpen |
| &New Viewer | mnuNew |
| &Toolbar Changer | mnuTool |
| &Close Window | mnuClose |
| &Exit | mnuExit |

You will see that it's not quite what we want. The items go across the screen, as part of the top level menu. We want our new entries to be part of the File menu structure. This is what the four arrow tools are for. These move the highlighted item around in the structure. Press the menu tool again, highlight the `&Open` entry, then click the right arrow. The entry has now been indented, which indicates that it is now a level below the File menu. Do the same for the others, up to the `&Exit` entry:

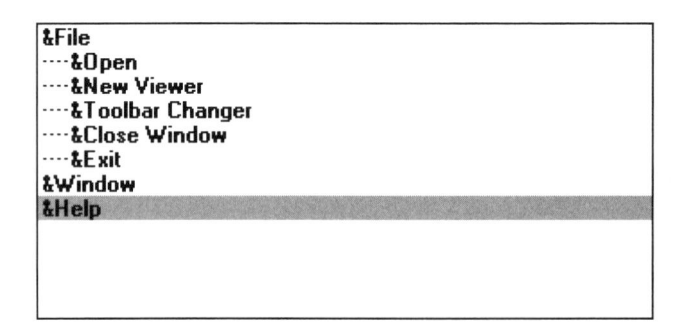

```
&File
····&Open
····&New Viewer
····&Toolbar Changer
····&Close Window
····&Exit
&Window
&Help
```

Now when you press the OK button, you'll see that the top level menu is back to its original state, which is as we want it. Click on the top level File menu on your MDI form, and you will see its entries drop down. This is very useful for checking that the menu is correct, and this is how it will appear at runtime. However, you'll notice that it's still not the same as the screenshot - we need to do some further work. Load the menu tool, and indent the new and tool entries a further level. This now makes them part of the Open menu.

# Menu Structure

```
&File
····&Open
········&New Viewer
········&Toolbar Changer
····&Close Window
····-
····&Exit
&Window
&Help
```

You'll see that we've also inserted an extra menu item before the exit entry, with a hyphen in the **Caption**. This is the separator and is a valid menu control, so it must have a name. When you are done, press OK, and see if your menu structure is as it should be - if not alter it to match the screenshot. This covers most of the functionality that we actually want, so let's add those extra value features that we mentioned.

## The Window Menu Structure

Within most Microsoft products, there is a facility to control how the desktop looks, and these functions usually live under the Window menu. We'll allow the users to tile or cascade the open windows, arrange the icons for minimized forms, and also display a dynamic list of loaded windows.

191

# Chapter 7 - Objects, Menus & Dialogs, and MDI

Alter your menu structure to match the screenshot. We've highlighted the `&Window` entry, because we've now checked the `WindowList` property. Visual Basic only allows one menu to have this property checked in an MDI application, and will produce a dynamic list of windows loaded at the end of the Window menu. Run the project and see what happens. If you look at the Window menu, both our forms are loaded and listed at the end of the menu.

## Short Cut Keys

Assigning short cut keys is really simple. All you need to do is to highlight the menu item in the list box, and then select the short cut key that you wish to assign to that menu item from the combo box. We've assigned three short cut keys to the items in the Window menu.

That's all there is to it. Once again, you'll find that Microsoft does use some standard keys, such as *Ctrl* and *C* for copy to the clipboard, *Ctrl* and *X* for cut to the clipboard, and *Ctrl* and *V* for paste from the clipboard.

> See *The Windows Interface - An Application Design Guide*, **Microsoft Press for Microsoft's own standards.**

# Short Cut Keys

## Coding Menu Items

The only event that a menu item receives is a **Click** event. You've probably discovered that by clicking the lowest level item in a menu brings up its Code window. We'll write code for the Windows menu, and code the **Exit** event and disable the rest of the menu items. We'll enable them as we write code for them.

> This is useful where you are prototyping. You may wish to convey the functionality of your application to the users, but have yet to complete all the functions. You can give the users the feel of the finished product and get some early feedback.

In the exit **Click** event enter the following:

```
Unload MDIForm1
```

This will unload the form and any child forms that are loaded, thereby ending the application.

In the MDIForm load event we need to disable the menu items that we are not using, so add the following code:

```
mnuOpen.Enabled = False
mnuNew.Enabled = False
mnuTool.Enabled = False
mnuClose.Enabled = False
mnuHelp.Enabled = False
```

Since we are disabling the New menu option for our prototype, we need to add a piece of code to the **Form_Load** event to load the Icon Viewer form to give us something to play with. We will return to these menu items shortly, but first a short interlude on the methods available to you to display your child forms, and how to display a menu as a popup.

## Using the Arrange Method

To allow the user to arrange the windows on the desktop, unsurprisingly we use the **Arrange** method. This will do all the work for us to tile, cascade, and arrange the minimized icons. In each case, the method is the

193

# Chapter 7 - Objects, Menus & Dialogs, and MDI

same, it is just a different argument. So for the tile **Click** event add this code:

```
MDIForm1.Arrange 2
```

The argument **2** tells Visual Basic to tile the open windows vertically. The other arguments are: **0 - Cascade**, **1 - Tile Horizontally**, and **3 - Arrange Icons**. So to cascade our windows, add the line **MDIForm1.Arrange 0** to the cascade **Click** event and **MDIForm1.Arrange 3** to the arrange icons **Click** event.

The Window menu is now fully functional, although we can't yet try it out. We can also use the short cut keys on the menu items to tile, cascade or arrange our icons. Also, if you minimize the forms, and then select one of the windows off the window list, it is brought back to its normal state.

Save the project, and we'll come back to it later, after we've looked at the other menu type that Visual Basic supports, the **popup** menu.

## PopUp Menus

The popup menu is a menu that can be displayed anywhere on a form. Any menu that you've designed with a sub-menu can be used as a popup menu. As you would expect, the command to call a popup menu is **PopupMenu**. This is becoming more common in applications, where the user clicks the right mouse button to pop up a menu (such as in Word or Excel). By using the mouse events for a form or control, you can code context sensitive popup menus.

> A few words of caution. When a popup menu is displayed, the code in the module that called the menu has its execution interrupted until the user selects an item, or closes the menu. If the user selects an option, the **Click** event code for the menu item selected will be executed before the code in the event that called the popup menu continues executing.

We'll add a popup menu to the Alter Icons form, but not display it at the top of the form, so uncheck the Visible check box on the top level. Select the Alter Icon form, then the menu tool. Now add the same entries as the screenshot:

# PopUp Menus

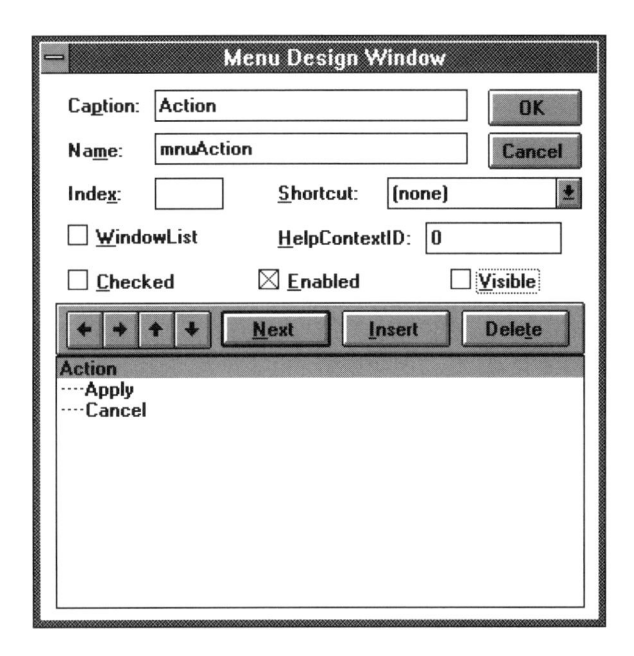

[Menu Design Window screenshot showing Caption: Action, Name: mnuAction, with Action/Apply/Cancel menu items]

To view the popup menu add the following code to the **MouseDown** event of the Alter Icon form:

```
If button = 2 Then
    mnuAction.Visible = True
    PopupMenu mnuAction
End If
```

We are checking if the button pressed is the right button. If it is, our menu will popup at the same position as the mouse pointer.

> It's not normally necessary to make the menu visible before you pop it up, unless you are going to unload the form. There's a bug in Visual Basic that will cause it to crash if you try to unload the form from a non-visible menu via a popup. Comment out the visible line, then try it. If you select **Cancel**, Visual Basic will cause a GPF. This is a documented bug, and for those of you who have access to the Knowledge Base, further information is in the VB_BUGS Knowledge Base article Q116058 *Incorrect Popup Menu Events*.

**195**

Chapter 7 - Objects, Menus & Dialogs, and MDI

Now in the `mnuApply_Click` event, enter `cmdApply_Click`, and in the `mnuCancel_Click` event enter `cmdCancel_Click` to call the corresponding `Click` events. We now have a popup menu for our application.

## MDI Re-visited

There are not too many more features of the MDI that you've not already encountered. So far, we've created child forms, and now added some functionality with the menus. To round MDI off, we'll look at how menus behave, then extend the functionality to allow for multiple instances of the viewer form, and finally we'll add the status bar as promised way back in Chapter 4.

### Menus With the MDI

Menus act slightly differently within an MDI application. If a child form has a menu associated with it, it will replace the MDI menu when the child form has focus, even if it is hidden. Run the MDI viewer application, and give the Alter Icons form the focus by clicking on it with the left mouse button. You'll notice that the menu disappears! This is because a non-visible menu on the child form is now being displayed (or not as the case may be).

> The menu on the MDI form will be displayed only if there are no child forms loaded, or if a child form without a menu structure has focus. To return to the MDI menu structure you'll need to cancel the Alter Icon form.

If you click the right mouse button to display the popup menu when the Alter Icon form is loaded, you get a slightly disturbing jump effect because the Action menu is being displayed as a work around for the popup bug fix. This can be cured by setting the `Visible` property to `True` in the menu design window, although it does detract somewhat from the usefulness of popup menus.

## Multiple Viewer Form Instances

To allow the user to open multiple instances of the viewer form, add the following code to the `mnuNew_Click` event:

```
Dim frmNewView As New frmView
frmNewView.Show
```

This is the same code that we used in Chapter 2 to load multiple instances.

Remove all the code from the MDI form load event, and run the application. Now when you select New viewer from the menu, a new form instance is loaded. Also, the first time that an instance is loaded, the Alter Icon form is loaded, but when you try to apply changes to the toolbar an error occurs. This is because our form reference **frmView** no longer applies. We need to use a **Global** form variable to hold the last active viewer form. Within the MDI we can use the **ActiveForm** property to determine the last active form. Add a code module, and in the general declarations section enter **Global frmCurrent As form**. Now change the references to **frmView** in the whole project to **frmCurrent** using the Replace option from the Edit menu. Now, in the active event in the viewer form, set **frmCurrent** to **Me**. The tool bar will now be altered on the most recently active viewer form.

When you run the project, you'll find that it works fine except when you click on the exit button on the view form toolbars. This is a case for the **Me** keyword, so change the code to **Unload Me** in the **imgTool** array **Click** event.

To close the correct form we also need to know which is the active form. So to close the correct form, add the following code to the **mnuClose_Click** event:

```
Unload MDIForm1.ActiveForm
```

The final bit of tidying up is to move the code to load the Alter Icon form from the **form_load** event of the viewer form to the **mnuTool_Click** event. All the options on our menu should now be fully functional, except the Help, so you can try out the Tile, Cascade and Arrange Icons menu options.

# Status Bar

As promised in Chapter 4, we'll use the picture control to add a status bar to the bottom of our MDI viewer application. Click on the MDI parent form, then double click on the picture toll in the toolbox. Visual Basic draws a picture control for us, as it did in the viewer forms. Change the

**Align** property to **2 - Align Bottom**, the **BackColor** to gray, and the name to **picStatus**. We're going to use this as a container control, to hold a text box that will display the status text. Draw a text box on the picture control, call it **txtStatus**, change the **BackColor** to gray, and clear the **Text** property. Now all we need to do is use the **MouseMove** events of the forms and controls as we did in the hotspot project to display details of where the user is at any given time.

We've added this to the **MouseMove** event for the Icon View form:

```
MDIForm1!txtStatus = "You are on an Icon View Form"
```

and this to the **MouseMove** event for the Alter Icon form:

```
MDIForm1!txtStatus = "You are on the Icon Changer Form".
```

# Common Dialogs

So far we've used the **Open File** common dialog in Chapter 2. The **Save As** dialog is identical, apart from the caption, so we've already covered this too! This leaves us with the **Print**, **Color** and **Font** dialogs available with the common dialog control and the two other common dialogs that we can use: the input box and the message box. All these dialogs get information from the user that we then use in our applications.

# Input Boxes

These are a quick and dirty way to get input from a user. Generally, you'll design your own dialogs to get input from the user. You use an input box as a function. For instance, to get the users name using an input box, you'd use the following code:

```
sUserName = InputBox("Enter Your Name:", "User ID")
```

The message box will be displayed for input:

# Common Dialogs

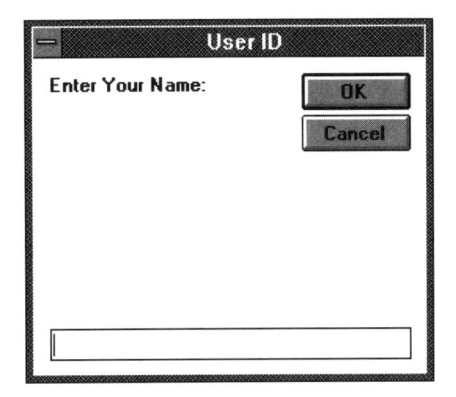

You can only alter the **Prompt** string and the caption of the input box. By default the input box will appear in the center of the screen, but you can specify your own coordinates after the caption if you want to. The returned value when OK is clicked will be a string of the contents entered. If Cancel is pressed, a zero length string will be returned.

## Message Boxes

We've used the most basic form of the message box which simply displays some information, and allows the user to close it. This is the message box statement. We can also use it as a function to return an integer that will refer to the key pressed. We'll use the message box in the Alter Icon form **cmdClick** event as an example.

Firstly, declare an integer variable **iReturn**. This will hold the value of the key pressed by the user. We will display a stop graphic, and a Retry and Cancel button in the message box. If the user clicks Cancel, then unload the form. Change your code to the following:

```
If imgIconUp.Picture = 0 Then
    iReturn = MsgBox("You have not loaded an 'Up' picture. Please retry", 16 + 5, "Icon Up Error")
```

The first string is the message that's displayed, the **16** tells Visual Basic to display the stop icon, and the **5** displays the Retry and Cancel buttons. We could have entered **21** here for the same effect, but take care with this method as it is very easy to make mistakes and end up with the wrong style of message box.

> For the other constants that are used in displaying the message box, and the return values for the buttons, search the <u>H</u>elp file for *Message Box*. There is also a file that contains all the constant declarations for Visual Basic called CONSTANTS.TXT in your Visual Basic directory. You should cut and paste the declarations that you require for each project, rather than load the whole file, to save resources.

```
If iReturn = 4 Then
```

If the <u>R</u>etry button is pressed, then `iReturn` will be set to `4`, so we pass the focus back to the last active instance of the view form.

```
        frmCurrent.SetFocus
        Exit Sub
    Else
```

Otherwise, we unload the form, because the <u>C</u>ancel button is pressed.

```
            Unload frmalter
            Exit Sub
        End If
    End If
```

# The Color Common Dialog

The Alter Icon form might look better with different background colors. We'll add a color dialog box which will allow the user to change the color. Firstly, add an extra item to the menu for the form called **mnuColor** (this will call the dialog box), and set the color, and then add a common dialog control to the form. We've renamed ours to **dlgColor**. Now add the following code to the **mnuColor_Click** event:

```
Sub mnuColor_Click ()
    dlgColor.CancelError = True
```

If the user clicks the <u>C</u>ancel button, generate an error:

```
On Error GoTo ErrCancel
```

Here we are picking up the error generated by the <u>C</u>ancel button click, and jumping to our error code.

```
dlgColor.Action = 3
```

This action setting displays the color common dialog.

```
frmAlter.BackColor = dlgColor.Color
```

Now set the forms **BackColor** property to the selection made by the user.

```
ErrCancel:
    Exit Sub
End Sub
```

Finally, if the Cancel button is pressed we exit the procedure.

# The Font Common Dialog

The use of the font common dialog is identical to the use of the color dialog, except that you are able to alter font properties. Before you call the dialog, however, you'll need to set the **Flags** property to tell Visual Basic where to look for the fonts. You can select the screen fonts (**Flag** property set to **1**), printer fonts (**Flag** property set to **2**), or both (**Flag** property set to **3**). If you don't do this, you'll get an error, **No Fonts Exist**. We'll allow the users to alter the font details for the labels on the Alter Icon form. To save coding effort, rename all the labels **lblClick**, so that we can use the **Click** event for the control array to set each label as it is clicked. Now add the following code to the **lblClick_Click** event:

```
Sub lblClick_Click (Index As Integer)

    dlgColor.CancelError = True
    On Error GoTo ErrCancel
```

These lines are the same as in the previous example.

```
dlgColor.Flags = 3
```

Setting the **Flags** property to **3** will allow us to use all the available fonts. There are many **Flag** settings available (too numerous to mention), and you can look them up in the Help file under common dialog properties.

```
dlgColor.Action = 4
```

Setting the **Action** property to **4** will display the font dialog.

```
lblClick(Index).FontBold = dlgColor.FontBold
lblClick(Index).FontItalic = dlgColor.FontItalic
lblClick(Index).FontName = dlgColor.FontName
lblClick(Index).FontSize = dlgColor.FontSize
```

Now we can set the properties of our label control to the ones selected in the common dialog.

```
ErrCancel:
    Exit Sub
End Sub
```

The final code is identical to our previous example.

You can see how easy it is to let the user control the look and feel of your system with the common dialogs. Also by using the common dialogs, you'll ensure that your application has the same look and feel as the version of Windows that it is running under.

We'll save the print common dialog for Chapter 9 where we cover input and output.

# Summary

In this chapter we learnt about object variables, and how to use them to create new form instances, as well as reference the controls on a form. We looked at how to design a menu structure that goes across the top of our forms, as well as popup menus that can be displayed anywhere on the form.

We learnt how the menus behave in an MDI application, and further explored object variables and creating new form instances.

We rounded up the chapter by using some of the other common dialogs available in Visual Basic. Because we've covered a lot of ground in this chapter, we'll go easy on the exercises.

# Summary and Exercises

## Exercises

**1** Extend the use of the color custom control to allow the user to change the foreground and background colors of the Alter Icon form.

**2** Now set up the color change as a function, and allow the user to change the colors of the all the controls on the form. (You'll have to pass the control as an object variable to the function.)

**3** Re-create the MDI form menu in the Alter Icon form, but disable the functions that can't be used. This will stop the jump effect, and allow you to once again have the Action menu hidden and only available as a popup. Remove the Cancel option from the popup to stop the GPF, and add it to the MDI Menu instead.

# Chapter 8

# Introducing Graphics

Windows is a very graphical environment, and Visual Basic is designed to take advantage of this. In this chapter, you'll get an introduction to this rather complex and detailed subject, which is almost worthy of a book in itself.

In Chapters 3 and 4 we looked at the two picture handling graphic controls, image and picture. There are two other graphic controls, line and shape, which can be used to draw lines and shapes. Visual Basic also has the facility to draw directly onto the screen, or draw directly to the printer. Conversely, you can print to the printer or to the screen!

Apart from textbox and label, Visual Basic treats everything you place on the screen as a graphic, so you can resize it, change fonts, and so on. The main controls that you can draw and print to are the picture control and the form. But before we can do any of this, you'll need to learn about the coordinate and scale systems that Visual Basic uses, and in this chapter we'll also look at color in more detail.

In this chapter we'll cover:

- System objects
- The coordinate system
- Simple animation
- Lines and shapes
- Grapics methods drawing
- Colors

## System Objects: Concepts

There are five objects that we've yet to encounter. These are system objects that are looked after by Visual Basic and Windows. They are the reason that you can draw to a printer and print to the screen:

| Object | Use |
|---|---|
| **App** | This object supplies information about the application |
| **Clipboard** | This provides access to the clipboard |
| **Debug** | Used to control the debug window |
| **Printer** | Enables the printing of text and graphics to the printer |
| **Screen** | Supplies the current form, control, and other screen data, such as the mouse pointer |

To use these objects, simply precede the method with the object name. For instance to print to the printer you would use this:

```
Printer.Print "This is the First Line".
```

To change the mouse pointer for the whole screen you would use the following:

```
Screen.MousePointer = 7.
```

## The Coordinate System in Visual Basic

The coordinate system in Visual Basic is a two dimensional system X, Y, where X is the horizontal axis, and Y is the vertical axis. By default, the top left hand point of a control is at coordinates 0, 0, with X and Y increasing as you move right and down by the scale amount.

Each control you can draw or print in has its own set of coordinates, as illustrated in the following figure:
In some circumstances, you'll want to create you own coordinate system. For instance, you may want the center of the screen to be coordinates 0,0

# System Objects

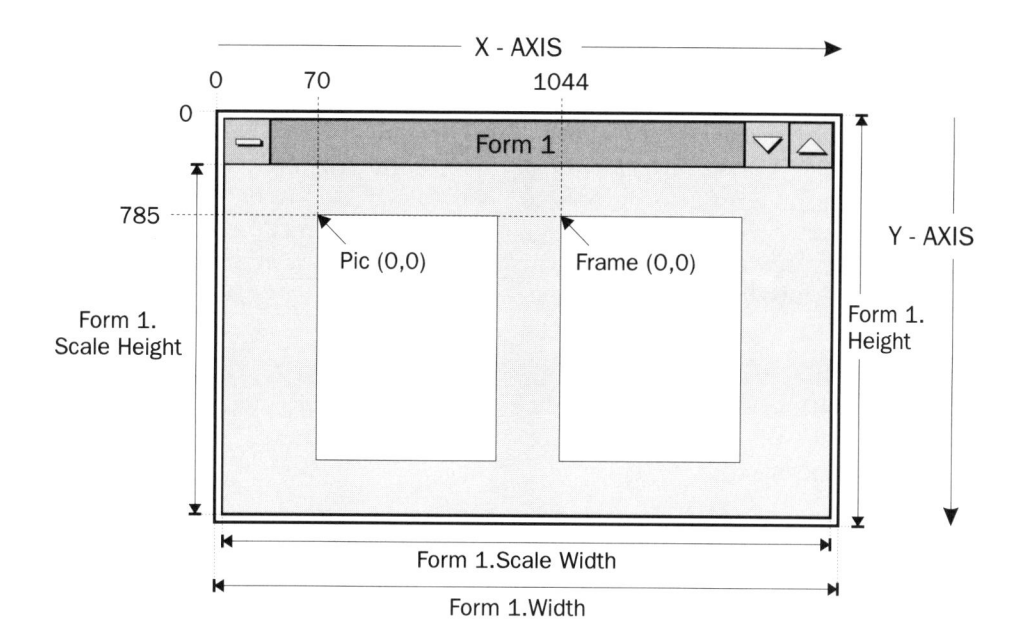

[Diagram: Form 1 showing X-AXIS with values 0, 70, 1044; Y-AXIS with values 0, 785; Pic (0,0) and Frame (0,0) inside Form 1; labels for Form 1. Scale Height, Form 1. Height, Form 1.Scale Width, Form 1.Width]

for drawing graphs, rather than the inconvenient 0,0 at the top left of the screen. Visual Basic will allow you to define your own coordinate system, and we'll see how to create a custom system after we've looked at the measurement systems in Visual Basic.

## Scale Width and Height

There are areas on each control, such as the title bar of a form, that you can't draw to, but these are included in the **Width** and **Height** properties. So how do we determine the size of the area (the **client** area) we can use? It is determined by the **ScaleWidth**, and the **ScaleHeight** properties of the control. So a form's **Width** and **Height** properties will refer to the whole form including the title bar and border (useful for positioning on the screen), whilst its **ScaleWidth** and **ScaleHeight** will refer to the area available for drawing and printing. This is very useful for formatting and centering output, and making sure that it will all fit on the screen or printer.

**207**

## Cursor Positioning

Where on a control your drawing or printing begins is dependent on the position of the cursor. This is independent of the position of the mouse and is invisible, but to layout your graphics correctly you will need to know its position. There are two properties maintained by Visual Basic which hold the location of the cursor, `CurrentX`, and `CurrentY`. The `CurrentX` and `CurrentY` details are only updated when you draw or print, so when the control loads they will be set to the first available position.

> This may not be 0,0 because you can only print or draw within the client area. When the control loads, `CurrentX` and `CurrentY` will be equivalent to a `ScaleWidth` of 0, and a `ScaleHeight` of 0.

You can alter these properties at runtime to allow you to format your display or print.

## Scales and Measurements

Having got to grips with the coordinate systems in Visual Basic we now encounter its scales and measurements. The default scale is `Twips`, which were briefly mentioned in Chapter 4 in our hotspot resize code. A `Twip` is about 1/567th of a centimeter, or 1/1440th of an inch. These are device independent, so a line that you draw in `Twips` will be the same size on a CGA, VGA, or SVGA screen, or on the printer. There are several other scales that you can use, and these can be set for each object using the `ScaleMode` property. Here are the settings:

| Mode | Setting |
|---|---|
| 0 | User-defined. Use this when you want your own coordinate system. |
| 1 | `Twips`. This is the default for all controls. |
| 2 | `Points`. A point is a 1/72nd of an inch. |
| 3 | `Pixels`. The smallest unit of resolution for the screen. A pixel is a single dot on the screen. |

*Continued*

# Custom Coordinates

| Mode | Setting |
|------|---------|
| 4 | **Characters**. A character is 1/6th of an inch high and 1/12th wide. |
| 5 | **Inches**. |
| 6 | **Millimeters**. |
| 7 | **Centimeters**. |

When you change the **ScaleMode** in code, **ScaleWidth** and **ScaleHeight** are reset to reflect the new values. However, anything currently displayed is not affected.

If you change the **ScaleWidth**, **ScaleHeight**, **ScaleTop**, or **ScaleLeft** properties, Visual Basic will assume you are now using your own coordinate system, and set the **ScaleMode** to **0** to reflect this.

## Creating a Custom Coordinate System

To create a useable system, you'll need to consider the scale that you want to use, and the orientation of the coordinate system. Most mathematical calculations use the X-Y Cartesian system, where X measures how much you move across, and Y how much down from the center point.

To create a scale where the screen is 200 units wide, and 200 units high, with the center point at 0,0 we'd need to set the properties to the following:

```
ScaleHeight = 200
ScaleWidth  = 200
ScaleLeft   = -100
ScaleTop    = 100
```

The problem with this is that the Y scale counts up from the top down, so that the center point is actually at **X = 0** and **Y = 200**. To correct this we set the **ScaleHeight** to **-200**. This tells Visual Basic that the top coordinates are higher than the bottom. This also applies for **ScaleWidth**, in that if it's negative then the left-hand coordinates are higher than the right-hand coordinates.

**209**

Visual Basic has a simpler way of setting up a custom scale, with the **Scale** method. This will allow the setting of the top left, and the bottom right coordinates. It will also set the **ScaleWidth andScaleHeight** from the coordinates that you've used. The syntax of this is:

```
{object}.Scale (LeftX, TopY) - (RightX, BottomY)
```

So for the example above, we'd use the following **Scale** method:

```
Scale (-100, 100) - (100, -100)
```

The four corners are now top left (**-100,100**), top right (**100,100**), bottom left (**-100, -100**), and bottom right (**-100, 100**). The center is now at 0,0. Visual Basic will calculate the **ScaleWidth** and **ScaleHeight** for you.

# Simple Animation With Print and Move

Let's look at some of this stuff in action. We're going to use the **Print** method to print details on our form, and control the position with the **CurrentX** and **CurrentY** properties, to provide a simple animation, and then try out another method with **Move**.

# Animation With Print

Start a new project, and set the Form1 properties to: **BackColor** as Black (**&H00000000&**), its name to **frmPrint**, **WindowsState** as **2 - Maximized**, and **BorderStyle** to **0 - None**. This will display a black screen.

Include **Unload frmPrint** in the **DblClick** event procedure for the form (as there will be no buttons on the screen).

Now add the following code to the form's **Click** event.

```
Dim izoom As Integer, iPrvX As Integer, iPrvY As Integer, iWait As Integer
Const cBlack = 0
Const cYellow = 6
```

We've declared the integers and constants that will be used in the code.

```
Cls
```

# Animation

The `Cls` command will clear the screen, and set the cursor to the top left of the screen, (in this case at coordinates `0,0`).

```
frmPrint.FontSize = 6
```

Although the default font of `MS Sans Serif` doesn't get this small, others do, so we've chosen `6` as the initial font size.

```
For izoom = 1 To 12
```

With the combination that we've used, after 12 times through the loop, the string will be at the bottom of the screen. Different fonts, font sizes and screen resolutions will end in different results.

> This can be a problem if your application is to be distributed to different system set ups. Unfortunately there's no quick fix for this, but as a rule, design for the lowest screen resolution, then you can at least guarantee that your application will run on all systems, although the display may not be quite as you intended.

```
iPrvX = frmPrint.CurrentX
iPrvY = frmPrint.CurrentY
```

The first thing that we're doing in the loop is to store the current cursor position.

```
frmPrint.ForeColor = QBColor(cYellow)
frmPrint.Print "Steve Dolan"
```

Next, set the `ForeColor` to yellow, so that we can see what is being printed, and then print the string `"Steve Dolan"` on the form.

```
For iWait = 1 To 10000
    'Just take up processor time
Next iWait
```

This loop is simply to slow the animation down. We're running on a 486DX266, so the number is quite high. Experiment until you get a number that gives a reasonable animation.

## Chapter 8 - Introducing Graphics

> As this is a loop to tie up the processor, in its current state it's very Windows unfriendly. However, we haven't put a `DoEvents` in the loop for two reasons. The first is that generating too many `DoEvents` will also consume resources, and eventually you'll run out of stack space. This could be addressed by only generating a `DoEvents` every 1000 iterations. We'll explain the other reason at the end of the example.

```
frmPrint.CurrentX = iPrvX
frmPrint.CurrentY = iPrvY
```

Now we're setting the cursor position back to what it was prior to the **Print** statement being executed. If you remember, the cursor will move after you've executed a **Print** statement.

```
frmPrint.ForeColor = QBColor(cBlack)
Print "Steve Dolan"
```

The reason we've set it back is so that we can overwrite the yellow **"Steve Dolan"** with a black one. This in effect deletes it, as we now have a black name printed on a black background.

```
frmPrint.FontSize = frmPrint.FontSize + izoom
```

Now make the font size larger, so that the next time we print, the name expands.

```
Next izoom
```

Now loop back, and print the string in yellow again.

```
frmPrint.ForeColor = QBColor(cYellow)
Print "Steve Dolan"
```

At the end, we're printing a final yellow version, because the last print in the loop will have hidden the string.

To run the animation, click anywhere on the screen. To end, double click the screen.

You probably noticed that it ran the animation again. We did this to show you that a double click is actually more than one Windows event; in this case the click, followed by the double click. You need to remember this when you've coded multiple mouse events. The order that the events are triggered is: **MouseDown**, **MouseUp**, **Click** and then **DblClick**.

## Unexpected Results With DoEvents

Try running the project again, with **DoEvents** in the idle loop. Single click on the form, and it works just fine. Now double click on the form. At first it looks like the project has ended without the print being displayed, but if you look at the title bar, the project is still running. You can stop the project by clicking the End button. So what happened?

When you double clicked the form, the **Click** event was triggered. All was proceeding nicely as the loop started. Then a **DoEvent** was triggered, so Windows processed all waiting events. This included the **DblClick** event, which then unloaded the form. The project has not ended because the **Click** event procedure is still running when the form is unloaded. If this was compiled and run as an executable, you wouldn't be able to stop it running until you closed Windows.

## Persistent Graphics

Forms and picture boxes have a property called **AutoRedraw**. By default, this is set to **False**. This means that the graphics that you display are not saved in memory, and if covered by another form will disappear. You will then need to write code to recreate the graphics on the screen, and the **Paint** event is provided for this purpose. It will only be triggered when **AutoRedraw** is **False**.

However, if you set **AutoRedraw** to **True**, your graphics will slow down because Visual Basic is now making a copy in memory as it is drawing onto the screen.

To see the effect of **AutoRedraw**, add another form to the Print Animation project, and call it **frmOver**. Make it quite small, and display it at the end of the **Click** event. Now to end the project, we need to move the **Unload frmPrint** statement from the **DblClick** event of the print form, to the **QueryUnload** event for the new form.

# Chapter 8 - Introducing Graphics

> The `QueryUnload` event is called just before a form unloads. Generally, tidy-up code is placed in this event. In our example, if we don't do this then it's difficult to get the project to end, because of the triggering of the click before the `DblClick` event.

First of all, stick with the **AutoRedraw** as **False**. When you run the project, the string is displayed after the loop, and then the new form is displayed. Now move the form over some of the string, and then move it away. The section covered by the form has disappeared.

## Using the Paint Event

The **Paint** event is triggered when part of the form needs to be redrawn, such as when a form is moved, resized or uncovered by another form being moved. It will only be triggered if the **AutoRedraw** property is set to **False** (when this is **True**, Visual Basic itself handles all the necessary painting). It seems fairly obvious that we need to re-display the string in the **Paint** event, so give it a try.

```
Sub Form_Paint ()
    Const cYellow = 6
    frmPrint.ForeColor = QBColor(cYellow)
    Print "Steve Dolan"
End Sub
```

Now when you run the project, it starts with the string displayed in the top left, because a **Paint** event is triggered when the form is displayed. Click the screen to run the animation, then move the form. The **Paint** event is triggered, and the string is printed, but because we have not reset the cursor, it's not printing in the right place. It's actually printing off the screen, and our graphics are still being erased.

The cure for this is to hold the **CurrentX** and **CurrentY** coordinates at the form level, and then reset them when the **Paint** event is triggered. Add two integers to the (general) declarations section of the print form called **iX** and **iY**. Now change the code after the **Print** loop in the **Click** event of the print form to the following:

```
    . . .
        Next izoom
    iX = frmPrint.CurrentX
```

# AutoRedraw

```
        iY = frmPrint.CurrentY
        frmPrint.ForeColor = QBColor(cYellow)
        Print "Steve Dolan"
        frmOver.Show
End Sub
```

This will save the last print position. Now add these two lines to the start of the **Paint** event code:

```
Const cYellow = 6
    frmPrint.CurrentX = iX
    frmPrint.CurrentY = iY
```

When you re-run the project, you'll find that covering part of the string will not now delete it, because we are re-painting the string when the form is moved. This is the principle behind using the **Paint** event to create persistent graphics. It saves on memory resources, but uses processor resources, especially for complex graphics.

## Setting AutoRedraw

The other method of producing persistent graphics is to set the **AutoRedraw** to **True**. This saves a duplicate of the graphics in memory, so that they can be restored if they are covered and then re-exposed.

We'll try this out, so in **frmPrint**, delete the code in the **Paint** event, set the **AutoRedraw** property to **True**, and see what happens. You'll notice that the effect here is poor. This is because Windows is not getting a chance to repaint the screen between iterations of the loop. Visual Basic is too busy printing into memory to allow any Windows events to run. Even if you remove the **Wait** loop, it still doesn't work. Replace the **Wait** loop with **frmPrint.Refresh**, and the animation will now work. The **Refresh** method causes an immediate repainting of the form, including calling the **Paint** event. Windows itself only repaints the screen during idle time, so there are times when we need to call the refresh ourselves.

> We could have also used the `DoEvents` method to cause Windows to process all the waiting events, including our pending form repaint.

Our animation is really jerky because the system is now doing twice the work it was before, but that's the overhead of using **AutoRedraw**.

**215**

## Clipping

The other property that affects repainting is the `ClipControl` property. This property exists for the form, the picture control and the frame control. It is used to determine the amount of the screen that needs to be repainted, and works in close conjunction with `AutoRedraw`. With `Autoredraw` set to `False`, your application will receive `Paint` events. With `ClipControls` set to `True`, you can redraw any area on the screen, except the **clipping region**, which is placed over non-graphical controls by Visual Basic to stop you drawing over them. With `ClipControls` set to `False`, Visual Basic will only allow you to repaint the areas that it thinks need repainting. Obviously the less that there is to repaint, the faster the repaint operation will be, so setting `ClipControls` to `False` will speed up the display. With `AutoRedraw` set to `True`, and `ClipControls` set to `True`, Visual Basic will repaint the whole form, whereas with `ClipControls` set to `False`, it will only repaint affected areas.

> There are other aspects that affect clipping, autoredraw, and painting, such as layering, but these really fall outside the scope of this book. Layering is covered in the *Programmer's Guide* manual.

Here's a brief summary of the different effects you can get:

| AutoRedraw | ClipControls | Paint Event | Effects |
| --- | --- | --- | --- |
| `True` | `True` | Ignored | Clipping region defined over control. Whole screen repaint. |
| `True` | `False` | Ignored | No clipping regions defined. Only affected areas repainted. |
| `False` (default) | `True` (default) | Triggered | Clipping region defined. Whole repaint. |
| `False` | `False` | Triggered | No clipping region. Only pixels that were covered, or are exposed in a resize are re-drawn. |

# Animation With the Move Method

It's also possible to provide simple animation for controls with the **Move** method, or the **Left** and **Top** properties. Start a new project, and add three option buttons as a control array called **optDirect**, a command button called **cmdExit**, a frame, and an image control within the frame called **inmAnim**. Our form looks like this:

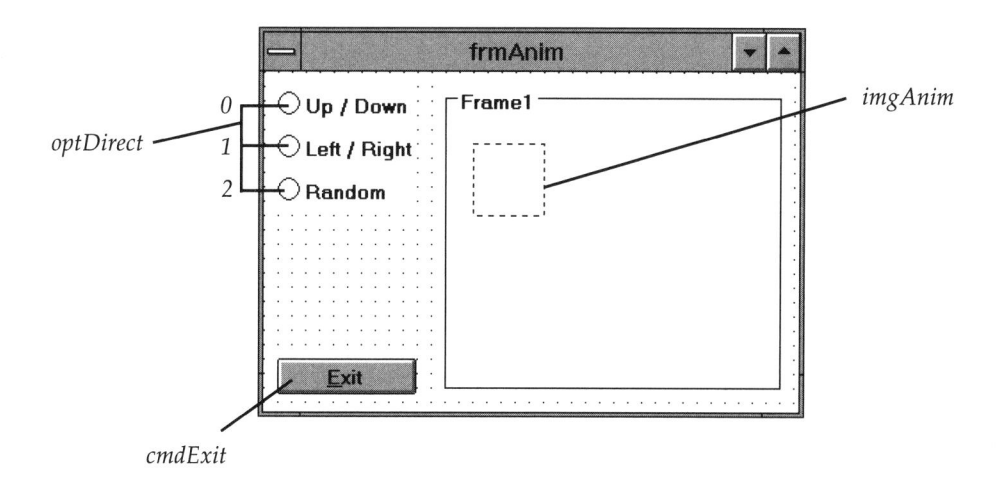

*optDirect*

*cmdExit*

*imgAnim*

The code for the **Exit** command button is as follows:

```
Sub cmdExit_Click ()
    End
End Sub
```

This is the rest of the code is in the option array **optDirect_Click** event:

```
Sub optDirect_Click (index As Integer)
    Dim iMoveAmt As Integer, iMoveTop As Integer
    iMoveAmt = 100
    iMoveTop = 100
```

The two integers are the movement factors.

```
    Select Case index
    Case 0  ' Up/down selected
        Do
```

## Chapter 8 - Introducing Graphics

Here is the code for the up and down option. The **Do**... loop is used to create an infinite loop to keep the animation running.

```
            If imgAnim.Top < 104 Then
                DoEvents
                iMoveAmt = 50
                imgAnim.Picture =
LoadPicture("C:\vb\icons\traffic\trffc03.ico")
            End If
```

If the image is at the top of the form, carry out **DoEvents**, otherwise nothing else will run because of our infinite loop. Set the movement factor to positive so that the movement is down the screen, and change the picture to a down arrow.

```
            If imgAnim.Top > 4605 Then
                DoEvents
                iMoveAmt = -50
                imgAnim.Picture =
LoadPicture("C:\vb\icons\traffic\trffc01.ico")
            End If
```

If we're at the bottom of the screen then use **DoEvents**, change the movement factor, and load the up arrow picture.

```
            imgAnim.Visible = False
            imgAnim.Top = imgAnim.Top + iMoveAmt
            imgAnim.Visible = True
```

Hide the image, move it and re-display it. This helps reduce flicker, but the animation will still have some flicker on it.

```
            frmAnim.Refresh
        Loop
```

Call the **Refresh** method so that the screen is repainted. Try it without this and see what happens. Finally, loop back.

```
        Case 1   'Left/Right selected
            Do
```

If **Left/Right** is clicked, then we change the movement to an infinite left/right loop.

# The Move Method

```
            If imgAnim.Left < 50 Then
                DoEvents
                iMoveAmt = 50
                imgAnim.Picture =
LoadPicture("C:\vb\icons\traffic\trffc02.ico")
            End If
            If imgAnim.Left > 6500 Then
                DoEvents
                iMoveAmt = -50
                imgAnim.Picture =
LoadPicture("C:\vb\icons\traffic\trffc04.ico")
            End If
            imgAnim.Visible = False
            imgAnim.Left = imgAnim.Left + iMoveAmt
            imgAnim.Visible = True
            frmAnim.Refresh
        Loop
```

All the code here is the same as the top/bottom loop except it changes the **Left** property.

```
    Case 2 'Random selected
        imgAnim.Picture = LoadPicture("C:\vb\icons\traffic\trffc06.ico")
        Do
```

If the **Random** movement is selected, then we set up an infinite loop with the image moving diagonally. This uses the **Move** method for a control, so we need to set the **Left** and the **Top** of the image. Here we're only loading one icon, at the start of the animation.

```
            If imgAnim.Left < 50 Then
                iMoveAmt = 50
                DoEvents
            End If
            If imgAnim.Left > 6500 Then
                iMoveAmt = -50
                DoEvents
            End If
            If imgAnim.Top < 104 Then
                iMoveTop = 50
                DoEvents
            End If
            If imgAnim.Top > 4605 Then
                iMoveTop = -50
                DoEvents
            End If
```

These **If** statements check to see if the icon has reached the edge of the frame. If it has, then the relevant movement factor is altered, and a **DoEvents** is executed.

```
            imgAnim.Visible = False
            imgAnim.Move imgAnim.Left + iMoveAmt, imgAnim.Top + iMoveTop
            imgAnim.Visible = True
            frmAnim.Refresh
        Loop
    End Select
End Sub
```

Next the icon is hidden, and moved, using the **Move** method, before being redisplayed. The screen is then refreshed before looping.

The **Move** method parameters are **Left**, then **Top**, **Width** and **Height**. Only **Left** is mandatory, all the other parameters are optional.

# Lines and Shapes

These two controls are pretty simple to use, but fairly limited. The line control allows you to draw a line in a form at design time, and the shape control allows you to draw a shape. There are also methods that let you draw lines and shapes at runtime.

## The Line and Shape Controls

The best way to learn about these controls is to use them, so start a new project, and draw a line and a shape control on it. Our form looks like this:

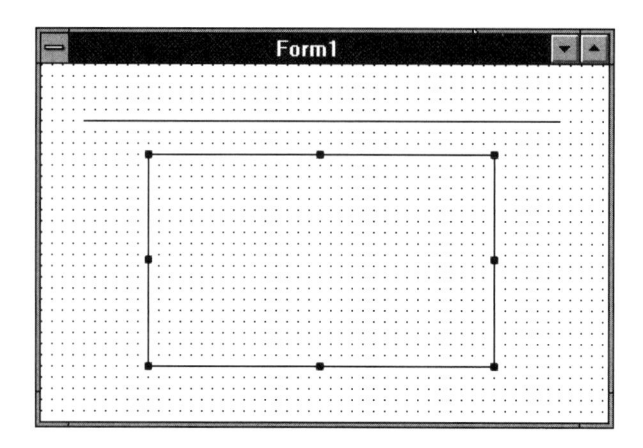

# Lines and Shapes

Now run the project and you'll see a rectangle and a line displayed. These controls are useful for grouping or separating details on a screen, to make it easier to understand.

> If you don't need the facilities and functions which a frame can give you (for example if you just want to group some controls visually), then use the shape control, as it uses less resources.

There are several pre-defined shapes available, and these can be altered by setting the **Shape** property. **0** is a rectangle (the default), **1** is a square, **2** is an oval, **3** is a circle, **4** is a rectangle with rounded corners, and **5** is a square with rounded corners.

You can also use the line to produce 3D effects, but this is very time-consuming. In the next screenshot, we've drawn two rectangles, then two white lines which we've placed just inside the top, and left of the inner rectangle. Then we've placed two black lines just outside the bottom and right hand of the inner rectangle. To do this, we had to switch off the Align to Grid option in the Options, Environment... menu. You could also use the **Top** and **Left** properties of the lines to place them where required. This is sometimes easier than trying to line them up exactly with the mouse.

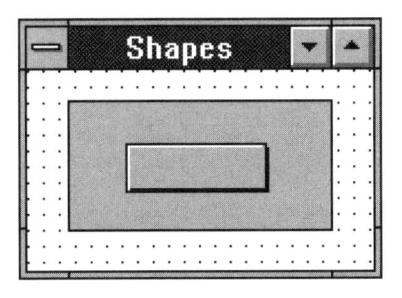

There are no events associated with the line and shape controls, so our nice 3D rectangle can't actually do anything, but we can simulate a 3D button with the form mouse **Down** and **Up** events. This is a very resource-friendly method, and you may need to do this in large, complex applications.

To make it work, we need to determine the location of the mouse pointer when the mouse button is pressed. Fortunately the location is passed as part of the event. To determine the button region you can use its **Top**, **Left**,

**221**

## Chapter 8 - Introducing Graphics

`Height` and `Width` properties. Ours are `Top = 480`, `Left = 660`, `Height = 330`, and `Width = 960`. So for the user to click our button we need the following code in the form `MouseDown` event:

```
Sub Form_MouseDown (Button As Integer, Shift As Integer, x As Single, y As Single)
    If (x > 660 And x < 1620) And (y > 480 And y < 810) Then
```

We're using the `x` and `y` coordinates passed by Visual Basic to check that the mouse pointer is over our button.

```
        linLeft.Visible = False
        linTop.Visible = False
        linRight.Visible = False
        linBottom.Visible = False
```

Next we're hiding the lines, so that it looks like the button has been pressed.

```
    End If
End Sub
```

In the `MouseUp` event, we have written the following code:

```
Sub Form_MouseUp (Button As Integer, Shift As Integer, x As Single, y As Single)
    If (x > 660 And x < 1620) And (y > 480 And y < 810) Then
        linLeft.Visible = True
        linTop.Visible = True
        linRight.Visible = True
        linBottom.Visible = True
```

This is the opposite of the `MouseDown` code, and restores the lines to let the button pop up.

```
        'Put your click event code here
        MsgBox "You've simulated a 3D Command Button!!"
        Unload frmShape
```

Next comes the code that you'd normally write in the `Click` event, which in this case is a message box. We then end the application.

```
    End If
End Sub
```

222

# Screensaver Program

## Graphics: Implementation

With the graphics methods, you can draw lines, shapes, and set individual pixels on the screen. These methods can be used to draw graphs and charts, and produce some stunning effects with very little code.

> A brief word of warning. If you want to display graphics you have drawn using the graphics methods when the form loads, use the `Paint` event. This is because the form is not displayed until the end of the `Form_Load` event, so the graphics methods are ignored. Also, by default the graphics that you produce with the graphics method are not persistent (`AutoRedraw` won't save these graphics to memory), so form resizing and task switching will erase your graphics unless you take steps to re-create them.

You can use the graphics methods with a form, picture box, and the printer object. To tell Visual Basic which to use, prefix the method with the object name, (in the case of the printer object, it's printer!). The default is the form on which the code is attached.

## Drawing at the Pixel Level

To set a pixel, the **Pset** method is used. It's really easy to use - start a new project and type the following code into the **Click** event:

```
Dim iX As Integer, iY As Integer
    For iX = 300 To 20000 Step 100
        For iY = 500 To 1500 Step 500
            PSet (iX, iY)
        Next iY
    Next iX
```

The nested **For** loops are being used to determine the **X** and the **Y** coordinates in **Twips** for the pixels that are being set by the **Pset** command. This loop actually draws three dotted lines across the screen. We do have the option to also specify the color we want the pixel to be, after the coordinates. The color can be specified by using the `QBColor()` function that we've encountered before, or the `RGB()` function that's covered later in the chapter. For example, to make the pixels yellow in the above example you'd use:

```
PSet (iX, iY), QBColor(6)
```

Let's try something a little more complex with `Pset`. This program is similar to the star screen saver, and does much the same thing. You could adapt it with a timer event to use it as a screen saver yourself. Start a new project, and set the Form1 properties to `BackColor` as Black, `WindowState` as `2 - Maximized`, and `BorderStyle` to `0 - None`.

What we're going to do is create a moving star field, with the star movements as a sub procedure. Add the following code to the (general) declarations section of the form:

```
Option Explicit
    Dim iCount As Integer
    Dim iCurX(150) As Integer, iCurY(150) As Integer
    Const cBlack = &H0&
    Const cWhite = &HFFFFFF&
```

There are **150** stars in our starfield, so we've created two arrays of 150 elements to hold the **x** and **y** coordinates of each star. The more stars that you have, the slower the animation will be, so if it's too slow on your machine, adjust the number of stars accordingly.

```
Sub Form_Click ()
    Scale (0, 0)-(200, 200)
```

In the `Form_Click` event we're setting up our own screen scale. This is so that the stars move a reasonable distance each time. The top left of the screen is **0,0**, and the bottom right is **200, 200**.

```
    Randomize
    Cls
```

Seed the random number generator, then clear the screen.

```
    For iCount = 0 To 149
        iCurX(iCount) = Int((200 * Rnd) + 1)
        iCurY(iCount) = Int((200 * Rnd) + 1)
        PSet (iCurX(iCount), iCurY(iCount)), cWhite
    Next iCount
```

# Seeing Stars

Now place the 150 stars on the screen in random positions, within the bounds of the form.

```
    Do
        ShowStars
    Loop
End Sub
```

Finally, there is an indefinite loop that calls the **ShowStars()** sub procedure, to move each star along its x,y axis. Next, create the sub procedure **ShowStars()**, and enter the following code:

```
Sub ShowStars ()
    DoEvents
```

Because we're tying the whole machine up with indefinite loops and procedure calls, **DoEvents** will ensure that the system doesn't grind to a halt.

```
    For iCount = 0 To 149
```

Next, move each star in turn. If you have less stars, adjust the loop.

```
        PSet (iCurX(iCount), iCurY(iCount)), cBlack
```

Firstly, remove the star by setting the pixel back to black.

```
        If iCurX(iCount) < 100 Then
            iCurX(iCount) = iCurX(iCount) - 1
        Else
            iCurX(iCount) = iCurX(iCount) + 1
        End If
```

Because we want the stars to move out from the center of the screen, we need to determine whether to add 1 to the x coordinate, or subtract 1 (100 is the halfway point along the x axis).

```
        If iCurY(iCount) < 100 Then
            iCurY(iCount) = iCurY(iCount) - 1
        Else
            iCurY(iCount) = iCurY(iCount) + 1
        End If
```

Then do the same for the y-axis.

# Chapter 8 - Introducing Graphics

```
        If iCurX(iCount) < 0 Or iCurX(iCount) > 200 Then iCurX(iCount) =
    Int((200 * Rnd) + 50)
```

This line checks if the star has reached the edge of the screen. If it has, generate a new star in a random position (loaded toward the center section of the screen).

```
        If iCurY(iCount) < 0 Or iCurY(iCount) > 200 Then iCurY(iCount) =
    Int((200 * Rnd) + 50)
```

Then do exactly the same for the y-axis.

```
        PSet (iCurX(iCount), iCurY(iCount)), cWhite
    Next iCount
End Sub
```

Finally, display the star in its new position, and loop to the next star. Because the loop that controls the display is indefinite, it won't end, so we need a way to stop the application. The `MouseDown` event is ideal for this, by checking for a right mouse click:

```
Sub Form_MouseDown (button As Integer, Shift As Integer, X As Single, Y
    As Single)
    If button = 2 Then
        Unload frmStar
        End
    End If
End Sub
```

If the right button is pressed, unload the form, then end the program. The `End` statement ends the program, destroys any forms, and any variables.

## Using the Line Method

Although you can draw lines using `Pset`, it's much easier to use the line method. To draw a line we need to specify the start x and y coordinates, and the end x and y coordinates. As with `Pset`, we can also specify a color code. Start a new project and set the Form1 properties to `BackColor` as White, `WindowState` as `2 - Maximized`, and `BorderStyle` to `0 - None`. Now add the following code to the `Click` event:

```
Sub Form_Click ()
    Dim iCount As Integer, iX As Integer, iY As Integer
    Dim iRed As Integer, iGreen As Integer, iBlue As Integer
```

# The Line Method

```
Scale (0, 0)-(200, 200)
Randomize
Cls
```

For this project, we're using the same custom scale that we did in the previous project, seeding the random number generator, then clearing the screen.

```
For iCount = 1 To 20000
    iX = Int((200 * Rnd) + 1)
    iY = Int((200 * Rnd) + 1)
```

The loop will run 20,000 times, producing 20,000 lines on the screen. Don't worry - the effect looks really good! Next set the **x** and **y** coordinates to a random number within our custom scale.

```
iRed = Int(255 * Rnd)
iGreen = Int(255 * Rnd)
iBlue = Int(255 * Rnd)
```

This batch of random numbers will result in a random color. We'll look at this in more detail later.

```
    Line (100, 100)-(iX, iY), RGB(iRed, iGreen, iBlue)
Next iCount
Unload frmLines
End Sub
```

The last section of code displays a line, starting at the screen center, and going to the random **x** and **y** coordinates. The color is a random mix of red, green and blue. Having drawn the line, loop round to draw the next. (When the loop ends, so does the program, because we are unloading the form.) Now run the program. It's surprising what effects you can get with a little code!

There are a couple of other things that you can do with the **Line** method. If you do not specify a set of start coordinates, Visual Basic will draw the line from the current cursor position. Try taking out the start coordinates from the line project above. Visual Basic will now draw a single continuous line, which has the effect of creating a very colorful spider's web!

There are times when you may want to specify a starting point for a line, but specify offsets for the end points. This can be achieved with the **Step** keyword. For instance, the following both achieve the same result:

**227**

## Chapter 8 - Introducing Graphics

```
Line (100, 100) - (150, 150)
Line (100, 100) - Step(50, 50)
```

The following code snippet will draw a line one **Twip** at a time from the current cursor position:

```
Sub Form_Click ()
    Dim iCount As Integer
    For iCount = 1 To 3000
        Line -Step(1, 1)
    Next iCount
End Sub
```

You can also have negative offsets. For instance:

```
Line -Step(-1, -1)
```

Less usefully, you can specify offsets for the start of the line. In this case, the line will start from the current cursor position moved by your offset, and move to the end point, or the offset you've specified. This also uses the **Step** keyword. For example:

```
Line Step(10, -5) - Step(-20, 48)
```

This will start a line at the current **x** position plus 10, and current **y** position offset by minus 5, then draw it using the end point offsets.

### Boxes With the Line Method

You can draw a box with four line statements by leaving off the start coordinates, but this is not the best method. There are two further optional parameters that can be used with the **Line** method. To draw a box, add a '**B**' after the color parameter.

If you don't want to specify a color, then you'll still need a comma, otherwise Visual Basic will think that the color is held in a variable called **B**. The start coordinates are the top left of the box, and the end coordinates are the bottom right of your box. Start a new project, with a maximized form. Now add the code below to the **Click** event for the form:

```
Sub Form_Click ()
    Dim iCount As Integer
    For iCount = 1 To 15
        Line -Step(500, 500), QBColor(iCount), B
    Next iCount
End Sub
```

# Circles and Arcs

This code will produce a row of fifteen boxes down the screen. Each box is a different color, as specified by the **QBColor()** function, and is 500 by 500 **Twips**. The last parameter that we can add to the **Line** method is **F**. This tells Visual Basic to fill the boxes that we've drawn. To try it out, add an **F** to the **Line** statement. You'll now have fifteen filled color boxes down the screen. (Actually, there's fourteen because the last box is white.)

## Drawing Circles and Arcs

You can draw circles and arcs using the **Circle** method. This method is a little more complex than the others, especially if you want to draw arcs. Most of the trigonometric functions in Visual Basic are measured in *radians*, and the circle method is no exception. If you remember your school math, radians are calculated with this formula:

```
No. of Degrees * Pi divided by 180 (Pi is approximately 3.1415926 or 22/7).
```

We'll be using this later when we draw arcs, but for now we'll try out a few circles. To draw a circle, you specify its center point with **x** and **y** coordinates, then the radius of the circle where the radius is measured horizontally from the center to the right hand edge. Here are some examples:

```
Circle (1500, 1500), 1000
Circle (1500, 1500), 1500, QBColor(10)
```

The first example draws a circle from an **x** position of **1500** and **y** position of **1500** with a radius of **1000**. The second example is similar, but with a color of light green.

As with the **Line** method, you can specify the center of the circle as an offset with the **Step** keyword. Start a new project, and add this code to the **Click** event:

```
Sub Form_Click ()
    Dim iCount As Integer
    For iCount = 1 To 15
        Circle Step(500, 500), 500, QBColor(iCount)
    Next iCount
End Sub
```

This code does exactly the same as the box code in the previous example, producing a series of colored circles down the screen.

**229**

# Chapter 8 - Introducing Graphics

You may not wish to produce perfect circles, but ellipses. There is an argument called **Aspect** that is a single precision number specifying the ratio of vertical to horizontal dimensions. Replace the **Circle** statement in our example with this one, and give it a try:

```
Circle Step(500, 500), 500, QBColor(iCount), , , 1 / iCount
```

Here we're reducing the height of the circle, squashing it with each iteration of the loop. To reduce the width, invert the ratio, (take off the **1/**) so that it gets compressed with each loop.

## Arcs

You'll notice that there are a couple of arguments that were not specified in the previous example. These are used to produce arcs, and specify the start and end of the arc in radians. This is drawn in an anti-clockwise direction, so 0 radians is at 3 o'clock, and goes up so that 12 o'clock would be 90*Pi/180 radians. To illustrate this, start a new project, and we'll draw the above arc with the statement:

```
Const cPi = 3.1415926
Circle (1500, 1500), 750, , 0, 90 * cPi / 180
```

You'll see an arc drawn from 3 to 12 o'clock. An added feature is that if you make the start or the end angles negative, then Visual Basic will draw a line to the center of the circle. Try it out. You'll see a line drawn from the top, but not from the right. This is because 0 is a positive number - you can't have minus zero. Replace the **0** with **-360*cPi /180**, which is the same point on the arc. It'll now work fine.

To draw the inverse of this segment, reverse the start and end angles so that our circle statement is now this:

```
Circle (1500, 1500), 750, , -90 * cPi / 180, -360 * cPi / 180
```

To cut a piece out of our circle, add back the previous **Circle** statement, but move the center slightly so that it stands out:

```
Circle (1550, 1450), 750, , -360 * cPi / 180, -90 * cPi / 180
```

# Arcs

## Filling, Drawing and Coloring In

You can see how the above example could be extended to produce pie charts, but they're pretty bland at the moment. What they need is filling in. There are several properties that take care of this: the **FillStyle** property, and the **FillColor** property to control how and what color an object is filled, and the **DrawWidth** and **DrawMode** properties. To fill our two segments with color we would use a **FillStyle** of **0** for solid, and set the **FillColor** to the same as the outline. The code in our **Click** event now looks like this:

```
Const cPi = 3.1415926
FrmArc.FillStyle = 0 'Set the fill style to solid
FrmArc.FillColor = QBColor(3) 'Set the color
Circle (1500, 1500), 750, QBColor(3), -90 * cPi / 180, -360 * cPi / 180
FrmArc.FillColor = QBColor(5)  'set the color for the other segment
Circle (1550, 1450), 750, QBColor(5), -360 * cPi / 180, -90 * cPi / 180
```

This will produce two filled in segments. To look at the other **FillStyles**, reload the Box project we did earlier, and in the **Click** event alter the code to the following:

```
Dim iCount As Integer
    For iCount = 1 To 15
        If iCount < 9 Then
          frmBox.FillStyle = iCount - 1 'Go through each style
        Else
          frmBox.FillStyle = iCount - 8 'start again
        End If
        frmBox.FillColor = QBColor(iCount)
        Line -Step(500, 500), QBColor(iCount), B
    Next iCount
```

Here, we're cycling through each different **FillStyle**, and you can see the different effects. If you add the **F** to the end of your **Line** statement, this overrides the **FillStyle**, and all your boxes will be solid.

To see the effect of the different **BorderStyles**, remove the **Color** section from the **Line** command, and add the following statement before the **Line** command:

```
If icount < 8 Then frmBox.DrawStyle = icount - 1
```

This will cycle through the different **DrawStyles**. Now to expand the size of the outline, add **frmBox.DrawWidth = iCount** to the code before you draw the line.

## DrawMode Property

We've left the `DrawMode` property until last, because it's more complicated. These properties affect the way that your graphics are drawn, by changing the attributes of the pen and how the object your drawing interacts with what's already there. This moves beyond the scope of this book - you can look it up in the *Language Reference*, or in the Help file. We will mention the most common settings now:

| Setting | Name | Effect |
| --- | --- | --- |
| 4 | Not Copy | Inverts the current line pattern, regardless of the background. The pattern is the current `FillStyle`. |
| 7 | Xor | Allows you to draw an object over a background, then when you re-draw the object, the background is restored. Useful for animation. |
| 11 | Nop | No operation. Turns drawing off. |
| 13 | Copy | This is the default, and applies the object, no matter what's in the background. |

# How Colors Work in Visual Basic

During this book, we've encountered three different methods of specifying a color. There are the two functions, `QBColor()` and `RGB()`, and the specifying of a hexadecimal number. We'll look at each in turn below.

## Color Specification with QBColor

The easiest to understand is the `QBColor()` function which we've used quite extensively in this chapter. This function is a carry over from Quick Basic, and has a range of sixteen colors from **0** to **15**. The only parameter is a number that corresponds to the color that you want to use. Go back through some of the exercises to determine exactly what the colors are. If you want to use a more detailed pallet or different hues, then you'll need to use one of the other two methods.

# Colors

## The RGB Function

The `RGB()` function mixes different levels of color for the three primary colors to produce the required color. The exact amount of color to mix is a number between `0` and `255` for red, green and blue. The two extremes are black (which is the absence of any color), and white (which is a mix of all the colors). The specification for these two colors using the `RGB()` function is therefore `RGB(0, 0, 0)` for black, and `RGB(255, 255, 255)` for white.

If you look back at the first example we used to demonstrate lines with the multicolor lines, then you'll see that we used random amounts of red, green and blue to produce our colored lines. We'll look at how different levels of red, green and blue produce color. Start a new project, and add three horizontal scroll bars, six labels, and a picture box to the form. The scroll bars **Max** property has been set to `255`, and they have been set up as a control array, as well as the right hand labels. Our form now looks like this:

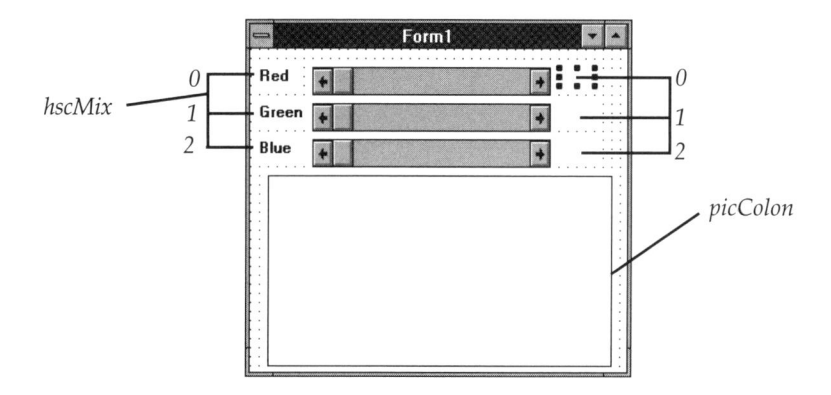

The only code you need are these two lines in the scroll bar array **Change** event:

```
Sub hscMix_Change (index As Integer)
    lblAmt(index).Caption = hscMix(index).Value
    picColor.BackColor = RGB(hscMix(0), hscMix(1), hscMix(2))
End Sub
```

As the scroll bars are moved, their value changes, and the **Change** event is triggered which displays the new color mix by setting the **BackColor** of the picture box with the `RGB()` function.

**233**

# Chapter 8 - Introducing Graphics

Basically, the scroll bar controls are used as graphical input devices. You specify the **Max** and **Min** values in the properties, and the user can input new values by using the arrows to scroll along the bar, or by clicking the scroll bar itself. The actual values that the scroll bars change by are controlled by the **SmallChange** and **LargeChange** properties. The **SmallChange** property is linked to the scroll bar arrows, and the **LargeChange** to clicking on the scroll bar itself. The default for both properties is **1**, so you'll get the full range in the example. Try changing these properties, such as **15** for **LargeChange**, and see the effect.

## Specifying Hex Values

If you want to use Visual Basic colors directly, then you'll need to use the hex equivalents of the red, green, and blue values. These are **0** - **FF**. Just to confuse you, Visual Basic expects the colors in reverse, so to specify full blue only you would use **&HFF0000**. The **&H** tells Visual Basic that the number is a hexadecimal number, then the first two digits are the amount of blue, the next two are the amount of green, and the last two the amount of red. Black is **&H00**, and the other extreme, white, is **&HFFFFFF**. You should now be able to make some more sense of the color values in the Properties window.

# Summary

In this chapter we were introduced to the five system objects. You then learnt about how the coordinate system in Visual Basic works, and the different measurements that can be used. You saw how to create your own custom coordinates and scales, and some of the reasons why you'll want to do this.

We looked at some of the effects of using clipping and **AutoRedraw**, both on the screen and on performance.

You learnt about the line and shape controls before moving on to the graphics methods for drawing lines, circles and ellipses, as well as setting individual pixels. On the way through this chapter we tried out several simple bits of animation, before finishing with a look at the way Visual Basic handles colors.

# Summary and Exercises

This is by no means an extensive look at the graphic facilities, but we hope that you've learnt enough to try out some of the combinations of properties to produce unusual effects, especially **Xor** animation.

This has been a very fast paced chapter, covering a lot of ground, so see how you get on with the exercises.

## Exercises

**1** Using the Name animation, try out some different fonts to see the effect. See if you can stop the name going off the screen.

**Hint: use** `ScaleHeight` **properties**

**2** Still with the Name animation, at the end flash the name five times before ending the program.

**3** While the Name animation is running, you don't actually need **AutoRedraw** as **True**. See if you can create speedy, but persistent graphics.

**4** In the Lines project, make the line display a function in a similar manner to the stars project so that it will run indefinitely, but stop on a mouse click.

**5** Using the **Circle** method, see if you can produce a bouncing ball animation. As the ball bounces, it'll squash, so you'll need to use an ellipse or two.

**235**

INSTANT
INSTANT
INSTANT
INSTANT
INSTANT
INSTANT
INSTANT
INSTANT
INSTANT

# Chapter 9

# Input and Output

So far, we've manipulated data of all types, but have yet to save any of it to disk. In reality, this is the main reason for an application. Data is read in, manipulated in some manner, then saved. Visual Basic provides two ways of saving data, and the next two chapters will cover each of them. In this chapter we are going to look at how to use the Visual Basic file system, and the different types of files that can be manipulated with Visual Basic. We'll save databases for the next chapter.

Although databases can be great for storing and retrieving structured information, and lots of it, there are times when they are not appropriate. For example, you may want to write the next ground breaking wordprocessor or spreadsheet application. Your users are going to expect to be able to store their data on their hard disks, and embedding it inside an Access database does not fit the bill, so you'll need to use files.

In this chapter we'll cover:

- File handling
- File types
- Printing
- The printer object

# Chapter 9 - Input and Output

## File Handling: Concepts

Visual Basic provides you with the necessary methods and controls to create and manipulate files of information. You could use a random access file to create your own custom database format where the user can jump around from record to record. On the other hand, you may just want to create a sequential file of information, a file where your program expects to have to read the whole file in, starting at the beginning of the file and working through to the end (a wordprocessor document, or a temporary file, for example).

The other side of input and output is printing. No matter what application you are developing, it's more than likely that, at some point or another, you'll be asked to produce reports from the data that you've created and manipulated. Visual Basic comes complete with two built in methods for printing, as well as support for the printer common dialog which we'll be covering later in this chapter.

## The Three Visual Basic File Types

In terms of reading and writing information to files, Visual Basic supports three file types: random access, binary access and sequential access. We'll be looking in detail at sequential and random access here since they represent the most common application needs, but first we'll just mention binary access files.

## Binary Access Files

**Binary access** does have some advantages over the other two (for instance, the ability to create variable length records in a flat file) but is in fact very rarely used in these days of Access databases and such like. This type of file is generally only used now where you need to access binary data, such as the details of a `GIF` (Graphic Interchange Format), or `PCX` file. Obviously, to be able to do this you'll need to understand the format of these files.

To use a binary file, you'll need to know exactly what has been written in every byte of every record, so that the information is retrieved in the correct format. For instance, if you retrieve data at byte 56 as an integer,

# File Handling

Visual Basic will take bytes 56 and 57 to be an integer even if you've saved them as a string, and this can lead to unexpected results. If you wish to investigate binary files further, then they are covered in the *Programmers Guide*, Chapter 19.

## Sequential and Random File Access

For the rest of this section we are going to look at the two most commonly used access methods: **random** and **sequential**. Despite the rather daunting names, the difference between the two is really quite easy to grasp. A random access file is one which contains data broken down into a number of pre-defined fixed length blocks of data. You can use Visual Basic methods to jump from record to record in any order you want - since Visual Basic doesn't know the order in which you intend to get to the records, it considers the order random and access is achieved by using a **unique key**.

With sequential files you tend to `Read` and `Write` data in them, starting at the beginning of the file and working your way through to the end. For example, think about storing a wordprocessor document on the disk. There really is no point in being able simply to update the middle section of the document file whenever a change is made. Most wordprocessors work by saving the whole document, starting at the top and finishing at the bottom.

If you have never come across sequential and random access files before, then an easier way to think of them is to draw an analogy to CDs and tapes. CDs are like random access files with each track on the CD representing a record in the file. You can jump to any particular track you want whenever you want, and with most CD players you are able to set up a list of tracks that you want played, which may not be the order that they are actually stored on the CD. Sequential files are like tapes. You have very little choice but to put the tape into the machine and play it from its current point forwards. Sure, most tapes allow you to rewind or fast forward to a specific point but the process is hardly speedy. Also, if you'd never seen either a tape player or CD player, tapes are far easier to understand and use. The same applies to Visual Basic: sequential files are far less powerful in use than random files, but they are somewhat easier to code.

# Chapter 9 - Input and Output

## Sequential Files

Whether you are dealing with random access files or sequential files, the steps required to manipulate them remains the same:

**1** `Open` the file, telling Visual Basic what kind of file it is and its unique number

**2** `Read` or `Write` the information in the file

**3** `Close` the file

The difference between the two file formats comes in the `Read`/`Write` part of the operation. In this section we're going to look at the easier of the two, sequential file access.

To open a file you use the `Open` command, followed by the file name, the access type and the unique file number. The syntax is:

```
Open <filename> For <access type> As <filenumber>
```

The filename bit should take very little explaining - its simply the path and name of the file that you want to open enclosed in quotation marks.

As in DOS, the case of the letters in the filename is irrelevant. The `<access type>` part of the command tells Visual Basic what you intend to do to the file. When dealing with sequential files, there are only three access types, as shown in the table below.

| Access Type | Description |
| --- | --- |
| `Input` | Tells Visual Basic that you intend to just read information from the file. |
| `Output` | Tells Visual Basic that you intend to just write information out to a NEW file. |
| `Append` | Tells Visual Basic that you intend to add information onto an existing file. |

# Sequential Files

With the `Input` access type the file that you are reading from must exist. If it doesn't then you get a runtime error which you can catch with the `OnError` method (the error number is 53 - File not found). When using files in applications, we would recommend that you have an error handler that will handle all the likely errors. This is explained fully in Chapter 11, where we develop a file error handler. However, for most of the examples in this chapter we're not going to develop error handlers.

> With the `Output` and `Append` types, if the filename specified doesn't already exist then a new one will be created. If the file does already exist and you use the `Output` type then Visual Basic will delete the file and overwrite it with any new information you `Write` out. This is an important point - `Output` will always create a new file and should not be confused with `Append`.

The `Append` type will also create a new file, if one doesn't already exist. However, if the file specified does currently exist then `Append` will let you add information to the end of it.

> These access types highlight one of the main problems with sequential files. There is no obvious way to overwrite information in only a part of the file. Sequential files are really supposed to be read and written in their entirety.

The `<filenumber>` part of the `Open` command is necessary because in Visual Basic you can have a number of files open at any one time. You need a way to tell Visual Basic which files to use and that is where the `<filenumber>` comes in.

You don't have to worry about working out and keeping track of unique file numbers for yourself. The `FreeFile()` function returns a unique file number which you can then use in the `Open` command.

**241**

# Chapter 9 - Input and Output

> A word of warning. Make sure that for each file you intend to open you create a file number variable for it, otherwise you will be using the wrong file numbers for your files. For instance, if you have three files that you want to use, create three integers that will hold the unique file numbers for each file returned from `FreeFile`. If you use meaningful names, you're unlikely to use the wrong file numbers and corrupt all your data.

Let's look at an example of opening the **AUTOEXEC.BAT** file for sequential input:

```
Dim iFileNumber As Integer

iFileNumber = FreeFile
Open "c:\autoexec.bat" For Input As iFileNumber
            :           'Code to look at the data in Autoexec.bat
            :
            :
Close iFileNumber
```

As you can see, prior to opening the file we call the `FreeFile()` function to allocate a unique number for the file, then use it in the `Open` command. This is the usual way of doing things since the `Open` command expects you to use either a number or a variable for the filenumber.

```
Open "c:\autoexec.bat" For Input As FreeFile          ' This is bad
```

It's not advisable to open a file like this because we have no idea of the number allocated by the `FreeFile()` function, so we can't use the file number for subsequent methods such as `Close` (which is as simple as typing `Close` followed by the file number).

Now we know how to open and close a sequential file, we need to find out how to read and write the data. Visual Basic provides us with a set of new methods for reading and writing data, some of which will appear quite familiar.

# Reading and Writing Data

| Method | Description |
| --- | --- |
| `Input$` | Lets you read in a specific number of characters from the file into a variable. |
| `Input#` | Reads a list of values into a list of variables. Each value in the file is separated by either spaces or commas. |
| `Line Input#` | Reads all characters from your current position in a file, up to the first carriage return, into a string variable. |
| `Print#` | Works in the same way as `Print`, allowing you to dump strings to a file, instead of to a form or control. |
| `Write#` | Writes a list of variables out to a file, separating them with commas. |

It's time to try an example in which we'll be reading information from the **AUTOEXEC.BAT** file, so start a new project in Visual Basic, and in the **Form_Load** event enter the following code:

```
Sub Form_Load ()

    Dim iAutoNumber As Integer, sInputData As String
```

The integer will hold out unique file number, and the string will hold the data input from the file.

```
    frmAuto.WindowState = 2
    frmAuto.Show
    iAutoNumber = FreeFile
```

Here we show the form in a maximized state, and allocate the unique file number. We are going to print the details on the form as you saw in Chapter 8. The print details will not be persistent unless you set **AutoRedraw** to **True** for the form.

```
    Open "c:\autoexec.bat" For Input As iAutoNumber
```

243

## Chapter 9 - Input and Output

Next we open the file for input, using the unique number.

```
Do While Not EOF(iAutoNumber)
```

All files have a start (the beginning of the file or **BOF**) and an end (the **EOF**). The **EOF()** function lets you test whether or not the end of the file specified by the file number has been reached. If it has then the result of the function is **True**, otherwise it is **False**. The **Do**... loop is set up to run for as long as the **EOF** of the file is not reached.

```
Line Input #iAutoNumber, sInputData
```

The **Line Input#** method is used to read the lines from the **AUTOEXEC** file into **sInputData**.

> `Line Input#` **is an ideal method to use when you need to read text files like** AUTOEXEC.BAT. **The reason for this is that it reads data from a file up to, but not including, the next carriage return.**

```
frmAuto.Print sInputData
```

Now we print the details that we have just read into **sInputData** on the form.

```
    Loop
    Close iAutoNumber
End Sub
```

Finally, we loop back until the end of the file is reached, when we **Close** the file. The form will now hold a copy of your **AUTOEXEC.BAT** file.

OK, let's change the code a little, replace the **Line Input #** line with the **Input$()** function and see the effect:

```
sInputData = input$ (4, nFilenumber)
```

Now run the code again. This time, instead of seeing the entire **AUTOEXEC** printed onto the form, you only receive 4 characters at a time printed on

# Comma Seperation

each line of the form. The chances are the program will also crash with an 'Input past end of file' error message. The `Input$()` function reads the number of characters you specify from the file (in this case 4). Unless the length of your **AUTOEXEC** is exactly divisible by 4 then you will get an error which can be trapped with an error handler. To do so add the following:

```
On Error GoTo errhandle
```

This line should be entered before the `Open File` statement and activates the error handler.

```
    Exit Sub
errhandle:
    MsgBox Err & " " & Error
    End
```

These lines should go after the `Close File` statement and will trap the error, display the error details, then end the application.

## Comma Separated Variables

`Input$()` is still a very useful function, though, especially in those cases where you need to read one character at a time from a file. A good example of this might be where you are reading comma separated variables. You can read from the file a character at a time, and check whether you have read a comma. If you have, then you have completed the input of the current variable, and are at the start of the next variable. Comma Separated Variable (CSV) format is quite common, and is used to pass data from one package to another.

To try it out, create a text file using **NOTEPAD.EXE**, which contains the following (and without pressing *Enter*):

```
This,is,the,Instant,Guide,to,Visual Basic3,comma,separated,example
```

You'll need to remember the name of the file, so that you can open it. Now start a new project, and add two command buttons and a list box. Our form looks like the following:

## Chapter 9 - Input and Output

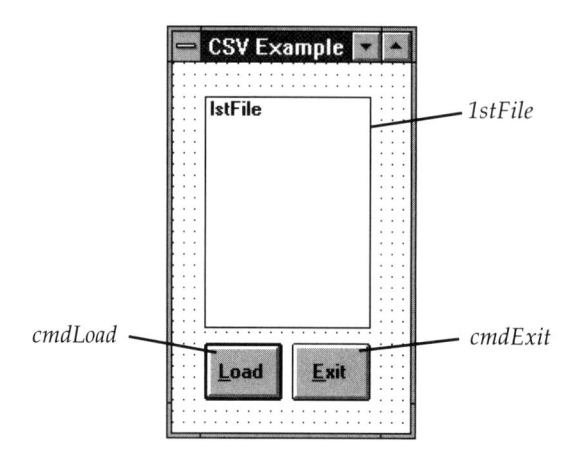

*cmdLoad* — *cmdExit* (CSV Example window with lstFile listbox and Load / Exit buttons)

In the **Click** event code for the Exit button enter the following:

```
Sub cmdExit_Click ()
    End
End Sub
```

In the **Click** event for the Load button, enter the following:

```
Sub cmdLoad_Click ()
    Dim iCSVNumber As Integer, sInputchr As String * 1, sWord As String
```

The first string will hold the next character read from the file, and **sWord** will hold the word that we are building up.

```
    iCSVNumber = FreeFile
    Open "c:\temp\csvtest.txt" For Input As iCSVNumber
```

Allocate the next unique file number, and open the file, which you created in Notepad.

```
    Do While Not EOF(iCSVNumber)
        sInputchr = Input$(1, iCSVNumber)
```

Start a **Do** ... loop that will run until the end of the file, and read the next character from the file.

```
        If sInputchr = "," Then
            lstFile.AddItem sWord
            sWord = ""
```

246

If it's a comma, then we have a complete word (or variable) in **sWord**, so add it to the list box and set **sWord** to nothing, ready for the next word. This also has the effect of ignoring the commas in our list box.

```
        Else
            sWord = sWord + sInputchr
        End If
    Loop
```

If it's not a comma, add it to **sWord**, and loop round for the next character.

```
        lstFile.AddItem sWord
        Close iCSVNumber
    End Sub
```

At the end of the file, remember to add the last word to the list, then **Close** the file.

## Input to Variables

An easier way to read variables from a sequential file is to use the **Input#** method. This will read data from a sequential file into a list of variables that you specify. The fields in the file should be separated by commas (as in the above example), or by spaces, or by the end of the line. Be sure to input the correct fields from the file into the correct data types - don't try to input a string into a numeric variable.

Let's see the effect of entering the data in our **AUTOEXEC.BAT** file to two string variables. Start a new project, and in the **Form_Load** event enter the following code:

```
Sub Form_Load ()
    Dim iAutoNumber As Integer
    Static sInput(2) As String
```

The first variable is our file number - we then have an array of two strings.

```
        frmMess.Show
        iAutoNumber = FreeFile
```

Next display the form, and allocate the file number.

```
        Open "c:\autoexec.bat" For Input As iAutoNumber
        Do While Not EOF(iAutoNumber)
```

# Chapter 9 - Input and Output

As per our previous examples, open the file, and read through it with a **Do**... loop.

```
Input #iAutoNumber, sInput(0), sInput(1)
```

This is the line that reads the next two fields from the file, and places them in the two strings that make up our array.

```
frmMess.Print "1: " & sInput(0) & "   2: " & sInput(1)
```

Next print the details on the form. So that we can make some sense of the output, we are placing a **1** before the first string and a **2** before the second.

```
    Loop
    Close iAutoNumber
End Sub
```

Finally, loop back to read the next two fields and close the file at the end. The details that are being printed are a bit of a mess, because **AUTOEXEC.BAT** is not structured to be read in this manner. Try this example with the comma separated text file of the last example, and you'll get more meaningful output. Ours looks like this:

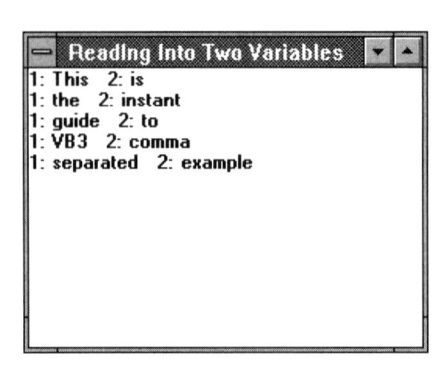

```
┌─ Reading Into Two Variables ──────┐
│ 1: This   2: is                   │
│ 1: the   2: instant               │
│ 1: guide   2: to                  │
│ 1: VB3   2: comma                 │
│ 1: separated   2: example         │
│                                   │
│                                   │
└───────────────────────────────────┘
```

If you want to use a comma as part of the data rather than as a delimiter, then it will need to be embedded in quotes. Add the following to our **CVTEST.TXT** file as a second record:

```
With,"Some, Embedded",commas,in!!
```

Now re-run the project, and you will see that the string **"Some, Embedded"** has been treated as a single variable.

# Write #

## Using Write# to Create a Structured File

The **Write#** command lets you produce a file in the format expected by the **Input#** method. We will create a file that can be read by the example above. The file will contain two random numbers between 1 and 99 in each record.

Start a new project, and add the following code to the **Form_Load** event:

```
Sub Form_Load ()
    Dim iOutNumber As Integer
    Static iRnd(2) As Integer, iCount As Integer
```

This is similar to the previous example, except our array is now an integer array which will hold our two random numbers for writing to the file. We are going to use a **For** loop to write twenty records.

```
frmWrite.Show
Randomize
iOutNumber = FreeFile
```

Show the form, then seed the random number generator, and allocate a file number.

```
Open "c:\test.dat" For Output As iOutNumber
```

This time we want to open the file for output, so that we can write details to it. You can call the file any name you like, and store it anywhere on your system. If you run out of room on the disk, a trapable error will occur.

```
For iCount = 1 To 20
    iRnd(0) = Int(Rnd(1) * 100)
    iRnd(1) = Int(Rnd(1) * 100)
```

Next we start the **For** loop, and allocate two random numbers to our array variables. You do not have to use array variables for the **Write#** and **Input#** methods, but it saves typing!

```
        Write #iOutNumber, iRnd(0), iRnd(1)
    Next
    Close iOutNumber
    End
End Sub
```

249

Finally, we write the two numbers to our file, and loop back. When all the data has been written, the file is closed, and the application ended.

Now, if you take a look at the new **TEST.DAT** file which this code creates, you will see that it is in exactly the format expected by **Input#** in the above example. Each set of values in the file is separated by a carriage return, with each value in each set (each physical line) being separated by a comma. Our output looks like this:

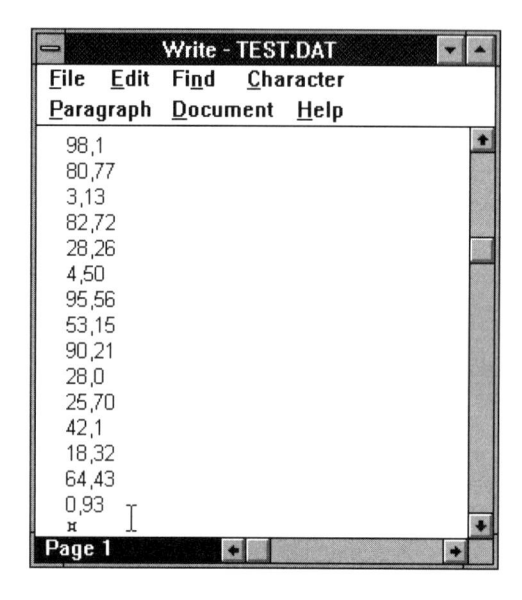

```
Write - TEST.DAT
File  Edit  Find  Character
Paragraph  Document  Help
98,1
80,77
3,13
82,72
28,26
4,50
95,56
53,15
90,21
28,0
25,70
42,1
18,32
64,43
0,93
```

## Random Access

With random access files you have a file which essentially consists of records (fixed length groups of data), generally described by a Visual Basic user-defined type. There isn't really anything overly complex about random access files, it's just that you have to be careful when managing the data inside them, especially when you realize you are now able to overwrite data in the middle of a file, add data to the end of it, and even delete records, and all with the minimum of effort.

All this is accomplished using only two methods, **Get** and **Put**.

```
Get <filenumber>, <recordnumber>, <data>
Put <filenumber>,<recordnumber>,<data>
```

# Random Access

The `<filenumber>` is exactly the same as you are used to with sequential files, the `<recordnumber>` is just what it says - the number of the record starting at 1 for the first record. Data is usually the name of a user-defined type variable, which reflects the structure of the data.

Let's try an example that writes data to a random file. Start a new project, and remove the form from the project. You'll need to add a code module, and enter the following code into it:

```
Option Explicit
Type Contact
    sName As String * 40
    sAddress As String * 75
    sPhone As String * 20
End Type
```

Firstly, we define the **Type** that will represent the records in our random access file. This is the declaration for our user-defined type **Contact**. It holds a name, an address, and phone number. The records must be fixed length, so you must make certain that any strings you declare are fixed length strings:

```
        sName As String * 40
```

This defines the **sName** string within the type as being a fixed length **40** character string.

Then we need to create a **Sub Main()** procedure, and enter the following code into it:

```
Sub main ()
    Dim typContact As Contact
    Dim iContNum As Integer, lLength As Long
```

The first declaration is a variable **typContact** which is based on our user-defined type **Contact**. Then we declare an **Integer** for our file number, and a **Long** that will hold the length of our records.

```
    iContNum = FreeFile
    lLength = Len(typContact)
```

Here we allocate the file number, and determine the length of our records by using the **Len()** function which returns the length of our variable. We saw the **Len()** function in Chapter 5.

**251**

## Chapter 9 - Input and Output

```
Open "c:\test2.dat" For Random As iContNum Len = lLength
```

The **Open** file statement has changed, because we are now using random files. We state that the file is a **Random** file, and use the length held in **lLength** to notify Visual Basic of our record length for this file.

```
typContact.sName = "Bill Smith"
typContact.sAddress = "12 Roland St, London"
typContact.sPhone = "0181-344-3455"
```

This section allocates data to each element of our variable **typContact**, which sets up our first record.

```
Put iContNum, 1&, typContact
```

Information is written using the **Put** keyword. Since this is a new file and we want to write just two records into it, it makes sense that they are numbered one and two. You'll need to remember that the record numbers have to be **Long** values and so we have appended the **&** symbol to the end of the number to signify to Visual Basic that it is a **Long** value.

```
typContact.sName = "John Doe"
typContact.sAddress = "4402 High Tower, 46th Street, New York"
typContact.sPhone = "1233-44-55-66"
Put iContNum, 2&, typContact
```

This is the second record being set up and written to the file.

```
    Close iContNum
    End
End Sub
```

Finally, close the file and end the application. You have just written two records to a random file. You can look at them using Notepad, as they are text. You'll see that all the data is on a single line.

Getting the information using **Get** is exactly the same, only we use **Get** instead of **Put**. With just these two commands you can add records to a file, change existing records in the file, and read information from the file either into controls in your form, or simply into a variable.

Start a new project, and add a list box with the **Sorted** property set to **True**, a large text box with **MultiLine** property set to **True**, a small text box, a status label, and two command buttons. Our form looks like this:

# Get and Put

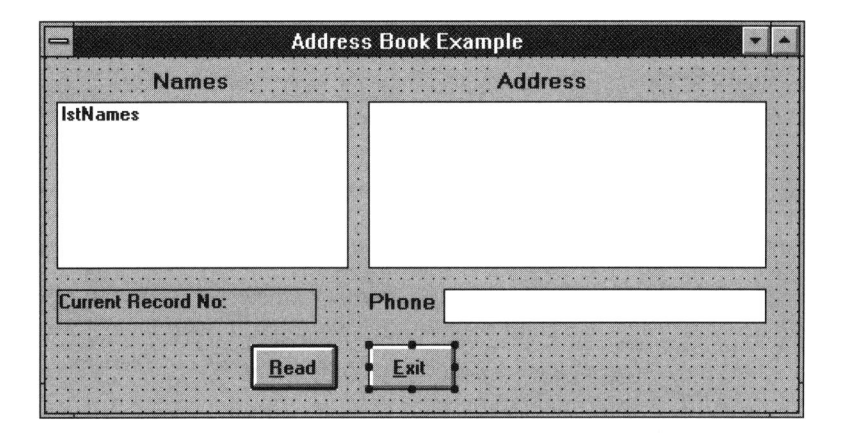

```
                Address Book Example
        Names                    Address
   lstNames

   Current Record No:        Phone

              Read        Exit
```

You'll also need to add a code module, and use the **Contact** type definition above for our record structure. Apart from the type definition we've also added two global variables:

```
Global glCurrent As Long
Global glNext As Long
```

These will hold the current record number, and the next available record number for our file. In the **Form_Load** event enter the following code:

```
Sub Form_Load ()
    Dim typContact As Contact
    Dim iContNum As Integer, lLength As Long
    iContNum = FreeFile
    lLength = Len(typContact)
    Open "c:\test2.dat" For Random As iContNum Len = lLength
```

All this should now be familiar. It's essentially the same code as in the previous example.

```
    For glNext = 1 To FileLen("c:\test2.dat") / lLength
```

We're using a **For** loop to read all the records in the file. The **FileLen()** function returns the size of the file in bytes, and by dividing this by the record length determines the number of records in the file.

```
        Get iContNum, glNext, typContact
```

## Chapter 9 - Input and Output

Now read the record from the file, and add the name to the list box.

```
lstnames.AddItem typContact.sName
lstnames.ItemData(lstnames.NewIndex) = glNext
```

We're also using the **ItemData** property as discussed in Chapter 4 to hold the record number. The **NewIndex** property is another runtime property which returns the index number of the item most recently added.

```
    Next
    Close iContNum
End Sub
```

Finally, close the file and exit.

In the **Read_Click** event we've entered the following code:

```
Sub cmdRead_Click ()
    Dim typContact As Contact
    Dim iContNum As Integer, lLength As Long
    iContNum = FreeFile
    lLength = Len(typContact)
```

This code should be very familiar by now!

```
glCurrent = lstnames.ItemData(lstnames.ListIndex)
lblCurRec = "Current record number " & Str(glCurrent)
```

Here, we're using the **ItemData** property to get the record number of the selected item, setting **glCurrent**, and displaying the details in the label at the bottom of the screen. Although this doesn't add anything to the application, it does help us see what's going on.

```
    Open "c:\test2.dat" For Random As iContNum Len = lLength
    Get iContNum, glCurrent, typContact
```

Open the file, and get the selected record.

```
txtAddress.Text = typContact.sAddress
txtPhone.Text = typContact.sPhone
```

Then display the details in the appropriate text boxes before closing the file:

```
    Close iContNum
End Sub
```

# I/O and Printing

We've also coded the **DblClick** event of the list box to display the address details and the exit command button:

```
Sub lstNames_DblClick ()
    cmdRead_click
End Sub
```

When the <u>E</u>xit button is clicked, unload the form and end the project.

```
Sub cmdExit_Click ()
    Unload frmAddress
    End
End Sub
```

## I/O and Printing: Implementation

No matter how graphical your system there is one area of input/output that you can't escape from, and that is printing. There will always be a requirement to produce hard copy details. For good or bad, people are still comfortable with a piece of paper in their hands - and it's easier to fit a piece of paper into a briefcase, rather than a whole computer. To print in Visual Basic we use the printer object, which is one of the system objects mentioned in Chapter 8.

## The Printer Object

You can think of the **Printer** object as the paper-based equivalent of a form. Anything you can draw or write direct to a form at runtime, you can also write direct to the **Printer** object at runtime. Unlike a form, the **Printer** object and its properties are not available to you at design time. For this reason, you can't draw controls on the printer object, or set up the fonts to be used when printing at any time other than at runtime.

### Using the Common Dialogs

The font common dialog, as discussed in Chapter 7, is really useful for giving the user the option of setting up their own fonts, and the print common dialog can be used to control the printing. You'll need to use the

# Chapter 9 - Input and Output

**Flags** property to determine what you will allow with the print dialog. They are all explained in the Visual Basic Help file - search for **Flags** property.

## The Print Common Dialog

To display the print common dialog just set the **Action** property of the common dialog control to **5** at runtime. We'll try out a print common dialog, so, start a new project and add the common dialog control and four labels to the form. Ours looks like this:

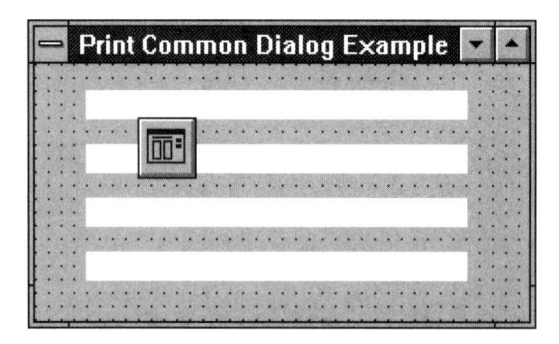

In the `Form_Load` event enter the following:

```
Sub Form_Load ()
    cmdialog1.Action = 5
```

This line displays the print common dialog.

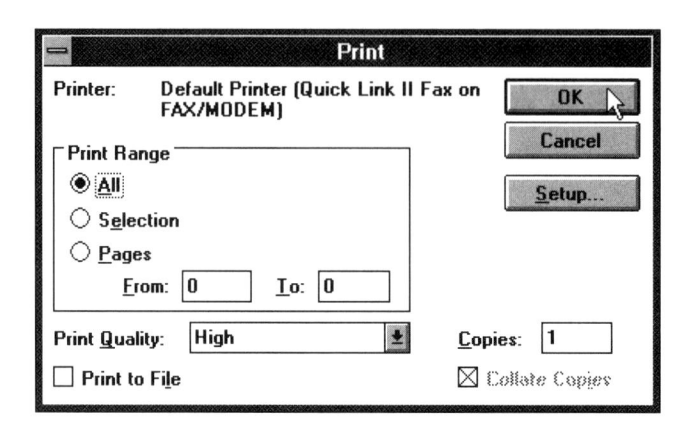

# The Printer Object

As you can see, ours is currently set up for a fax. From within this dialog, you can change the printer settings in the `WIN.INI` file by clicking on the Setup... button, providing that the `PrinterDefault` property is `True` (the default). Also with `PrinterDefault` set to `True`, you can print to the printer object:

```
    lblFrom.Caption = "Starting to Print From " & cmdialog1.FromPage
    lblTo.Caption = "The Print Will End at Page " & cmdialog1.ToPage
    lblCopies.Caption = "The Number of Copies Is " & cmdialog1.Copies
    lblHdc.Caption = "The Printer Device Context Is " & cmdialog1.hDC
End Sub
```

These are the properties that are returned from the dialog that you can make use of in your applications. All the other controls are accessed via flags. The `hDC` is something called a **device context handle**, and is used in calls to the Windows API - this is discussed in Chapter 12.

## Printing to the Printer Object

Actually printing something is really simple:

```
    Printer.Print "I've Just Printed This Line On The Printer!!"
```

This prints the message at the current position on the printer, and the following code prints a dot on the printer at position `1000,1000` (depending, of course, on the current coordinate system which you saw in the last chapter).

```
    Printer.Pset 1000,1000
```

Actually, what's happening is that the print is going to the printer object, and from there Visual Basic will pass the details to Windows for printing to the selected printer through Print Manager. This all happens in the background so you don't really need to worry, except that the details that you print to the printer object will not be printed immediately. The printer object acts as a print buffer for Visual Basic. The details that you build up will only be printed when an `EndDoc` statement is encountered, or when the application ends.

However, the printer does have some new properties of its own:

**257**

## Chapter 9 - Input and Output

| Property | Description |
| --- | --- |
| Page | Holds the number of the current page so that you can print it at the top of reports and other documents. |
| TwipsPerPixelX | Tells you the number of **Twips** that equals one dot on the printed page going from left to right. |
| TwipsPerPixelY | Tells you the number of **Twips** that equals one dot on the printed page going from top to bottom. |

The **TwipsPerPixel** properties are quite useful when drawing graphics on the printer since they help you when scaling graphics and such like. You may know that a line is 1000 **Twips** long and 12 **Twips** in height, but the printer may be using a coordinate system so large that it only equals half a pixel in length and a quarter of a pixel in height, which may be too small. Using these properties before you start printing you can make adjustments to your graphics to scale them up or down.

> The Printer object also has the Newpage method which allows you to create a page break from code. This is very useful for ensuring that important information is not split across a page break.

Let's try some of this, by printing 100 lines, 40 to a page. Start a new project, remove the form and add a code module. Now enter the following code:

```
Sub main ()
    Dim iNoLines As Integer, iCurrentLine As Integer, iIndex As Integer
    iNoLines = Int(printer.ScaleHeight / Printer.TextHeight("X"))
```

The first thing this code does is figure out how many lines of text the printer can actually display, using the printer's **TextHeight** and **ScaleHeight** properties. The **ScaleHeight** is the same as we saw in the last chapter. The **TextHeight** property will return the text height, based on the currently selected font. You can use this property to ensure that your current line of text will fit on the page. There is also a **TextWidth** property which returns the width of a variable or string, and this can be used in association with **TextHeight** to ensure that important details are not split across pages.

# Changing Fonts

```
    iCurrentLine = 1
    For iIndex = 1 To 100
```

Set the current line indicator, and start the **Print** loop.

```
        Printer.Print "This is a test line, of which you will only see 40
   on this page"
        iCurrentLine = iCurrentLine + 1
```

Now print the line to the **Printer** object, and add **1** to our line count.

```
        If iCurrentLine > 40 Then
            iCurrentLine = 1
            Printer.NewPage
        End If
```

If we've printed **40** lines, then reset the line counter and start a new page.

```
    Next
    Printer.EndDoc
End Sub
```

Finally, use the **EndDoc** method to actually print all the details held in the **Printer** object. For those of you who have coded reports in other languages, the structure may be familiar. In the real world, after the new page, we'd probably print some header details. We find it useful to write most of our printing in procedures, such as **PrintPageHeader**, which we can then reuse, and this also makes the report logic easier to read.

Further, in reality we may want to change the fonts being used in the report, so how can we keep track of where we are on the page? Just as with graphics on a form, the **Printer** has a **CurrentX** and a **CurrentY** property which can be used here. You know how big the actual page is using **Printer.ScaleHeight**. You can check **Printer.CurrentX** to see if it is approaching this number and create a page break using **Printer.NewPage** accordingly. If you are using footers, you'll need to use this method.

The unfortunate thing about using the **Printer** object is that your printed reports can be just as graphical as the displays you put on a form, but you have no tools in Visual Basic to help you in designing the layout of your reports. With the **Printer** object, actually achieving a layout that looks presentable is really nothing more than a question of trial and error.

**259**

# Chapter 9 - Input and Output

> There are, however, report painters and generators which can be used. A report generator called *Crystal Reports* ships with the Professional version which allows you to produce reports from database tables, and there is also a commercial version of this package available, which will allow you to produce reports for many different file and database formats.

The printer's **ScaleMode** property can be a help here, especially if you stick to a fixed width font such as Courier. By setting the printer's **ScaleMode** to **4** you can tell Visual Basic to measure the form in terms of characters. In this way you can treat the page you are printing to like a grid, with each square on the grid representing a single character.

We'll try this out, so replace the code in **Sub main** with the following:

```
Sub main ()
    Dim iNoLines As Integer, iIndex As Integer
    Dim iX As Integer, iY As Integer
    Randomize
```

Declare the integers to be used, and seed the random number generator.

```
Printer.ScaleMode = 4
```

Set the scale mode to characters for the **Printer** object.

```
Printer.FontBold = True
Printer.Print "A random collection of Xs - current X = ";
```

Set the **Font** to bold, then print the first line. The semi colon at the end of the line is used to suppress a carriage return and line feed, so printing will continue from the end of the string.

```
Printer.Print printer.CurrentX
```

The **CurrentX** position will be printed at the end of the above string.

```
Printer.FontBold = False
For iIndex = 1 To 10
```

Turn off **Bold** printing, and start the **Print** loop.

260

# Printing Forms

It's possible to alter all the **Font** properties during printing, but this can cause you layout problems, and you may need to use the **TextWidth** and **TextHeight** properties.

```
iX = Int(Rnd(1) * printer.ScaleWidth)
iY = Int(Rnd(1) * printer.ScaleHeight)
```

Set the two coordinate variables to a random number within the bounds of our printer page.

```
Printer.CurrentX = nX
Printer.CurrentY = nY
Printer.Print "X";
```

Now we set the **Printer** object **X** and **Y** properties to the random numbers, and print an X at that position. The semi colon is again used to suppress a carriage return and line feed so that an unwanted page throw isn't generated.

```
    Next
    Printer.EndDoc
End Sub
```

When you run the project, after printing a nice bold report heading, X symbols are printed at random positions all over the page using **ScaleMode** set to **4**. This means that by setting the **CurrentX** and **CurrentY** properties of the **Printer** object we can position the print head at specific character positions on the page. Indeed, the first line of the print even checks **CurrentX** and prints the result 40 to indicate that you have currently printed 40 characters.

Using **Scalemode**, **CurrentX** and **CurrentY** in this way you can greatly reduce the hit and miss element of designing a print. For example, one technique we use a lot involves nothing more than designing the report on 80 column graph paper, then translating that into **CurrentX** and **CurrentY** values to set at runtime.

## Printing Forms

Although setting scalemode to **4** can reduce your workload greatly, especially if you stick to just textual printouts, printing complex graphics, even reproducing a form on paper, can be an horrendous task. Visual Basic comes to the rescue here as well with the `PrintForm` method.

```
<formname>.PrintForm
```

This method attempts to faithfully reproduce a form on the printer, and involves nothing more than typing the form name followed by `PrintForm`. You can try this out yourself. Put some controls on a form, then link the `<formname>.PrintForm` method to a command button on that form. When the button is pressed, the form prints.

Using `PrintForm` you don't have to worry about `CurrentX`, `CurrentY` or `ScaleMode` at all. Nor do you have to worry about `NewPage` and `EndDoc` - Visual Basic does it all for you.

# Summary

In this chapter you saw how to use both sequential and random files for storing and retrieving data. Generally, with more complex data handling and the designing of databases you will avoid some of the methods we have outlined in this chapter. Before you do go leaping off to the next chapter, try out the exercises, which enhance the Address application.

# Exercises

There are quite a few things that you can do with the Address project.

1   Constantly opening and closing the file is not very efficient. See if you can determine a way of opening the file at the start of the project, and closing it at the end.

   **Hint: try using a `Sub main` procedure and load the form from this.**

2   Change the listbox to a combo box, and add an `&Add` command button which will allow the user to add an entry into the list, and also write it to the file. You'll need to use the global variable `glNext`.

# Summary and Exercises

**3** Now add an **&Update** command button that will allow the user to alter and save new details of a selected record. Here you'll need to use the **ItemData** property.

**4** Try out some ways of better structuring the address, such as delimitimg each section with a comma, and reformatting in the text box.

**5** Using the **Printer** object print your name and address details. You'll need to use **TextWidth** and **TextHeight** to make sure that you don't split an address over two pages.

# Chapter 10

# Database Development

All modern day applications deal with data of some kind. It doesn't matter if you are holding something in a couple of variables, or whether you are doing a full blown client-server database application - ultimately you are still dealing with data. Visual Basic makes it easy to deal with all types of data manipulation. Variables provide an easy way to deal with temporary data - files make it easy to deal with data on a more permanent scale.

The most powerful data manipulation features of Visual Basic come from its Jet database engine. This is a slightly cut down version of Microsoft's Access Database engine, and if you have Access, then the two sets of databases are totally interchangeable (depending on version numbers).

In this chapter we will look at how Visual Basic uses its native database. Although the Standard edition is an ideal entry point into the world of database programming, real database power can only be achieved with the Professional edition, or by using one of the numerous add-on database engines that are available.

In this chapter we'll cover:

- Relational databases
- Creating a database
- The data control, and the recordset
- SQL

# Chapter 10 - Database Development

## Relational Databases: Concepts

Relational databases represent an extremely flexible and powerful way to manage and maintain large amounts of data. However, the relational database facilities in Visual Basic are also ideal for storing medium and large amounts of temporary data, which means that memory is freed up as Visual Basic and Windows takes some of the strain of information storage via the database.

The worse point about relational databases, including Visual Basic, is the number of confusing terms that people use. Before we go much further it's worth taking a look a what these terms are, and also how the relational database stuff in Visual Basic relates to the other MS Office applications, in particular Microsoft Access.

## Access

As you spend more time with your nose in Visual Basic books and magazines, you will come across the term **Jet engine** a great deal. At its simplest, the Jet engine is the code used both in Microsoft Access and Visual Basic to provide control over the databases themselves. In Visual Basic, any command you execute which has something to do with a database gets translated into a Jet command and sent to the Jet engine. From there its out of your hands. You don't have to worry about complex file handling, accessing files that are currently being accessed by other users and so on. Jet does it all for you.

There are two unfortunate side effects to this. First of all, speed. Unless you pay careful attention to what you are doing with your databases, the speed of your application can go through the floor. We will take a look at some of the things you can do to keep your database code slick and fast a little later.

The other drawback of the Jet engine is that since it represents the tricky stuff behind Microsoft Access, you really need Access to be able to create and manage the databases outside of your Visual Basic programs. There are ways to create an Access database from within Visual Basic, but really Access is the best tool for the job. Don't panic yet though, we'll take a look at the alternatives later, in particular the Visual Basic **Data Manager** application.

# Relational Databases

# What is a Relational Database?

As we've already pointed out, the world of databases, in particular relational databases, is populated with a mass of confusing names and keywords. Thankfully you need to know only a few of them in order to survive in Visual Basic, although you really *do* need to know these few.

## Databases

First off we have **database**. A business may have many databases, one holding accounts information, another for the sales team and so on. Alternatively, some businesses have only one database which simply holds everything to do with the business. A database therefore, is a repository of related information. In the case of the business with just one database, all the information in that database relates specifically to the business. A sales database would have a lot of information in it relating only to sales - it's unlikely that you would find the company payroll information in the sales database.

## Tables

The actual information within the database is once again broken down into separate, related groups called **tables**. Think of the sales database again - it may have a customer table to hold information on all the company's customers, an invoice table holding the details of all the invoices ever produced, and a stock table which is used to check on the stock levels in the warehouse.

## Records

In the customers table, information is once again broken into smaller subgroups, this time called **records**. Where the customers table holds information about *all* the customers, a customer record holds information about one specific customer.

## Fields

The final level of breakdown is that all items of information in a record are stored in **fields**. Getting back to the sales database and the customer table, you may have fields in that table to hold the customer's unique customer number, name, address and so on.

Let's illustrate all of this:

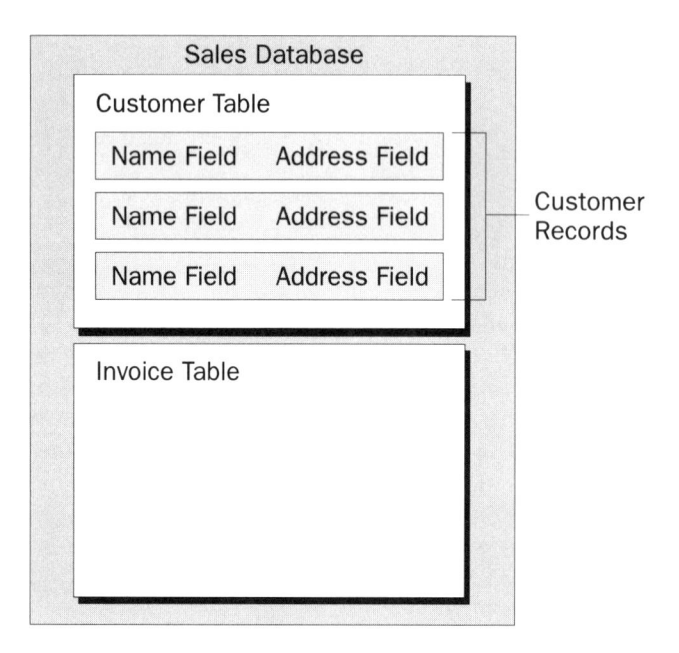

```
                    Sales Database
    ┌─────────────────────────────────────┐
    │  Customer Table                     │
    │  ┌───────────────────────────────┐  │
    │  │ Name Field    Address Field   │  │
    │  ├───────────────────────────────┤  │  Customer
    │  │ Name Field    Address Field   │  │  Records
    │  ├───────────────────────────────┤  │
    │  │ Name Field    Address Field   │  │
    │  └───────────────────────────────┘  │
    │                                     │
    │  Invoice Table                      │
    │                                     │
    │                                     │
    │                                     │
    │                                     │
    └─────────────────────────────────────┘
```

## Relations

Next, we come to the relational bit - let's stay with the sales database example. Whenever the company invoices, it is going to send that invoice out to a specific customer. In days of old that would mean copying certain customer information (specifically the name and address) into the invoice record to indicate where and to whom it was sent.

With a relational database the idea is to keep the amount of duplicated information to a minimum, so instead of copying the customer information to the invoice record you find some way of uniquely identifying each customer (usually by using a long number) and put that number in the invoice records. This way, when you pull up an invoice in your code, you know from the customer number on that invoice precisely which customer record to locate, display, print, or whatever.

That's fine in principle, but what if there are 10 million customers in the database and 50 million invoices? How can we locate individual records in such a number quickly and easily, even with customer numbers? How do we know where to look on the hard disk to find the specific customer?

### Indexes

The answer to all these questions is to use something called an **index**, and that is something that the Jet engine handles for you automatically, once the database has been properly set up. This book covers a lot of subjects, or information about a specific Visual Basic keyword and would be really hard to use without the aid of the index at the back. Access databases work in the same way. When you set up a database and define the tables and fields in it, you can tell the Access engine to automatically keep track of some or all of the fields in indexes. Then, when you need to find a record in a hurry (for instance, the customer related to an invoice) you just fire the value of the index at the Jet engine and Access does all the leg work for you.

This is getting a little complicated now, and those of you who have never programmed a database application before are probably feeling a bit confused. Let's put the theory into practice.

## Creating a Database

Since the databases that Visual Basic uses all revolve around the Access Jet engine, it makes sense that the best tool to set up the databases and later maintain them is, of course, Access. If you don't have it though then don't panic - Visual Basic comes with an alternative.

If Visual Basic is not already running then load it up now. Although the following section looks long and complex, after you've been through it you'll find that it's all fairly easy to follow.

When the familiar Visual Basic menu bar appears take a look at the Window menu.

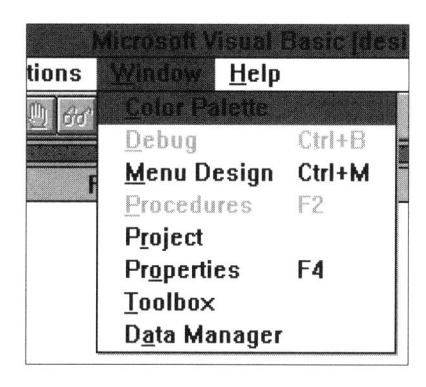

**269**

# Chapter 10 - Database Development

The bottom entry on the list says D<u>a</u>ta Manager which is your link to the Visual Basic database manager, a tool which lets you create and maintain the format of Access databases. Click it now. After a short while a blank window and menu bar will appear declaring itself to be Data Manager.

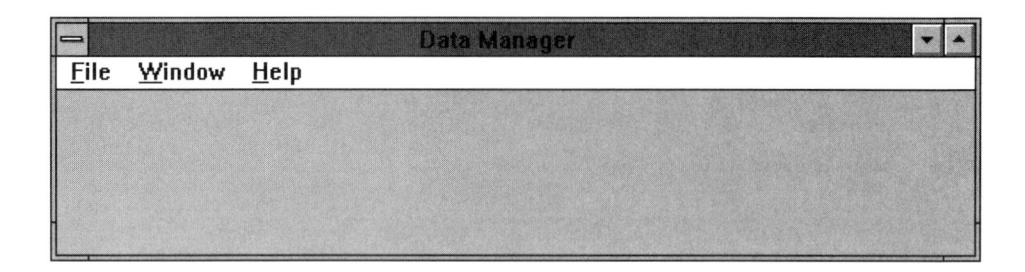

Let's see how it works by creating a very simple contacts database. From the <u>F</u>ile menu select <u>N</u>ew Database. Another menu will appear asking you for the format you require.

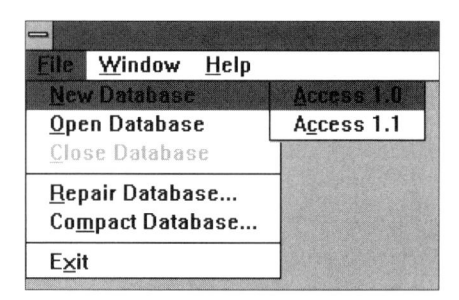

> Visual Basic 'out-of-the-box' only lets you deal with Access 1.0 and 1.1 format databases. However, as you will see later, Microsoft does supply a set of files known as the compatibility layer which you can use to gain entry to Access 2 format databases.

Select Access 1.1 to tell Data Manager that you want to create an Access 1.1 database. A File dialog will pop up asking you for the file name.

# Using Access

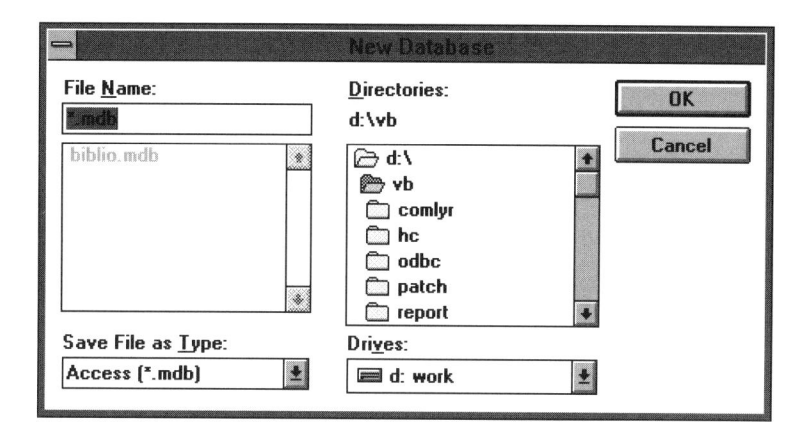

All Access databases end in **.MDB** so for the moment just enter **TEST.MDB** as the file name and press *Enter*.

You have now created your Access database. We now need to add at least 1 table, some fields and an index to the database to make it of any use. You can do this using the buttons across the top of the database control form.

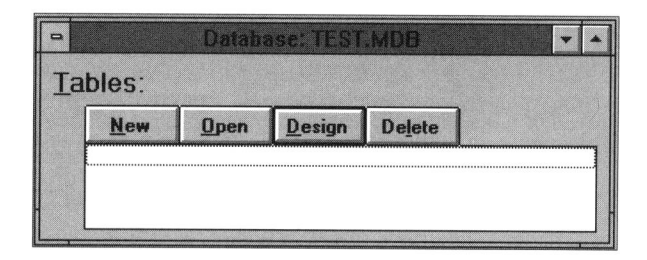

Click on the New button to create a new table. A fairly familiar Input box will appear (Data Manager was written in Visual Basic after all) asking for the database name - enter Contacts and press *Enter*.

271

# Chapter 10 - Database Development

Data Manager then goes ahead and creates the table, dropping you into the table designer. From here we can start to add fields to hold the contact information, and an index or two to make retrieval of the information in the table nice and quick.

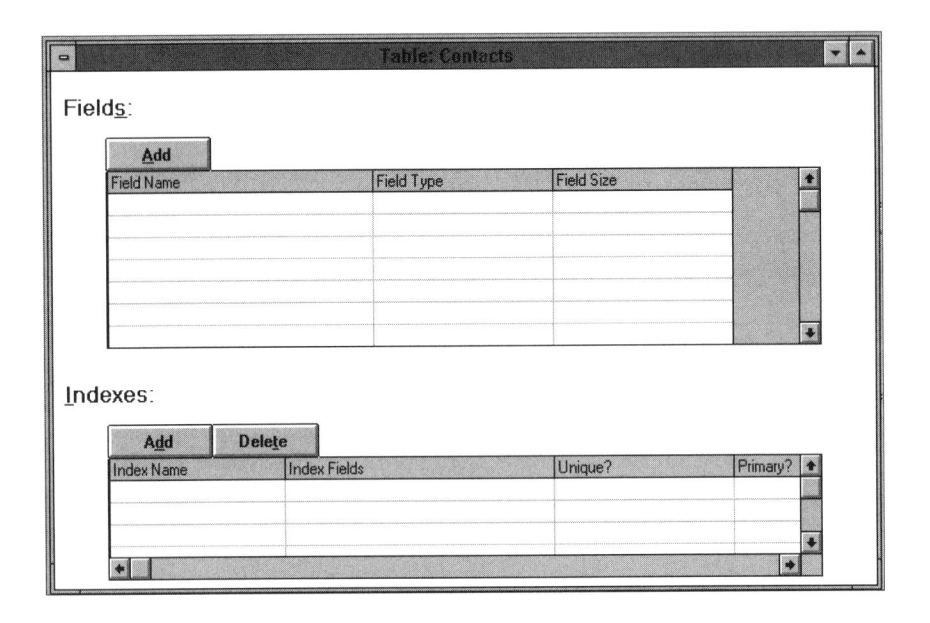

Click on the Add button at the top of the table design window. Up pops the new Add Field dialog box, where you need to enter information about the field so that Access, and ultimately your own Visual Basic code, knows how to deal with it.

# Adding Fields

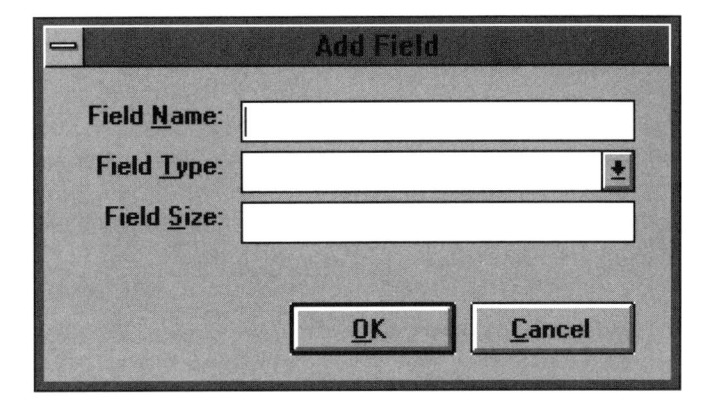

The first entry in the dialog is the Field Name - this is a textual name which you will later use in your code to refer to that field. It's really very similar to assigning a variable name.

Field Type is similar to the data type you would specify when you create a normal Visual Basic variable. This is really only for the Access engine's use since when you pull data out of a database, as you will see later, the values you retrieve are always of type `Variant`.

Finally, Field Size specifies how big the data in the field is going to be. Unlike variables, you must tell Access how much data you intend to store in a field, so that it can allocated enough space to hold it in the database file itself (`TEST.MDB`).

We are going to replace our contacts file used in the last chapter, so add these fields in the table designer:

| Field Name | Field Type | Field Size |
|---|---|---|
| Contact_Name | Text | 40 |
| Contact_Address | Text | 75 |
| Contact_Phone | Text | 20 |

At the end of it all the table designer window should look like the following:

273

## Chapter 10 - Database Development

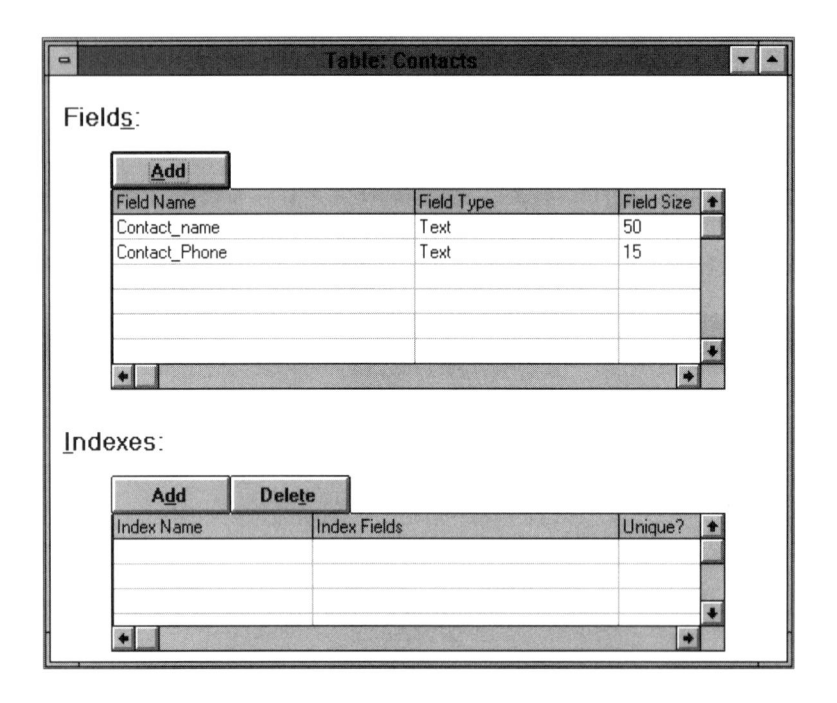

This gives us fields to hold the contacts name, address and phone number. You have told Data Manager (or rather Access), that these fields will hold text (same type of data as a **String** in Visual Basic) and that the contacts name will be up to 40 characters in length, the address will be up to 75 characters, while the phone number will be 20 characters.

The last stage in creating any table is to define the indexes that will be used to actually access the data in the table itself. The index works the same way as in this book - it tells Access where it can find information in the database so that it can do so quickly when your actual application is running. All you need to do is tell Access which fields to keep an eye on.

Click on the Add button on the bottom section of the table designer form - the indexes section. The Add Index dialog pops up.

# Adding Indexes

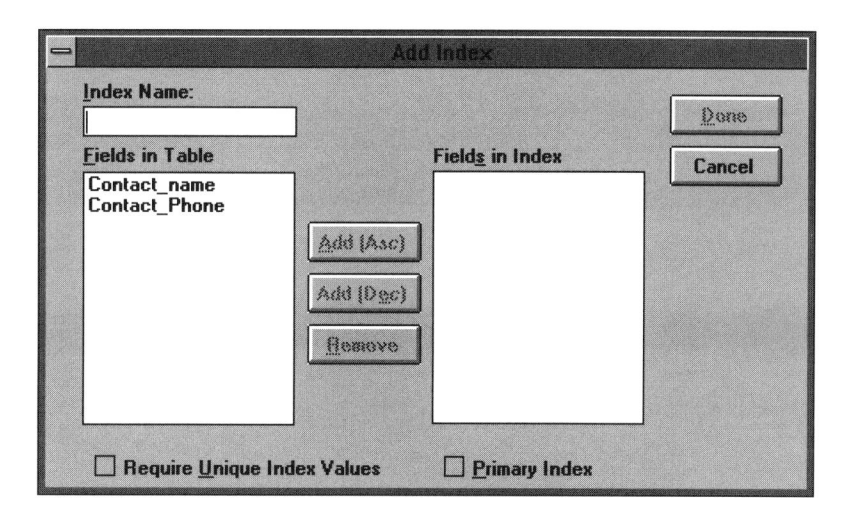

![Add Index dialog box showing Index Name field, Fields in Table list (Contact_name, Contact_Phone), Fields in Index list, Add (Asc), Add (Desc), Remove buttons, Done and Cancel buttons, and checkboxes for Require Unique Index Values and Primary Index]

Despite its rather daunting name, the above index designer is really easy to use. The text box at the top of the dialog expects you to give a name to the index in the same way that you thought of a name for the fields themselves. For example, if you were setting up an index to make it easy to get at a person's surname you could call the index **Surname_Index**. In our example simply key in *Contact_Idx* to give the index a name of **Contact_Idx.**

The listbox beneath the index name holds the fields in the table which you are currently working with. What you need to do now is select those fields that are going to form the index and click on either of the Add buttons. Notice that there are two add buttons there, Add (Asc) and Add (Desc). The top one Add (Asc) means that the index will be sorted according to values in this field in ascending order. The Add (Desc) sorts the field within the index in descending order. When you later write code to find records these buttons directly affect how the data you get back is sorted.

For now, just click on the **Contact_Name** field and click on Add (Asc). This means that the **Contact_Idx** index refers to our contact names, and sorts them in ascending order.

The final stage in setting up the index is to decide whether or not this index is the primary one, and whether the values in it are unique. Every table must have at least one unique index, called the primary index that will be used by default. You can, however, set up more than one index on a table, and they don't have to be unique.

**275**

In the case of our contacts database, if you were to click the Require Unique Index Values checkbox then any data you add to your database later must have a unique contact name. In our simple example this is fine, but in a real-world application you would probably want to give each contact a unique number and set that as the primary index because names are not really unique.

Now you know how to create a database, let's go take a look at how to write code to use it. Obviously, we wouldn't get far with a database like your new one - it has no data! So, in the examples to follow we will use the **BIBLIO** database which is supplied with Visual Basic. Before we go any further make sure that you have this database (**BIBLIO.MDB**) on your hard disk. If you don't then now is the time to grab the Visual Basic installation disks and re-install the sample applications that come with it.

# The Data Control

Your primary tool for reading and updating databases is the Data Control. In the toolbox it looks like this:

When it is drawn onto a form it looks like this:

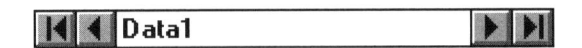

At either design or runtime you can link the data control to a database and one or more tables. In addition to that, you can even tell the data control to select only a subset of all the data available. For example, you may want to select only those customers who have not yet paid their bills in a sales database.

At runtime you can either leave the data control visible, in which case the user can use the data control's VCR style interface to move through the records, or you can leave it invisible, in which case you need to write code to tell the data control what to do next.

# The Data Control

Let's take a look at how the data control works for real.

## Binding

Visual Basic databases are all about bondage ... no, really! On its own, a data control is nothing more than a set of on-screen VCR buttons. To make it do something useful it needs to be bound to a database (bondage). This is all accomplished with a set of properties:

| Property | Description |
| --- | --- |
| `DatabaseName` | The name of the database to which you want to bind. |
| `RecordSource` | The name of the table you want to play with, or an SQL selection (see later). |
| `Connect` | A special string called a `Connect` string, for connecting to ODBC databases. |
| `RecordSet` | Lets you send SQL commands straight to the database, bypassing the control. |

### Binding the Data Control

The first step in binding the data control is to set the `DatabaseName` property. Start a new project and draw a data control on it. Then bring up the Properties window (select the data control and press *F4*).

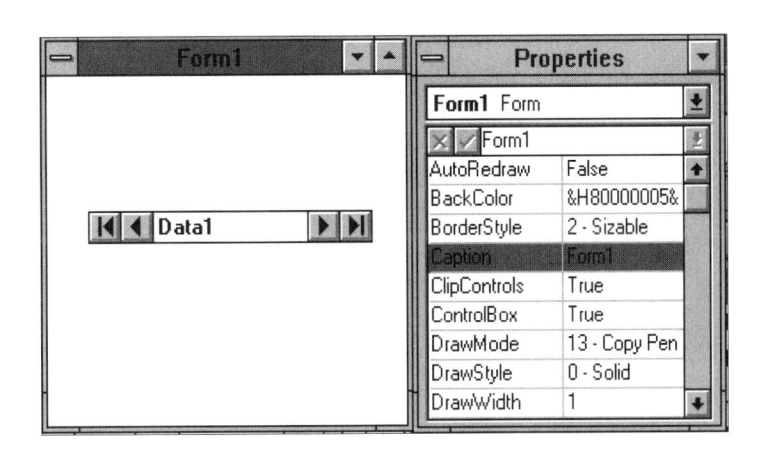

**277**

# Chapter 10 - Database Development

Find the `DatabaseName` property and either type in the full path and name of the database, or double click the property to bring up a File dialog and select the data base that way. Whatever method you use, make sure that the `DatabaseName` property ends up holding the path of your Visual Basic directory, followed by `BIBLIO.MDB`; for example:

```
c:\vb\biblio.mdb
```

Having told the data control which database to use, the next step is to tell it which table to use. We do this by setting the `RecordSource` property.

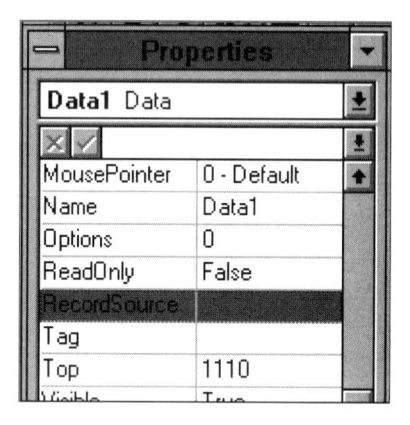

Click on the down facing arrow to the right of the property entry area to bring up a list of tables in the database.

Select the Titles table so that we can use the data control to browse all the books in the database.

# Binding Controls

That's really all there is to binding a data control to a database. You can now use the arrows on the data control to move through the Titles table, but you have no visible indication of what is taking place because we are not displaying any data. To actually view and change the data we need to bind some other controls to the data control.

## Binding Other Controls

To be able to manipulate the data we need to bind in other controls, so add a text box and label so that the form looks like this:

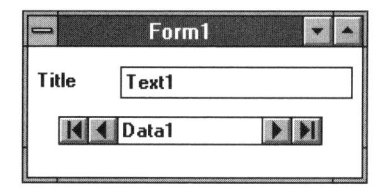

To bind a control such as a text box, to a data control, you need to set two more properties: **DataSource** and **DataField**. Bring up the Properties window for the text box and find the **DataSource** property.

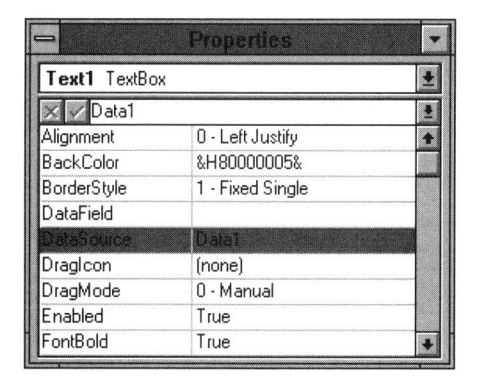

Having set the **DataSource** property to tell the text box which data control to use, we now need to tell the text box which field to display inside itself. That can be done with the **DataField** property. Select it now and drop down the list box beside the property entry area to view all the fields in the table:

**279**

# Chapter 10 - Database Development

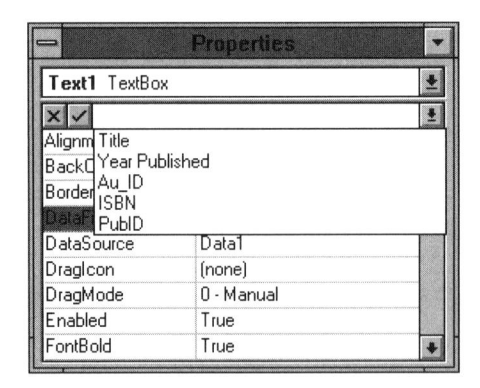

*[Properties window screenshot showing Text1 TextBox properties with a dropdown list of DataField options: Title, Year Published, Au_ID, ISBN, PubID]*

Select the **Titles** field, which will bind this text box to the titles field of the titles table. That's it. Now you can use the icons on the data control to move through the titles in the database.

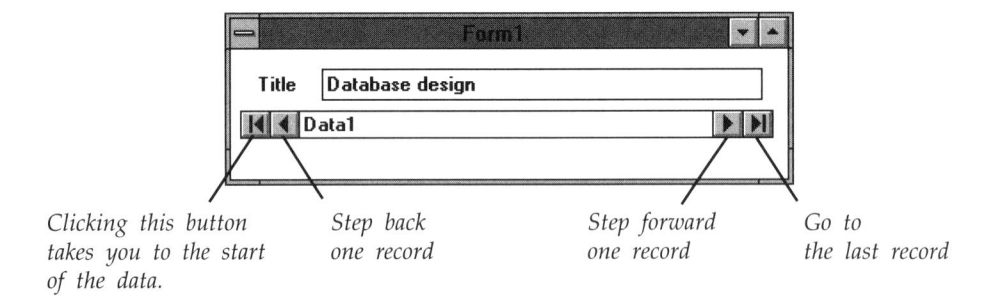

*[Form1 screenshot showing a Title text box with "Database design" and a Data1 control with VCR-style navigation buttons]*

*Clicking this button takes you to the start of the data.*   *Step back one record*   *Step forward one record*   *Go to the last record*

## Data Control Events

Simply being able to move around the database using the data control is fine, but what we really need is to be able to find out and respond to what the user is doing from within code. The data control only has a few events, including **Validate** and **Reposition**. If you still have the last example loaded, add some code to the **Reposition** event of the data control.

```
Sub Data1_Reposition ()
    MsgBox "We have moved"
End Sub
```

If you run the program now you will see that a message box pops up whenever you use the VCR controls on the data control to move to a new record. As you can see, the **Reposition** event is really quite simple to handle.

# Data Control Events

The **Validate** event, however, is an altogether different ball game.

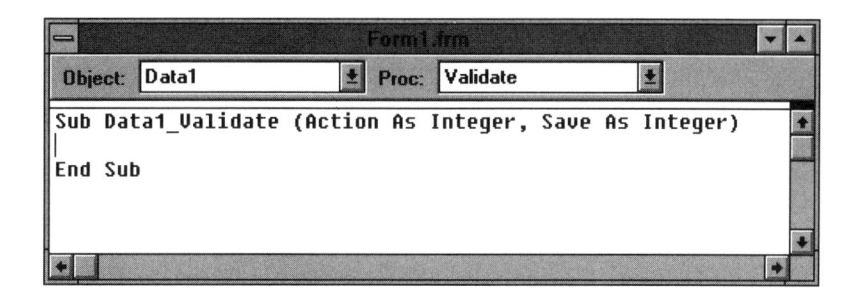

```
                          Form1.frm
Object:  Data1            ±    Proc:  Validate          ±
Sub Data1_Validate (Action As Integer, Save As Integer)
|
End Sub
```

The **Validate** event comes complete with two parameters, and it is these that make the event slightly tricky to handle: **Action** and **Save**.

The **Validate** event occurs before a new record becomes the current one. For example, if you use the VCR controls to move to a new record then the **Validate** event occurs just before the move takes place (the **Reposition** event always occurs after the current record has changed). Also, if you delete a record, find a new one or even unload the form, then the **Validate** event occurs before the change takes place. The **Action** parameter tells us what is about to happen.

Since the **Action** parameter is an integer, numbers represent the action that is about to take place, and these are in the **CONSTANT.TXT** file you came across earlier in the book.

| Value in CONSTANT.TXT | Description |
|---|---|
| DATA_ACTIONCANCEL | Set **Action** to this to cancel the current action. |
| DATA_ACTIONMOVEFIRST | We are about to move to the first record. |
| DATA_ACTIONMOVEPREVIOUS | About to move back one record. |
| DATA_ACTIONMOVENEXT | About to move forward one record. |
| DATA_ACTIONMOVELAST | About to move to the last record. |
| DATA_ACTIONADDNEW | A new record is about to be added. |

*Continued*

## Chapter 10 - Database Development

| Value in `CONSTANT.TXT` | Description |
| --- | --- |
| `DATA_ACTIONUPDATE` | The current record is about to be updated. |
| `DATA_ACTIONDELETE` | The current record is about to be deleted. |
| `DATA_ACTIONFIND` | We are about to find a new record. |
| `DATA_ACTIONBOOKMARK` | About to move using bookmarks (see later). |
| `DATA_ACTIONCLOSE` | The database or table is about to be closed. |
| `DATA_ACTIONUNLOAD` | The form is about to be unloaded. |

The first value `DATA_ACTIONCANCEL` gives you a method to cancel an operation before it even takes place. For example, you may want to cancel any `UPDATE`s so that if the user changes the data in a bound text box, you can prevent it from being saved to the database permanently.

The other parameter in the event, `Save`, indicates whether or not the data in the bound controls has changed. For example, if the data in the text box has changed then the `Save` parameter is `True`, otherwise it will be `False`.

By now you know how to display data on the screen, using the bound controls. Once the data is displayed, you can update it on the screen and move to a new record to save your changes into the database. However, you can't access the underlying data through code yet, nor can you create new records or delete existing ones. For that you need to learn how to use the recordset. Let's take a look.

# Introducing the Recordset

The data control provides you and your users with a view of data in the database. You can also access this view using the `Recordset` object. Now things get a little confusing. The data control is like a visual view of the data in a table. The recordset is the behind the scenes view. What the data control actually does is provide you with a way to see and manipulate

# The Recordset

what is actually in the **Recordset**. However, there are times when you don't really want to see the data control but you do still need to access the data itself.

Take a password dialog, for example. The user enters an ID which your code should use in the database to check the password entered. By leaving the data control visible, the user would be able to move through the records one-by-one viewing them on the screen. If you don't bind the text boxes to the data control the user would still see a redundant control on the form. By using the data control's **Recordset** object, you can leave the data control invisible but still use the database.

## Accessing the Recordset

As we have already said, the **Recordset** is an object of the data control. In this sense you access it very much like a normal property. The difference between it and a normal property is that it, in turn, has properties of its own.

We'll use our current project to see this in action, so bring up the **Form_Load** event and add the following code:

```
Sub Form_Load ()
    frmTitles.Show
```

Firstly, show the form.

```
    data1.Refresh
```

Next, we refresh the data control. Even though you have set up the **DatabaseName** and **RecordSource** at design time, the data control doesn't actually 'get' the records and make them available to you until the **Load** event has finished. Running the **Refresh** method on the data control tells it to get the records you have now asked for. In the case of the example, that means going to the database and binding itself to the Titles table.

```
    Do While Not data1.Recordset.EOF
```

This line starts a **Do**... loop which will run while the **EOF** property of the **Recordset** is **False**. **EOF** is set to **False** until the end of the **Recordset** is found. Since our `Recordset` is essentially all the records in the Titles table, the loop will run until the `Recordset` moves to the end of the Titles table. There is another property worth remembering called `BOF` which stands for `Beginning of File`. It is set to `True` when you try to move backwards through the `Recordset` to before the first record.

```
        MsgBox "Title : " & data1.Recordset("Title")
        data1.Recordset.MoveNext
```

Display the value of the titles field in a message box, then move to the next record in the `Recordset` using the `MoveNext` method. If you reach the end of the `Recordset` and attempt a `MoveNext` then the `EOF` property of the `Recordset` becomes `True` and the loop ends.

```
    Loop
End Sub
```

If you run the program now you will find that a message box keeps popping up, each time showing you a new title from the Titles table in the database. You'll notice that the title also changes in the text box because it's bound to the data control.

## Accessing Fields in a Record

The `Recordset` can also be considered as an array. Because tables can have many fields in them, so the `Recordset` is also an array of fields. The properties of the `Recordset` itself relate to the records in the table.

In turn, each element of the `Recordset` array has properties, such as `Value` (which is the value of the field in the current record), `Name` which is the name of the field, and so on. Time for a figure:

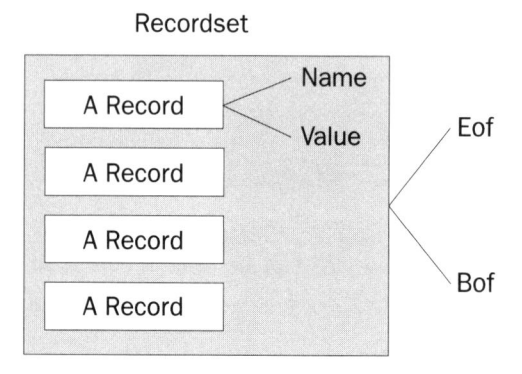

# Accessing Fields

More often than not you will want to access the value of a field in a record. You can do this in a number of ways:

```
Data1.Recordset(0)
```

This means the first field of the current record (just as with normal arrays, the first element is **0**). The next field is **1** and so on for all the fields in the record.

```
Data1.Recordset("Title").Value
```

This means the field called **Title**. A more common notation, however, is this:

```
Data1.Recordset!Title
```

or this

```
Data1.Recordset("Title")
```

Both mean the same thing. Since the **Value** property of a record is the default property it is not necessary to type **Value** each time you want to access it. Indeed, just as with normal controls and their properties, your Visual Basic code will run faster if you don't name the default property (such as **Text** of a textbox, or **Value** of a checkbox) when you want to use it, because then Visual Basic won't have to evaluate the reference.

> Just as you used the **Data Manager** previously to create a database and define the tables and fields within it, you can also use **Data Manager** to find out the tables and fields in an existing database. Have a go with the **Data Manager** and the BIBLIO database to see this in action.

The first line within the **Do**... loop in our example is the line which displays the value of the title field:

```
Msgbox " Title : " & Data1.Recordset("Title")
```

This simply displays the word **Title** followed by the value of the **Title** field using a technique we have already seen.

# Chapter 10 - Database Development

## Moving Around

You have already seen the **MoveNext** method and how it can be used to advance through a **Recordset** record by record. However, **MoveNext** is one of four similar methods that are available to you to deal with a **Recordset**. These reflect the four buttons that are on the Data Control.

| Method | Description |
| --- | --- |
| `MoveFirst` | Moves to the first record in a recordset |
| `MoveLast` | Moves to the last record in a recordset |
| `MovePrev` | Moves to the previous record in a recordset |
| `MoveNext` | Moves to the next record in a recordset |

> There is a little more to these methods than meets the eye. Since they all act on a **Recordset** of a data control each time they move through the **Recordset**, they also update any bound controls that are showing data from that **Recordset**, so any changes made will be saved to the database. This also applies to moving through the data control on the screen.

## BookMarks

There are times when you'll want to jump around from record to record. The Jet engine uses **BookMark**s for just that purpose. Each record in a **Recordset** has a string available, known as its **BookMark**. You can use this to jump quickly to a record for which you have previously retrieved the **BookMark**. For example in one place in your application you could use the following:

```
sOldBookMark = data1.RecordSet.BookMark
```

Then, when you needed to return to that record, the code is as simple as this:

```
data1.Recordset.BookMark = sOldBookMark
```

The `Recordset` will jump instantly to the record pointed to by the `BookMark`. `BookMarks` come in especially handy when you are modifying data in some way, as you will see in a moment.

## Data Maintenance

Holding data in a database is great, but not much use if you have no way to get the data in there in the first place, delete unused data, or change data that may be wrong or out of date. This is where the `AddNew`, `Edit`, `Update` and `Delete` methods come into play.

Count them up - that's four methods for three operations! The reason for this is quite simple. The `Update` method simply saves the changes that `AddNew` and `Edit` may have already done - so `Update` is not strictly an operation like creating, editing or deleting.

`AddNew` and `Edit` both prepare the `Recordset` for changes to take place. In the case of `AddNew`:

```
Data1.Recordset.AddNew
```

the `Recordset` moves to the blank area beyond the last record and prepares it to receive information. You can copy this information in roughly the same way that you pull it out.

```
Data1.Recordset("Title") = "Instant Visual Basic"
Data1.Recordset("ISBN") = 10000
```

Using the `Update` method then saves this new information to the blank area, creating a new record.

```
Data1.Recordset.Update
```

The `Edit` method works in roughly the same way.

```
Data1.Recordset.Edit
```

The difference between `Edit` and `AddNew` is that `Edit` simply prepares the current record to have its field values changed. You change them in the same way as you did when putting values into the new record above, and then save them to the database with `Update`.

**Delete** is even simpler to use - simply put the word **Delete** after the **Recordset** object and the current record gets deleted:

```
Data1.Recordset.Delete
```

Now we come to the interesting part. Which record is current after a new one is added, or after the current one is deleted? This is where the **BookMarks** come into play. The **Recordset** has two special **BookMark** properties called **LastUpdated** and **LastModified**. The **LastUpdated** property is the **BookMark** of the last updated record. If at any time you need to jump instantly to the last updated record, then you can simply use this:

```
Data1.Recordset.BookMark = Data1.Recordset.LastUpdated
```

**LastModified** is much more specific though, jumping to the last updated or created record. This is useful for when you add a new record. The process that Visual Basic goes through when you use the **AddNew** method is to first move to the end of the **Recordset** and wait for the changes to take place, followed by the **Update** method. Then the **Recordset** moves back to the record that was current before the **AddNew** operation. Using the **LastModified** method you can get back to your newly created record.

```
Data1.Recordset.AddNew
Data1.Recordset("Title") = "Instant Visual Basic"
Data1.Recordset("ISBN") = 1874416486
Data1.Recordset.Update
Data1.Recordset.BookMark = Data1.Recordset.LastModified
```

This snippet of code would create a new record in our Titles **Recordset**, set up two fields in that record, update the **Recordset** to save the changes and then jump back to the new record.

Finally, the **AddNew** and **Edit** methods can also be used to cancel themselves out. If you need to cancel an **AddNew** operation, simply do it again.

```
Data1.Recordset.AddNew
        :
        :
        :
        :
Data1.Recordset.AddNew   ' Cancels the first addnew
```

# SQL

The second **AddNew** cancels the first out, leaving the recordset in the same state that it was in before the first **AddNew**. The same applies to **Edit**. This is useful for those times where you have a command button on a dialog box to add or edit a record, but you also have a Cancel button and need to cancel the previous operation. You could, of course, put code in the **Validate** event and cancel the operation that way, as you saw earlier. The changes to the **Recordset** are not applied until the **Update** method is called.

So far you have seen how the **RecordSource** property of a data control can be used to give you access to all the records in a single table. However, you can also use the **Recordsource** property to access more than one table, and also to locate a subset of the records available.

## SQL: Database Implementation

In larger more traditional database systems, such as Oracle or Informix, SQL (Structured Query Language) is used to rapidly select groups of records, sort them and search them.

Visual Basic supports a subset of this language, the most useful command of which is **Select**. Using **Select** you can tell the Jet engine which records to select, how to **Join** two or more tables into a single **Recordset** and much more. The syntax of **Select** is quite simple: you type **Select**, followed by what you want (which fields), where it comes from (the tables) and what the selection criteria are (in order to limit the number of records you get back). For instance, to select all records and all the fields in the records from the Titles table, you would code this into the **RecordSource** property of the data control:

```
Select * from Titles
```

This selects all fields (* means all), from the Titles table with no criteria to exclude any records.

To select only the Instant Visual Basic title record from the Titles table you would put the following into the **RecordSource** property:

**289**

# Chapter 10 - Database Development

```
Select * from Titles where Title = 'Instant Visual Basic'
```

Notice how single quotes (') are used to surround text in a SQL string, instead of the usual double quotes (") you are used to. SQL can also be used to link two or more tables together, and this is where the relational elements of the database come into play.

Let's see some of this in action. Start a new project and on the form put a data control, two labels and two text boxes. Our form looks like this:

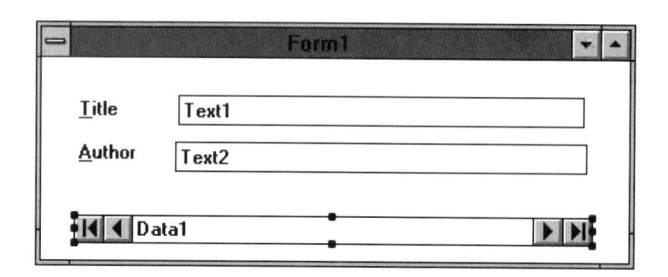

Set the **Databasename** property of the data control up so that it points to our **BIBLIO** database.

We need to display the title of the books and the authors who wrote them. The problem is that the titles and authors come from different tables within the database; the title of a book comes from the **Title** field of the Titles table, while the author comes from the **Author** field of the Authors table. Both tables have an **Au_ID** field, which we will use to link them by, and we can use this in our **Select** statement to restrict the records that the Jet engine transfers to the recordset. Put this into the **RecordSource** property of the data control in the Properties window:

```
Select Title, Author from Titles, Authors where Authors.Au_Id = Titles.Au_Id
```

This tells the data control to form a **Recordset** containing only a **Title** and **Author** field. It also tells the data control to get these fields from the Titles and Authors tables respectively and that the link is the **Au_Id** field in both tables.

Now set up the **DataSource** and **DataField** properties of the two text

290

boxes in the normal way: **Text1** is bound to the **Title** field, **Text2** to the **Author** field. If you run the program now you will see that you can move through the **Recordset** in the normal way, but this time you get to see the title and the author of the books.

Using the SQL **Select** statement you can even write a query (that's what they are called), which selects or finds a single record. A much better way to do it though is to use the **Find** methods: **FindNext**, **FindFirst**, **FindPrev** and **FindLast**. These work in the same way as the **Move** methods, but let you use SQL to move to the first, last, next and previous records that match your selection string:

```
Data1.Recordset.FindFirst "Title = 'Instant Visual Basic'"
```

The text after the quotes is the text that you would normally put after the **Where** clause in the **Select** statement. If the find fails then you can check the **Recordset**'s **NoMatch** property, which will be **True** if the find operation failed.

```
Data1.Recordset.FindFirst "Title = 'Instant Visual Basic'"
If Data1.Recordset.noMatch then
        MsgBox "Couldn't find the record you were after"
End If
```

You now have the basics at your disposal to start using databases with the data control in your own applications. However, there are still a number of finer points which are best used by doing away with the data control totally. However, for that you need to look beyond Standard Visual Basic.

## The Alternatives

By now you have seen what the Standard edition has to offer: the data control and bound text boxes. However, what happens when you need access to a table throughout your application? What about talking to two databases at once, or how about deleting or updating a couple of thousand related records? When we start looking at issues like these in the Standard edition then we start to look at large chunks of slow Visual Basic code.

The Professional edition, and the various other database add-ons that are available for Visual Basic provide you with a much easier life as a programmer.

# The Professional Edition

Let's take a look at how the Professional edition of Visual Basic compares first of all. In standard Visual Basic you talk to the database and its underlying tables with the data control. However, Access databases support a number of different ways in which to retrieve data; tables can be used to get at the pure table data, dynasets let you process complex SQL commands to create 'pseudo tables' or queries - speedy read-only selections of data are handled by Snapshots.

When you talk to a data control, Visual Basic takes time to convert your requests into something that the Jet engine can understand. The Jet engine may then in turn have to convert those requests into ODBC calls if you are not directly talking to an Access database. The Professional edition lets you remove one of these layers by allowing you to talk to the Jet engine directly.

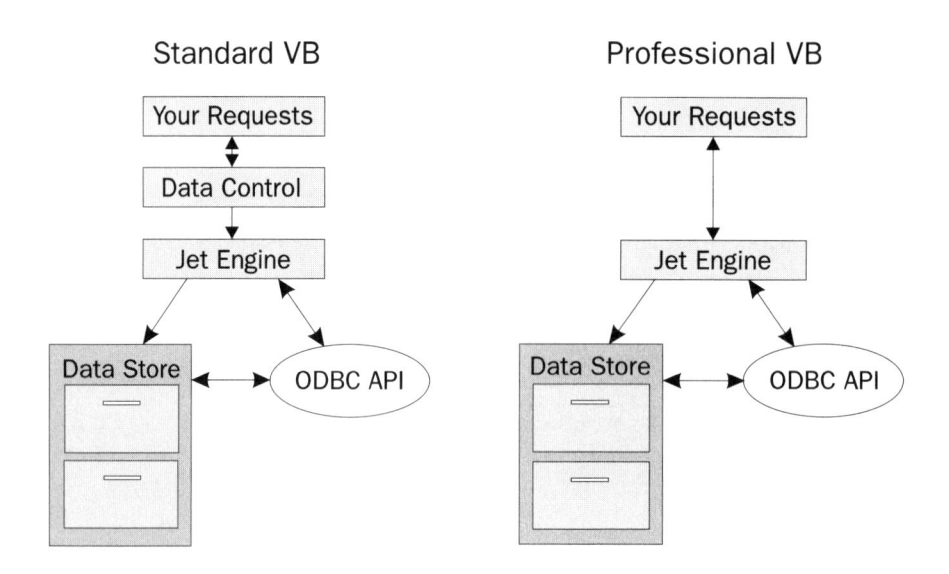

**Standard VB**

Your Requests → Data Control → Jet Engine → Data Store ↔ ODBC API

**Professional VB**

Your Requests → Jet Engine → Data Store ↔ ODBC API

Using the Professional edition's new database methods you are able to select records, examine tables and process queries from within your code without the need for the data control. You also have complete control over how you select records, create them, update them and delete them.

Of course, you can do these things with the data control. However, by bypassing the data control your code soon finds itself with a considerable performance increase. In addition, there are yet more commands to let your process SQL to perform mass database updates.

Consider this: you need to open a table called **TABLE1** in a database called **DATA1.MDB**. When you have it open you need to delete all the records in it. With standard Visual Basic you would need to produce a form, put a data control onto that form, and then put something like this somewhere in the form's code:

```
Datacontrol.Databasename = "data1.mdb"
Datacontrol.Recordsource = "table1"
Datacontrol.Refresh
Do While Not Eof Datacontrol.recordset
        Datacontrol.Recordset.Delete
Loop
```

The Professional edition code to do the same job would look a lot more elegant and also run a lot faster

```
Dim DB as Database
```

Declare a database object variable.

```
Set DB = OpenDatabase("data1.mdb")
```

Set it to reference the required database.

```
DB.Execute("Delete from table1")
```

Execute the SQL statement (called an action query) which will delete all the records in the table.

This is much better, and since you can keep the database open and held in a global variable throughout an application, the above code would really end up as just the last line (`DB.Execute("Delete from table1")`.

# Code Basic and Q+E

An alternative to the Microsoft offering is to purchase a whole new database add-on. Two of the more popular are Code Basic and Q+E Multilink/VB. Both essentially dump the Jet engine totally, and all the bound controls with it.

# Chapter 10 - Database Development

In their place you get a whole new set of controls, properties, functions and methods. They have certain advantages, particularly if you don't just write Visual Basic code: both have libraries for sale which slot in nicely with C and C++. Both libraries are also slightly faster in use than the Jet engine, but both are also quite a lot more complex and prevent you from using your library of bound controls.

It's horses for courses - if you want to re-use the libraries in your C and C++ developments, or have a need to access a database format that the Jet engine doesn't natively support, then take a look at these two.

## Summary

In this chapter you were introduced to the concept of the relational database, and how it is structured. You learnt how to set up your own databases by using the Data Manager application, and set up a database that reflects the example in the previous chapter.

Using the database that is shipped with Visual Basic you saw how to create a data control, bind it to a database, and use a bound text box to view details in a table. We also reviewed the events and methods associated with the data control. We then moved on to controlling the database in code via the `RecordSource` object. You saw how to access records and the fields within the records, how to jump to records by using bookmarks and how to add, amend and delete data using the `RecordSource` properties and methods.

You were then introduced to SQL and saw how to access data in different tables by using the `Select` statement. Finally we discussed some of the alternatives to database access using the Standard edition. If you're serious about using databases, then we'd strongly recommend that you use the Professional edition as a minimum.

## Exercises

For this chapter, rather than go through some small specific exercises, you're going to develop a whole application, based on the Contacts application. As a starting point, you'll need two tables, one that holds names and phone numbers, the other structured address details.

# Summary and Exercises

Create a new directory to hold all your project details, then create a new database in the directory called Contact. The first table call Names, and add the following fields:

| Field Name | Type | Size | Description |
|---|---|---|---|
| `IdNo` | `Integer` |  | A unique id starting at 1 and going up 1 for each new record |
| `Surname` | `Text` | 30 |  |
| `FirstName` | `Text` | 20 |  |
| `HomePhone` | `Text` | 20 |  |
| `OfficePhone` | `Text` | 20 |  |
| `Fax` | `Text` | 20 |  |

Create a primary index on the `IdNo` called `NameIndex`. Now create an address table and insert the following fields:

| Field Name | Type | Size | Description |
|---|---|---|---|
| `IdNo` | `Integer` |  | Used to link to the Name table. It will also be the unique primary key |
| `Address1` | `Text` | 40 | Line 1 of the address |
| `Address2` | `Text` | 40 | Line 2 of the address |
| `Address3` | `Text` | 40 | Line 3 of the address |
| `Address4` | `Text` | 40 | Line 4 of the address |

Create a primary index called `AddIndex` on `IdNo`. Unfortunately, we can't hold an array in a database, so each line of the address has been split individually.

Now create an application that will allow you to enter, amend and delete contact details in your database. Bear in mind that you can only have an address if you have created a name record. Good luck!

# Chapter 11

# Debugging and Error Handling

Producing perfect, bug-free programs is the goal of every programmer, but in today's complex environments it's rarely achievable. How your code reacts to the errors it receives, therefore becomes of paramount importance. In this chapter, we'll look at the ways of reducing the amount of bugs in your applications using the Visual Basic debugging tools and then at ways of handling errors in your code, so that your system doesn't crash, but degrades gracefully.

In this chapter we'll be covering:

- Program design
- Debug facilities
- Procedure stepping
- Runtime Errors

## Good Program Design: Concepts

We can attempt to reduce the amount of bugs before we write a single line of code. One of the reasons for the introduction of structured programming in the late 1970s was part of an attempt to reduce the number of bugs in programs, as well as to write code that is easy to maintain. These reasons still hold true today, in fact more so with the rise of the use of object-oriented programming.

## Modularity and re-Usability

If you wrote a program which allowed a user to enter a password and check that it was valid, you could be fairly confident that the five or so lines of code required would be bug free, and that the application would work. Now imagine that you've been asked to write an application which is password-protected and allows valid users to view or amend details on your marketing database, depending on their access level. This may well take over a thousand lines of code, use a multitude of screens and have a menu structure attached. How confident would you be that your application was totally bug free?

## Modules

Part of the problem is that in a password program, only one function is involved, with only one route through the code. In fact, it's a completely stand alone module, whereas the second example undertakes many functions, some of which are dependent on one another, and there are many routes through the code. So how do we minimize the number of possible bugs? The key is to break up your code into modules, each undertaking a particular function, as in the password function. Testing five or fifty lines is much easier than testing a thousand in one go. When you're happy that the module is bug free, go on to the next one, until all the modules are bug free. Then put them all together to test the application, (sometimes called link testing). You couldn't guarantee that your application was totally bug free, but you would have drastically reduced the chance of a bug occurring.

# Program Design

## Design for Reuse

The other advantage of using this method is reusability. Once you've written and debugged a module, you may find that it can be used in other applications. You already know that there are no bugs in it, so it won't only save coding time, but testing time too. Eventually you can build up a code library of useful modules which will drastically reduce the time taken to produce applications (this is one of the objectives of object-oriented programming).

This does take some forethought before you start coding. You need to ask yourself if the function that you're about to write could be used in other applications. If it's an actuarial calculation for premium levels on schedule 'd' policies for the next 15 years, then it's unlikely. A function to validate the input from a text box may well be used in several different places in your application, and elsewhere, so why re-invent the wheel?

A reusable function or module must be totally stand-alone, and may not make any reference to variables that are specific to the application for which it was first written. This isn't as difficult as it might seem. In fact, our password application from Chapter 1 could fairly easily be packaged into a stand-alone function which gets a username and password from a user, checks it (probably against a table of users in a database), and returns a boolean that is **True** for a valid user and password, or **False** for an invalid entry. You would have to pass the location and name of the database (and possibly table) to the function to make it totally stand-alone. The function call would look something like this:

```
iValid = GetUserPassword(ByVal sDataBaseLocation, ByVal sTableName)
```

**iValid** is the return boolean which will indicate whether or not the user name and password is valid, and the two strings **sDataBaseLocation** and **sTableName** are string variables which hold the location and name of the database, as well as the relevant table.

## Parameter Passing by Val

We've sneaked in a new keywords here, **ByVal**. In Visual Basic, there are two ways to pass variables to a procedure or function. So far we've passed all out parameters **by reference**. This means that within the function or procedure you have called, the variables used as parameters can be altered.

# Chapter 11 - Debugging and Error Handling

This is useful if you want to pass back more than one value, such as writing a function that is passed three numbers, and returns the square of all three numbers, in the variables used as parameters.

In many cases, you don't want the actual parameter values to be altered, as this can cause certain bugs that are difficult to find. To avoid this problem, use the **ByVal** keyword. This stops the values in your parameters being accidentally overwritten. It's also more efficient, because Visual Basic doesn't have to load it into memory in case it has changed. You'll find that when you deal with the Windows API in the next chapter, all the parameters have to be passed **ByVal**.

## The Visual Basic Debugging Facilities

No matter how hard you try, and what techniques you use, bugs will manage to creep into your code. Visual Basic has extensive facilities for testing and debugging your code.

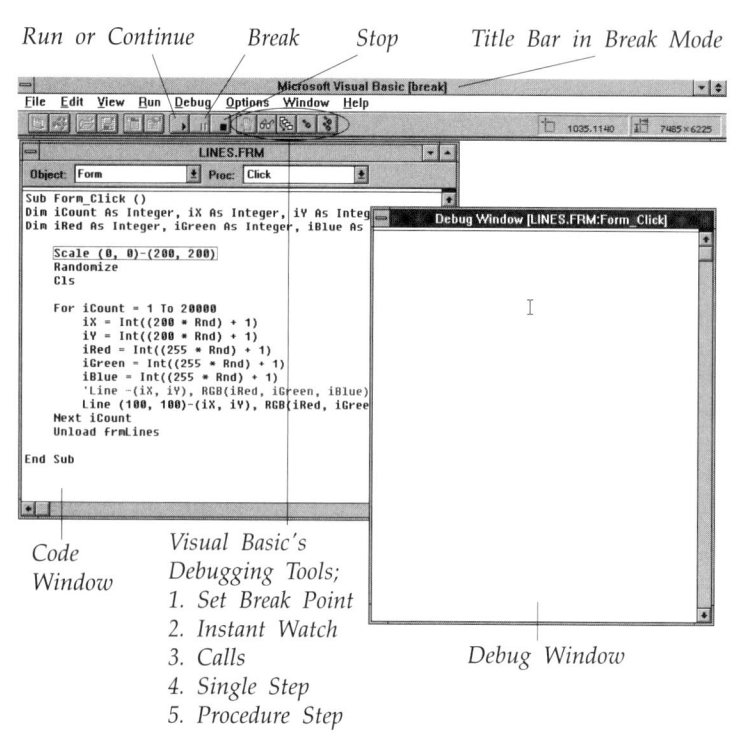

*Run or Continue*    *Break*    *Stop*    *Title Bar in Break Mode*

*Code Window*

*Visual Basic's Debugging Tools;*
1. Set Break Point
2. Instant Watch
3. Calls
4. Single Step
5. Procedure Step

*Debug Window*

*Debug window - Used to display details, and change variables and properties whilst in break mode*

*Title bar in break mode for debugging*

*Run Icon - Run or continue running the application (Run Mode)*

*Break - Put the application into break mode*

*Stop Icon - Stop execution and return to design mode*

*Set Breakpoint Icon - Set a breakpoint (puts application into break mode)*

*The Instant Watch Icon - Look at the value of a variable*

*Calls Icon - Shows all procedures called that have not yet finished*

*Single Step - Run the next executable line of code*

*Procedure Step - Run the next executable line, without stepping through the procedures code*

*Code Window showing the current executable line*

# Debugging

Here's what you'll see when you're in break mode. You can step through your code, changing variables and properties as you go, and even change the next line to be executed. Let's see how these elements fit into Visual Basic.

## The Debug Window

If you remember, `Debug` is one of the five system objects available. This allows us to write code that prints directly to the Debug Window. This output will only be visible when the debug window is visible, either during runtime while Visual Basic is waiting for an event, or during break time. Start a new project, and type the following in the `Form_Load` event:

```
Debug.Print "This will be printed in the Debug Window"
```

Now run the program, and press *Ctrl + B* to bring the debug window to the top, (or select Debug from the Window menu).

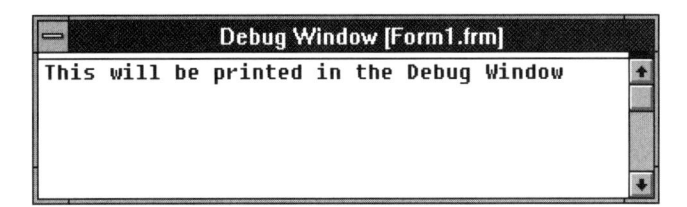

```
Debug Window [Form1.frm]
This will be printed in the Debug Window
```

You'll notice that the title of the Debug Window shows which procedure or function is currently being executed.

> **Printing to the Debug window will not affect your system's functionality at runtime, but if you leave debug code in your application, the executable file will be larger and slower, as it will still execute the `Debug.Print` statements.**

**301**

# Chapter 11 - Debugging and Error Handling

Stop the program from running, and then delete the line. In the `Form_Click` event create an array of five strings, and then enter the following code:

```
Sub Form_Click ()
    Static sJunk(5) As String, iCount As Integer
    For iCount = 1 To 4
        sJunk(iCount) = "This is Element No. " & Str(iCount)
    Next iCount
```

There are two bugs here, which may not be obvious at first glance. You may well have spotted them, but they would be harder to see if this was part of a multi thousand line application.

```
    For iCount = 0 To 4
        Debug.Print sJunk(iCount)
    Next iCount
End Sub
```

Here we're printing all the array details to the Debug Window. When you run the program, you'll end up with the following:

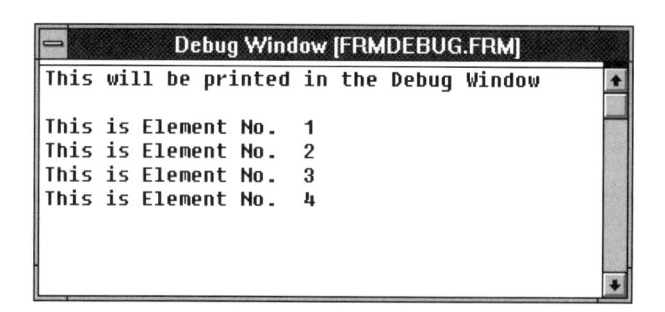

```
Debug Window [FRMDEBUG.FRM]
This will be printed in the Debug Window

This is Element No.  1
This is Element No.  2
This is Element No.  3
This is Element No.  4
```

You'll notice that the previous message is still in the Debug Window. The details are never overwritten, but they do scroll off the top. The next line is blank. This is the print of the first array element, and is our first bug. The loop should have run from 0 to 4, not 1 to 4 (remember array indexes start at 0). We're going to fix this on the fly, so run the project again but don't click on the form, instead put the project into break mode by pressing the break icon

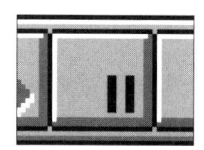

# Breakpoints

We now have control of the execution of the project. If the Code Window isn't visible press *F7*, or select it from the <u>V</u>iew menu. Now select the **Form_Click** event, and our code is displayed.

## Setting BreakPoints

We suspect that the first **For**...**Next** loop may not be working correctly, so we'll stop the program at this point. To set a breakpoint move the cursor to the line, then click the Breakpoint icon, or press *F9*. The line will now be highlighted in a similar way to this screenshot:

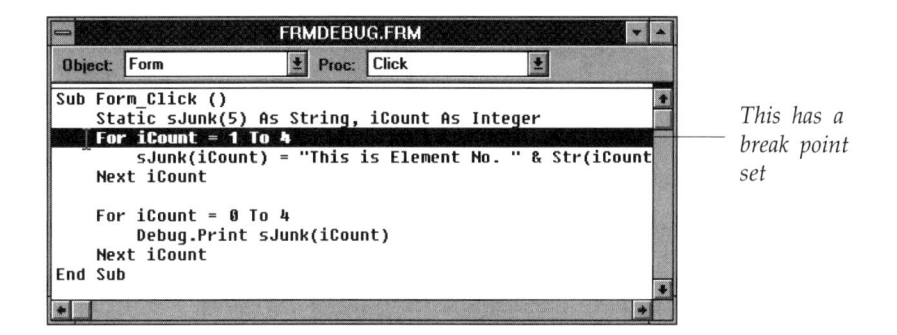

```
                 FRMDEBUG.FRM
Object: Form              Proc: Click

Sub Form_Click ()
    Static sJunk(5) As String, iCount As Integer
    For iCount = 1 To 4
        sJunk(iCount) = "This is Element No. " & Str(iCount
    Next iCount

    For iCount = 0 To 4
        Debug.Print sJunk(iCount)
    Next iCount
End Sub
```

*This has a break point set*

Now press the Run icon to continue running the program, then click on the form to execute the code. Visual Basic has reached the breakpoint, halted execution, and put the project into break mode. Now that we are in the code, we can control its execution, look at the value of variables and properties, and alter them if we want to. It's also possible to alter the code in the Code Window and try out the new code.

> Altogether you can completely take apart your code. Beware if you change code on the fly, because any alterations will remain after you've ended the project.

## Single Stepping

To execute the **For** statement, and subsequent statements, we need to single step through each line. This will keep the project in break mode and allow us access to the code, properties and variables. To single step, click the

**303**

# Chapter 11 - Debugging and Error Handling

Single step icon, or press *F8*. You'll see that a dotted box is now on the `Next` statement:

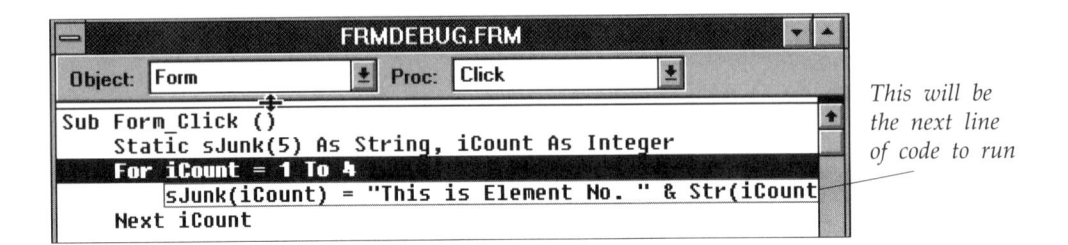

```
┌─────────────────── FRMDEBUG.FRM ───────────────────┐
│ Object: Form          ▼  Proc: Click            ▼  │
├────────────────────────────────────────────────────┤
│ Sub Form_Click ()                                  │
│     Static sJunk(5) As String, iCount As Integer   │
│     For iCount = 1 To 4                            │
│         sJunk(iCount) = "This is Element No. " & Str(iCount
│     Next iCount                                    │
└────────────────────────────────────────────────────┘
```
*This will be the next line of code to run*

Now in the Debug Window type `?iCount`. The number `1` will be displayed. What we have asked Visual Basic to do is run a `Print` statement, using the shortcut `?`. In fact, it's possible to type any valid Visual Basic statement in the Debug Window for execution, although you can't declare variables. For this run through type `iCount = 4` in the Debug Window. We've now set the value to `4`, so that only one iteration of the loop will occur. Press *F8*, and you'll see the `Next iCount` statement highlighted. Press *F8* again, and instead of going back up the loop, the `Next` statement is now the start of the `Print` loop because we set `iCount` to `4`. Press F5 to continue running and you'll see that only the last element of our string array has been set and blank lines are printed for the unset elements.

Click the form again, and we're back at the breakpoint. To switch off the breakpoint, press *F9*, or click the Breakpoint icon. This key toggles the breakpoint on and off.

## Altering the Running Order

We can change the order that our code is executed by using Set Next Statement from the Debug menu. Move the cursor to the start of the `Print` loop, then select Set Next Statement. You'll see that Visual Basic has now set the `For`... line as the current statement. Press *F8* a few times to run through several iterations of the loop, then look at the Debug Window. All we have now is blank lines. Print the value of `iCount` to see what it is, then move the cursor to the first loop, and again use Set Next Statement. We've determined that the loop should start at `0`, so change the `1` to a `0`, and run the program. All elements of our array are now set as required. End the project, and you'll see that the change you made is now part of the code.

# Watches

## Using Stop

An alternative to setting a breakpoint in your code is to enter the **Stop** command where you want an execution to stop. Enter **Stop** before the first loop and run the project again. Execution is halted at the **Stop** command and we're back in break mode. This is a hangover from older versions of BASIC and is less versatile than breakpoints because you have to type them in and remove them yourself. If you leave them in when you compile, a message box will be displayed when you run the program, and the program will then end. Breakpoints have no effect on the executable.

Now we're back at the start of our first loop, we can correct the other bug. Our users have informed us that the element count should start at **1**, not **0**, so we need to add **1** to **iCount** before adding it to the string. That's it - our project is bug free! Well almost - we need to remove the **Stop** statement and print to the form instead of the **Debug** object.

## Watching

Obviously, this is a very simplistic example, but it does illustrate most of the debugging facilities. For larger projects, it can become difficult to keep breaking and then printing the value of a variable to the Debug Window. Visual Basic has the facility to set a **watch** on an expression.

> An expression on which a watch can be set can be a variable, a property, a function call, or any valid expression.

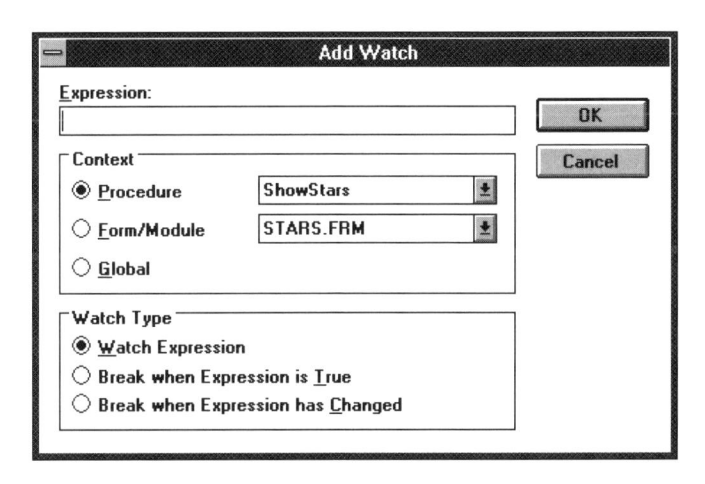

305

Within the Context options, you can set the scope of the expression to be evaluated. For instance, you can restrict the scope of the watch of a global variable or function to a single procedure or form. Visual Basic can evaluate the expression more quickly if the scope is narrowed. This is because if you choose Procedure, the watch expression will only be evaluated after every line of code while the selected procedure is open. If you choose Form/Module or Global, the expression is evaluated after every line is executed. If you try to set a global watch on a local variable, then you'll get a variable undefined message when you try to run the project.

Within the Add Watch dialog the radio buttons allow you to create an expression that, when true, puts the project into break mode or puts the project into break mode when the expression changes. If you select the Watch Expression radio button, then you'll have to set breakpoints to break the project. The details of the expression being watched will be displayed in the Debug Window. We'll try out some of the watch facilities using the Stars project we wrote in Chapter 8.

## Setting and Editing a Watch

Load the Stars project, and bring up the Code Window. We're going to set a watch on `iCount`, and there are several ways to do this. The easiest way is to highlight `iCount`, then select Add Watch from the Debug Menu, and click the OK button. You've now set a watch on `iCount`, but to see the effect, we need to set a breakpoint. The `For`... statement in the `Form Click` event is a good place. Now run the project.

The project halts at the breakpoint, and the code window is displayed, but where's the title bar, and the Debug Window? Because our form is maximized and borderless, we need to press *F10* to bring the title bar into view, and *Ctrl+B* to get the Debug Window to be displayed. The Debug Window is now split into two parts. The top section shows our watch expressions, and their current status, and the bottom section (also called the **immediate pane**) shows `Debug.Print` statements and so on.

# Editing a Watch

*This pane holds all our watch expressions*

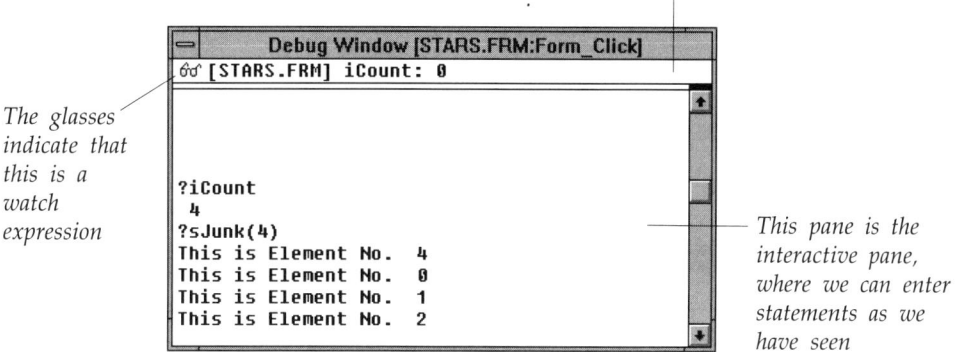

*The glasses indicate that this is a watch expression*

```
    Debug Window [STARS.FRM:Form_Click]
 6d [STARS.FRM] iCount: 0

?iCount
 4
?sJunk(4)
This is Element No.  4
This is Element No.  0
This is Element No.  1
This is Element No.  2
```

*This pane is the interactive pane, where we can enter statements as we have seen*

Click in the immediate pane, and type the following:

`frmStar.WindowState = 0.`

This will change the **WindowState** property of our form from maximized to normal. Start stepping through the loop by pressing *F8*. You'll see the watch expression change every time you step through the **Next** statement.

We can also set a watch whilst in break mode. First take the breakpoint off the start of the loop, then select Add Watch, and type the following expression, then click OK:

`iCount = 30.`

You'll now see the new expression in the watch pane. Ah, this has been entered as a watch, whereas what we require is a break when **True**, so we'll need to edit the watch. This can be done by selecting Edit Watch from the Debug Menu, or double clicking on the expression. Now select the Break When Expression is True radio button, and click OK. The icon in the watch pane has changed and so has its status (notice the <False> at the end).

Now to continue, but first, set the **WindowState** back to **2** in the immediate pane. To save having to retype the whole line just change the **0** to **2** in the last statement. Visual Basic will re-evaluate the whole line when you press the *Enter* key and the window will maximize. Press *F10*, and select Continue from the Run menu (or press *F5*).

**307**

# Chapter 11 - Debugging and Error Handling

Providing you didn't single step past **30**, the project will break when **iCount** reaches **30**. There should be a few stars on the screen when this happens. If you bring up the Debug Window, you'll see that the watch expression is highlighted, and that **iCount** is now equal to 30.

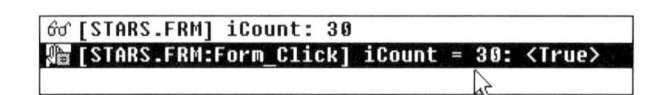

```
👀 [STARS.FRM] iCount: 30
📄 [STARS.FRM:Form_Click] iCount = 30: <True>
```

Press *F5* to continue, and the project will break when **iCount** next reaches **30** (this time in the **ShowStars** procedure). Stop the project by typing **End** in the immediate pane, then choose Edit Watch from the Debug menu.

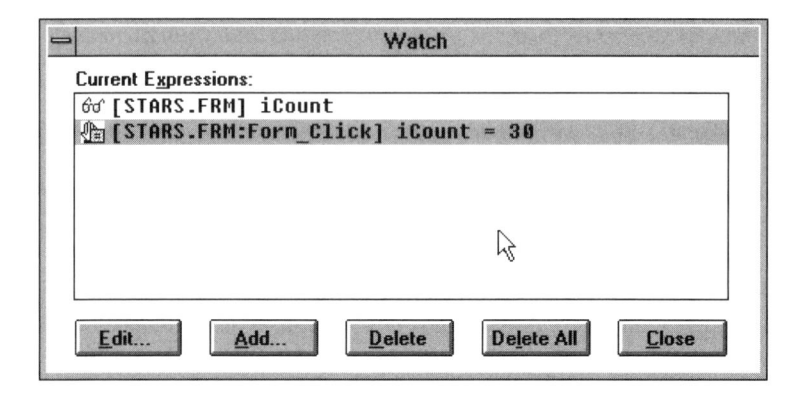

```
                        Watch
Current Expressions:
 👀 [STARS.FRM] iCount
 📄 [STARS.FRM:Form_Click] iCount = 30



        Edit...   Add...   Delete   Delete All   Close
```

From this dialog, you can see all the current watches for the project, and undertake any watch function. Highlight the **iCount = 30** watch, and select the Edit ... function. In the procedure dialog box, select the **ShowStars** procedure, and click OK. We've now changed the scope of the watch statement, so run the project to see the effect. Now the project doesn't break in the **Form_Click** event, even though **iCount** will have been equal to **30** whilst setting up the stars. The first time that it breaks is in the **ShowStars** function. This is because we've narrowed the scope of this expression to the **ShowStars** prodedure only.

308

# Procedure Stepping

## Tracing Procedure Calls

In complex projects, you may need to see the path that was taken to arrive at a function or procedure (such as **ShowStars**). You can quickly see the procedure call tree by clicking the Calls icon, or pressing *Ctrl+L*, or selecting Calls... from the Debug menu. The Calls window is then displayed, with all the currently active procedures displayed:

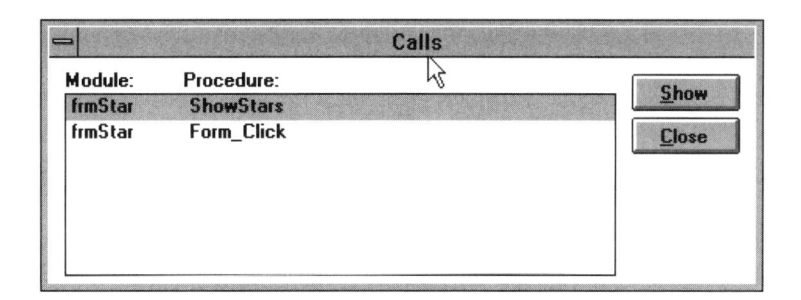

| Module: | Procedure: |
|---|---|
| frmStar | ShowStars |
| frmStar | Form_Click |

The earliest is placed at the bottom, and each successive procedure above it. The current procedure will be at the top. If this is highlighted when you click the Show button, then the current statement will be displayed in the Code Window. If you select any others, then the statement that called the procedure will be displayed.

## Procedure Stepping

Where you've written modular code, or included working modules from your code library, you won't really want to step through all the code in the function or procedure, but you will want to execute the code. The Procedure stepping icon will do this for you. Let's try it out. Remove all the watches in the project, and set a breakpoint on the **Loop** statement in the **Form_Click** event. Now run the project, and click on the form. All the stars will be displayed, moved one unit, and we are then dropped into break mode. Press *F10* to display the title bar, and click the single step to take you into the **ShowStars** procedure.

**309**

# Chapter 11 - Debugging and Error Handling

After single stepping, you'll agree that this is a bit of a drag, especially as we know that the function has no bugs. Press F5 to continue, and the project will stop at the next loop statement. Now click the Procedure step icon. The first click will make **ShowStars** the current statement. If you click the Procedure step icon again, the whole procedure is run, without having to step through each individual statement.

## Instant Watching

The final facility available to help you debug your code is the **instant watch**. This can be used at any time while you are in break mode to look at the value of a variable. You should currently be on the loop statement, so we can investigate the values in the variables. Bring up the title bar and then highlight the **iCurX(iCount)** variable. Now press the Instant watch icon and you'll see the following:

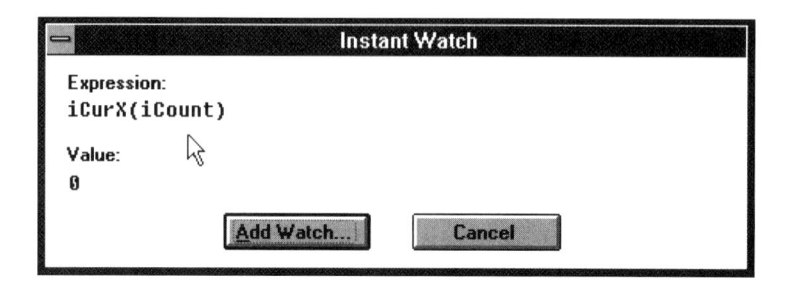

```
                    Instant Watch
Expression:
iCurX(iCount)

Value:
0

         [ Add Watch... ]    [ Cancel ]
```

You can set a watch from here, or cancel, and look at another variable.

That about rounds up the debugging facilities available in Visual Basic, with just a final word of caution. Because of the way that Windows handles events, setting breakpoints in the following events will not work as expected:

- **MouseDown** - you'll never run the **MouseUp** code, because **MouseUp** occurs outside of your programs control in the Visual Basic environment.

- **KeyDown** - this is the same problem as setting a breakpoint in the **MouseDown** event

- **GotFocus** and **LostFocus** - the timing of Windows will give inconsistent results with breakpoints in these events.

# Error Handling

The solution is to use `Debug.Print` statements in these events to determine what is happening.

## Handling Errors at Runtime

No matter how hard you try, and how much testing your system is subjected to, from time to time the unexpected will happen and errors will occur. It may be that a user has done something that you could never have anticipated, or it could be that the file server just crashed, or that when accessing a floppy drive there is no disk in the drive. All these will cause **runtime** errors, and if you don't write code to handle them your system will crash. The code that you write is called an **error trap** code, and we saw it briefly in Chapter 3. If you managed to do the exercise in that chapter, then you've already got a good idea of how error trapping works - if not, the next couple of pages should make it clearer for you.

## On Error Goto...

You can write error traps for specific events, to handle general errors, or to ignore errors and continue (although ignoring errors is not recommended!).

No matter what type of error trap you wish to set, they all have the same format:

```
On Error Goto...
```

The elipses are a label which holds the code to be executed in the case of an error. The **OnError** statement can occur anywhere in the function or procedure, but can't jump to an error trap that is written in a different function or procedure. This doesn't stop you calling other procedures and functions within the error trap itself.

### Setting Error Traps

So what happens when an error occurs? This depends on where you are in your code, and where you've set an error trap (if, indeed, you have set one). If you are in a procedure which has been called by another procedure, and an error occurs and there's no error trap in this called procedure, Visual Basic will check back up the procedure chain to see if there are any enabled error traps higher up the chain, and then uses the first enabled error trap it finds. There may well be several error traps, some of which are enabled, in the structure. The error trap is enabled by the **On Error Goto...** statement, and can be disabled with **On Error Goto 0**. It's also disabled when the procedure is exited. In either case, the error trap will be enabled when that procedure is next executed.

Generally, you should always handle the error in the procedure where it occurred because if you use this style to handle errors, you may get unexpected results. This will be explained later.

## Resuming Execution

When an error occurs, Visual Basic passes control to an enabled error trap (usually the one in the procedure), and then expects you to handle the error. It will remember the line that caused the error, so that after rectifying the problem you have the option of retrying the line that caused the error with the **Resume** command. If you ignore the line, you can carry on by using the **Resume Next** command. Generally, you'll use the **Resume** command to allow the user to undertake certain actions (such as putting paper in the printer). In certain cases you will use **Resume Next** when you can recover within your code (such as allowing the user to cancel an attempt to read a floppy disk).

> There is also the facility to resume at a specific point in the procedure with **Resume ...**, where the elipses are a line number or label. This is not recommended, however, because you will have to manually decide what to do next, and it can lead to spaghetti code.

## Using Error

The other method of exiting your error handler is to generate an error yourself by using the **Error** statement. In fact, you can generate an error from anywhere within your code by using the **Error** statement. All Visual Basic errors are integer numbers, and the full list is included in the back of the *Language Reference* manual. To generate an error, such as an I/O error you'd use:

# Error Statement

```
Error 57
```

where **57** is the error number (which in this case is an I/O error).

To help you at runtime when an error occurs, Visual Basic uses two functions which return information about the most recent runtime error to you. These are the **Err()** and **Error()** functions. **Err()** returns the integer value of the error that has occurred, and **Error()** provides a string which holds the error message.

There are two reasons why you might want generate your own errors. The first is to test your error trapping and handling. By using **Error** and an error number, you can generate all the errors that you are expecting to handle and ensure that your system reacts as expected. In this case, you would remove all the **Error** statements in the final version of your program.

The other reason is to do with where the error handler in a particular procedure has an unexpected error. When you call the **Error** statement from within an error trap, Visual Basic will look back up the call list for another enabled error handler (this enables you to pass the error on with the statement **Error Err**).

This error handler may be able to cope with the unexpected error. However, if a **Resume** or a **Resume Next** is present in the error handler, then execution will continue within the procedure that has the error trap, and *not* the procedure where the error occurred. A **Resume** will rerun to the last statement executed in the procedure (which will be the call to the next procedure in the list), and a **Resume Next** will start execution at the next line after the last one executed. This may well cause unexpected results in your system!

As we've already said, the safest thing is to try to handle the error in the procedure where it has occurred. This will give you the best chance to recover the situation, and if an unexpected error occurs (such as a network crash), you'll find that in most cases you wouldn't have been able to recover anyway. In these cases, it's best to close your application in an orderly manner.

# Chapter 11 - Debugging and Error Handling

You should also be aware of the `Error()` function. This simply returns the error message as a variant. If you don't supply a positive integer to the function then you will the receive the message of the most recent runtime error. This could be useful if you wanted to keep a logfile of runtime errors while handling the actual error in your code.

## Error Handling : Implementation

In large complex projects, you may well find yourself writing the same error handling details several times, and over time, the same details in different projects. Error handlers are an ideal use for functions, which can be written to handle specific error classes, such as file errors, or you may want to write a single error handler that can handle all errors. We prefer to write a handler for each class that we want to handle - they're easier to maintain and understand.

We're going to write and test a generic handler for file errors. Start a new project and add a code module that will hold the generic error handler. To test the error handling function, enter the following code in the `Form_Load` event:

```
Sub Form_Load ()
    Dim iErrgen As Integer, iErrReply As Integer
    On Error GoTo ErrHandler
```

Declare the variables used and enable the error trap.

```
    For iErrgen = 50 To 80
        Error iErrgen
    Next iErrgen
```

All of the errors that we're interested in occur between `50` and `80`, so we're going to generate each error in turn. There are file errors outside of this range, but we're not handling them in this error routine.

```
    Exit Sub
```

To ensure that execution doesn't proceed into our error handler, we exit the procedure just before the error label.

# Error Handling Program

```
ErrHandler:
    iErrReply = FileError(iErrgen)
```

Call our error handling function and place the response in **iErrReply**

```
    Select Case iErrReply
        Case 1 ' User has fixed problem, so retry
            Resume
```

The user has requested a retry, so resume. In our test routine, this will cause the same error again because we will call the **Error** statement again. In real life, the user will choose this after rectifying the fault (such as putting a disk in the floppy drive).

```
        Case 2 'Code can recover so carry on
            Resume Next
```

The user has chosen to ignore the error - for instance, they selected the wrong drive letter when they didn't intend to access a floppy disk.

```
        Case 3 'Close the application in a tidy manner
            MsgBox "Aborting the Application"
            End
```

The user has chosen to abort the application. In a real system, you'd run some tidy-up code to leave the system in a reasonable manner before closing.

```
        Case 4 'Close in a tidy manner
            MsgBox "An Unexpected error has occurred - (" & Str(Err) & ") " _
            & Error & " - Closing Down"
```

In this case we're closing if an unexpected error has occurred. You may well have other error handler functions that you'd want to call before closing down.

```
            Resume Next 'Used to test the error handler only
        End Select
End Sub
```

For test purposes we have a **Resume Next**, so that the next error in the sequence can be generated and tested.

315

# Chapter 11 - Debugging and Error Handling

In the code module, we've entered the following code:

```
Function FileError (iErrNo As Integer) As Integer

    Dim sErrorMessage As String, iMessBoxType As Integer, iButton As
Integer

    'Set the error message, and the type of message box to
    'be displayed to the user.
    'Return values are:
    '1 = Resume
    '2 = Resume Next
    '3 = Abort the application
    '4 = Error outside the scope of this handler

    Select Case iErrNo
        Case 52, 64
            sErrorMessage = "Unknown File Name"
            iMessBoxType = 2 + 16 + 256
        Case 53
            sErrorMessage = "The Specified File cannot be found"
            iMessBoxType = 2 + 16 + 256
        Case 54
            sErrorMessage = "You cannot open the file in this mode"
            iMessBoxType = 2 + 16
        Case 55
            sErrorMessage = "This File is already Open"
            iMessBoxType = 5 + 16 + 256
        Case 57
            sErrorMessage = "A Disk access error has occurred"
            iMessBoxType = 2 + 16 + 256
        Case 58
            sErrorMessage = "The File already exists"
            iMessBoxType = 2 + 16 + 256
        Case 61
            sErrorMessage = "The Disk is Full"
            iMessBoxType = 2 + 16
        Case 62
            sErrorMessage = "An error has occurred at the End of the file"
            iMessBoxType = 5 + 16 + 256
        Case 68
            sErrorMessage = "The device is currently unavailable"
            iMessBoxType = 2 + 16 + 256
        Case 71
            sErrorMessage = "The Disk is not ready"
            iMessBoxType = 2 + 16 + 256
        Case 75, 76
            sErrorMessage = "A Path/File error has occurred"
```

# Select Case

```
            iMessBoxType = 2 + 16 + 256
        'Any other error is outside the scope of this handler
        'So set the return value and exit
        Case Else
            FileError = 4
            Exit Function
    End Select
```

The first **Select Case** traps the errors this error handling function is interested in, sets an error message string and decides on the style of message box that this error requires. The **Case Else** at the end captures all the other error values and sets the unknown error return value, leaving the calling routine to decide the action to be taken (which may well be to call other error functions).

```
    'Display the message box, and analyze the button pressed

    iButton = MsgBox(sErrorMessage, iMessBoxType, "File Error")
```

Now display the message box, and capture the button pressed by the user. This is a modal message box so that no further action can be taken until some response is made.

```
        Select Case iButton
            Case 4 'Retry Button pressed so resume
                FileError = 1
            Case 2, 5 'Cancel or ignore  Pressed so resume next
                FileError = 2
            Case 3 'Abort Pressed so return abort
                FileError = 3
            Case Else 'This should never occur!!
                FileError = 4
        End Select

End Function
```

Finally, we use another **Select Case** to determine the button clicked and set the appropriate return value. The **Case Else** in this case block should never be executed, but it's better to be safe than sorry!

**317**

# Chapter 11 - Debugging and Error Handling

# Summary

There is no tried and trusted method for producing error free systems. Testing and debugging is something of an art with no hard and fast rules (except the one rule that it must be done!). There are, however, ways of producing systems that can reduce potential errors.

In this chapter we looked at structuring the applications that we write and some of the reasons why this might prove useful in producing error free systems, as well as saving time and effort in coding and testing.

You learnt about the tools available within Visual Basic to test and debug an application by using the Debug Window, setting breakpoints, stepping through code and using watches to observe the behavior of the application.

You also learnt about handling runtime errors and produced a generic file error handling function that can be used in many applications.

# Exercises

**1** The only way to become familiar with the debugging tools is to use them. You'll find that the Debug Window is also very useful for testing your application, by altering the value of variables as you go through the code.

Load the circles application that you wrote in Chapter 8 and set a breakpoint which allows you to alter the parameters to the `Circle()` function. Now try out different positions sizes and colors.

**2** Load the MDI icon viewer program and link in our generic file error handler to trap any errors that may occur. Test it by selecting your floppy drive without a disk inserted.

# Summary and Exercises

INSTANT
INSTANT
INSTANT
INSTANT
INSTANT
INSTANT
INSTANT
INSTANT
INSTANT
INSTANT
INSTANT

# Chapter 12

# Communicating With Other Windows Applications

This chapter concentrates on the Windows **API** (**A**pplication **P**rogram **I**nterface), which provides functions that can be called from *within* Visual Basic so as to undertake tasks directly *within* Windows. This provides two main advantages. The first advantage is speed. By directly controlling Windows you are bypassing all the Visual Basic stuff, especially in the areas of graphics and multi-media. The second advantage is that using the API allows you to undertake tasks that simply aren't supported within Visual Basic.

Within this chapter we will introduce you to the API, and we'll look at some of the more useful API calls. But first, we'll look at the Windows clipboard, and its use as a communications device between applications.

In this chapter we'll cover:

- The clipboard
- The Windows API
- DLL functions
- .INI files
- DDE and OLE

# Chapter 12 - Communicating with Other Windows Applications

## The Clipboard: Concepts

There are very few professional Windows applications written today that do not use the clipboard to allow users to edit their work, whether the application is text or graphic based. The clipboard can support a variety of formats for graphical and text based files.

The clipboard is the most commonly used method of passing data across different Windows applications, as well as the most common method of allowing you to edit the details within your own application. Although it's a manual procedure, it's one that is easy for a user to understand, and it's also simple to code within Visual Basic. Access to the facilities of the clipboard is usually supported via menus, so that the controls you are editing can retain focus throughout the operation.

## Clipboard Methods

The clipboard object has no properties and can't be accessed at design time, as it's one of the five system objects. There are six methods that are used within Visual Basic to interact with the clipboard:

| Method    | Usage                                                                   |
|-----------|-------------------------------------------------------------------------|
| Clear     | Deletes all data in the clipboard.                                      |
| SetText   | Transfers text from a string or control to the clipboard.               |
| SetData   | Transfers data which is not in text format, such as bitmaps or metafiles. |
| GetText   | Transfers text from the clipboard.                                      |
| GetData   | Transfers the specified data format from the clipboard.                 |
| GetFormat | Used to find out if the clipboard is holding a specified format.        |

# The Clipboard

## Using the Clipboard for Text

Start a new project, add an MDI Form and change the name to **mdiClip**, as well as a code module. Set the **MDIChild** property to **True** for Form1 and change its name to **frmName**.. For the MDI form, add a picture control, and on the picture control add two text boxes. On the child form we have added just a text box. For both forms, we've added a menu structure, with Exit under File on the **MDIform1**. Code has been added to the View menu section of the code which provides another menu item (with the caption Text Window), which in turn, when clicked, loads the child form. For both forms, we have Cut, Copy and Paste under an Edit menu. (We are using the Windows standard short cut keys of *Ctrl+X*, *Ctrl+C*, and *Ctrl+V* for cut, copy and paste respectively.)

> Don't forget to make the MDI parent the start up form in the Options, Project ... menu.

Our two forms look like this:

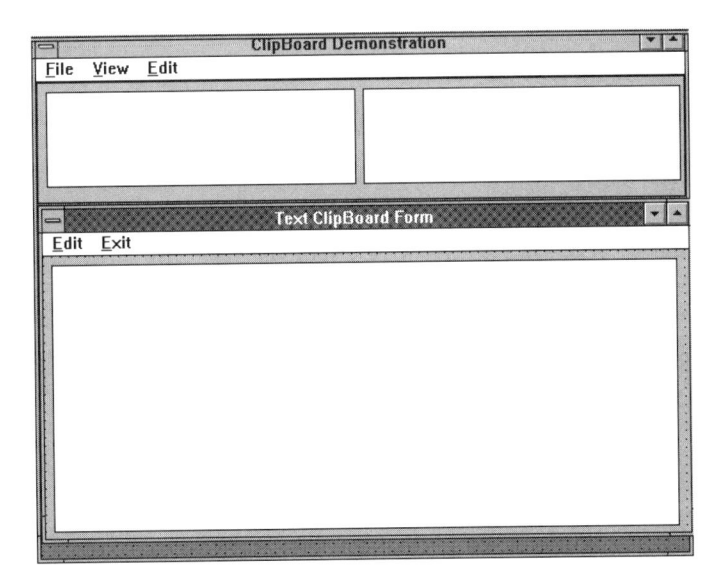

# Chapter 12 - Communicating with Other Windows Applications

The MDI menu structure is as follows:

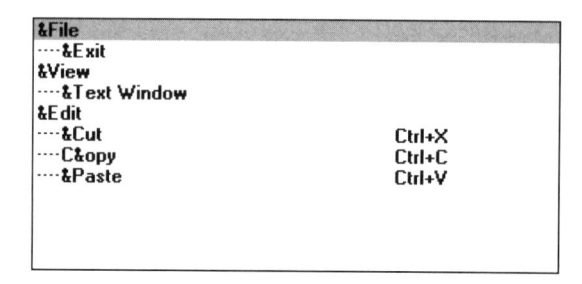

```
&File
----&Exit
&View
----&Text Window
&Edit
----&Cut              Ctrl+X
----C&opy             Ctrl+C
----&Paste            Ctrl+V
```

This is the form:

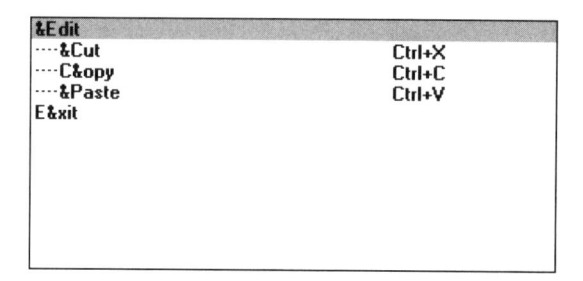

```
&Edit
----&Cut              Ctrl+X
----C&opy             Ctrl+C
----&Paste            Ctrl+V
E&xit
```

We'll start the code description with the code module, as we're using this as a generic clipboard handler for text. You'll find that this is a function used in many of your applications, so it's a useful generic function to add to your library.

> We've cheated a bit by also declaring our global variables here - in a real application you'd have a module that just holds all the declarations that you use in the application. This makes them easy to find and maintain, and doesn't fill all your general functions with specific globals.

```
Option Explicit
    'Program Globals
    Global giTxtFocus As Integer
```

We're using this global to determine which of the text boxes has the focus, and (therefore) which should have the action undertaken on it.

# Set Text

```
Sub ClipText (nAction As Integer, oTxtBox As TextBox)
    Select Case nAction
```

There are two parameters being passed to the procedure. The first is the action selected: **1** = cut, **2** = copy and **3** = paste. The second is an object variable, which is the text control that currently has the focus. The `Case` statement controls the action to be undertaken.

```
Case 1 'cut selected
    Clipboard.Clear
    Clipboard.SetText oTxtBox.SelText
    oTxtBox.SelText = ""
```

This is the code for cut. The first line clears all data from the clipboard. The next line uses two methods. The `SelText` method is used with text boxes, and tells Visual Basic to use the text that has been selected in the text box (this text will be highlighted). The `SetText` method is used with the clipboard, and transfers text to the clipboard, so in this case we are transferring the currently highlighted text to the clipboard. The final line sets the selected text to blank, which has the effect of erasing it from the textbox.

```
Case 2 'Copy Selected
    Clipboard.Clear
    Clipboard.SetText oTxtBox.SelText
```

The code for copy is almost identical, except that we don't clear the selected text.

```
Case 3 'Paste Selected
    oTxtBox.SelText = Clipboard.GetText()
    End Select
End Sub
```

To paste the text, the `GetText` method is used. This copies the text from the clipboard to the current cursor position in the textbox. If you have any text highlighted, it will overwrite the highlighted text.

We now have a generic text handler, so let's add the code to out project to enable us to use it, starting with the MDI form:

```
Sub MDIForm_Load ()
    giTxtFocus = 0
End Sub
```

**325**

In the `Form_Load` event, set the text focus variable to `0`.

```
Sub mnuTxt_Click ()
    Load frmText
    frmText.Show
End Sub
```

In the Text Window menu `Click` event (from the View menu), the `frmText` child form is loaded.

```
Sub txtClip_GotFocus (index As Integer)
    If index = 0 Then
        giTxtFocus = 1
    Else
        giTxtFocus = 2
    End If
End Sub
```

On the MDI form, we've set the two textboxes up as a control array. Depending on which has the focus, `giTxtFocus` is set to the relevant number.

```
Sub mnuCut_Click ()
    Select Case giTxtFocus
        Case 1
            ClipText 1, txtClip(0)
        Case 2
            ClipText 1, txtClip(1)
        Case 3
            ClipText 1, frmText!txtOnForm
    End Select
End Sub
```

In the `Click` event code for the Cut option on the menu, the generic function is called with an action of 1 for cut, and `giTxtFocus` is checked to see which text control the action should be taken on. The control for which the operation is to be carried out is passed as the second parameter.

```
Sub mnuCopy_Click ()
    Select Case giTxtFocus
        Case 1
            ClipText 2, txtClip(0)
        Case 2
            ClipText 2, txtClip(1)
        Case 3
            ClipText 2, frmText!txtOnForm
    End Select
End Sub
```

The same code is used for the **Copy_Click** event, except the **nAction** parameter is set to **2** for copy.

```
Sub mnuPaste_Click ()
    Select Case giTxtFocus
        Case 1
            ClipText 3, txtClip(0)
        Case 2
            ClipText 3, txtClip(1)
        Case 3
            ClipText 3, frmText!txtOnForm
    End Select
End Sub
```

Not surprisingly, it's also the same for the **Paste** event, except the **nAction** parameter is now **3** for the paste action.

```
Sub mnuExit_Click ()
    Unload mdiclip
    End
End Sub
```

The final code for the MDI form is in the Exit event, which also unloads the form, to end the application.

In the child form we have the following code, most of which will look very familiar!

```
Sub txtOnForm_GotFocus ()
    giTxtFocus = 3
End Sub
```

If the textbox on this form has focus, then set **giTxtFocus** to **3**.

```
Sub mnuCut_Click ()
    Select Case giTxtFocus
        Case 1
            ClipText 1, mdiClip!txtClip(0)
        Case 2
            ClipText 1, mdiClip!txtClip(1)
        Case 3
            ClipText 1, frmText!txtOnForm
    End Select
End Sub
```

This code is almost identical to the code in the **Clip_Click** event on the MDI parent form. The only difference is that we've added the form identifier to the first two textbox references as they are on a different form.

```
Sub mnuCopy_Click ()
    Select Case giTxtFocus
        Case 1
            ClipText 2, mdiClip!txtClip(0)
        Case 2
            ClipText 2, mdiClip!txtClip(1)
        Case 3
            ClipText 2, frmText!txtOnForm
    End Select
End Sub
```

It's the same for the **Copy_Click** event and the **Paste_Click** event:

```
Sub mnuPaste_Click ()
    Select Case giTxtFocus
        Case 1
            ClipText 3, mdiClip!txtClip(0)
        Case 2
            ClipText 3, mdiClip!txtClip(1)
        Case 3
            ClipText 3, frmText!txtOnForm
    End Select
End Sub
```

Finally the **Exit_Click** event unloads the child form:

```
Sub mnuExit_Click ()
    Unload frmText
End Sub
```

When you run the project, you'll be able to cut, copy and paste between the forms. If you run up Notepad, you'll be able to cut and paste data between the two applications.

# Other Clipboard Formats

The clipboard can also support the Windows standard graphic formats. To determine which formats are currently held within the clipboard use the **GetFormat** method. This will return **True** if the format you specify is currently held in the clipboard. The actual format type is a number as in the following table:

| Constant | Data Type |
|---|---|
| &HBF00 | DDE link data. Used to set up DDE links with other applications. |
| 1 | Text, as used in the examples above. |
| 2 | Bitmap. |
| 3 | Metafile. |
| 8 | DIB. (Device Independent Bitmap). Another bitmap format. |
| 9 | Color Palette. Current color information. |

To determine if the clipboard has any text the following statement would be required:

```
If Clipboard.GetFormat(1) Then.....
```

To copy a graphic to a picture box from the clipboard if there is a bitmap, the following statement would be required:

```
If Clipboard.GetFormat(2) Then picPaste.Picture = Clipboard.GetData()
```

# The Windows API

There have been a few references to the Windows API throughout the book, so what actually is the Windows API, and why is it useful? It's actually a collection of **DLL**'s (**D**ynamic **L**ink **L**ibraries) which give you access to many functions that are not available in Visual Basic itself.

A DLL is basically a collection of functions that can be called from other programs, usually in C or C++, but we can also use them from within Visual Basic. Windows is composed of several DLLs, and it's these that form the API. If you look under the windows directories, you'll see many DLLs and, if you are experienced in C, then you can create your own custom DLLs to use with your Visual Basic applications.

# Declaring DLL Functions

This is where many Visual Basic programmers eyes start glazing over, and they start to worry about understanding complex C calls. Don't worry - you call the functions in a DLL in a similar way to other functions calls. The one exception is that you have to declare the function to Visual Basic before you can use it (which is similar to declaring a variable). If you have the Professional version, then all the standard declarations, constants and user-defined types used are in a file called **WIN30API.TXT** in the **VISUAL BASIC\WINAPI** directory, and can be cut and pasted into your code. There is also a file called **WIN31EXT.TXT** which holds the extra declarations and constants for Windows 3.1.

> If you want to investigate the API further, we'd recommend Daniel Appleman's *Visual Basic Programmers Guide to the Windows API*, published by Ziff Davis Press. It's an invaluable reference work, even if you have the Professional version of Visual Basic.

To be able to declare an API call, we need to know the procedure or function name, the DLL that contains it and the parameters that it expects to be passed.

## Passing Parameters to DLLs

All DLL parameter passing is **ByVal** rather than by reference. There is a very good reason for this. When you pass a parameter by reference, as we have most of the time, what you actually pass is the memory address where the data is held. This is not a problem while you're safely within the Visual Basic environment, but DLLs behave differently.

For example, suppose you were passing an integer to the DLL function. If you omit the **ByVal** keyword, instead of passing say **2**, the DLL would receive the memory address such as **123,545**. This will almost certainly cause an error. Unfortunately, because you are now outside of Visual Basic, the errors can't be trapped and will usually crash Windows.

# DLL Functions

> When you are testing DLL calls, save your work before you run your project. You have been warned!

## Declaring Functions and Procedures

Let's look at a couple of declarations we'll be using in the next example. All declarations should be typed on the same line, but because they don't fit on the page they have been split.

Visual Basic has no method of monitoring resource usage, and currently the only way that we have is to look on the About Program Manager menu option from the Help menu in Program Manager or some other Windows package. However, there are a couple of API calls that we can make to get much more detailed information on resource usage.

```
Declare Function GetFreeSpace Lib "Kernel" (ByVal wFlags as Integer) as
Long
```

This is a function that is in the **KERNEL.DLL**, has a single integer parameter and returns a **Long** variable type. It is the amount of free memory currently available.

```
Declare Function GetFreeSystemResources Lib "User" (ByVal fuSysResource as
Integer) as Integer
```

This function is in the **USER.DLL** and will return the amount of free resource depending on the parameter passed to it. Between them, they will give a fairly good picture of the amount of resource used.

You'll find it's conventional that DLL call parameters and return values are declared as constants, along with the declaration of the DLL function. This is so that the call is more readily understandable - it's impossible to know even a fraction of the parameters and return values.

All declarations which use DLLs have to be declared in the declarations section of a form or a separate code module. To try these out, start a new project and add a code module. On the from, add 8 label controls and a command button. Our form looks like the following:

331

## Chapter 12 - Communicating with Other Windows Applications

[Free Resources in Your System dialog showing labels: Free Memory, Free System Resources, Free GDI Resource, Free User Resource, and an Exit button]

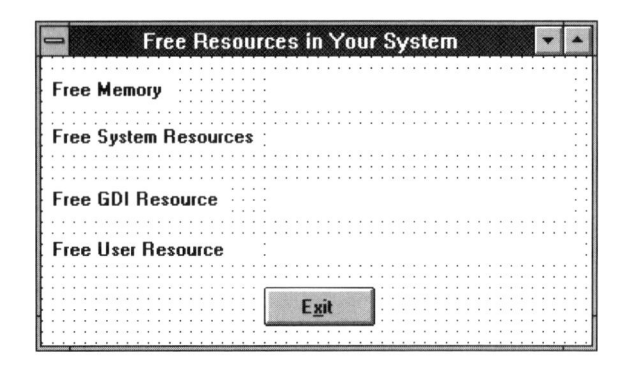

The code in the code module declares both the functions and the global constants used to pass parameters to `GetFreeSystemResources`:

```
Option Explicit
    'API Declarations

    Declare Function GetFreeSpace Lib "Kernel" (ByVal wFlags As Integer) As Long
    Declare Function GetFreeSystemResources Lib "User" (ByVal fuSysResource As Integer) As Integer

    'These are the global constants required for GetFreeSystemResources
    Global Const GFSR_SYSTEMRESOURCES = 0
    Global Const GFSR_GDIRESOURCES = 1
    Global Const GFSR_USERRESOURCES = 2
```

The code in the form is fairly simple. In the `Form_Load` event we have:

```
Sub Form_Load ()
    labmem.Caption = GetFreeSpace(0)
```

This calls the `GetFreeSpace()` function with a parameter of `0`, which is the only valid value of the parameter. The caption of the first display label is set to the amount of free memory currently in the system. This includes any virtual memory that you may have specified in the Windows Control Panel.

```
    labsys.Caption = GetFreeSystemResources(GFSR_SYSTEMRESOURCES) & " Percent"
    labgdi.Caption = GetFreeSystemResources(GFSR_GDIRESOURCES) & " Percent"
    labuser.Caption = GetFreeSystemResources(GFSR_USERRESOURCES) & " Percent"
End Sub
```

`GetFreeSystemResources` is called three times with different parameters to determine the amount of free resources, free GDI resources (this is the amount of graphic workspace left) and free user resources.

# INI Files

Finally, we end the project in the exit button **Click** event:

```
Sub cmdExit_Click ()
    Unload frmResource
    End
End Sub
```

When you run the project, it will give you the amount of free resource that you currently have. Opening and closing other Windows applications will affect the values displayed if you re-run the project.

> There are also API calls which will tell you what you have in your system, what version of windows you are running, what mouse driver you are using and so on. The Windows API has over a 1000 functions and procedures, most of which will work with Visual Basic. This means that there are some that either don't work, or give unexpected results.

# Using .INI Files

One of the most common uses that the API is put to is to read and write **.INI** files. These are the initialization files used by most of the professional Windows applications to hold user options, as well as other data required between runs of an application. This can be a difficult and laborious task if you use the Visual Basic files functions, but is well supported within the API. There are two sets of functions, one to handle **WIN.INI** and another to handle all other **.INI** files:

| Function | Usage |
| --- | --- |
| `GetProfileInt` | Retrieve an integer setting from **WIN.INI** |
| `GetProfileString` | Retrieve a string from **WIN.INI** |
| `WriteProfileString` | Write a string to **WIN.INI** |
| `GetPrivateProfileInt` | Retrieve an integer from a specified **.INI** file |
| `GetPrivateProfileString` | Retrieve a string from a specified **.INI** file |
| `WritePrivateProfileString` | Write a string to a specified **.INI** file |

333

## INI File Structure

To fully understand the functions we need to understand the structure of `.INI` files. To be honest, they are pretty simple. Here's an extract from the start of our `WIN.INI` file:

```
[windows]
run=
spooler=yes
load=C:\MSMOUSE\POINTER.EXE
Beep=yes
NullPort=None
BorderWidth=3
CursorBlinkRate=530
DoubleClickSpeed=1043
Programs=com exe bat pif
Documents=
DeviceNotSelectedTimeout=15
TransmissionRetryTimeout=45
KeyboardDelay=2
KeyboardSpeed=31
```

The `.INI` file is broken down into sections that are headed by square brackets [ ], as in `[windows]` above. The entries under the section header are called keys, with the string to the left of the equal sign being the keyname, and string to the right is the key value. Apart from this structure, there are no other standards for `.INI` files, you can hold pretty much anything that you wish under any section headings that you wish.

## Getting Information From WIN.INI

We're going to read all the key names in the Windows section of `WIN.INI`, and display them in a list box. Then we can select a key name and display its value. The function declaration to read from `WIN.INI` is as follows:

```
Declare Function GetProfileString Lib "Kernel" (ByVal lpAppName As String,
lpKeyName As Any, ByVal lpDefault As String, ByVal lpReturnedString As
String, ByVal nSize As Integer) As Integer
```

The integer returned is the size of the return string `lpReturnedString`. The parameters passed are as follows:

# INI File Structure

| Parameter | Description |
|---|---|
| `lpAppName` | The section header that you want to search. |
| `lpKeyName` | The key that you are interested in. If you want all keys returned, then pass a zero in long format (`0&`). Because this parameter can be either in `String` or `Long` format, it's specified `As Any` for the variable type. |
| `lpDefault` | If the specified entry is not found, then this is the default return string. |
| `lpReturnedString` | This holds the details string returned from the function. |
| `nSize` | The size in bytes of the `lpReturnedString` buffer. Generally set at about 4k or 4095 bytes. |

> You'll notice an odd variable type in the declaration, `As Any`. This will allow us to pass any type of variable in this parameter. The type of parameter you pass will determine the exact API function that will be called. In this case `lpKeyName` can be either a `Long`, or a `String`. You'll see this in quite a few API calls.

Start a new project, and add a code module to hold the declarations for the functions required. Although this example only uses `GetProfileString`, we've included all the other `.INI` file handling function calls for you to include in your own programs.

On the form we've added a text box in which to enter the section name, `txtSection`, then a simple combo box to display the key names, `comIni`, a blank label to display the key value, `lblValue`, and a menu at the top that allows you to list the key names, `mnuView`, used to display a key value, and `mnuExit`. Our form looks like the following:

**335**

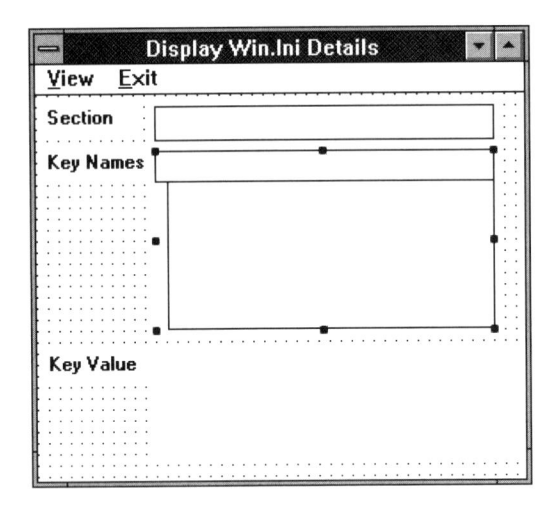

# Chapter 12 - Communicating with Other Windows Applications

It has a menu structure like this:

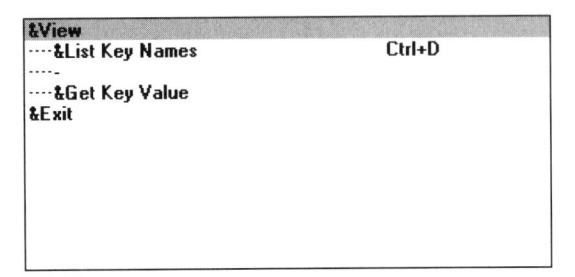

The code in the `.BAS` file in this case holds only the declarations for handling `.INI` files:

```
Option Explicit

Declare Function GetProfileInt Lib "Kernel" (ByVal lpAppName As String,
ByVal lpKeyName As String, ByVal nDefault As Integer) As Integer

Declare Function GetProfileString Lib "Kernel" (ByVal lpAppName As String,
ByVal lpKeyName As Any, ByVal lpDefault As String, ByVal lpReturnedString
As String, ByVal nSize As Integer) As Integer

Declare Function WriteProfileString Lib "Kernel" (ByVal lpApplicationName
As String, ByVal lpKeyName As Any, lpString As Any) As Integer
```

# WIN.INI

```
Declare Function GetPrivateProfileInt Lib "Kernel" (ByVal lpApplicationName
As String, ByVal lpKeyName As String, ByVal nDefault As Integer, ByVal
lpFileName As String) As Integer

Declare Function GetPrivateProfileString Lib "Kernel" (ByVal
lpApplicationName As String, ByVal lpKeyName As Any, ByVal lpDefault As
String, ByVal lpReturnedString As String, ByVal nSize As Integer, ByVal
lpFileName As String) As Integer

Declare Function WritePrivateProfileString Lib "Kernel" (ByVal
lpApplicationName As String, ByVal lpKeyName As Any, lpString As Any, ByVal
lplFileName As String) As Integer
```

These can be cut and pasted from **WIN30API.TXT**, but check that all the parameters are preceded with the **ByVal** keyword, otherwise they will not work.

Let's look at the rest of the code. The first event is the **Click** event for the List Key Names menu entry:

```
Sub mnuKeys_click ()

    Dim sReturned As String * 4096, iReturnSize As Integer
    Dim sKeyVal As String, iStart As Integer, iEnd As Integer
```

The string **sReturned** is a 4K string which will hold the details of all the key values for the section specified, up to a limit of 4K. The integer **iReturnSize** is the return value from the function and is the actual size in characters of **sReturned**.

```
If txtSection = "" Then
    MsgBox "You Must enter a Section Name", 16, "Section Entry Error"
    Exit Sub
End If
```

The check is to ensure that a section header has been entered.

```
comIni.Clear
iStart = 1
```

Clear any details out of the combo box and set the string start position to 1.

337

## Chapter 12 - Communicating with Other Windows Applications

```
    iReturnSize = GetProfileString(txtSection.Text, 0&, "None", sReturned,
4095)
```

Get all the key values with **GetProfileString**. Now we need to extract all the key values with some string manipulation. Each individual key value is terminated by a **null** character, with the whole string being terminated by two **null** characters.

> The **null** character referred to here is not the Visual Basic **null** character, but the C **null** character. The Visual Basic equivalent is a **String 0** or **Chr$(0)**.

```
    Do While (Asc(Mid$(sReturned, iStart, 1)) <> 0)
```

Check if the start character of the next entry is not the **null** character. If it is, then the end of the loop has been reached.

```
    iEnd = InStr(iStart, sReturned, Chr$(0))
```

Set the end position of the next key value, by checking from the current position to the next **null** character.

```
    sKeyVal = Mid$(sReturned, iStart, iEnd - iStart)
```

Now using the start and end positions, extract the next key name

```
    comIni.AddItem sKeyVal
```

and then add it to the combo box:

```
    iStart = iEnd + 1
    Loop
End Sub
```

Set the current position to the end position **+ 1**. This will step over the **null** character, which we do not want to display. It's this line which makes the check at the top of the loop work, because if the next character is another **null** character then we've had two in a row, which is the end of the string.

# Running Applications

The code to display a particular key value is in the `Click` event for the Get Key Value menu entry:

```
Sub mnuValue_click ()
    Dim sReturned As String * 1000, iReturnSize As Integer
    iReturnSize = GetProfileString(txtSection.Text, CStr(comIni.Text),
"None", sReturned, 1000)
    lblValue.Caption = sReturned
End Sub
```

Because we are only getting back the value of a particular key, we don't need to worry about any string manipulation - we just need to display the result in the label at the bottom of the screen. To make the application more friendly, we are also calling this event from the `DblClick` event of the combo box:

```
Sub comIni_DblClick ()
    mnuValue_click
End Sub
```

Finally the Exit menu `Click` event ends the application:

```
Sub mnuExit_Click ()
    Unload frmIni
    End
End Sub
```

# Running and Controlling Other Applications

Within Visual Basic there are several commands which allow you to *run* other applications, and in the case of Windows applications, *control* the running of other applications. The `Shell` command is used to launch another application from within Visual Basic, (either DOS or Windows), `AppActivate` passes focus to another application, and `SendKeys` passes key strokes to the current active window.

# Running Other Applications

The `Shell` command will launch any executable file. The files with a `.BAT`, `.COM`, `.EXE`, `.PIF`, `.BAT` are all valid executables, so it's possible to launch DOS programs by using `.PIF`s or `.BAT`s. If you don't include an extension on the name of the file that you are launching, then `.EXE` is assumed.

You can also decide the window state, and focus with the window style parameter. The values are as follows:

| Value | What it Gives |
|-------|---------------|
| 1,5,9 | Normal with focus. |
| 2     | Minimized with focus. This is the default. |
| 3     | Maximized with focus. |
| 4,8   | Normal without focus. |
| 6,7   | Minimized without focus. |

The `Shell()` function will run other programs asynchronously. What this means is that your code will launch the required program and then continue. This may not be what you wish, especially if you launch a DOS program. You may well want your program to wait until the launched program has completed before continuing. We'll look at some possible solutions to this later on.

Firstly, let's try out the `Shell()` function. Start a new project, add two textboxes, and two command buttons. The first textbox will be the application that we're going to run, and the second is the **WindowStyle**. The two command buttons run the selected program and end our project. Our form looks like this:

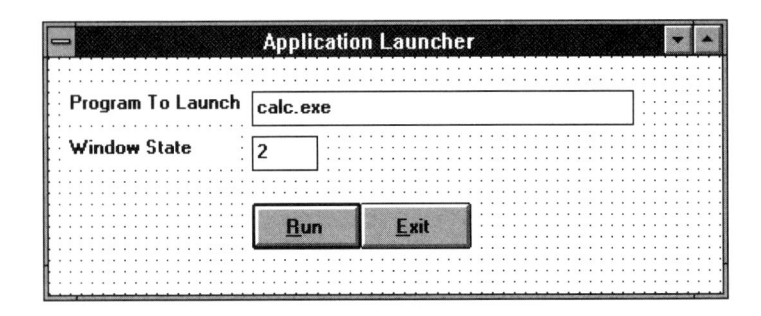

```
┌─────────────── Application Launcher ─────────▼▲─┐
│                                                  │
│   Program To Launch  ┌──────────────────────┐   │
│                      │ calc.exe             │   │
│   Window State       ┌───┐                      │
│                      │ 2 │                      │
│                      └───┘                      │
│                                                  │
│              ┌──────┐    ┌──────┐               │
│              │ Run  │    │ Exit │               │
│              └──────┘    └──────┘               │
│                                                  │
└──────────────────────────────────────────────────┘
```

# Shelled Tanks

There's very little code for this project. This is the run command button code:

```
Sub cmdRun_Click ()
    Dim ihMod As Integer
    ihMod = Shell(txtLaunch.Text, Val(txtState.Text))
End Sub
```

The **Shell** function has two parameters: the first is a string which contains the executable to run, and the second is an integer to indicate the **WindowState**.

The return value from **Shell** is something called an **instance handle**. This is a unique identifier to the running program, allocated by Windows when the program starts. You'll see something similar, called the **Windows handle**, used in many of the API functions. This is a unique identifier allocated by Windows to every window, whether active, maximized or minimized.

> In fact, all the objects that make up the Windows environment, such as bitmaps, pens, brushes, modules, windows and instances, are uniquely identified by their 16-bit handle. It's this handle that is used by Windows (and the API), to talk to the correct object.

If **Shell** can't start the named program, a runtime error occurs.

The Exit command button has the **End** code:

```
Sub cmdExit_Click ()
    Unload frmShell
    End
End Sub
```

Try out the different window styles, and also see what happens if you end the project. You'll find that the program you launched continues to run after your project has finished.

## Monitoring Shelled Tasks

There are several methods of determining if the shelled task has finished. All use the API. The first method is to use **GetNumTasks**. This returns the number of tasks currently running under Windows. You can call this after

# Chapter 12 - Communicating with Other Windows Applications

you have started your shelled application, then monitor the number of tasks in a loop. When it drops by **1**, the shelled task has ended. The problem with this is that, unless you can guarantee that it was actually the shelled task that ended, you may get incorrect results.

The declaration for **GetNumTasks** is this:

```
Declare Function GetNumTasks Lib "kernel" () As Integer
```

The second method uses two API functions. The first **GetActiveWindow** returns the Windows handle of the currently active window, and the second **IsWindow** returns **True** if the window exists and **False** if it doesn't. The declarations are as follows:

```
Declare Function GetActiveWindow Lib "user" () As Integer
Declare Function IsWindow Lib "user" (ByVal hWnd As Integer) As Integer
```

After you've started your shelled application, call **GetActiveWindow** to access the handle of the window, then create a loop that checks if the window still exists with **IsWindow**. When it doesn't, your shelled task has ended. The problem with this is if you have to launch a program without giving it the focus. The handle returned may not be the one that is your shelled process, so you'll be monitoring the wrong process.

The other method used the identifier returned by the shell program, so it does monitor the correct process. The API call is **GetModuleUsage**, and returns the number of times that a particular module has been loaded. When it reaches **0**, then the module is no longer in use, so it has ended. This is the declaration:

```
Declare Function GetModuleUsage Lib "kernel" (ByVal hModule As Integer) As Integer
```

We'll try this one out. Add the function declaration for **GetModuleUsage** to the (general) declarations section of the form:

```
Option Explicit
Declare Function GetModuleUsage Lib "kernel" (ByVal hModule As Integer) As Integer
```

The **Run_Click** event code is now this:

# Activating Applications

```
Sub cmdRun_Click ()
    Dim ihMod As Integer
    ihMod = Shell(txtLaunch.Text, Val(txtState.Text))
```

These lines are the same as before.

```
    Do While GetModuleUsage(ihMod) > 0
        DoEvents
    Loop
```

The program will now loop here until the shelled task has ended. The **DoEvents** ensures that Windows doesn't lock up while we're looping.

```
    MsgBox "Its Done"
End Sub
```

Just to prove that it carries on at the end, a message box is displayed. In a real application you would have the rest of the processing code here. You can still end the Visual Basic application, leaving the shelled process running if you wish to.

## Activating Other Applications

To activate another application, you need to know the caption in the title bar of the application. The check on the title bar is not case sensitive. For example to pass focus back to Visual Basic you would use the following:

```
AppActivate "Visual Basic"
```

The main reason for doing this is to pass **keystrokes** to the active application. Keystrokes are passed in the form of a string, with a second parameter stating whether or not to wait until the keystrokes have been processed. If this is omitted, Visual Basic doesn't wait.

This is useful for self running demos, or where you need to control another application. The details passed in the string are treated as if you had typed them on the keyboard with these exceptions: ~, +, %,^, [,],{, and}. If you wish to use these they must be enclosed in { }. So to add 2 + 2 in the calculator you would use this:

```
AppActivate "calculator"
SendKeys "2{+}2=", True
```

**343**

If you have to send special keys such as *F1*, *Shift*, *Enter* and so on, then a table is provided in the Visual Basic help file under **SendKeys** of the codes that you should use. It's also printed in the *Language* reference. A final word on passing key strokes - you can only pass them to other Windows applications, not to applications that are running in a DOS window.

## DDE and OLE

The other two methods of transferring data to and from Visual Basic applications are Dynamic Data Exchange (DDE), and Object Linking and Embedding (OLE). You can only use these methods with applications that have been specifically set up to support them. They both allow you to dynamically pass data back and forth between your application and another, such as Word for Windows or Excel. The downside of this is that both methods are very complex and resource hungry. They are really advanced topics and beyond the scope of this book, so in this section we'll look briefly at DDE and OLE. Full details on both can be found in the *Programmers Guide*.

> Visual Basic now supports the most recent version of OLE, called OLE2, which is replacing the original OLE, so that's what we'll be looking at.

## DDE

DDE is a kind of automated clipboard and keystroke passer which allows data to be simultaneously updated in your Visual Basic application and the application to which you are linked. The passing of this data is called a **conversation**, with the application that starts the conversation being the **destination** and the responder being the **source**. Your application can be both source and destination.

For example, a marketing department may have details of a new product in a Word file, together with a database of contacts. You could write an application that starts a conversation with Word to produce a mail shot of the new product details with the contacts. However, the Word document would need to be set up so that it expects data to be passed via DDE.

# DDE

When you start a conversation, you need to specify two things:

**1** The **source name** of the application which will be provided in the documentation that came with the package, for example the DDE name for Word is WinWord and Excel is Excel. The source name is not case sensitive.

**2** The **topic** of the conversation. This is usually a file such as a **.DOC** for Word, or **.XLS** for Excel.

If either the source or the destination change the application name, or the topic, then the conversation is terminated.

The details passed between the two applications are called **items**, and these are units of data that are meaningful to both applications. For instance, Excel recognizes cell references, such as **R1C1**, and Word recognizes bookmarks and the special bookmark **\DOC**. During a conversation, either the source or destination application can change the item without terminating the conversation.

There are three different kinds of conversation or **link**.

**1** An **automatic** (or hot) link passes updates to the items specified from the source to the destination as they occur.

**2** A **manual** (or cold) link will only pass updates when the destination requests them.

**3** A **notification** link will notify the destination when an update has occurred, but will only pass the update across when the destination requests it.

> To make full use of DDE, you will need to know how the application that you are linked to handles DDE conversations, topics and items. This will be supplied with the documentation for the package.

# Chapter 12 - Communicating with Other Windows Applications

## OLE

OLE goes beyond the functionality of DDE, and Microsoft are putting a lot of effort into OLE to improve communications between Windows applications. It is expected that OLE will replace DDE as the method of communication. One of the main advantages of OLE is that the information is presented in the same format as application to which you have linked. This means that if you link to a Word document, then it appears as a Word document and you can use all the Word functions to alter the document, as Visual Basic actually runs Word.

A real life example may be where you have several departments all working locally on their budgets in Excel. When they have completed their budgets, they consolidate them with the central consolidated budget spreadsheet for all departments. The accounts department can then link via OLE to the consolidated spreadsheet.

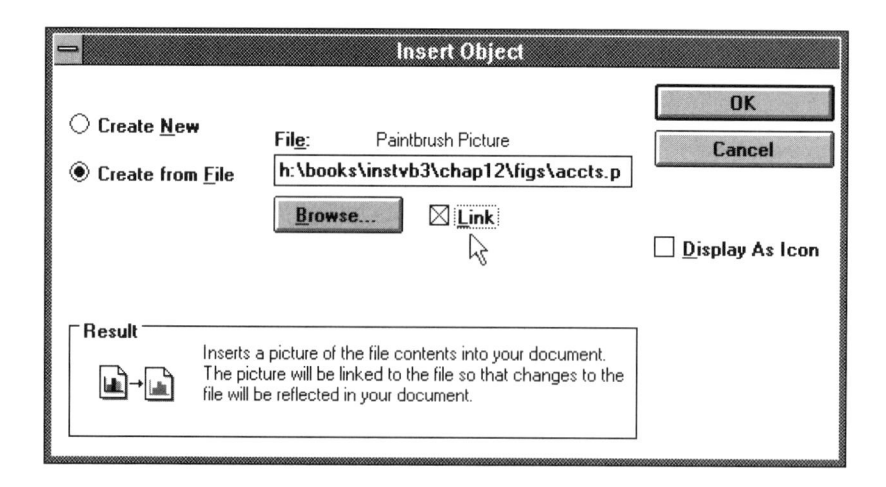

# OLE

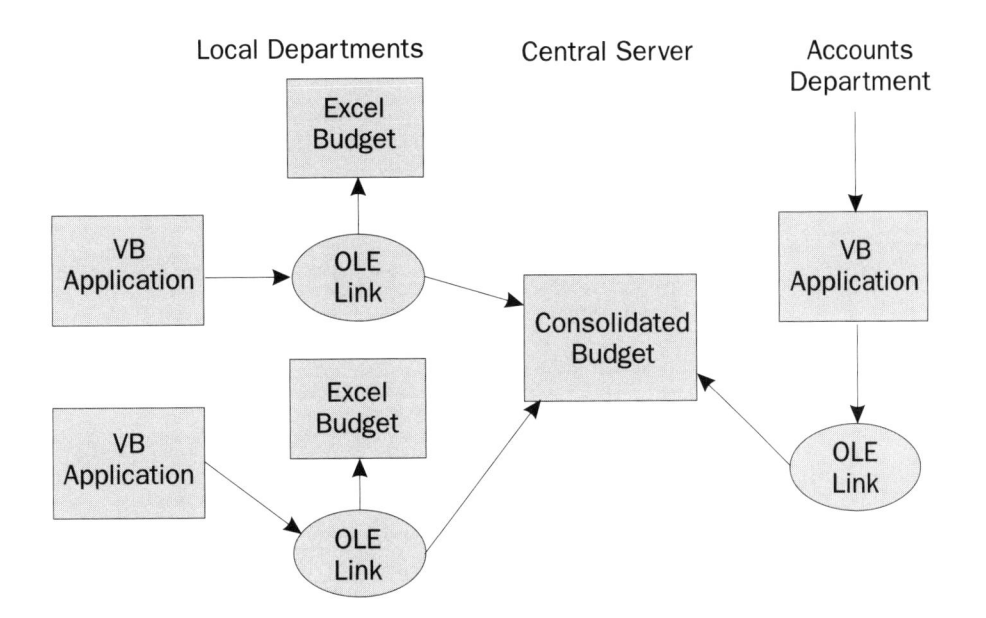

**Local Departments** — Excel Budget, VB Application → OLE Link → Excel Budget
**Central Server** — Consolidated Budget
**Accounts Department** — VB Application → OLE Link

OLE is very useful where several different users all wish to work on the same set of data (in this case the consolidated budgets). This is an example of linking using OLE. What is happening is that when the link is created a reference to the data, called a **placeholder**, is created, and an image of the data is stored in the OLE control. This allows other applications to also use the data.

The other way of using OLE is to embed the object in your application. In this case, all the data is included in the control, so that when you save the contents to a file, the file will also contain the name of the application that produced the object, the object's data and a metafile image of the object. This means that no other application will have access to the data.

You can create the objects at design time, or at runtime by setting properties. If you create at design time, your executable will be larger as it will contain the object. If you create at runtime, the user will experience a delay while the system creates the object. While this is happening, all other tasks are suspended.

## Linkage: Implementation

We'll look at an example of creating a link at design time. You'll notice the delay while the system creates the object.

### Linking At Design Time

The object that we're going to use is the paintbrush. Before you start a new project, create a drawing with the paintbrush, then save it. Now start a new project and on the form draw an OLE control. The Insert Object dialog is displayed:

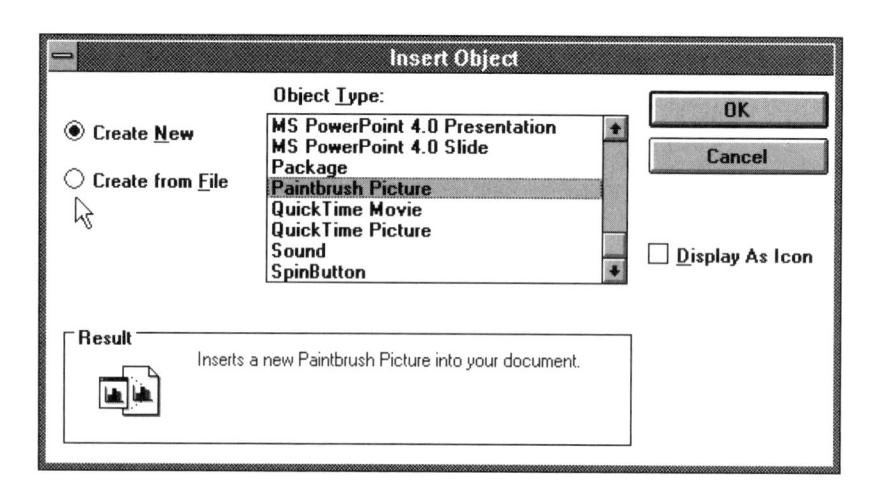

Select the paintbrush picture in the Object Type combo box, then click the Create from File radio button. The next dialog appears.

You can use the Browse... button to find the file that you've created, then check the Link check box to create a link to the file. If you check the Display as Icon check box, the control will be iconized at runtime. When the display type has been selected, it can't be changed. When you click the OK button, there will be a delay while the system sets up the link, and a copy of the current contents will be copied into the control on your form.

One of the most useful properties of the OLE control is the `SizeMode` property. Change it to `2 - Autosize`, so that the size of the control will alter to the size of the underlying data - in this case our picture.

Now run the project, and the picture will be displayed in the OLE control. If you double click on the control, Visual Basic will run paintbrush with the picture already loaded, after a suitable delay! You can now alter the picture (although it will be much slower than running paintbrush by itself). When you save the file and close paintbrush, you'll notice that the picture in your OLE control has also been updated.

# Summary

In this chapter we looked at the different methods available to us to communicate with other applications within Windows, and also with Windows itself. You learnt how to use the clipboard to cut and paste data both within your own application, and also swap data with other applications that support the clipboard.

We then looked at the Windows API, and how to call the functions in the DLLs that make up the API. Using the API you learnt how to keep an eye on resource usage, then how to manipulate `.INI` files.

You then learnt how to launch other applications with the `Shell` command, and monitor the progress by using API calls. You also learnt how to swap focus to other applications, and pass key strokes to control the application.

## Chapter 12 - Communicating with Other Windows Applications

The chapter was completed with a brief look at DDE, and the method of the future, OLE. Before you move to the final chapter, here are a few exercises.

## Exercises

**1** As mentioned, the clipboard can hold different data types. Alter the clipboard procedure to handle all the different data types. This can then be used in any project that requires access to the clipboard.

**2** In the Resource project, the display of free resources is static. Create a timer control that creates and updates a display of the free resources every few seconds. Then try loading and closing other windows applications to see the effect on resource usage.

**3** Extend the **.INI** viewer to allow the user to enter an **.INI** file to be looked at. You'll need to change the function call to **GetPrivateProfileString**, with the last parameter as the name of the .**INI** file, such as '**WIN.INI**'. If you don't include the path, then the **WINDOWS** directory will be searched for the **.INI** file.

**4** Alter the application launcher program to run up the calculator, and allow the user to enter a string of keystrokes that will be passed to the calculator when a command button is pressed.

# Exercises

# Appendix A

# The Professional Version

The body of the book covers Visual Basic Standard Edition, version 3. Using this you can produce excellent Windows applications, so why buy the Professional Edition? Well, the Professional Edition is much more than a few extra controls. It's an extensive upgrade to the functionality and use of the language, especially in the area of database handling.

This is reflected in the documentation, with two extra volumes which are, in effect, five extra manuals, covering the custom controls, the control development guide, the help compiler guide, the data access guide and the Crystal Reports users manual.

# Appendix A - The Professional Version

# The Professional Version Extras

The Professional Edition ships with the Windows help compiler so that you can produce the context sensitive help files that are a standard feature of any professional Windows package, although you'll also need a word processor which can produce files in Rich Text Format (RTF). There is also a hotspot editor which allows you to place hotspots on any graphics included in the help file.

The support for using and manipulating data using the Access database engine is all via the data control in the Standard Edition. The Professional Edition allows you to access the data directly via tables, snapshots and dynasets, and gives you much more control over the structure of the database as well as expanding on the SQL commands available.

There is a full report writer called Crystal Reports available and this can be linked into your applications via a custom control. Crystal reports is very easy to use. You just paint the report, add sorts and breaks and then you can run the report to the screen, printer, or to a file.

There are also extensive documentation files, such as the API files, the Visual Design Guide, which outlines the standards for design that Microsoft use, and the Windows SDK (Software Development Kit) help file. This allows you to add your own custom controls to Visual Basic.

The extra controls cover all areas of Windows. If you've loaded the samples, then you can run the professional demonstration which will show you all the features of the Professional Edition and run examples of all the custom controls. We'll look briefly at them in turn.

# The Professional Version

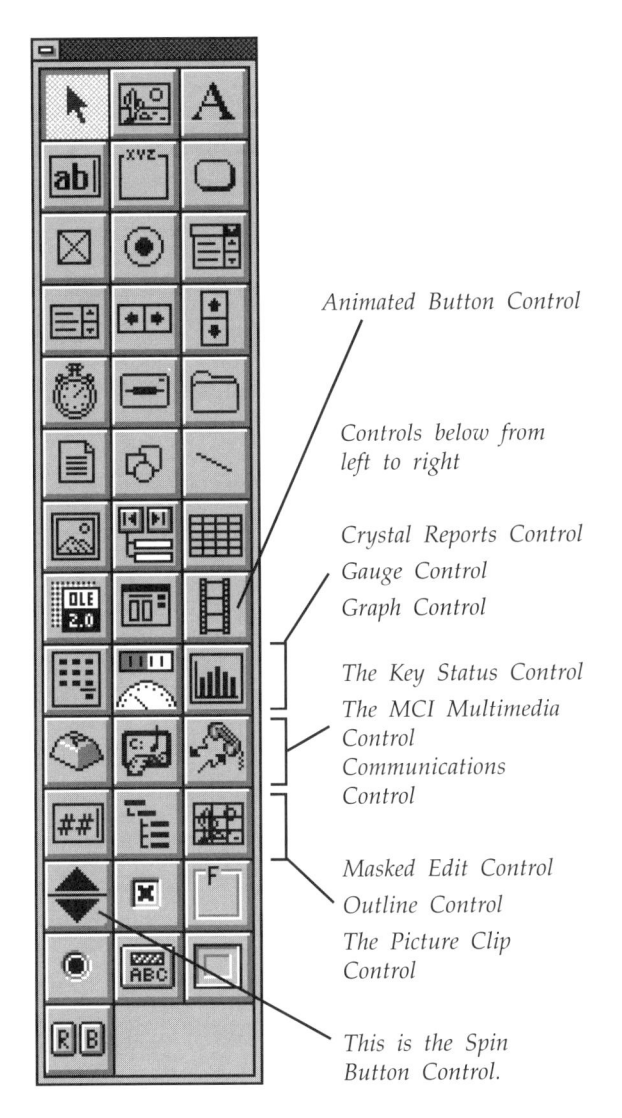

## The Animated Button Control

This is a much better implementation of our attempt to create an animated click button, in Chapter 4. You can use this anywhere where you would use a normal command button. The way it works is that the button contains images and an optional caption. The images can be considered as a control array, and you can decide which image is currently displayed in your code.

## The Crystal Reports Control

This control links the reports that you've written in Crystal Reports to your Visual Basic application. Using this control, you can pass the report run-time parameters, control which reports are run, and decide whether to print the report to the screen, printer, or a file. The full explanation of the Crystal Reports System is in the *Professional Features Book 2*.

*Animated Button Control*

*Controls below from left to right*

*Crystal Reports Control*
*Gauge Control*
*Graph Control*

*The Key Status Control*
*The MCI Multimedia Control*
*Communications Control*

*Masked Edit Control*
*Outline Control*
*The Picture Clip Control*

*This is the Spin Button Control.*

*The final six buttons of the toolbox are 3D versions of the standard controls*

**355**

# Appendix A - The Professional Version

## The Gauge Control

The gauge control lets you add either linear (filled), or circular (needle) gauges to your applications. The Professional Edition comes with several gauges built in, but you can create and display your own. It is used in tasks such as indicating percentage completion, amount filled, and so on.

## The Graph Control

This is a very useful control for producing graphs. Manually coding each graph with the Standard Edition can become very time consuming. This control reduces the effort required by allowing you to create many different styles of graph interactively. These can be cut into the clipboard and pasted into other applications such as Word. As you change the properties at design time, the representation of the graph is redrawn so that you can see the effect. Then at run time, you can pass the data from your application to the graph, which will redraw whenever new data is passed to it, or if any of its properties are changed.

## The Key Status Control

The key status allows you to display and monitor the status of certain keys, such as *Caps Lock*, *Scroll Lock* and *Num Lock* on the keyboard, depending on the `Style` property.

## The MCI Multimedia Control

This control will allow you to record and play multimedia files via the MCI (Media Control Interface), if your PC supports them. Files such as Wave Audio, (`WAV`), Video, (`AVI`), and MIDI (`MID`) files can be played via this control. It appears as a set of buttons, rather like the front of a video recorder. Multimedia is a whole topic within itself, and how much use you can make of this control will depend on the configuration of your PC. To be honest, we don't use this control - we prefer to use direct calls to the Windows API.

# The Professional Version

## The Communications Control

The communications control allows you to control the settings of a serial port, and transmit and receive data. There are two ways of using the control. Using the event code, you can monitor for things like CD (Carrier Detect), RTS (Request To Send), and so on. The other way is to poll the serial port and monitor the `CommEvent` property.

## The Masked Edit Control

This is a replacement control for the textbox, which allows for restricted input and formatted output to the control. It acts in a similar manner to the standard textbox, but it does have DDE capabilities. You can define input masks to restrict the input, with invalid entries generating a `ValidationError` event. We can also declare an output format, much like the format command we used to display the result of our Repayment Calculator in Chapter 5.

## The Outline Control

This is a special type of list box which presents the information in a hierarchical manner similar to the way that File Manager displays directories and files. The different legs of the hierarchy can be expanded and contracted as required. There are two styles that can be utilized, the tree type, which is the same as File Manager, or the +/- style.

## The Picture Clip Control

This control will allow you to display a selected area of a bitmap at runtime in a form or picture box. The control itself is invisible at runtime. This is useful if you have many different bitmaps to display. You can hold them all as one source bitmap, then use the picture clip control to display the required images at runtime, thereby saving resources.

## The Spin Button Control

The spin button control is another way of entering counter or volumetric data, and can be used in place of the horizontal and vertical scroll bars. The main advantages are that this control can take up a lot less space, and also its events are continually generated whilst the user holds down the mouse button.

## The 3D Controls

The 3D controls are a set of six controls, some of which replace standard controls in the toolbox.

### 3D Check Box

This control can be used in place of the standard check box. It gives a 3D effect to the check box, provided that your background color is gray. Use it in exactly the same way as a normal check box.

### 3D Command Button

This button can be used in the same way as the standard command button, except that you can have 3D text, and also display a bitmap or an icon on the button.

### 3D Frame

This is the 3D version of the frame control, which also supports 3D text.

### 3D Ribbon Buttons

These buttons are similar to the ribbon buttons of Word. They are like small command buttons, but act like radio buttons, as they are used in groups. Pressing one button in the group raises the previous one. You can also display bitmaps on these buttons.

## The Professional Version

### 3D Option Button

This control is the 3D version of the standard option button, and can be used where you would use the option control.

### 3D Panel

This is a container control that can be used in place of a frame, or picture control. It can also be used to display text. It's useful as a status panel in MDI applications.

## The MAPI Control

MAPI is the Message Application Program Interface and allows you to create mail-enabled Visual Basic applications. To use this custom control, you'll need to have Microsoft Mail. The control is split into two: the session control, and the message control. They are used in a similar manner to common dialogs in that they are invisible at runtime and controlled through the `Action` property.

## The Pen Controls

The pen controls are a set of three controls which allow you to develop pen-based systems. To use these controls you'll need to be running Pen For Windows operating system. The pen edit control is a replacement for the textbox and accepts pen input. The pen Ink-On-Bitmap is a replacement for the picture control which allows the user to draw and erase in the control. The details can then be saved. The pen on screen keyboard displays a standard keyboard and allows the user to select the keys on screen by pointing with the pen.

**359**

# Appendix B

# What Next?

Now you have most of the tools in your hands to produce professional quality Windows applications. One of the most frequently asked questions is whether industry strength applications can be produced with Visual Basic. The short answer is that they can. Visual Basic is a fully-functional Windows language, and with access to the API and the many add on custom controls - it is also much quicker than traditional C methods.

If you are experienced in writing Windows applications in C, then you'll also have another string to your bow. Use Visual Basic for most of your work, especially in the user interface. Any *complex* code that you require to be optimized, or code which requires speed, can be written in C and compiled as a DLL, and called from your Visual Basic code as you would any other function in the API. If you have the Professional Edition you will be able to package these DLLs as custom **V**isual **B**asic**X** controls.

# MultiMedia and Visual Basic

It's possible to create complex multimedia applications without having to resort to using C at all. Many of the requirements for multimedia are covered in the API, and for some of the specialist files, such as `.FLI` files produced from Autodesk's 3D-Studio, there are shareware custom controls available. (See the forthcoming *Revolutionary Guide to Multimedia using Visual Basic* from Wrox Press.)

# Client Server Visual Basic

One of the minor revolutions which is currently sweeping through the industry is the move to Client/Server. So how does Visual Basic fit into this revolution? Well, for small applications, using Visual Basic with its native Access database may well prove to work well, although we would recommend that you bought a copy of Access to fully maintain the database. For larger systems, you'll need to move to SQL Server, or one of the other major databases such as Oracle. It's still possible to use Visual Basic as a front end controlling the client, and accessing the backend database through Open Database Connectivity (ODBC). You'll find that all the major database vendors support ODBC.

In reality, the actual front end language that you decide on may well need to take many factors into consideration, and it's possible that several front end languages are used. Visual Basic shouldn't be ruled out just because it's cheap and easy to use.

# Further Help

## Talking to Other Visual Basic Users

Visual Basic is a very popular language world wide, and is supported on many bulletin board services. There are two forums on CompuServe, the MSBASIC and Visual BasicPJ forums, where you can get help and advice, as well as custom controls and other code, from the Visual Basic community in general. Microsoft actively participate in the MSBASIC forum, often posting bug fixes and software there first. There are also several news groups on the Internet that deal with Visual Basic, and if you live in the UK you can also try out the Visual Basic conference on CIX. In most on-line services there'll be an area dedicated to Visual Basic, so if you have access, check them out.

## Other Add Ons

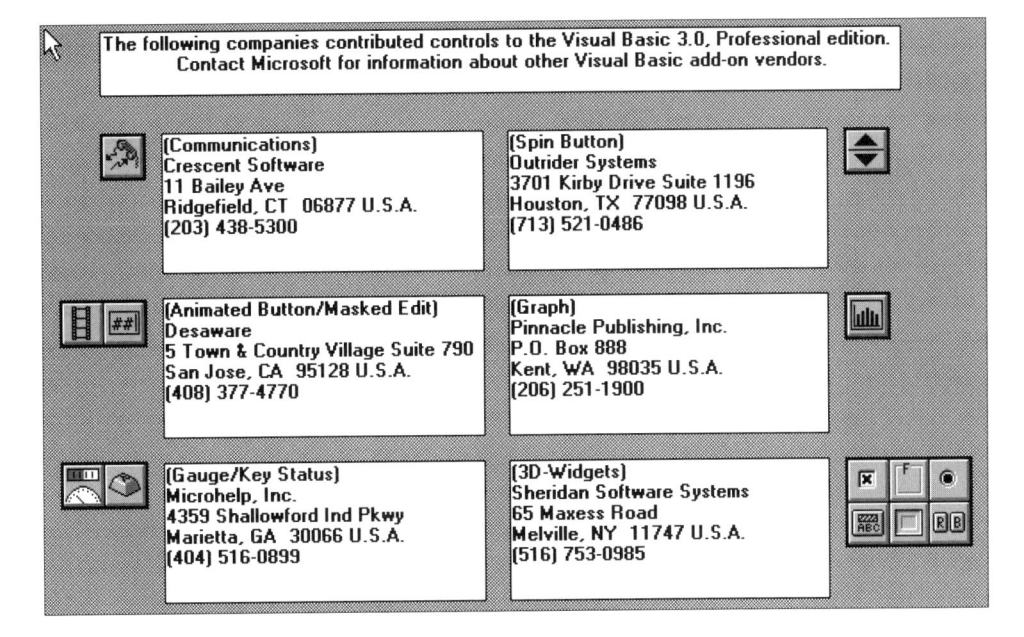

The following companies contributed controls to the Visual Basic 3.0, Professional edition. Contact Microsoft for information about other Visual Basic add-on vendors.

(Communications)
Crescent Software
11 Bailey Ave
Ridgefield, CT 06877 U.S.A.
(203) 438-5300

(Spin Button)
Outrider Systems
3701 Kirby Drive Suite 1196
Houston, TX 77098 U.S.A.
(713) 521-0486

(Animated Button/Masked Edit)
Desaware
5 Town & Country Village Suite 790
San Jose, CA 95128 U.S.A.
(408) 377-4770

(Graph)
Pinnacle Publishing, Inc.
P.O. Box 888
Kent, WA 98035 U.S.A.
(206) 251-1900

(Gauge/Key Status)
Microhelp, Inc.
4359 Shallowford Ind Pkwy
Marietta, GA 30066 U.S.A.
(404) 516-0899

(3D-Widgets)
Sheridan Software Systems
65 Maxess Road
Melville, NY 11747 U.S.A.
(516) 753-0985

The custom controls mentioned in Appendix A are all part of the Professional Edition of Visual Basic. There are, however, many more custom controls available which cover almost every topic imaginable. Companies such as Sheridan, Microhelp and Crescent (who all contributed to the custom controls in the Professional Edition) have an extensive catalog of **V**isual **B**asic**X** controls, including bound grids, graphics controls, and replacement text and combo boxes.

# Appendix C

# Exercise Hints and Tips

You didn't think we would leave you completely on your own, did you? As you start each exercise, save all the project files to new files so that you don't spoil the examples as we work through them in the book. You'll find that there are quite a few examples used throughout the book. Don't worry too much if you mess them up - we have kept the amount of typing to a minimum intentionally, so you should be able to quickly re-create a project if required.

We'll replay the questions and then offer one way of solving each problem.

# Appendix C - Exercise Hints and Tips

# Chapter 2

**1** Set the `Filename` property to the default `*.ICO` when the view button is pressed.

> *You shouldn't need any help here. Just reset the* `Filename` *property before calling the open dialog.*

**2** Extend the viewer to also view `.BMP`s and .WMF's

> *You will need to extend the default* `Filename`. *The format is filename;filename;filename.*

```
cmdialog1.Filename = "*.ico;*.bmp;*.wmf" is the solution.
```

**3** Add the password dialog you designed in Chapter 1, make it the startup form, and only load the MDI form if a valid password is entered.

> *You'll need to add the password from to the MDI Viewer project, with* Add File... *from the* File *menu, then change the* Start Up Form *on the* Options/ Project... *When a valid password has been entered,* `Load` *then* `Show` *the MDI parent form, and unload the password form.*

**4** Save the project and compile it, so that it can be run from Program Manager.

> *No problems here, just select* Make EXE File... *from the* File *menu.*

# Chapter 3

Using the Buttons project:

**1** Change the check boxes into a control array and re-code the `Click` event

366

# Hints and Tips

*Look at the control array example to see how this is done. When you re-code the* `Click` *event you'll have to check the* `Index` *to see which control has been clicked. The quickest way is to cut and paste the code from the old* `Click` *events, then rename the controls. You'll notice that Visual Basic doesn't remove your old code. You can delete this when you've re-coded the* `Click` *events.*

**2** When a new option is added, set the focus to the new button, and automatically change the mouse pointer.

*You can do this by altering the properties in your code.*

**3** Add a new control array of options that change the color of the label text, using `Qbcolor()`. Allow the user to add and remove controls at runtime.

*Look at the examples for any help you need here. It shouldn't be too difficult.*

Using the View Icon project:

**4** In the `drvSel_Change` event add an error handler to stop the project from crashing if a floppy drive is selected without a disk in the drive.

**Hint: we saw how to trap run time errors in the MDI View project in Chapter 2.**

*Use the* `On Error Goto...` *statement. In the error handler display a message box, then put in a* `Resume` *statement. This will re-try. This is covered fully in Chapter 11.*

**5** Add the View Icon form to the MDI View project replacing the old viewer, and recompile the project to a new `EXE`.

*Use Add File... from the File menu to add the View Icon form. You'll need to alter some of the code to load the new form.*

# Appendix C - Exercise Hints and Tips

# Chapter 4

Using the Hot Spots project:

**1** The resizing/relocating looks messy on the screen. Hide this activity from the user.

> At the start of the **Resize** event, change all the image and label **Visible** properties to **False**, then at the end, change them back to **True**. You'll notice that the **Resize** event now speeds up quite a lot, because Windows doesn't have to re-display (called **Repaint**) the screen for every control.

**2** If the user changes the size of the window disproportionately, the icons won't be square. Write code to prevent this from happening.

> Choose one of the dimensions of the form to control what the final resized form should be scaled to, and use this to determine the ratio of change for the size and location of the hotspots. If you are using the **Width** to determine the final size of the form, remember to change the **Height** property of the form proportionally to this.

Using the Contact project:

**3** Change the combo style back to a drop down style and sort it. When you add an item from the text box, empty the text box.

> All you need to do here is set the **Sorted** property to **True**, and in the **Add_Click** event set the textbox **Text** property to **""**.

**4** Disallow duplicate entries to be added to the combo box.

> You'll need to write a **For**...**Next** loop starting at **0** and ending at **comNames.ListCount -1**, checking the **comNames.List(index)** against the string entered in the text box.

**5** Allow the user to add a name by double clicking the textbox, and also pressing the *Enter* key.

> No problem, just call the add button click event from the double click event of the text box, and set the **Default** property of the add button to **True**.

# Hints and Tips

# Chapter 5

**1** In the Variant project we occasionally get a type mismatch error when converting between the different types. Write some code in the **Click** events to prevent this.

> *Check* **vEntered** *is either numeric or a date before converting. If the data is not in the correct format then display a message box asking for re-input.*

**2** In the Contacts project, assume that the end of each address line is delimited by a comma. Using this delimiter write some code to extract each individual address line and the phone and fax numbers.

> *Set up labels on the form to hold each line as you extract it. You'll need a couple of integers to hold the current start and end positions. Use the* **Instr()** *function to find the next comma and the* **Mid$()** *function to extract the strings.*

**3** When entering a name in the Contacts Project, ensure that the first character of the first name and surname is upper case, and the rest of the name is lower case.

> *Use the* **Ucase()** *and* **Lcase()** *functions. You'll also need to use* **Mid$()** *function to check each letter. The* **Len** *function will return an integer that is the length of the string. Use a* **For**...**Next** *loop.*

**4** In the dice project, generate dice throws between 6 and 12.

> *This should be no problem, just change the lower and upper limits as in the code to get your required range of values.*

**5** In the financial project, validate the input from the text boxes to make sure that it is in the correct format.

> *Use the* **IsNumeric()** *function to check the input is numeric. A good place to put the check is in the* **Change** *event.*

# Appendix C - Exercise Hints and Tips

# Chapter 6

**1** Extend our top of form procedure to also center a form when it's loaded.

> This should be no problem. Simply calculate what the **Left** value should be based on the **Width** of the form and of the **Screen.Width** properties.

**2** You'll notice that the age calculation isn't accurate, because it doesn't take into account when in the year the birth date occurs. Extend the function to check the system day and month against the date entered day and month, and adjust the DOB accordingly.

> Use the **Month** and **Day** functions to compare the two. If the date entered is greater now, you'll need to subtract **1** from the number of years, because the birthday has not yet been reached. If the month is the same you need to extend the check to the day of the month as well.

**3** In our looping number project, you'll notice that if you use an odd number and set the descending check, the numbers displayed are odd. Write a check to make sure that even numbers are displayed.

> What you will need to do is see if the number is odd or even. The function to use is the **Mod** function. This divides one number by another, and returns the remainder. Use

```
iRemainder = lNumber / 2
```

> and check if **iRemainder** is **0**. If not, then delete **1** from **iNumber**.

**4** Extend the check, by turning it into a function which will be passed an integer, and return an indicator saying whether the number is odd or even. You can now extend the loop numbers project to allow the user to select whether odd or even numbers are displayed.

> This should now be easy - try using the **Mod** operator.

**5** Create a project which uses `Sub main` as its start. Now add a `.BAS` file, and in the `Sub main` procedure `Load` the password form. Using a loop in the `Sub main` procedure, allow for five tries. (This code could be used to restrict access to your applications.)

*Change the start up form in the project options to Sub Main. The rest is fairly easy.*

# Chapter 7

**1** Extend the use of the color common dialog control to allow the user to change the foreground and background colors of the Alter Icon form.

*Add a common dialog control to the form. Set the `Action` property to `3` in the code and use the `Color` property of the dialog for your form.*

**2** Now set up the color change as a function, and allow the user to change the colors of the all the controls on the form. (You'll have to pass the control as an object variable to the function.)

*When you pass a control via an object variable, all its properties go with it, so you'll be able to use the object variable to alter the controls `Color` properties.*

# Chapter 8

**1** Using the Name animation, try out some different fonts to see the effect. See if you can stop the name going off the screen.

**Hint: use `ScaleHeight` properties.**

*You may get stuck here. There is a function called `TextHeight()` which will return the height of text. So to check that the text will fit on the screen use the following:*

**371**

# Appendix C - Exercise Hints and Tips

```
If (frmPrint.ScaleHeight - frmPrint.CurrentY) < TextHeight("The Print
String") Then (OK to Print)
```

**2** Still with the Name animation, at the end flash the name five times before ending the program.

> Use a **For...Next** loop. Don't forget to reset the **CurrentX** and **CurrentY** properties.

**3** While the Name animation is running, you don't actually need **Autoredraw** as **True**. See if you can create speedy, but persistent graphics.

> The way to do this is to set **Autoredraw** to **False** in design, and only set it to **True** after the animation has finished. This speeds up the animation, yet still gives persistent graphics.

**4** In the Lines project, make the line display a function in a similar manner to the stars project so that it will run indefinitely, but stop on a mouse click.

> The Stars project should provide all the necessary clues to this one.

**5** Using the **Circle** method, see if you can produce a bouncing ball animation. As the ball bounces, it will squash, so you'll need to use an ellipse or two.

> The Circle project should give you the idea here. Draw a circle, then the next one, and redraw the first in the background color. You'll need to keep track of the **CurrentX**s and **CurrentY**s for the circles, and experiment with the squashing to get it right.

# Hints and Tips

# Chapter 9

**1** Constantly opening and closing the file is not very efficient. See if you can determine a way of opening the file at the start of the project, and closing it at the end. As a hint, try using a **Sub main** procedure and load the form from this.

> At the start of **Sub main** open the file, then load and show the form. You'll need to make the variables global so that they can be used in the form. In the **QueryUnload** event for the form, close the file. Don't forget to change the project options so that the start form is **Sub main**.

```
Sub main ()
    iContNum = FreeFile
    lLength = Len(typContact)
    Open "c:\test2.dat" For Random As iContNum Len = lLength
    frmAddress.Show
End Sub
```

**2** Change the listbox to a combo box, and add an **&Add** command button which will allow the user to add an entry into the list, and also write it to the file. You'll need to use the global variable **glNext**.

> This should be fairly easy. Look in the contact example to see how we did it, then use the **Put** statement to add a record to the file. Don't forget to add **1** to **glNext** after you've saved it, and also set the **ItemData** property in the combo box.

**3** Now add an **&Update** command button which will allow the user to alter and save new details of a selected record. Here you'll need to use the **ItemData** property.

> Allow the user to alter the textbox fields, place them in the user defined type variable, then using the **ItemData** property for the record number **Put** the record. This will overwrite the old details with the new ones.

**373**

# Appendix C - Exercise Hints and Tips

**4** Try out some ways of better structuring the address, such as delimiting each section with a comma, and reformatting in the textbox.

*This should be quite easy to do. In real world applications, there would probably be a variable for each address line, and each would appear in its own textbox to give the address structure.*

# Chapter 10

Create a new directory to hold all your project details, then create a new database in the directory called **CONTACT**. The first table call **Names**, and add the following fields:

| Field Name | Type | Size | Description |
| --- | --- | --- | --- |
| IdNo | Integer | | A unique id starting at 1 and going up 1 for each new record |
| Surname | Text | 30 | |
| FirstName | Text | 20 | |
| HomePhone | Text | 20 | |
| OfficePhone | Text | 20 | |
| Fax | Text | 20 | |

Create a primary index on the **IdNo** called **NameIndex**. Now create an address table and insert the following fields:

# Hints and Tips

| Field Name | Type | Size | Description |
|---|---|---|---|
| `IdNo` | `Integer` | | Used to link to the Name table. It will also be the unique primary key. |
| `Address1` | `Text` | 40 | Line 1 of the address |
| `Address2` | `Text` | 40 | Line 2 of the address |
| `Address3` | `Text` | 40 | Line 3 of the address |
| `Address4` | `Text` | 40 | Line 4 of the address |

Create a primary index called `AddIndex` on `IdNo`. Unfortunately, we can't hold an array in a database, so each line of the address has been split individually.

Now create an application that will allow you to enter, amend and delete contact details in your database. Bear in mind that you can only have an address if you have created a name record.

Creating the database should not prove too difficult, just follow the example in the book. There are many different ways to go from here. We would recommend that you create an MDI application which has two child forms. The first will allow you to maintain the `Name` table. If you add a record, you'll need to move to the last record to find out the last `IdNo`, then add `1`.

The second form has a listbox of all the name entries from the name table (and their `IdNo`s in the `ItemData` property). You'll need to hold the last `IdNo` used in a global in the same manner as the previous chapter. From here you can select a name to get its `IdNo`, then create, amend or delete the `Address` details as required.

**375**

# Chapter 11

**1** Really, the only way to become familiar with the debugging tools is to use them. You'll find that the Debug Window is also very useful for testing your application, by altering the value of variables as you go through the code.

*Load the Circles application you wrote in Chapter 8, and set a breakpoint which allows you to alter the parameters to the* `Circle` *function. Now try out different positions sizes and colors.*

*You don't need any help with this, just play around with it.*

**2** Load the MDI Icon Viewer program, and link in our generic file error handler to trap any errors which may occur. Test it by selecting your floppy drive without a disk inserted when selecting the icon file to be viewed.

*You should be able to manage here without any problems. Just add the module with the error handling function and call this function from your code when an error is received.*

# Hints and Tips

# Chapter 12

**1** As we have said, the clipboard can hold different data types. Alter the clipboard procedure to handle all the different data types. This can then be used in any project that requires access to the clipboard.

*Use the* **GetFormat** *function to determine which type of data is on the clipboard at any one time and write code in a format appropriate for it. Typically using a* **Select Case** *block of code.*

**2** In the Resource project, the display of free resources is static. Create a timer control which creates and updates a display of the free resources every few seconds. Then try loading and closing other windows applications to see the effect on resource usage.

*Simply write a procedure to work out the various resources (as is done in the* **Load** *event of the project), and call this procedure from within the* **Timer** *event. This will then update the labels periodically for you.*

**3** Extend the **.INI** viewer to allow the user to enter an **.INI** file to be looked at. You'll need to change the function call to **GetPrivateProfileString**, with the last parameter as the name of the **.INI** file, such as '**WIN.INI**'. If you don't include the path, then the Windows directory will be searched for the **.INI** file.

**4** Alter the Application Launcher program to run up the calculator, and allow the user to enter a string of keystrokes that will be passed to the calculator when a command button is pressed.

*To do this you will need to use the* **SendKeys** *statement. Prepare a string of characters to send to the calculator program first before* **Shell***ing to it.*

**377**

# INSTANT Visual Basic

## Index

### Symbols

! Qualifier  125
   # Date format specifier  130
# format specifier  140
&, hot keys  28
* (SQL)  289
?  304
3D controls  358

### A

Accelerator Keys  66
Access 2 Compatibility Layer  270
Access Database  266
Access Type  240
   Append  240
   Input  240
   Output  240
Accessing Database Fields  285
Accessing Fields in RecordSet  284
Accessing Multiple Tables  289
Accessing the Recordset  283

Action parameter.
   *See* Validate event: Action
Activating Other Applications  343
Active form
   Me  58
Active Form property  197
Add Field Dialog  272
Adding Controls at Run time 78, 81
Adding Files 18, 38
AddItem Method  113
AddNew Method  287
Align property  105
Align To Grid  44
Alter Icon example  182
Altering the running order  304
Animated button control  355
Animation
   example  217
   with Move Method  217
API  321, 329
   example  336
   project  332

# Index

App Object 206
AppActive 339
Application Communication 321
Arcs 230
Arrange Method 194
Array
   Object Variables 175, 176, 184
      Action / Methods 184
Array declaration 143
Arrays 142
   Changing size 143
   Control Arrays 76
   Multi dimensioned 144
   of Object Variables 184
   of Variable 97
   Preserve 143
Arrays of Object Variables 184
As Any keyword 335
Assigning Objects 178
autoload.mak 42
AutoRedraw effects 215
AutoRedraw property 213. *See also* ClipControls property

## B

BackColor Property 40, 111
Beginning Of File. *See* Files: Beginning Of File
biblio database 276
Binary Access Files 238
Binding controls 277, 279
BOF 244
   function 244
   property 284
Bookmarks 286
BorderStyle 25
BorderStyle property 100
Bound Controls 277
   DataField property 279

DataSource property 279
Break Mode 13, 304
BreakPoints 303
Buttons
   Check 73
   Commands. *See* Command Buttons
   Enabled property 70
   Grouping 73
   Option 73
ByVal keyword 299, 330

## C

Calling code 72
Calls 309
Cancel property 71
Caption 26
Caption property 22
Case
   Is comparison 159
   To keyword 159
Case Else Statement 158
Change event 85, 171
Changing Focus 67
Changing Name properties 77
Changing Properties
   At Run Time 68
Changing Tab Order 68
Check Buttons 73
Circle Method 229
   Aspect argument 230
   Drawing Arcs 230
Clear Method 115, 322
Clearing the screen 211
Click Event 65
Clicking Buttons 65
Client / Server 362
Clipboard 321, 322
   formats 328, 329

# Instant Visual Basic

Clipboard Methods 322
   GetData 322
   GetFormat 322, 328
   GetText 322, 325
   Clear 322
   SetData 322
   SetText 322, 325
Clipboard Object 206
Clipboard project 323
ClipControls property 216
Clipping 216
Close statement 242
Cls command 211
Code
   Modularity 298
   Modules 298
Code Basic 293
Code Labels 161
Code Module 150
   Sub Main() 47
Code window 19
Coding 31, 149
Coding Menu Items 193
Collections 185
Color common dialog 200
Color Example 233
Colors
   QBColor function 75
   RGB function 224
Colors in Visual Basic 232
Combo box 115. *See also* List box
   Drop down List box 116
   ItemData 117
   RemoveItem 116
   Style property 116
Comma Separated Variables 245
Command Button 65
   Cancel Property 71
   Default property 70
   Value property 70

Command Line Arguments 47
Common Dialog 24, 51, 198
   Print 256
   Flags property 201, 256
   Action property 202
   Font dialog 201
   CancelError property 200
   Color dialog 200
   Input box 198
   Message box 199
Communicating with Other
     Applications 321
Communications control 357
Comparison Operators 160
Compatibility Layer 270
Compiling Projects 47
Connect property 277
Const Keyword 142
constant.txt 141, 281
Constants 141
Contact project
   Using databases 273
   With file access 251
Container Controls
   Picture box 198
Control
   Arrays. *See* arrays: Object Variables
   MAPI 359
   MCI Multimedia 356
   Outline 357
   Values 63
Control Array 76
   Actions / Methods 184
Control Value 62
Controlling For Loops 162
Controlling Other Applications 339
   SendKeys 339, 344
Controls 10, 18, 61
   3D controls 358
   Adding at Run Time 78, 81

**381**

# Index

Animated Button  355
Buttons  65
Check Button  73
Combo box  115
Command Buttons  65
Common Dialog  24
Communications  357
Containers  104
Control Arrays  76
Crystal Report  355
Custom  61
Data Control  276
Disabling  69
File System  83
FileSystem
   Pattern property  84
Focus  67
Frame  73
Graph  356
Grid Control  24
Image  91
Image box  29
Key status  356
Line  221
List box  112
Masked edit  357
Naming  64
Object Variables  177
Objects  20
OLE Control  24
Option Button  73
Pen  359
Picture box  29, 104
Picture Clip  357
Removing at Run Time  82
ScrollBars  233
Shape  221
Source  182
Spin button  358
Standard  61
Tab order  31

Textbox  26, 111
Third Party  18
Timer  108
Coordinate Systems  206
Creating a Database  269
Creating a function  153
Creating Controls  78
Creating custom coordinate systems  209
Creating Errors  312
Creating New Instances  179
Creating Toolbars  104
Crystal Reports  260, 354
   control  355
CSng function  127
Currency  133
CurrentX & CurrentY property  208
Cursor  208
Custom Controls  39, 61
Custom Dialogs  51
Customizing Visual Basic  42

## D

Data Access
   Alternatives  291
   ODBC  292
Data Control  276
Data control. *See* RecordSet: Methods
   Connect property  277
   DatabaseName property  277, 278
   RecordSource property  277, 278
   Refresh Method 283
Data control events  280. *See* Validate event:
   Action & Save parameters
   Reposition  280, 281
   Validate  280, 281, 289
Data Maintainance  287
Data Manager  266, 270
   Add Field Dialog  272

# Instant Visual Basic

Index Designer 275
New Database 270
Table Designer 272
Database 267
   Access 266
   Action Parameters 281
   Adding Records 287
   Biblio.mdb sample 276
   BookMarks 286
   Creation 269
   Data Maintainance 287. *See* RecordSet
   Editing Records 287
   Execute Method 293
   Field Name 273
   Field Type 273
   Fields 267
   Indexes 269
   Jet Engine 266
   Moving through Records 286
   Objects 293
   Records 267
   Related Information 267
   Relational 266
   Relations 268
   Returned data format 273
   Sort order 275
   SQL 289
   Tables 267
Database Development 265
   Professional edition 265
DatabaseName property 277
DataField property 279
DataSource property 279
Date functions 131
   DateAdd function 131
   DateDiff 131
   Now 132
Date manipulation 130
DblClick Event 85
DDE 344
   conversation 344

destination 344
items 345
link 345
source 344
Debug
   ? 304
   Break Mode 304
   BreakPoints 303
   Editing Watches 306
   Example 302
   Immediate Pane 306
   Print 301
   Procedure Stepping 309
   Set Next statement 304
   Setting Watches 306
   Single Stepping 303
   Stop 305
   Tracing Calls 309
   Watch 305
Debug Menu 16
Debug Object 206, 301
Debug Window 301, 302
   Immediate Pane 306
Debugging 297
Debugging Facilities 300
Decisions 156
Declaring DLL's 330
Declaring Functions and Procedures 331
Declaring variables 122
Default Command Button 70
Default Font 211
Default name 27
Default names 22
Default Save As 45
Default Storage of Variants 127
Delete Method 287
Design Mode 13
   setting properties 22
Designing Menus 188
Device independence 9
Dialog Title property 52

**383**

# Index

Dialogs 51
   Common 51
      Action Property 56
      Open 52
   Custom 51
Dim keyword 57, 122, 123, 143
Disabling Controls 69
DLL 329
   As Any parameter type 335
   GetActiveWindow 342
   GetFreeSpace 331
   GetFreeSystemResources 331
   GetModuleUsage 342
   GetNumTasks 341
   GetPrivateProfileInt 333
   GetPrivateProfileString 333
   GetProfileInt 333
   GetProfileString 333. *See also* GetProfileString
   IsWindow function 342
   Null character 338
   Passing Parameters 330
   WritePrivateProfileString 333
   WriteProfileString 333
Do Loops 165
   Placing the test 168
   Until Statement 165
   While statement 165
DoEvents 212
   Unexpected Results 213
DoEvents Statement 169
Double 127, 133
Doubles 102
Drag and Drop 182
DragDrop event 182
   Source parameter 182
Drawing at Pixel level 223
Drawing Circles and arcs 229
DrawMode property 231, 232
DrawWidth property 231

Drive property 85
Dynamic Data Exchange 344
Dynamic Link Libraries 329

# E

Early functionallity 31
Edit Menu 15
Edit Method 287
Editing Watches 306
Empty String 113
Empty Variants 126
Enabled property 70
End Select 159
End statement 226
EndDoc Method 259
EndFunction statement 155
Enviroment
   Align To Grid 44
   Code Styles 44
   Customizing Start Up 42
   Default Save As 45
   forms design grid 44
   Options 43
   Require Variable Declaration 45
   Save Project Before Run 45
   Show grid 44
   Syntax Checking 46
EOF 244. *See* Files: End Of File
   function 244
   property 283
Eroor Handling
   Setting ErrorTraps 311
Err function 313
Error function 313, 314
Error Handler 56
Error Handling 297, 311
   Err function 313
   Error function 313, 314

example 314
Procedure Chain 311
Resume Command 312
Resume Next Command 312
Resuming Execution 312
Setting error traps 311
Testing handlers
    Error statement 313
    Unexpected Errors 313
Error statement 312, 313
Error Trap 311
Event Combo Box 20
Event-Driven Programming 7, 8, 9
Events 9
Example
    Buttons Project 66
    Option and Check Buttons 73
Password Project 24
EXE File 10
Execute Method 293
Exit For Statement 162
Exit Sub Statement 111, 161


## F

Field Name 273
Field Type 273
Fields 267
File handling concepts 238
File Menu 10, 14
    Add File 18, 38
    Make EXE File... 47
    New MDI Form 48
    Remove File 38
    New Project 19
File System Controls 83
    Directory List Box 85
    Drive List box 85

File List box 85
FileError example function 316
FileName Property 52
FileNumber 241
Files
    .BAS 151
    .INI 333
    .FLI 362
    .MDB 271
    Access Type 240
    Appending 241
    BAS 10
    Binary Access 238
    BOF function 244
    closing 242
    Code Modules 41
    End Of File 244
    EOF function 244
    Form Files 41
    Forms 10
    FreeFile function 242
    Get 250
    Help File 47
    INI file structure 334
        Sections 334
    Input# Method 243, 247, 249
    Input$ Method 243
    Line Input# Method 243
    Naming Conventions 30
    Open statement 240
    Print# Method 243
    Project .MAK 42
    Put 250
    Random Access 250
    Reading and Writing 239
    Save as Text 41
    Sequential and Random Access 239
    Sequential Files 240

**385**

# Index

Types 41
VBX's 10, 18, 39
WIN.INI 333
Write# Method 243, 249
FillColor property 231
FillStyle property 231
Flag Icons 94
Focus 67
   Disabled Controls 69
   Events 170
   LostFocus event 171
   Setting 68
Focus example 170
Font Common Dialog 201
For ... Next Loop 162
   Controlling the loop 162
   Exit For Statement 162
For Loop 103
Form control
   ClipControls property 216
   Height Property 207
   ScaleHeight property 207
   ScaleWidth property 207
   Width Property 207
Form Design Grid 44
Form files 10
Form Level Variables 96
Form Load event 49
Form object 20
Form Styles 48
   MDIChild property 48
   Modal 48
   Non-Modal 48
Form1 19, 22
Format function 140
Forms 11
   AutoRedraw property 213
   Collections 185
   Count property 185
   Files 10
   Loading 32

Printing 261
Unloaded 32
Windows 11
Frame Control 73
FreeFile function 241, 242
Functions
   AgeInYears example 155
   Creating 153
   EndFunction 155
FV (future Value) function 137

## G

Gauge control 356
Generic Objects 177
Get 250
GetActiveWindow 342
GetData Method 322
GetFormat Method 322, 328
GetFreeSpace function 331
GetFreeSystemResources 331
GetModuleUsage function 342
GetNumTasks function 341
GetPrivateProfileInt 333
GetPrivateProfileString 333
GetProfileInt 333
GetProfileString 333
   lpAppName parameter 335
   lpDefault 335
   lpKeyName parameter 335
   lpReturnedString parameter 335
   nSize 335
GetText Method 322, 325
Getting information from WIN.INI 334
Getting Table Information 285
Global keyword 123
Global Replace 116
GoSub Statement 161
GotFocus event 170
GOTO

Statement  56
Graph control  356
Graphical Controls  29,  89
Graphical development  8
Graphics  205
    Arcs  230
    Circle Method  229
    Drawing boxes  228
    Drawing at Pixel level  223
    DrawMode property  231
    DrawWidth property  231
    FillColor  231
    FillStyle property  231
    Layering  216.
        *See* Programmer Guide manual
    Line and Shape controls  221
    Line Method  226
    Loading  30
    QBColor  224
    Refresh Method  215
    RGB function  224
    simulating a button example  222
    Use of Paint event  223
Grid Control  24
Grouping Buttons  73

# H

Handling Errors at Run time  311
Heavyweight controls  90
Height  25
    property  207
Help File  47
Help Menu  16
Hot Keys  28,  66
Hot Spot project  94
    Improving the code  158
    Updating Status  97

# I

I/O and printing  255

I/O Methods  243
    Get  250
    Input#  243, 249
    Input$  243
    Line Input#  243
    Print#  243
    Put  250
    Write#  243, 249
Icons  17
    Flags  94
    quick icons  12
    Stop  31
Idle Loops
    DoEvents  169
If Then Else  156
Image box  29
Image control  91
    As a button  91, 93
    As a Hotspot  94
    As an Indicator  93
    Picture Property  56
    Stretch Property  55
Immediate Pane  306
Improving Projects  98
Index designer  275
Indexes  269
    Ascending/Descending  275
    Primary  275
    Unique  275
Infinite loops  72
INI file structure  334
INI files  333
    Keyname  334
    Keyvalue  334
    Sections  334
InitDir property  52
Initializing forms  150
Input box  198
Input to Variables  247
Input#  243

**387**

# Index

Method  247
Input$  243
Input$ function  245
Instance  57, 176
   Creating  179
   Multiple Instances  185
   Handle  341
Instant Watches  310
InStr function  135
Int function  139
Integer  133
Interval property  108
Input and Output  237
Is keyword  179
Is Statement  159
IsDate function  130
IsEmpty Function  126
IsNull  127
IsNumeric function  130
IsWindow funcion  342
ItemData Property  117
ItemData property  254

## J

Jet database Engine  265, 266
   BookMarks  286

## K

Kernel  331
Key status control  356
Keys  239
Keyname  334
keystrokes  343
Keyvalue  334
Knowledge Base  196

Known Bugs  196

## L

Label declarations  161
LargeChange property  234
LastModified property  288
LBound function  184
LCase function  137
Len function  135
Lifetime of Variables  122
LightWeight Controls  90
Line control  221
Line Input#  243
   Method  244
Line Method  226
   Drawing boxes  228
Lines and Shapes  220
Link properties  345
Link Testing  298
Linking  348
   at Design time  348
List box  112
   AddItem Method  113
   Clear method  115
   Columns property  115
   ItemData  117
   ListIndex  113
   Multiple Selections  114
   RemoveItem. *See* Combo box: RemoveItem
   Sorted property  114
ListIndex property  113
Load Statement  81
Loading Graphics  30
LoadPicture Function  56
Loan Repayment project  139
Local Variables  123
Logging Errors  314

Long  133, 252
Looping  162
LostFocus event  170, 171

# M

Managing Projects  38
MAPI control  359
Masked edit control  357
MaxButton  26
MCI control  356
MDI
  Menus  196
MDI Forms  48
Me keyword 58, 158, 197
Measurements  208
Menu
  options menu  16
Menu Bar  14
Menu Design Window  187
  Tools  190
Menu examples
  Arrange Method  194
  File Menu Structure  189
  Window Menu Structure  192
Menu Properties  189
Menu Short Cuts  192
Menus  186
  Checked  189
  Coding Items  193
  debug menu  16
  Designing Menus  188
  Edit  15
  example  189
  file  14
    Add File  18
  help menu  16
  Level  188

  MDI  196
  Popup menus  194
  run menu  15
  view menu  15
  Window
    Menu Design  187
  Window menu  16
  WindowList Property 189
Message Boxes 33, 72, 199
Mid function  135
MinButton  26
Modes  208
Modular Code  9
Modules  298
Monitoring Tasks  341
MouseDown event  107
  Button Parameter  195
MouseMove Event  96
MousePointer property  82
MouseUp Event  107
Move Method  217
MoveFirst  286
MoveLast  286
MoveNext  286
MoveNext Method  284
MovePrev  286
Moving through Records  286
MsgBox  33, 72
Multi Dimmensioned Arrays  144
Multi-Column List box  115
MultiLine property  112
Multimedia  362
Multiple Form Instances 185, 197
Multiple Selections  114

# N

Name property  52
Names

# Index

default 22
Naming Conventions 64
Navigating the properties window 23
New form instances 57
New keyword 177, 179, 185
NewPage Method 258
Next statement 304
NoMatch property 291
Nothing 178, 179
Now function 132
Null 113, 127, 338
Null Variants 126
Numeric function
   Format 140
   Int 139
   PMT 139
   Rnd 139
Numerical functions 137
   FV 137

## O

Object
   Databases 293
   Debug 301
   Declarations 176
   Handles 341
   Printer 255
Object Combo Box 20
Object Linking and Embedding 344, 346
Object Oriented 18, 62
Object Oriented programming 299
Object Variable Arrays 184
Object Variables 175, 176
   Is keyword 179
   Testing type 179
Objects 10
   As Control 177
   Assigning 178
   Controls 20

Generic 177
New keyword 177
properties 21
Set Statement 178
   Nothing 178
Specific 177
System 206
TypeOf keyword 179
Objects RecordSet 282
ODBC 292, 362
OLE 344, 346
   placeholder 347
   SizeMode property 349
OLE Control 24
On ... GoSub 160
On ... Goto 160
On Error 311
   Statement 56
   Method 241
OpenDatabase Method 293
Opening Files 240
Opening Files
   FileNumber 241
   FreeFile function 241
Operating Mode 13
   break mode 13
   design mode 13
   run mode 13
Operators
   Comparison 160
Option Base statement 143
Option Explicit 45
   Effects 55
Options Menu 16
Outline control 357

## P

Paint event 213
   Effects of ClipControls 216
Parameterized function 150

Parameters
    Passing by Reference  300
    Passing by Value  299
Passing Keystrokes  343
Passing Parameters to DLL's  330
Password Project  24
Pen control  359
Persistent Graphics  213
Picture Box  29
Picture Box control  104
    Align property  105
    ClipControls property  216
    AutoRedraw property  213
Picture clip control  357
Picture Property  56
Pixels  208
placeholder  347
PMT function  139
Popup Menus  194
    Bug  196
    MouseDown Event  195
PopupMenu statement  194
Positioning the cursor  208
Preserve keyword  143
Primary Index  275
Print Common dialog  256
Print method  210, 212
Print#  243
Printer Object  206, 255
    EndDoc Method  259
    NewPage Method  258
    Page property  258
    Scal properties  259
    ScaleMode property  260
    TextHeight property  258, 261
    TextWidth property  261
    TwipsPerPixel property  258
PrintForm Method  262
Printing  255

Crystal Reports  260
Forms  261
Using Common Dialogs  255
Printing to the Debug Window  301
Printing to the Printer Object  257
Procedure Calls  309
Procedure Stepping  309
Procedures  152
    TopForm example  152
Professional Edition  292, 353
    Crystal Reports  260
    Extras  354
    OpenDatabase Method  293
Program Control  156
    Case Else  158
    Do Loops  165
    Do Until  168
    Do While example  167
    End Select  158
    For ... Next Loop  162
    Idle Loops  169
    Looping  162
    Select Case  157
Program Design  298, 299
Program Manager
    Application Icon  47
Project Development
    Improving the Project  98
Project File  42
Project Options  46
    Command Line Arguments  47
    Start Up  46
Project Structure  150
Project Window  23
Projects  10, 38
    Compiling  47
    Management  38
    New project  19
    project files  10

**391**

# Index

Saving  41
Properties  21
   BackColor  40
   BorderStyle  25
   Caption  22, 26
   Changing  27
   Default name  27
   Height  25
   MaxButton  26
   MinButton  26
   Run Time only  71
   Text  33
   Width  25
   Window  21
Properties window  22
Property Identifier  63
Prototyping  193
Pset Method  223
Public Scope  155
Put  250

## Q

Q+E  293
QBColor function  75, 224, 232
Qualifier, !  125
QueryUnload event  214

## R

Radio Buttons  73
Random Access  250
Random Access Files  239
Random numbers  138
Randomize statement  138
Reading Files  239
Records  267
RecordSet 282
   AddNew Method  287
   BOF property  284
   Delete Method  287
   Edit Method  287
   EOF property  283
   Getting Table Information  285
   LastModified property  288
   Move... Methods  286
   NoMatch property  291
   Update Method  287
   Value  284
   Value property  284
RecordSet Methods
   MoveFirst  284
   MoveNext  284
RecordSet properties  284
Recordsets  282
RecordSource
   SQL  289
RecordSource property  277, 278
   SQL  289. *See* SQL
ReDim statement  143
   Preserve  143
Refresh Method  215, 218, 283
Relational Database  266
Relations  268
Releasing Resources  178
RemoveItem Method  116
Removing Controls  82
Removing Files  38
Replacing code  116
Reposition event  280, 281
Resize event  101
Resize Handles  26
Resizing the Graphic  101
Resizing Controls  26
   Proportional Scaling  103
Resizing Controls at Run Time  100
Resources  90
Resume Command  312

Resume Next Command 312
Resuming Execution 312
Reusable functions 299
RGB function 224, 232
Right function 135
Rnd function 139
RTrim function 133
Run Menu 15
Run Mode 13, 50
Run time Errors 311
Run time Properties 71
Running Other Applications 339
    AppActive 339
    Shell command 339
    Window Style 340
Running other applications 339
Running other events 72

## S

Save As Text 41
Save Project Before Run 45
Saving 30, 41
    Automatic Resaving 35
    Resaving 35
Scale Method
    Customizing coordinate system 209
Scale Method 210
Scale properties 209
Scale Width and Height 207
ScaleHeight property 207
ScaleMode property 208
Scales 208
ScaleWidth Property 207
Scope 122
    Functions and Procedures 155
    Private 156
Screen Measurements

Twips 102
Screen Object 206
ScrollBars
    LargeChange property 234
    Min / Max property 233
    SmallChange property 234
ScrollBars Property 112
SDK 354
Sections 334
Select (SQL) 289
Select Case 157, 158
    default comparison 159
    Is comparison 159
    To keyword 159
SelText Method 325
SendKeys 339, 344
Sequential Access Files 239
Sequential Files 240
    AUTOEXEC.BAT 242
Set Next statement 304
Set statement 178
    Nothing 178
SetData Method 322
SetText Method 322, 325
Setting BreakPoints 303
Setting Error Traps 311
Setting Focus 68
Setting properties 22
Setting Watches 305, 306
Shadowed Variables 124
Shape control 221
    property 221
Shell command 339
Shell function 340
    Instance Handle 341
    monitoring tasks 341
Short Cut Keys 192
Show Grid 44

# Index

Show Statement  50
ShowStart Sub procedure  225
Simulating a button
      with graphics example  222
Single type variable  133
Single Step Icon  304
Single Stepping Code  303
SizeMode property  349
SmallChange property  234
Sorted Lists  114
Sorted Property  114
Specific Objects  177
Specifying Hexadecimal values  234
Spin Button control  358
SQL  289
  *,  289
  Execute Method  293
  Joining tables  289
  Select  289
  WHERE  290
SQL example  290
Standard Controls  61
  Values  63
Starfield project  224
Startup template  42
Statements
  MsgBox  33
Static keyword  122, 143
Status Bars  198
Step keyword  228
Stepping through Procedures  309
Stop command  305
Stoping the program  302
Stopping the program  31
Stretch Property  55
String  133
String functions  133
  InStr  135
  LCase & UCase  137
  Len  135

Mid  135
Right Function  135
RTrim  133
Strings in strings  134
Sub Main()  47
Syntax Checking  46
System Objects  206

## T

Tab Key  67
Tab Order  31, 67
  Changing  68
TabIndex property  67, 68
Table Designer  272
Table Information  285
Tables  267
TabStop property  68
Tag Property  118
Terminating Routines  111
Terminating the program  226
Text  33
Text box  26
  Change event  171
  IsDate function  130
  IsNumeric function  130
  SelText Method  325
Text Controls  111
  MultiLine property  112
  ScrollBars property  112
TextHeight property  261
TextWidth property  261
threed.vbx  40
Time functions  131
  Now  132
Time manipulation  130
Timer Control  108

Limits 108
Timer Project 108
Title Bar 13, 50
To keyword 159
Toolbox 17
   icons 17
Toolbar 17, 104
   Adding Files 38
   coding the butons 107
   MouseDown event 107
   MouseUp event 107
Tracing Procedure Calls 309
Twips 102, 208
Type keyword 144
TypeOf keyword 179

## U

Ubound function 184
UCase function 137
Unexpected Errors 313
Unique Indexes 275
Unique key 239
Unload Statement 55, 82
Unloading controls 82
Until Statement 165
Update Method 287
User defined Properties 117
User defined types 144
User Input 33
Using .INI files 333
Using Buttons 65
Using Modules 151
Using the Clipboard for Text 323
Using the Line Method 226
Using the Paint event 214
Using the Printer 206

## V

Validate event 280, 281, 289
   Action Parameter 281
   Save parameter 281
Variable Arrays 97
Variable Declaration 122
Variable Input 247
Variables
   Currency 133
   Double 102, 127, 133
   Global 123
   Integer 133
   Lifetime 122
   Local 123
   Long 133, 252
   Me 185
   Object
      As Control 177
      New 177
   Object type 176
   Objects
      Set 178
   Scope 122
   Shadowing 124
   Single 133
   Static 122
   String 133
   Text (ACCESS) 274
   Variant 121, 126, 273
   Watching 305
Variant 114, 121, 126, 273
   Conversion function 127
   Default Storage 127
   disadvantages of use 127
   Empty 126
   IsEmpty function 126

# Index

IsNull function  127
Null  126, 127
Types  126
VarType Function  126
VBX's  18, 39
   threed.vbx  40
View Code  23
View Form  23
View Menu  15
Visual Basic
   Icons  93
   Debugging  300
   Project  23

## W

Watches
   Instant Watch  310
   Scope  306
Watching  305
WHERE (SQL)  290
While Statement  165
Width  25
   property  207
WIN.INI  333, 334
   file structure  334
   getting information  334
WIN30API.TXT  330
   *See* Declaring DLL's
Window
   Debug  301
Window Menu  16
   Data Manager  270
   Project  24
Windowlist Property  189
   Arrange method  194
windows  10
   Code window  19
   Forms  11

Project Window  23
Properties  22
Properties window  21
   navigating  23
Windows API  321, 329
   API project  332
Windows clipboard  321
Windows Handle  341
Windows programming  9
Windows Resources  90
   BAS files  151
   DoEvents  169, 212
         *See* DoEvents: Unexpected Results
   GDI  332
   How Much?  91
   Releasing  178
   Using DLL's  331
   Using Graphical Controls  221
Windows SDK  354
Write#  243, 249
WritePrivateProfileString  333
WriteProfileString  333
Writing Procedures  152
Writing to Files  239

# Instant Visual Basic

# WROX

## WIN FREE BOOKS

### TELL US WHAT YOU THINK!

Complete and return the bounce back card and you will:

- Help us create the books you want.
- Receive an update on all Wrox titles.
- Enter the draw for 5 Wrox titles of your choice.

---

**FILL THIS OUT to enter the draw for free Wrox titles**

Name _____

Address _____

_____

_____

_____ Postcode/Zip _____

Occupation _____

How did you hear about this book ?
- ☐ Book review (name) _____
- ☐ Advertisement (name) _____
- ☐ Recommendation
- ☐ Catalog
- ☐ Other _____

Where did you buy this book ?
- ☐ Bookstore (name) _____
- ☐ Computer Store (name) _____
- ☐ Mail Order
- ☐ Other _____

What influenced you in the purchase of this book ?
- ☐ Cover Design
- ☐ Contents
- ☐ Other (please specify)

How did you rate the overall contents of this book ?
- ☐ Excellent
- ☐ Good
- ☐ Average
- ☐ Poor

What did you find most useful about this book ?

What did you find least useful about this book ?

Please add any additional comments.

What other subjects will you buy a computer book on soon ?

What is the best computer book you have used this year ?

*Please do not put me on your mailing list* ☐

# WROX

*WROX PRESS INC.*

Wrox writes books for you. Any suggestions, or ideas about how you want information given in your ideal book will be studied by our team. Your comments are always valued at WROX.

Free phone in USA 800 814 4527
Fax (312) 465 4063

Compuserve 100063,2152.
UK Tel. (44121) 706 6826   Fax  (44121) 706 2967

*Computer Book Publishers*

**NB.** If you post the bounce back card below in the UK, please send it to: Wrox Press Ltd. Unit 16 Sapcote Industrial Estate, 20 James Road, Tyseley, Birmingham B11 2BA

## BUSINESS REPLY MAIL
FIRST CLASS MAIL    PERMIT#64    CHICAGO,IL

POSTAGE WILL BE PAID BY ADDRESSEE

**WROX PRESS**
**2710 WEST TOUHY AVE**
**CHICAGO IL 60645-3008**
**USA**

NO POSTAGE
NECESSARY
IF MAILED
IN THE
UNITED STATES